96
GAR3-3

A CALLING
AND ITS
COLLEGE

A History of
the American
College of Life
Underwriters

President Davis W. Gregg and President Emeritus S. S. Huebner in the reception area of Huebner Hall on dedication day.

A CALLING AND ITS COLLEGE

A History of
the American
College of Life
Underwriters

By Mildred F. Stone, C. L. U.

1963

RICHARD D. IRWIN, INC., Homewood, Illinois

First Printing, September, 1963

Library of Congress Catalog Card No. 63–21182

PRINTED IN THE UNITED STATES OF AMERICA

DEDICATED

TO

David McCahan

who saw the American College of Life
Underwriters of 1963 only in the vision
of faith, but whose strength is in it still.

C.L.U. PROFESSIONAL PLEDGE

In all my relations with clients I agree to observe the following rule of professional conduct: I shall, in the light of all the circumstances surrounding my client, which I shall make every conscientious effort to ascertain and to understand, give him that service which, had I been in the same circumstances, I would have applied to myself.

A MESSAGE FROM THE BOARD OF TRUSTEES
of the
AMERICAN COLLEGE OF LIFE UNDERWRITERS

A half century has passed since a young professor at the University of Pennsylvania proposed that "... a life insurance course of study leading to a degree or designation comparable to that of Certified Public Accountant, might ultimately be created and centered in a college of standing, commensurate with other degree-granting educational institutions." This volume tells the story of what happened subsequent to that proposal.

Fifty years is but a brief period in the building of a profession. However, as recorded in the pages of this history, much progress has been made by the American College of Life Underwriters in building the meaning of C.L.U. as a professional designation for persons who are engaged in the process of insuring human life values.

The History Committee of the College's Board of Trustees, composed of Dr. S. S. Huebner, Chairman, Paul F. Clark, and Julian S. Myrick, had only one choice as to who might do the historical research and prepare this history. Mildred F. Stone, biographer of Dr. Huebner, a life insurance historian, and a Chartered Life Underwriter herself, was their choice. In accepting the challenge, the author stated that her efforts would be a work of love since any financial return would not be compatible with her company responsibilities. It is believed that the quality of this volume proves the correctness of the Committee's decision to choose Miss Stone and the depth of her devotion to her task.

Mildred F. Stone, C.L.U., has spent her entire business career of almost forty years in insurance. Following her graduation from Vassar College in 1924 she joined the Mutual Benefit Life Insurance Company of Newark, New Jersey. She was elected Agency Field Secretary in 1934, the first, and still the only, woman officer of the company. She was named Director of Policy-holder Services in January, 1947, Staff Assistant to the President in June, 1954, and since 1962 has been Assistant Secretary. Miss Stone has many and varied business and community interests. In addition to being the author of Dr. Huebner's biography, Miss Stone has written *A Short History of Life Insurance, Better Life Insurance Letters,* and *Since 1845,* a history of the Mutual Benefit Life Insurance Company. She is also editor of *Life Underwriting—A Career for Women* and is a speaker before life insurance, civic, and club groups.

Although much historical material is included in this volume, it will be obvious to the reader that a multivolume history would have been necessary to tell the "whole story." An effort has been made to highlight the major policy actions taken by the College over the years in its goal of building a profession. Personal vignettes are included and will add to the flavor of the volume.

This history should be particularly meaningful to persons interested in insurance in either its institutional or academic aspects. It should be of particular interest to Chartered Life Underwriters and persons striving to attain this goal. Finally, because of the upsurge of interest in many segments of American life in developing programs of professional education and certification, the volume should have an interest far beyond the provinces of insurance.

THE AUTHOR'S FOREWORD

Man has two eyes to give depth to his vision. To know only the today of an institution is to see a flat picture with no proper relationships. History enables us to look with two eyes. History helps us know why things are as they are. History shows how problems have been solved. History leads us to appreciation of what has been done for us by people who have gone before. From this kind of understanding comes a proper evaluation of what we have today, guidance for the developments of tomorrow, and inspiration for us, in our turn, to serve our times.

For all these reasons it seemed that a history of the American College of Life Underwriters should be written. Its purpose is to give perspective and understanding to new generations. In addition, for many who have helped to make the history, this book should be a testimonial and an expression of thanks. It has been my purpose to include as many significant names as possible to remind us all that the College today is the creation of many, many people with diverse talents working with a united purpose.

This book is the history of the College, not of the Society. Frequently it was necessary to remind myself of that limitation. There are many persons who were key people in the history of the Society, and therefore of major importance also to the College, whose full service is nevertheless not reflected in these pages. Their contributions to the College are well recognized, but the real record of their work must be written in a history of the Society.

The preparation of this manuscript was accomplished through the help of a great number of cooperative friends. Preeminently, the members of the History Committee appointed by the College trustees: Dr. Solomon S. Huebner, Mr. Paul F. Clark, and Mr. Julian S. Myrick, have been most valuable. In many personal interviews, in correspondence and in telephone conversations they gave me information and guidance. Mr. Earl R. Trangmar, Mr.

Joseph H. Reese, Mrs. David McCahan, Mr. Roger Hull, Mr. Benjamin N. Woodson, Mr. J. Harry Wood, Mr. Leroy G. Steinbeck, Mr. Clarence B. Metzger, Mr. Gordon K. Smith, Mrs. Margaret Carlsen, and Mr. Howard H. Cammack were particularly helpful. Many others gave valuable suggestions and information during the years of research and preliminary writing or in offering suggestions after review of the first draft of the manuscript.

President Davis W. Gregg and Dean Herbert C. Graebner have helped, guided, and encouraged me from the start. Miss Esther M. Horr, Mrs. Helen L. Schmidt, and Mrs. Rose Thompson of the College staff have also given invaluable assistance through their personal memories and official records. Mrs. Schmidt, in the organization of the appendix material, and Mrs. Thompson, in preparing the American College bibliography, have made a particularly important contribution to the historical value of this book. Mr. James A. Ballew and Mrs. Patricia Chatburn helped immeasurably in assembling the interesting collection of historical pictures which illustrate the text.

To my secretary, Miss Claire M. Marra, especial thanks are due for tireless, cheerful and most accurate typing and retyping of manuscript. And over all I want to register appreciation to The Mutual Benefit Life Insurance Company for many hours of freedom to undertake the task of research and writing which represented a considerable corporate contribution to the cause of life insurance history.

MILDRED FAIRBANKS STONE

Newark, New Jersey
May, 1963

TABLE OF CONTENTS

Chapter 1

THE END FROM THE BEGINNING:
A PROLOGUE

"No peddlers, solicitors or insurance agents allowed." This inhospitable sign was seen not infrequently 50 years ago in lobbies of office buildings. How the life insurance underwriter in hardly more than a generation has moved in the public mind from the company of peddlers to association on equal footing with attorneys, bankers, accountants, and educators is a fascinating story. The physician was once a barber, the lawyer a man who had read Blackstone and perhaps Coke. These older professions developed slowly and in what might be called the course of nature. However, life underwriting as a professional activity is a concept which is achieving stature more quickly. It has crystallized during the working years of many men now living, and is the purposeful fulfilment of an ideal.

The profession grew from within the calling. Even life insurance peddlers were motivated by the good they saw resulting from their sales of $500 or $1,000 policies. Men who sold even small contracts for death benefit payments knew that their work often meant the difference between hope and despair for a bereaved family. From among such salesmen arose leaders who recognized how much greater was the potential of life insurance service.

These leaders saw the need for education—education for salesmen and the public—and for the establishment of life insurance courses in the colleges and universities of the nation.

1

They saw the need to formulate standards of ethics, to inspire commitment to common purposes and loyalty to fellow underwriters. Through conflicts of ideas but with unity of ideals these men worked to create an organization that would accomplish their aims.

The American College of Life Underwriters and the Chartered Life Underwriter program became an important channel for the tide of professional development in life insurance service. This book is written as a record for life underwriters of events, struggles, and personalities which many remember well. It will serve also as a guidebook to workers in many other fields. Those who seek to elevate their own callings, in service to the public and as a vocation for men and women of pride and ambition, will find that C.L.U.s have blazed a trail which they may follow.

Chapter 2

THE TEACHER FOR THE INDUSTRY

Young Solomon Huebner, his student work completed at the University of Pennsylvania, debated his next step. Should he teach high school in Philadelphia or join the faculty of the Imperial University of Japan? As he pondered this perplexing question he suddenly received inspiration from the pages of the *New York Journal of Commerce*. Here was a daily paper reporting the news of business and industry across the nation, devoting major sections to insurance and to the stock and produce markets. But these subjects were not taught at all in the oldest and biggest collegiate business school in the country.

With this realization came Solomon Huebner's challenge. He saw the road for him, and he started on it the next morning. The Wharton School of the University of Pennsylvania approved of the idea of insurance courses from an economic viewpoint, and also of courses in the stock and produce markets, and invited him to join the faculty to develop them. Thus, Dr. Huebner pioneered the world's first college-level study in these subjects.

As Dr. Huebner saw a need for university training of this kind, and took steps to bring it into being, so also he shared the vision which resulted in the American College of Life Underwriters. However, the time from the birth of the idea to the official launching of the College was not weeks but years. Agreement and cooperation had to come not from a few university officials in Philadelphia, but from scores of men from Texas to Boston.

Although Dr. Huebner's personal contribution to the founding

3

and development of the American College is beyond measure, the College today stands as the work of many men. In the early years Dr. Huebner was the architect and David McCahan was the man who daily helped him build. Even before Dr. Huebner, the leaders of the National Association of Life Underwriters had made efforts toward educational programs for life insurance salesmen and the public. A few companies and agencies were attempting to train agents for their jobs. Men like Ernest J. Clark, Paul F. Clark, Edward A. Woods, J. Stanley Edwards, John Newton Russell, Franklin W. Ganse, Julian S. Myrick, and many others gave Dr. Huebner hearing among life underwriters, and constantly supported and magnified his work. Later, James Elton Bragg, John A. Stevenson, Irvin Bendiner, Joseph H. Reese, Earl R. Trangmar, Charles J. Zimmerman, Roger Hull, and Orville E. Beal, with Davis W. Gregg and Herbert C. Graebner and their associates of today, brought their strength to the mission.

What Dr. Huebner calls the pre-incorporation period of the College lasted 13 years. Encouraged by Ernest J. Clark, he made in 1914 the first public suggestion of a professional life underwriting designation, comparable to the C.P.A. recognition, in a talk before the Life Underwriters Association of Baltimore. Later that year at the annual convention of the National Association of Life Underwriters, he made a major speech on education for life underwriters and for the public in the area of life insurance. He began soon afterward to spell out to other life insurance audiences proposals for a college-level course of study, centered in a recognized educational institution, and leading to a professional degree. The response to those addresses was overwhelming, and indicated to leaders of the National Association of Life Underwriters that here was a man who could blaze the trail they would be glad to follow. They knew they all wanted to go in the same direction—toward better life insurance service for the public. However, they could not quite visualize the specific objective, and there were many disagreements before the goal came into focus.

The American College of Life Underwriters probably could never have been born without the help of the National Association. On the other hand, Dr. Huebner recognized that the universities would not accept an educational program too closely allied with a trade association. To win the academic cooperation and respect that were desirable, the proposed College must be independent. All life insurance men did not accept this principle readily. In various phases it was a matter of conflict for many years.

In fact, the period was replete with conflicts and obstacles. The attitude of life insurance home offices was generally cool or definitely hostile to the whole idea of academic training. The vice presidents in charge of sales, as well as many general agents and managers in the field, thought book learning would ruin the salesmen. They wanted none of it.

A major obstacle was the lack of life insurance text books. A literature had to be developed as the basis for college-level study in life insurance. A curriculum and texts in related subjects had to be agreed on. With his pioneering enthusiasm, Dr. Huebner outlined a course of preparation for five professional examinations involving 23 books and 8,000 pages of reading. Even his strongest supporter, having had the books on his desk for months "trying to get used to them," could not go along with that. On the other hand, it was imperative that the proposed course involve real academic achievement. A diploma mill operation would be a distinct disservice to the public and to the industry. So there were years of compromise and discussion before the first study program was approved.

There was great difference of opinion too about honorary degrees. Some incorporators felt strongly that it would be appropriate for a group of leaders to be honored as Chartered Life Underwriters without examination. That had possibilities of financial advantage, which made it a tempting consideration, but Dr. Huebner was vehemently and adamantly opposed to the idea. He was actively supported by Edward A. Woods and Ernest J. Clark, and their decision finally prevailed.

Before incorporation and in the early days of the College there was little money for the project. Fees for candidates were low and students were few. Financial needs were met in many ways—by

Edward A. Woods.

a loan from the National Association of Life Underwriters, from private funds of life insurance leaders devoted to the cause, through special help such as Dr. Huebner's summer work with the Massachusetts Mutual Life Insurance Company, and especially by the willingness of Dr. Huebner and Dr. David McCahan to do large amounts of work for very small salaries.

The story of financing the College in its foundation years, and later in the great expansion of its program, is one of successive struggles, but also one of satisfactory victories. The sound financial leadership of Julian S. Myrick through his 22 years as chairman of the Board of Trustees of the College; the enthusiasm of Earl R. Trangmar as executive assistant to Henry E. North, chairman of the cooperating committee which brought into existence the Cooperative Fund for Underwriter Training; the most recent multimillion dollar triumphs of the Permanent Endowment Fund and the C.L.U. Development Fund, are but parts of the inspiring record.

The physical headquarters of the College naturally were dictated by financial resources. How well the progress of the College is symbolized in what was successively "home base" for the C.L.U. program! Look from a few files in the corner of Dr. Huebner's university office, to the attic walkup quarters in an old Philadelphia office building, to the originally commodious but later overflowing accommodations in the handsome old house at 3924 Walnut Street near the University of Pennsylvania, and now to Huebner Hall in Bryn Mawr, modern and beautiful in the midst of its acres awaiting the needs of tomorrow.

The organizations which have become associated with the College during its lifetime are also an important part of the story. The American Society of Chartered Life Underwriters unites the graduates to effectively support the development of the College. The Society is providing a growing program of continuing education for its members, and supplies valuable information services for the public.

The S. S. Huebner Foundation for Insurance Education, created to fill a need brought to light by the College, has given to colleges and universities scores of well-trained insurance teachers. Through its publishing program, the Foundation has stimulated the production of new textbooks on insurance subjects, and distributed them widely in this country and abroad.

The David McCahan Foundation, established in memory of the fourth president of the College, stimulates fundamental and creative thinking in areas relating to life insurance. Currently the Foundation is sponsoring a long-range study in depth of the American family.

But the army of men and women who have earned C.L.U. designations since 1927 can speak most feelingly of the College. They say they do better work since they have completed their C.L.U. studies. They believe that with the development of the C.L.U. and other education programs the public looks on them with more appreciation and respect. They know that they earn more money as C.L.U.s.

The first year, 36 candidates qualified for the new C.L.U. designation. In 1962 there were 785. The total since 1927 is 10,582. Behind those cold figures are people. One man achieved his C.L.U. after 10 years of sporadic work and personal encouragement by Dr. Huebner. Currently, 44 C.L.U.s are presidents of their companies. Some 50 C.L.U.s have proudly seen their sons or daughters follow in their footsteps and in their turns win the designation.

The C.L.U. is officially recognized in the English language. Since 1949, the designation has been listed in Webster's dictionary and other reference sources.

The American College of Life Underwriters was a pioneer in serving as a national professional examining body with uniform national standards leading to a legal diploma and professional designation. The C.P.A. and other professional designations and degrees vary in their standards from state to state. The American Institute for Property and Liability Underwriters, granting the designation of C.P.C.U. (Chartered Property and Casualty

Underwriter), was directly inspired by the American College of Life Underwriters, and Dr. Huebner was a key figure in the organization of that body. Now many other vocations, seeking to upgrade their service to the public and raise the sights of their workers, are coming to the American College to ask: "How did you do it? Give us your advice about how we can establish a similar program in our field."

The American public today has learned to respect and appreciate the service of professionally trained life underwriters. An outstanding life insurance salesman who lived to share in this honor was fond of reporting that when he entered the business, about 1910, his mother sat down and cried. She felt he had disgraced the family. In her mind, a half-century ago, life insurance selling was associated with high-pressure artists, shady characters, and failures from other businesses. The desirability today of life underwriting as a vocation attractive to the capable, keen, service-minded man and woman is in no small part due to the American College of Life Underwriters. The history of the College is the story of crusaders for ideals, of fighters against obstacles, of cooperators who resolved their conflicts. The College is a living memorial to its founders and to countless others who have believed in and worked for its program with unselfish devotion.

Chapter 3

FROM UNDER A DARK CLOUD

In 1960 the National Association of Life Underwriters, representing 77,000 members throughout the country, met in Washington, D.C., for its annual convention. President Eisenhower honored the business by receiving at the White House a delegation of life insurance dignitaries, including from the American College President Emeritus Solomon S. Huebner, Board Chairman Emeritus Julian S. Myrick, Board Chairman Paul F. Clark, and Counsel Robert Dechert. Mr. Eisenhower also sent a message to the convention expressing "the highest regard for the work and standards of the National Association of Life Underwriters," and continuing, "I know that the life insurance industry will continue to provide a broad base for the security and growth of America. As its representatives help us understand the need for financial responsibility, both public and private, they help us to maintain the stability and progress of the economy."

What a testimony these experiences are to the change the twentieth century has seen in the concept of the life insurance salesman! A popular writer in 1906 crystallized a common image with his description.

At the end of the long-armed systems of the . . . , the . . . , the . . . , and their like, [names of life insurance company executives notorious at the time] there was a deft, pocket-dipping hand. That hand was the agent. He was a mixture of the royal good fellow, the hypnotist, the sleight-of-hand performer, the poet, and the genial pirate; and whichever of these constituent parts would be most effective with a certain type of customer, that part instinctively assumed temporary command over him. He charmed you with his personality, till you couldn't say no; he manipulated figures with the skill and innocence of a pea-and-shell man, and you put down your money; he boarded you unaware, battered you down with his booming statements, and leaving you dazed and helpless carried off his loot in the shape of a signed application for a policy; with his gilded words he built you castles in the air, which seemed so real to you that you hastened to pay him rent in the form of a commission; or good fellow, hypnotist, juggler, pirate, poet, all charged upon you at once, and you yielded to numbers.

In 1906 the historian Burton J. Hendrick wrote:

For the last thirty-five years a constant warfare has been fought in the United States between the good and the bad in life insurance. On one side have ranged honesty, economy, and fair and liberal treatment of the insured; on the other, dishonesty, extravagance, and absolute disregard of policy-holders' rights. Certain companies have treated life insurance as a great beneficent institution, organized for the purpose of protecting the weak and the dependent against adverse fortune; others have regarded it largely as a convenient contrivance for enriching the few men who happened to have usurped control.

In this thirty-five years the history of American life insurance has been one of progressive degeneration. The people have forgotten the old ideals; have persistently abandoned good life insurance and taken up with bad. They have for the larger part ignored the teachings of our great American leaders—men like Elizur Wright, of Massachusetts, the originator of nearly everything that is best in the American system, Jacob L. Greene, of Hartford, and Amzi Dodd, of New Jersey; and have sought the leadership of men who have degraded the whole institution. They have thus displaced the United States from the world leadership in life insurance which it formerly held, and have made what was one of our greatest claims to national distinction the cause of what is, in many ways, our most shameful national scandal.

Mr. Hendrick was writing shortly after the famous Armstrong Investigation. An historian of today evaluates that inquiry.

The Armstrong Investigation of 1905 in New York contributed more to the sound development of life insurance in the United States than any other single factor, yet most of us now active in the life insurance business know relatively little about this important milestone in the progress of life insurance.

As indicated by Mr. Hendrick, life insurance operations in New York had become a national scandal. National magazines as well as the New York newspapers gave the investigation voluminous coverage. Several of the big life companies became known as "The Racers" because of their competitive drive for growth. One company president openly boasted that he cared not at all about the kind of life insurance he sold; his only objective was to be the world's biggest life insurance company. Naturally this led to abuses—high-pressure sales promotions, commission scales that favored big producers and fostered rebates, and prizes and bonuses beyond all reason.

Many of the evils were rooted in the tontine policies being sold by almost all companies. The appeal of the policies was in the fantastic profits which were said to be possible. In most cases, however, people actually suffered losses. These plans involved deferred payment of dividends and developed huge surpluses in the companies for which their officers made no accounting. With great amounts of money to use freely, it is not surprising that questionable procedures developed in investment practices, in legislative lobbying and in interlocking directorates among insurance companies, banks, and other business corporations. Life company officers used policyholder funds to finance transactions designed to be profitable to themselves. Stock market manipulations were another ready means of channeling money to the right pockets.

Some life company officers became completely insensitive to the demands of stewardship for policyholders. They acted as if the business were being operated primarily for their own benefit.

Cartoons ruthlessly highlighted the abuses. For example, nepo-

President Eisenhower with leaders of the American College and the National Association of Life Underwriters, 1960.

tism flourished and was frequently a subject for caricature. One cartoon, under a slogan "Insure in the . . . Insurance Company and see that the family is provided for," showed a long series of desks with name plates and large salary tags attached. The name plates read: "Pa, President"; "Ma, General Manager"; "Son-in-law, Vice President"; "Sis, Board of Directors"; "Gran'pa, Janitor"; "Kid, Secretary"; "Dog, Treasurer"; and finally at the end of the line in a rocking chair, "Gran'ma, Custodian of the Dog."

Shady practices regarding official expense accounts were common. Extravagant expenditures were made shamelessly. One officer of a large life company gave a party at the elegant Sherry's restaurant in New York. He had the place turned into a replica of Louis XVI's palace of Versailles, with grass, shrubberies, and fountains. Guests attended in fabulous court costumes, and were feted with entertainment by a famous actress and food and drink beyond description. The newspapers published lurid estimates of the costs running up to $200,000, and were not reticent about the business connections of the host. The public, especially life insurance policyholders, was outraged by the implications of this extravagant display of wealth. The hospitable gentleman found it expedient to seek refuge in the neighborhood of the real Versailles, safely across the Atlantic.

All these evils were documented in the Armstrong Investigation by the testimonies produced under the leadership of Charles Evans Hughes. They were blazoned abroad by news reporters and feature writers to a public which knew the results—by observation or unhappy experience.

When the Armstrong Committee prepared suggestions for new legislation regulating life insurance operations in New York, most of its recommendations were followed. The breadth of the changes which came appears in the summary by J. Owen Stalson in his classic, *Marketing Life Insurance:*

> New election machinery for mutual companies was set up; a new rebate law was passed; contributions to political parties were

barred; and so too were false advertising and false bookkeeping; lobbyists were required to make themselves known and other related regulatory measures were passed. The most notable legislation, however, was that which revised the general insurance law. This put an end to tontine dividends; established non-forfeiture values on policies other than term after three annual premiums had been paid; prohibited discrimination between policyholders; forced the companies to follow a revised procedure in the election of trustees, even requiring the preparation of a list of policyholders for public inspection; provided for the mutualization of stock companies; put a specified limit upon the amount of new business that could be transacted in a given year, varying the per cent of new sales to insurance in force according to the size of the company; placed a limit upon acquisition costs—including, for instance, commissions, salaries, medicals, inspections, and advances to agents— providing that they could not exceed the first-year loading plus the present value of probable mortality savings in the succeeding five years; outlawed bonuses and "extras;" limited renewals; required that the board fix salaries of certain officers and that all persons who were paid more than $5,000 per year must be named and the amount they received stated, in a report open to the public; ruled against pensions to officers or their families; provided for four standard policy forms but gave the commissioner power to approve certain other forms which might be presented to him; required that mutual companies issue no non-participating policies and that stock companies issue only participating or only non-participating policies; prohibited investments in equities; other revisions were also made, significant among them being those which required more detailed reporting to the commissioner.

Thus the standards set by New York brought life insurance in the United States to a new era of responsibility and true service to the public. There have been modifications of the New York legislation in particulars which proved impractical, but the basic principles have continued to be effective. This house cleaning gave the public new confidence in the business. That the institution survived the exposures of the Armstrong Investigation is testimony to the fact that there is no substitute for life insurance. Essentially the system meets a widespread human need. This survival also demonstrated the effectiveness of Elizur Wright's crusading idealism a generation earlier when he had persisted in the demand for a legal reserve system in life insurance. For years he doggedly fought for this principle which would make life insurance fundamentally safe regardless of the ethics of management. Of Wright's work and its relation to the basic stability of life insurance even during the scandalous days before the Armstrong Investigation, Burton J. Hendrick wrote:

> This was the beginning of the great modern life-insurance principle of the legal reserve. Wright's old abolitionist persistence, in the face of constant discouragement, redeemed the whole system in this country, popularised life insurance, made it one of the great safeguards of society, and saved millions of dollars to the beneficiaries of life-insurance policies. Not improbably he rescued from ultimate disaster [certain New York companies], but, more than that, he gave American life insurance a standing unattained up to that time by that of any other country. He thus forced through a measure which has since been adopted by practically every state and territory. Wright made the failure of a life-insurance company mathematically impossible. No company which has observed the Massachusetts legal reserve law has ever gone to the wall. The financial stability of the three great New York companies, in spite of recent disclosures, has caused general amazement. The greatest banks, in the face of such assaults, would almost inevitably have landed in the receiver's hands. But the [New York companies] have stood the awful tests of the last twelve months—and why? Simply because Elizur Wright, fifty years ago, "lobbied for the widow and orphan" in the Massachusetts legislature and thus made the life companies so strong that even the recent dishonest managements have not unsettled them. Thanks to Wright, life-insurance scandals to-day affect other things than the companies' solvency.

Moreover, as historian J. Owen Stalson pointed out, although the New York companies took the lurid limelight, that was not the whole picture.

> Yet no reader should permit himself to believe that all life insurance men of this era were unethical or that all life insurance practice was misguided. The core of life insurance practice in that era was

sound; thousands of honest men carried the life insurance ideal to millions of existing and prospective policyholders; millions and millions of dollars of claims were paid to innumerable beneficiaries; hundreds of millions of life company assets were conscientiously and wisely loaned to countless farmers, home owners, and business firms.

In spite of the basic soundness of the life insurance industry and the admirable work of many honest and unselfish life insurance agents across the country, the idea of professional life insurance selling might have withered away without the Armstrong Investigation. The professional ideal was not compatible with the evils of the business which had flourished and been widely publicized. They had to be dramatically and openly condemned. This the Investigation did. A new climate favorable to the growth of the C.L.U. movement then could develop. In a new era, foundations could be laid for the American College of Life Underwriters.

It is interesting to try to evaluate the effect of the Armstrong Investigation on Dr. Huebner. In the midst of older academic associates he, a young teacher, was attempting to develop appreciation of the unique services of life insurance. He was exposed constantly to criticism, not to say scorn, of the business as viewed by university professors of the day. They saw it in its commercial aspect, blighted by ruthless competition and management autocracy characteristic of all big business at the time, and tainted by many questionable practices. Faculty friends asked why he wanted to have anything to do with such operations.

After the Armstrong Investigation, Dr. Huebner felt that road blocks had been cleared. He made up his mind to move forward as best he could to help put the business on a professional basis in its sales contacts with the public. If the way had not thus been opened for him, it is possible that his vision and creative energy would have been turned away from life insurance. How long would the C.L.U. idea have been delayed without Dr. Huebner? Nobody now can say.

Chapter 4

THE AGENTS FIND AN ALLY

It was against this background of failure and public disapproval, but in an atmosphere of "now things may be better," that life insurance salesmen 50 years ago groped toward something new. They knew they sold what the public needed. Unscrupulous promoters had capitalized on that. Conscientious men, even in those days, had been drawn to their work by an evangelistic urge to give their economic gospel to the people it would help. Sales managers sought ways to enable salesmen to satisfy their ambitions for service or success, according to personal motivations.

The National Association of Life Underwriters had been organized in 1890. One of its major objectives was improvement of sales practices and ethical standards. Another aim was life insurance education for potential underwriters and for the public. At the Association's second convention, a committee was appointed to correspond with colleges and universities throughout the country in an effort to have life insurance made "a common class study," and activity along these lines was continued in spite of many discouragements.

The whole program of the National Association of Life Underwriters progressed slowly in the early years, but reflected a vital interest on the part of life insurance salesmen in improving their standards for service to the public. When the sensational revelations of the Armstrong Investigation were made public, the National Association undertook a wholesale educational campaign to present the basic safeguards of life insurance in plain words

18

for the layman. The Association was invited by President Theodore Roosevelt to send delegates to the famous Chicago Conference of 1906, called to consider the disturbed state of insurance affairs. The Association was the only direct representative of life insurance and the policyholders enrolled among state governors, attorneys general, and insurance commissioners.

The Association's efforts to educate itself and the public concerning life insurance were handicapped by lack of study literature. There was no material on which to base a curriculum. At the turn of the century, Harvard and Yale presented a series of lectures on insurance. Yale's was published in book form and widely distributed. When Dr. S. S. Huebner inaugurated, at the Wharton School in 1904, his pioneer course in insurance, he also had to provide his own study materials. The only textbook he found useful was *Elements of Life Insurance* by Miles M. Dawson, an eminent actuary. Naturally, that book was heavily mathematical and lacking in the economic interpretation of the product of life insurance, its uses and its place in human affairs, so necessary to develop real understanding. Dr. Huebner's plan, therefore, was to bring to his classes lecturers who actually were working in various phases of insurance. They spoke on topics carefully planned by Dr. Huebner to present a composite of the leading forms of insurance, with the principles and methods on which the business was based and conducted. These lectures were published in 1905 by the American Academy of Political and Social Science under the title *Insurance*.

As life insurance in force in the United States grew (the amount owned more than doubled from 1900 to 1909), and as life insurance people urged the universities to consider including the subject in their curriculums, many pioneer courses developed. The Association of Life Insurance Presidents devoted a large part of its 1910 meeting to consideration of college-level training for life insurance people. One speaker was Dr. Edmund J. James, then president of the University of Illinois, and, earlier, one of the first professors at the Wharton School. He discussed the expansion of university programs to include engineering, architecture, and agriculture, and concluded:

> In a word, we may sum up the result of this development in every direction in our American life somewhat to this effect: That the victory of the well-planned, well-taught curriculum of the vocational school over the haphazard training of the office, the farm, the shop, is becoming ever more certain, and that especially in all those departments of life in which the success of the profession, as a whole and in a large way, is dependent upon the development of certain underlying fundamental sciences, by training in which the young man may get some help and assistance in preparation for his actual life work.

> So complete has this change been wrought that the definition of a university, which is coming to command the acceptance of an increasing number of thoughtful men, describes the university as an institution which affords an adequate training for the learned professions and which defines a learned profession to be any calling for the highest success in which a thoroughly systematic training in the sciences underlying the development of that profession is of value to the men and women who wish to pursue it.

Dr. James also presented the case for life insurance in the university curriculum, recalling his own efforts in that direction before the business had awakened to the idea.

> Twenty-five years ago [about 1885] in an address before the Philadelphia Chamber of Commerce, to which the insurance men of the city of Philadelphia had all been invited, I urged upon that body more ample preparation, more ample provision in the university for the study of the great subject of insurance.

> My argument at that time ran somewhat as follows: The department of insurance is certainly one of the most important departments of business and social life in a great commonwealth like ours. The principle of insurance is capable of such widespread application, one might almost say of such universal application, that it may really be considered one of the most fundamental and vital char-

acteristics of any highly civilized society, and the more highly civilized the society becomes the more possible forms of application will this principle find.

We have here, then, to do with a very important department of social and business life—one of the characteristics of a learned profession.

The application of this principle has had a considerable and very interesting history, something worth studying on its own account as a part of the history of human life, of civilization, as a part of the development of social ideals and methods of meeting social difficulties. This is another characteristic of a study which may well form an element in the training for a learned profession. The application of this principle depends for its success upon a careful, underlying, scientific study of the phenomena in any particular department of human life to which it is proposed to apply this principle. It calls for the application of scientific methods; it calls for a study of the economy of the people, of the habits of the people, of the prejudices of the people when we come to a practical application of the same—in other words, for a scientific survey of large departments of human life and activity.

In the handling of this enterprise itself, in the accumulation of funds, in the investment of those funds, in the relation of the different elements in a scheme of insurance to one another, we find an ample field for the most severe and careful intellectual training on the practical side. If we are to secure the widest application of this principle upon a perfectly sound basis, bringing home its benefits to every member of society, in every possible side of life to which the insurance principle may be applied, we must have skilled men, trained men, men of insight and out-sight, and experience, and they will naturally get the training for this particular thing best of all, first of all, by a careful study of the sciences underlying this insurance business and the history of the attempts which different and other nations have made to develop this great business as it ought to be.

I urged then that the insurance companies in Philadelphia provide for adequate instruction in these fields in the University of Pennsylvania.

I found, I am sorry to say, considerable indifference manifested toward the whole project. They were polite, but they thought this was some vagary of an academic man who had no practical sense, or rather perhaps we might say no sense for the practical actualities of life. He was a theorist with little to justify such views as to the advantages of training in insurance principles. They granted that a certain amount of actuarial study might be of advantage to an actuary, but that seemed to be the limit to which their ideas or thoughts could go.

Twenty-five years have come and gone. The attitude of the public in these matters is changing. I think it is not too much to say that if there had been twenty-five years ago a large body of educated men trained in the history, in the practice, in the study of insurance and insurance problems this country might have saved a thousand times what it would have cost to establish and develop a school which should be a center for the study of these problems.

A survey presented at this 1910 meeting of the Association of Life Insurance Presidents indicated that 263 colleges and universities in the United States had some life insurance teaching. This ranged from specialized treatment of actuarial and legal matter to incidental reference in classes of economics and sociology. Some enlightening comments regarding university training in life insurance were made by Professor James W. Glover, of the University of Michigan.

I am here representing the University of Michigan at this meeting, and I came here with the idea and the hope that I might get some information and some light on this subject of college instruction in insurance in our universities. About eight years ago I organized courses in the University of Michigan, and have made them what might be termed professional courses, and I want to tell you very briefly in what respect they may be called professional, and what the real problems are in this question.

In the first place, what is meant by a profession? That was defined this morning by President James, but I think he failed to mention one thing, one necessary qualification, namely, that to command the respect of the University the profession, to command a four-year curriculum, must have sufficient material in it to employ the student during that period. We all know that it is unnecessary really to defend the nobility of the profession. The nobility of the profession has been very ably treated of in the papers to-day. But those who have to teach this subject must face the practical question: What is there to teach? Two things are necessary in the University to enable a thing to command the dignity of a profession. In the first place it must command the respect of the faculty and teachers of the University, and in the next place it must command the respect of business men. There can be no doubt that a course which has for its object the training of the actuary, or the specific training of the insurance manager would command that respect, because it would require more than six weeks to accomplish it. For example, in the University of Michigan, the University which I have represented, and represent here, four years are devoted to the course in business administration that is known as the insurance course. In the first year rhetoric, mathematics, analytical chemistry and modern languages are given. In that course chemistry and biology are recommended as additional studies. Now, a man cannot be an actuary unless he has an understanding of mathematics. He may be an insurance agent, as has been stated here, without a knowledge of a number of these things. He may not necessarily speak French, or German, but if he is going to be a first-class actuary he will have to read many papers. Some of the best papers on this subject are written in foreign languages....

Now, the light that I came here to learn of, from those who have read papers to us is this: What course do you propose for this profession of agent; what shall he study the first year; what shall he study the second, the third and the fourth year? We have to face this practical question. I might suggest as a subject for this Association and its executive committee that this matter be taken under advisement so that we may be told upon paper what would be the course leading up to the profession of the agent, if it is a profession.

If professional educators were confused about a proper academic basis for life underwriter training, it is no wonder that life insurance men were not clear about it either. The concept that life insurance selling was an art which could be taught also was developing. In the trend toward more informed selling and sales management, Edward A. Woods, of Pittsburgh, was outstanding. Historian Stalson says that he "probably originated or stimulated the development of more ideas for selling life insurance and training agents than any other man in the history of the business." Dr. George Woods, his father, who had been chancellor of Western University of Pennsylvania (later named the University of Pittsburgh), became general agent at Pittsburgh for the Equitable Life Assurance Society of New York in 1880. Edward, while attending Western University, worked as office boy and clerk in his father's agency from its beginning. He left the university in 1883 without a degree to be a full-time agent. When his father retired in 1890, Edward, aged twenty-five, succeeded him. His promotion of the agency enabled it to grow from $10 million in force when he took over to $750 million in 1930 just after he died. Mr. Woods was creative in his concepts of life insurance selling. He urged business coverage, life insurance for estate taxes, monthly income rather than lump sum settlements, life insurance for philanthropic purposes, estate analysis, and similar ideas considerably in advance of the industry's general appreciation of these features. He was instinctively a salesman rather than a student. He was persuaded of the power of scientific salesmanship, and glorified it beyond everything else in his visions of progress for life insurance agents. Mr. Woods was one of the men without whom the American College of Life Underwriters probably could not have been created. His bias toward the pre-eminence of salesmanship, however, was the cause of many battles in the pre-incorporation years of the College.

Edward A. Woods undoubtedly had something to do with a pioneer educational program for the Equitable of New York. The Society, apparently as the first among life insurance companies, for several years ran summer courses to prepare college men to sell life insurance. The courses were held in New York. The company paid expenses for the students and even treated them to recreation trips to Coney Island. Successful salesmen from the field, pre-eminently Edward A. Woods, helped teach the classes which were held in the morning. In the afternoon, students went out to practice on the public. Similar experiments were tried by several other home offices with the emphasis always on salesmanship. At the same time and along the same lines, Louis A. Cerf, general agent in New York for the Mutual Benefit Life of Newark, conducted his "Cerf School of Salesmanship" which continued for many years. This was, so far as is known, the earliest instance of modern class instruction conducted by a local agency office.

All these courses depended chiefly on oral instruction and had little academic study material. The need for fundamental life insurance literature was even more pressing in high school and college courses in life insurance. Leaders in the field were urging introduction of the subject into high schools and institutions of higher learning. They felt that life insurance progress would be limited until the public became better informed about the services and sound operational basis of life insurance. They thought young men with some educational background in the subject could more easily be attracted to the business as a vocation. But almost always educational institutions balked at introducing a subject into their curriculums for which no teaching material was available. The thought often was expressed, "We ought to have a book."

Hence, when the National Association of Life Underwriters created an Education and Conservation Committee in 1912, one of its first undertakings was the production of a textbook. This was completely in line with the purpose of the committee—to improve life insurance selling, and policyholders' subsequent satisfaction with their purchases, through education of both buyer and seller.

Warren H. Horner was chairman of the new Education and Conservation Committee. Remarks he made before the N.A.L.U. convention in 1913 are interesting because they reflect not only the objectives of the committee, but also the life value concept that Dr. Huebner was beginning to disseminate, and the agents' evaluation of their home office operations in developing salesmen. He spoke as follows:

The National Association of Life Underwriters has established an educational and conservation bureau for the dissemination of non-partisan information of fact and interest to the public on insurance matters in general. This bureau will co-operate with institutions of learning, public and private, to promote insurance education, better fitting the younger generation to intelligently buy Life Insurance or engage in the business as a vocation.

This bureau is an *institutional movement prompted by legitimate, practical* business motives and an altruistic desire by the leading agents of the country to render more efficient service to the public at large, and to create a better spirit of understanding between the people on one side and Life Insurance on the other.

Life Insurance has not been properly understood in its economic and beneficent relation to the people. It is in reality the conservation of human life. The public, and all too many agents, have not understood that an individual, commercially speaking, is in reality only a human machine, and a frail one at that, and as such has a definite but perishable value which must be insured against loss by death or wearing out in old age.

Too small a percentage of Life Insurance agents themselves recognize that they are called to a work of large import and have the opportunity to render a great service to humanity. A Life Insurance agent who does not understand the economic application of what he is doing, and rise to its professional attainments, is a positive detriment to the business. The Life Insurance companies are babes in the woods in the method of appointing and training agents, and the states are equally as lax and unscientific in licensing the agents whom the companies appoint. The proper and adequate purchase of a Life Insurance policy or the care and selection of an individual's insurance over a term of years calls for a professional service, *personally rendered* by a trained individual possessing integrity and intelligence of the highest order.

One of the leaders of the National Association of Life Underwriters particularly committed to the cause of life insurance education was Ernest J. Clark, general agent for the John Hancock Mutual in Baltimore. He had sent his nephew, Paul F. Clark, to the Wharton School to prepare for work with him in his agency. There, of course, young Paul studied with Dr. Huebner, and thus a tie developed which had far-reaching results for the life insurance business.

Ernest Clark nominated Dr. Huebner to write the long-desired life insurance textbook. After considerable difficulty, D. Appleton and Company, of New York, agreed to publish it. They had little confidence in the potential market for the book, and it was necessary for the Education and Conservation Committee to guarantee them against loss. An arrangement was made for all sales to life insurance agents, companies, or insurance journals to be channeled through the Committee, with profits on those sales to go to the Committee for the furtherance of its broad program.

After years of wishing and months of hard work incident to the publication, one can imagine the emotions of the Committee members when Ernest Clark announced the finished product at the N.A.L.U. convention in 1915. *Life Insurance: A Textbook* was a reality. Mr. Clark characterized it as "the very cornerstone to the future educational and conservation movement," and added:

> Gentlemen, none of us have or ever have had a text book in the practice and principles of Life Insurance written from a purely disinterested point of view by a Life Insurance educator. Consequently we have had no text book in the past which could be accepted by a high school, a college, a university, or which could constitute the foundation for agency instruction in our various offices.

The book was an immediate success. The guarantors never had to make good on their underwriting. In the first year the Committee had $1,000 of profits from sales to life insurance customers; and, as expected, colleges and universities adopted the text for their courses. Eventually, the book went through five editions in the United States and was translated into many foreign languages.

The book was important in itself. Far more important, however, its writing tightened the association between Ernest J. Clark and Dr. Huebner. Mr. Clark was a national leader in life insurance agency affairs. Naturally, as he discussed with Dr. Huebner their plans for the textbook they talked also of other needs of the industry. Edward A. Woods, a member of the Education and Conservation Committee, also talked often with Dr. Huebner and reported what he was doing to train life insurance salesmen in his own agency. Dr. Huebner recalls that with him, and particularly with Mr. Clark, he would sit in a hotel room until 2 o'clock in the morning. There they discussed their hopes and plans for making better life insurance salesmen. Mr. Woods was enthusiastic about improvements in sales techniques. Mr. Clark recognized the importance of a sound educational background in the whole area of business. Stimulated by these two great leaders, Dr. Huebner began to envision a broad academic program of preparation for a lifetime profession.

Mr. Clark was not slow to encourage Dr. Huebner and to enlist his talents in the cause. He did not wait until they could influence national affairs, but started immediately in Baltimore. He invited Dr. Huebner to speak to the life underwriters in his home city, and Dr. Huebner enjoyed it. He found stimulus in combining his ideas with the experience of active salesmen. Repeatedly Dr. Huebner and Mr. Clark met and talked about the strategy of their crusade to organize professional life insurance education.

In February, 1914, Mr. Clark asked Dr. Huebner to speak to the Baltimore life underwriters on the general subject of life insurance education. There, for the first time publicly, Dr. Huebner referred to the idea of having a life insurance course of study on the college level leading to a professional degree, as did certified public accountants.

Young Paul Clark knew his teacher was to speak for his uncle's group in Baltimore. He asked Dr. Huebner if it would be all right for him to go along. Dr. Huebner said, "Of course. Your being there will probably help me make a better speech."

Paul Clark remembers that the underwriters sat him on the platform and introduced him as exhibit A, a young man who was going to college to prepare for a life insurance sales career. He said they regarded him like a man from Mars. They crowded around afterward with questions: "You are studying life insurance in college?" "What do you study?" They thought it was a strange thing.

The reaction to Dr. Huebner's talk indicated that the strategic time had come to seek a larger audience. Ernest Clark was then president of the National Association of Life Underwriters, and in the spring of 1914 he recruited four key men from the Association to work actively on development of a broad-based professional course of study for life insurance salesmen. These men were Edward A. Woods, John Newton Russell, J. Stanley Edwards, and Franklin W. Ganse.

These leaders felt that the life insurance fraternity as a whole needed conditioning before it was given the idea of a college course and a professional degree. Through their influence, "Life Insurance Education" became the theme of the 1914 convention of the National Association in Cincinnati. Dr. Huebner was invited to give the keynote address. Paul Clark is one of the few men now living who heard that speech. He was not yet in the business, but with a student's enthusiasm for his favorite professor he went from his home in Dayton at the end of the summer to be present for what proved an historic occasion.

In 1914 the life insurance business was still shadowed by the evils exposed in the Armstrong Investigation. People were still thinking of life insurance as a few thousands, or even hundreds, of dollars for burial purposes. The country was overrun with part-time agents—school teachers, bankers, storekeepers, practically anybody—who picked up occasional sales from friends or

Ernest J. Clark. (*Harris & Ewing*)

John Newton Russell.

J. Stanley Edwards.

neighbors, and demonstrated that selling life insurance required no particular talent or preparation. Even the full-time agent stood rather low in the scale of social approval. Sources of life insurance information were few, and ignorance of life insurance was widespread.

When Dr. Huebner, a high-ranking university professor, appeared on the convention platform speaking with respect about the importance and dignity of its calling, the life insurance audience was thrilled. That was a new experience. When he strengthened and expanded their sales ideas they could hardly believe their ears. Here was reinforcement from an unexpected source. When he opened to them the vision of educational possibilities for themselves and the public, they caught fire. Few had ever dared to think in such terms.

The Cincinnati audience broke into overwhelming applause as Dr. Huebner finished his talk. By formal resolution they went "on record in the most emphatic way" to express "gratitude of this magnificent address." Their enthusiasm led to invitations for repetition of the talk in other places. In the next few years, Dr. Huebner spoke on similar lines many, many times, sowing far and wide seeds which flowered wonderfully in later years.

The following quotations from the *Proceedings* of the convention indicate the foundation Dr. Huebner laid for the life underwriters' new concepts of themselves and their business.

Life Insurance, because of its complexity, is probably the most academic in character of all business subjects. Yet education in this field has, until recently at least, been limited almost wholly to those who are engaged in its various departments. The general public for whom Life Insurance really exists have been largely overlooked. The result has been that the institution not only suffers from unwise legislation, but the general public manifests only a faint idea of its great mission and seems to show a spirit of indifference to its welfare and a distrust of its methods. Probably no human agency so universally needed is so little understood. It will be conceded that it is high time that a proper public opinion should be developed and that much of the opinion now existing must be changed. The only way to do this, I believe, is through a comprehensive system of non-partisan education, which in the course of time will gradually mould the habit of thought on the part of the masses. . . .

I believe that there are six main lines of thought that should be emphasized through every available channel of education . . .

(1) First and foremost, all who have assumed family responsibilities should be impressed with the sacred duty of using Life Insurance as a means to protect their loved ones against the want that may be occasioned by premature death. Life Insurance is a bulwark of the home and the only safe method of hedging it against the uncertainties of life. Men must be made to recognize the value of a human life both from the family and business standpoint (the two being nearly always closely interrelated) and to capitalize and perpetuate that value in compliance with the dictates of Christian duty. The capitalization of the value of a human life for the benefit of the dependent members of the household is a fundamental duty that should be preached from every pulpit, be taught in every school where students are old enough to comprehend, and be given the widest publicity through the press by means of articles, editorials and non-partisan advertising. Emphasis should be laid on the "crime of not insuring" and on the biblical injunction, so frequently quoted, that "If any provide not for his own, and especially for those of his own house, he hath denied the faith, and is worse than an infidel." Let it be taught that the finger of scorn should be pointed at any man who, although he has provided well while alive, has not seen fit to discount the uncertain future for the benefit of his dependent household. Let it also be known that such a man, as Dr. Talmage well said, "is a defalcation, an outrage, a swindle. He did not die, he absconded." [Dr. DeWitt Talmage was a prominent New York clergyman who had preached a famous sermon in defense of life insurance.]

Life Insurance is the only sure means of changing uncertainty into certainty and is the antithesis of gambling. He who does not insure gambles with the greatest of all chances and, if a loser, makes those dearest to him pay the forfeit. . . .

(2) Writers on Life Insurance assert over and over again that insurance is not a producer of wealth and that its function is merely to distribute funds from the fortunate to the unfortunate. I feel that the public should be shown that Life Insurance, besides protecting against misfortune, is also a powerful force in the production of wealth, and that premium payments should not be regarded merely as an expense to be grudgingly borne. Constant worry is one of the greatest curses that can fall to the lot of man, and Life Insurance, if universally used, would lift that curse from innumerable shoulders. The knowledge of an assured estate from the moment the premium is paid will enable the insured to feel freer in assuming initiative. By removing a load of care from the mind it promotes efficiency and makes life happier. In my own case my Life Insurance is my most sacred possession, and I have often felt that I would not be without it even though the premiums were twice what they are. Because of it, I eat better, sleep better, feel better, and as a result of these, work better.

(3) Agents constantly meet with those whose argument against Life Insurance is that they prefer to save. This view should be strenuously opposed in our educational program. The habit of saving should by all means be encouraged, but it should be made clear that the saving of a competence involves the necessary time to save, and that Life Insurance is the only certain method to use as a hedge against the possibilities of the saving period being cut short. It must be made clear that a policy of saving can yield only a small amount at the start, while a policy of insurance from its beginning guarantees the full face value. Moreover, the roseate views which so many have concerning their resolution and ability to accumulate and keep should be tempered by a frank statement of the harrowing facts as they actually exist. Eighty-five per cent of this country's adults leave no estate at all, and about one-third of the widows in the country lack the necessities and 90 per cent the comforts of life. Let us also emphasize the fact that, in addition to guaranteeing an estate at once, Life Insurance contains an investment feature which is absolutely safe, that it is one of the greatest forces to inculcate the saving instinct, that it is admirably adapted to put small sums of money to prompt and profitable use, and that, to use the choice expression of one underwriter, it is "compound interest in harness." Let it also be known how easily and how frequently the competence which a husband or father has provided through saving or insur-

ance is lost by the heir or beneficiary, and that modern income policies furnish a guarantee against such a contingency.

(4) Life Insurance also lends itself to numerous business uses and it is highly essential in an educational program that a knowledge of these should be given as wide circulation as possible. I recently received a circular from a leading company outlining no less than 25 such cases, and unfortunately the limits of an address do not permit an enumeration of the same. Suffice it to say that they are little understood today by the great mass of business men, and it is certain that a readable and illustrated explanation of the uses of insurance as a means of indemnification against the loss by death of a valued official or employe, of providing a sinking fund to meet future liabilities, or safeguarding credit, of covering a mortgage, or raising further capital without additional tangible collateral, etc., is sure to attract attention and produce results. I venture to say that there is hardly a business man who is not at one time or another confronted with some business situation the solution of which can be rendered easier and safer through the proper application of Life Insurance . . .

But what is needed now is the immediate education of the adult population along the lines just indicated. This, I think, can be accomplished best (1) by having the great mission of Life Insurance explained, wherever possible, through the medium of the pulpit, the lecture platform and the editorial column; (2) by disseminating readable and carefully prepared information, of a strictly non-partisan and educational character and with the subject-matter so copiously and simply illustrated as to be readily grasped by the average mind, through the pages of the leading newspapers and magazines, and (3) by disseminating the same kind of information, as well as short articles explaining the specific business uses of Life Insurance through the leading trade journals of the country . . .

Let us not forget that the student of today becomes the family head, business manager, teacher, agent and community leader in the pulpit, the press, the school and the legislative hall tomorrow; and if a knowledge of the uses and sacred functions of Life Insurance is drilled into the minds of the young, and they are given the proper habit of thought, we may be sure that they will at the proper time translate that thought into action not only as regards themselves, but also in advising their fellow man.

I may be pardoned for feeling deeply on this subject, because in my own humble little way I am doing my best to teach Life Insurance to about 200 students a year. My meaning can best be expressed by a few examples. Every year an hour's lecture on the use of Life Insurance as a means of safely financing a young man without tangible collateral, except his health, good name and a willing relative or friend, has caused a number in the class to use the plan as a means of financing themselves through college, thus enabling them to give their undivided attention to the work before them. Every year, judging from the interviews, a fair percentage of the boys induce their fathers to take out insurance on their lives, and some take it themselves for the protection of a parent. Hardly a week goes by but what some former student writes me concerning some type of policy and some particular use to which Life Insurance may be put, and they often add that I may still remember their having been in the class in such and such a year. Only about a month ago a student who seven years ago took the general insurance course in our Evening School of Accounts and Finance as a part of a general business education asked me to meet him to talk over some insurance matters. This young man has been eminently successful and has worked his way to a directorship in a manufacturing corporation employing some 1,200 men. At our meeting it was evident that he still remembered the explanation of the business uses of Life Insurance and that he had not only amply supplied himself with protection, but has been instrumental in convincing the directorate to hedge the company against the loss by premature death of the one man in the business who was its chief asset financially and mentally. Not only had $250,000 of insurance already been taken on this man's life in the interest of the business, but the management had just decided to take $500,000 more. This ex-student frankly told me that he was deeply concerned personally because he has his nearly all in that business.

I trust I may be pardoned for making these references. They are merely mentioned as little incidents to show that the young men—the students—of today become the managers of business establishments and the heads of families tomorrow, and that if the uses of Life Insurance are forcibly brought to their attention it is not unreasonable to expect that in time that knowledge will be put to profitable use. . .

The attitude of the average agent toward the whole broad plan of Life Insurance education will necessarily depend upon his attitude toward the professional standing of his work, i.e., does he regard his business as a profession or merely as an occupation? Life Insurance salesmanship must be given the status of a profession— a high calling—both as regards the methods pursued and the quality of the service rendered. If this is done you will certainly have the right to feel that you are identified with one of the noblest professions in existence, ranking with those of the ministry, law, medicine and teaching . . .

The term "profession" implies expert knowledge and has been defined as "a vocation in which a professional knowledge of science or learning is used by its practice to the affairs of others, either in advising, guiding or teaching them, or in serving their interests or welfare in the practice of an art founded on it." If Life Insurance salesmanship is to have a professional standing, it is necessary for its representative in the field to meet the standards of this definition . . .

To this end he should understand the scientific features of the business, such as the fundamental principles underlying rate making, the operation of the reserve, the sources of the surplus and their interpretation, etc. . . .

As already stated, Life Insurance salesmen should be students throughout their career. They should strive to keep abreast with the best that is said and written about Life Insurance. And permit me to make the further suggestion that, if possible, agents should acquaint themselves with the leading facts surrounding various business activities, especially in view of the growing importance of so-called "Business Life Insurance."

With public life underwriter interest in education now aroused, Mr. Clark and Dr. Huebner decided to take further steps to shape their program. The Baltimore Life Underwriters again scheduled a talk by Dr. Huebner, this time on education for *life underwriters* and the professional aspects of life insurance selling. Now Dr. Huebner definitely described the goal of a life insurance course of study leading to a degree like the C.P.A., and originating in a college of standing commensurate with other degree-granting educational institutions.

Dr. Huebner's definition of a profession as he gave it to the Baltimore life insurance men in 1915 reflected contemporary problems, some of which are still with us. He repeated this speech the next week for the life underwriters of New York City, and later for other groups. His ideas were quoted widely. Also, the speech was published as an appendix in the first edition of his textbook, *Life Insurance*, promoted by the National Association of Life Underwriters. But the influence of his ideas did not stop there. They are still quoted in material furnished currently to C.L.U. students.

These fundamental observations about the four major aspects of a profession are:

First, that the vocation should be so essentially useful to society and so noble in its purpose as to inspire sufficient love and enthusiasm on the part of the practitioner to make it his life's work. One cannot regard highly the services of a professional man who looks upon his vocation as a side issue and who is not willing to devote to its practice his entire time and his best thought and energy.

Second, that the vocation involves a science and in its practice an expert knowledge of that science.

Third, that in applying this expert knowledge the practitioner should abandon the strictly selfish commercial view and ever keep in mind the advantage of the client. Conscientious and disinterested service—proper advice and guidance—is the very essence of professional conduct, and in the long run the best policy.

Fourth, that the individual practitioner should possess a spirit of loyalty to his fellow practitioners, of helpfulness to the common cause that they all profess and should not allow any unprofessional

Franklin W. Ganse.

acts to bring shame upon the entire profession. Unfortunately the public has a habit of jumping to general conclusions, and too frequently the selfish unprofessional conduct of a few leads to a distorted and unfair view of an entire group. The Golden Rule is applicable in this respect quite as much as in individual transactions.

Chapter 5

THE TIME GROWS RIPE

The first quarter of the twentieth century saw the development of an interesting variety of enterprises and conditions related to selling, and particularly to life insurance selling. Throughout much of the business world the idea was fermenting that selling was an art and a skill which could be taught and learned. Edward A. Woods fervently believed that himself. He was a wealthy man, with wide contacts among leaders of business and industry. With imagination and enthusiasm he shared their conferences and contributed his own ideas from his life insurance experience. Mr. Woods was in 1916 president of the National Association of Life Underwriters, and was a moving spirit of a new organization that year. At the N.A.L.U. convention that fall, Ernest J. Clark, reporting as chairman of his committee, gave him full credit:

> What your Scientific Salesmanship Committee regards as the most important achievement of President Woods' administration, was the founding of the Carnegie Bureau of Salesmanship Research on May 25, 1916, and this great, and what will doubtless become historic, piece of work was accomplished by the initiative and personal influence of President Woods.

> The object of the Bureau of Salesmanship Research is "for the purpose of reducing the cost of selling through a co-operative study of the best methods of employing and training salesmen."

In the beginning, the Edward A. Woods Company, the Equitable Life Assurance Society, the Metropolitan Life, the Phoenix

Mutual Life and the Prudential were life insurance company members of the Bureau. The other original members were world famous companies in many types of business: Carnegie Steel Corporation, Ford Motor Company, Armstrong Cork Company, H. J. Heinz Company, Westinghouse Electric and Manufacturing Company, Chalmers Motor Company, Page-Detroit Company, Burroughs Adding Machine Company, Aluminum Company of America, Pittsburgh Steel Company and Lilly and Company.

The new Bureau was associated with the Carnegie Institute of Technology in Pittsburgh. Its director was Dr. Walter Dill Scott, well-known professor of psychology, advertising, and salesmanship, and later president, at Northwestern University. The Bureau started immediately on its studies of the sales organizations of cooperating members to learn the best methods of finding, selecting, training, and supervising salesmen. They gave particular attention to psychological tests being used experimentally by some companies. This was in the midst of World War I when the United States was drafting its first huge citizens' army. The Bureau became interested in the possibilities of psychological tests for the selection and placement of military personnel, and soon most of the staff was employed by the War Department for that work. After the war, the Bureau resumed its study of life insurance salesmen.

Some of the group who originated the Bureau of Salesmanship Research at Carnegie in 1916 participated in another historic project that same year. They helped stage a world sales congress. Through Mr. Woods and others of the National Association of Life Underwriters, the life insurance business was well represented. E. J. Clark, chairman of the N.A.L.U. Committee on Scientific Salesmanship, reported to the 1916 N.A.L.U. convention:

> On July 9th to 13th, inclusive, there was held in Detroit the first World's Sales Congress, in which life insurance again, led by President Woods of the National Association, played a most im-

portant part. On Monday, July 10, 1916, the official opening of the Congress occurred in Arcadia Hall, the President of the United States making the first principal address, and followed by such able speakers as Hugh Chalmers, President of the Chalmers Motor Company; Norval A. Hawkins, General Sales Manager of the Ford Motor Company; Arthur Brisbane, Editor of the New York *Evening Journal*, and the Honorable William C. Redfield, Secretary of Commerce.

On Tuesday, July 11th, President Woods addressed the Congress on "Selling Schools." The program for Wednesday, July 12th, was made up of sectional meetings—each line of business with a sufficiently large attendance of representatives holding a separate meeting. Life Insurance was most creditably represented and enjoyed a valuable session in considering some of its own scientific salesmanship problems. . . .

One of the by-products of the Congress, and an outgrowth which we anticipate will constitute a monument of much value and interest to the life insurance field men, was a decision on the part of the agency executives of the respective companies participating in the Congress to appoint a committee, of which Mr. Winslow Russell is chairman, to consider a plan for organization of an Association of Agency Officials. We sincerely trust that this may be accomplished as such an organization can be made of the greatest value in the study of life insurance salesmanship, elimination of waste, conservation and training of field forces, etc., in co-operation with the work of the National Association.

The waste of time, money, and manpower in the sales phase of the business affected the whole industry. Winslow Russell emphasized that a bad sales force could "undo all the mathematics of the actuary." He promised that an organization of selling officials could do things "to gladden the heart of the actuary" who currently was harassed by results of bad selling. He urged that as the organizations of life company presidents, of medical directors, and of actuaries had proved valuable to the business, so an association of selling executives could benefit the industry. Thus, in the fall of 1916, the Association of Life Agency Officers came into being.

The experiences of war time were having their influence on life insurance selling. Primarily, the government offer of War Risk Insurance to the amount of $10,000 to every doughboy set a new standard for judging adequacy of life insurance ownership. War deaths were not heavy in the United States armed forces, but young people throughout the country were struck down in shocking numbers by the influenza epidemic. In 1918, the peak year for the disease in the United States, the average age at death was thirty-three years. Families in every community gratefully thanked the life insurance agents who had persuaded healthy young men and women to buy the policies which were proving so important for their families.

An editorial in a life insurance magazine gave a vivid description of a changing public attitude toward life insurance and its salesmen.

Life insurance. These words should only be uttered with respect, while many who have benefitted by its protecting mantle utter these words almost with a feeling of reverence ...

The months just passed have thrown a halo around the business of life insurance, possessed of a magnetic power which draws all manner of men to its shrine. The first flicker came with the information to be found in the financial statements of the respective life insurance companies, in connection with its losses from influenza and pneumonia sustained by the different offices. As the losses from this terribly devastating plague are made known, men in all walks of life marvel at the disclosure. Millions of dollars are being transferred from the coffers of the great provisional storehouses of life insurance companies to the beneficiaries of the policyholders.

Over one hundred millions of dollars has already been distributed over the country into the cottage of the poor and the mansion of the rich alike, according to the measure of protection secured through the agent back yonder, not now considered a pest or a bore.

Though the business and social worlds have rocked almost unceasingly in the throes of pestilence and war for months, and unnumbered deaths have followed in their wake, the policy obligations of life insurance companies have been liquidated according to contract and there is not a quake in the stability of the legal reserve life insurance companies. Life insurance stands today adamant in strength, and glorified through its service.

When the armistice came in 1918, the United States had two million soldiers in Europe. To occupy their time pending their return home and to help prepare them for civilian life, many educational courses were offered. Under the sponsorship of the Association of Life Agency Officers life insurance was included in this vast program. The course for the doughboys was the first formal educational course ever developed by the industry.

Two men who subsequently had an important part in the American College of Life Underwriters were among those sent to France to conduct the classes. One was John Marshall Holcombe, Jr., then of the Phoenix Mutual. The other, Frank L. Jones of the Equitable Life Assurance Society of New York, was in charge of the life insurance activities with the title "head of department of insurance, A.E.F." He reported that the overall educational plan for the men overseas had four objectives:

1. To send to French and British universities as many college grade men as can be accommodated for a period of four months.
2. To establish a University at Beaune for 20,000 men of high grade.
3. To maintain districts of education at embarkation points along the lines in Germany.
4. To give educational courses at every point where 500 or more men are in camp.

Life insurance found its place especially in the last two categories. Mr. Jones' first official report reflects considerable credit to the business.

You will be glad to know that we are on the ground with the only complete equipment there is. No other department has its course or prospectus printed and few have enough textbooks. I brought with me enough supplies for 100 teachers and 600 students. Mr. Alexander's book is at Chaumont in large quantities. I have not heard whether Huebner's text has reached there or not, but we can go ahead without it for the time being and the American Library Association here has 100 copies in cloth anyhow, and they will be available. I'm glad indeed we had our printing done in the United States. We are most fortunate; the fact that we came fully equipped is in itself a big advantage for life insurance. I have heard already many complimentary references to our foresight and alacrity.

Four months later, Mr. Jones reported that the course had had 1,200 students in organized classes, 1,800 in reading and study groups, and more than 120,000 in lectures given "in 'Y' huts, in tents, out-of-doors, before or after picture shows in assembly halls." The instructors had featured life insurance as an academic study rather than as a selling course. He explained their approach and evaluated the program:

Particular emphasis was given to the bearing of the various phases of life insurance upon American economic and social life. The by-products of insurance, such as thrift, investment, public health activities and other economic factors of insurance and insuring were emphasized. . . .

There was nothing that your association could do in the way of advertising life insurance as an institution which would bring it into more favorable notice than the conducting of classes such as was done among American boys in the foreign field. The impact of the whole plan will be seen in future years in the better understanding of life insurance, in the addition of men to the ranks of the agency forces, and, we trust, in the more favorable attitude which many of these men will take in legislative halls toward the subject of life insurance.

While the courses in Europe were going on, the Association of Life Agency Officers was not neglecting opportunities at home. It was planning a major educational project—a school of practical life insurance salesmanship at the Carnegie Institute of Technology in Pittsburgh.

Edward A. Woods, Winslow Russell, and three Carnegie professors were members of the committee in charge of organizing the school. Two other men, through membership on the committee, began careers of long-range importance in life insurance education. These men were Griffin M. Lovelace and John A. Stevenson.

Mr. Lovelace did much of the groundwork in planning the school. He became its secretary, and taught an economics course as well as life insurance principles and practices. He had had broad experience in selling and sales management with two companies.

Mr. Lovelace's part in the actual organization of the Carnegie school was important, but his leadership in its educational philosophy was even more important, and had a revolutionary influence on the whole life insurance business. Vincent B. Coffin, one of his students in the Carnegie school's first year, looked back over 30 years and wrote his appraisal:

> In the judgment of the writer, the one individual most responsible for the newer ideas (popping up in the 1920's) was Griffin M. Lovelace. . . . Mr. Lovelace introduced a new concept . . . completely accepted today . . . that life insurance ought to be sold on the basis of definite and specific needs. If it seems incredible to you that this truth was revolutionary, then you need to be reminded that up until about this time companies had distributed their wares almost exclusively on the comparative merits of one policy contract over another. . . . The needs concept caught the imagination of the field with great vigor in the 1920's and laid the foundation for the development of programming and ultimately estate planning.

When Mr. Lovelace was commissioned to organize the new life insurance education program at Carnegie Tech, he had first a double task. He had to find a director qualified to meet both Carnegie's scholastic standards and the life underwriters' practical requirements. Dr. Stevenson was then an assistant dean of education at the University of Illinois, and, as a college student, had been a part-time life insurance salesman. Mr. Lovelace went

John Marshall Holcombe, Jr.
(*Bachrach*)

John A. Stevenson.

to Urbana and spent a week with Dr. Stevenson. The plan for Carnegie students was to combine classes with actual selling. This method of teaching especially interested Dr. Stevenson. After prolonged discussions with Mr. Lovelace and Carnegie officials, he agreed to become director of the proposed new school, provided Mr. Lovelace would be part of the staff. Dr. Stevenson was a determining influence on life insurance education through the school and later through his work as vice president in charge of training at the Equitable Life of New York, and as agency vice president and president of the Penn Mutual Life.

Friends of life insurance other than the committee were enthusiastic about the proposed school. The *Eastern Underwriter* was one of the life insurance journals which reflected their interest and enthusiasm:

At last there is to be a real school for insurance agents. Not a mere lecture course, not a few hours a week, not a series of talks by overworked professors, but a real college where insurance salesmanship will receive the attention which it deserves.

The course is to be established at the Carnegie Institute which in its department of salesmanship research, which was headed by Dr. Walter Dill Scott, has been far in advance of other educational institutions in studying salesmanship as a science.

Cooperating with the Carnegie Institute, lending every possible help, is the Association of Agency Managers [*sic*], which includes many of the leading agency superintendents of the life insurance companies, and which is responsible for the introduction of life insurance courses in France for the American army and navy; and Edward A. Woods, who has been collecting facts for years in an effort to wipe out the tremendous waste of hours and money caused by the drifting of unsuitable men into and out of the insurance business.

Later, quoting "a spokesman for the school" who sounds very much like E. A. Woods, the *Eastern Underwriter* wrote again:

It must be remembered, too, that salesmanship is an art, the under-lying principles of which are founded on psychology. At the present time there are no satisfactory courses in the application of psychology to salesmanship. Both life insurance and life insurance sales-manship are to be taught at Carnegie. Thorough knowledge of the first will be required as a basis of a proper understanding of the second . . . Carnegie Institute's interest in the subject is easily under-stood. First, it is the leading institution in the field of vocational training, and sees in life insurance a vocation which touches the eco-nomic life of the people at a most vital point. Its department of applied psychology is also strong; in fact there is no better one in the country.

The Carnegie school opened in the fall of 1919. The course was offered three times a year for eleven weeks. Most students attended on scholarships provided by life insurance companies. They mastered academic work on principles and functions of life insurance, learned several organized sales presentations, and did actual sales work in Pittsburgh.

The Carnegie school's success inspired others during the next few years. Some were operated according to the Carnegie plan and approved by the Committee on Educational Standards of the National Association of Life Underwriters. Among these were the schools of New York University, Boston University, University of Denver, and University of Oklahoma. Also, summer schools were conducted by the Carnegie and N.Y.U. faculties at several universities on the West Coast, in St. Louis, at Marshall College in West Virginia, and Syracuse University in New York State.

The United Y.M.C.A. Schools—an important educational force after World War I—also offered an evening life insurance course which attracted thousands of men. These students were prospective salesmen as well as working life underwriters. The curriculum for these schools was submitted to the National Association of Life Underwriters and approved by the Committee on Educational Standards.

The New York University program attracted to life insurance teaching a number of young men who afterward became leaders in the business, and at every step cooperated with the American College program. Among them were Vincent B. Coffin, who became senior vice president of the Connecticut Mutual Life Insurance Company and later the first chancellor of the University of Hartford; and James Elton Bragg, who became general agent in New York City for the Guardian Life Insurance Company. He also continued for many years to teach life insurance at N.Y.U., and gave valuable service to the American College as chairman of the Examination Board, as will be described later.

The Carnegie school was the fertile soil from which grew a series of study books for life insurance salesmen. Dr. Stevenson wrote *Meeting Objections* (1921) and *Selling Life Insurance* (1922). Mr. Lovelace wrote *The House of Protection* (1921) and *Analyzing Life Situations for Insurance Needs* (1922), these two, a discussion of income insurance and simple programing, and *Life Insurance Fundamentals* (1923). Dr. Edward K. Strong wrote *The Psychology of Selling Life Insurance* (1922). Harper and Brothers published these books as part of the "Harper Life Insurance Library," which also included *Life Underwriting as a Career* (1923) by Edward A. Woods, and *Inheritance Taxation* (1925) by Leon Gilbert Simon.

The National Association of Life Underwriters also had sponsored a primer on life insurance for beginners, *What Life Insurance Is and What It Does*, by William Alexander, secretary of the Equitable Life Assurance Society. The book was used first by the Society for its own agents, but became generally available when it was published by the Spectator Company in 1917. It was used in the courses in Europe after the armistice, and for a long while it was the introduction to the book study of life insurance for many salesmen.

A life insurance literature was growing slowly. Dr. Huebner and the men looking forward to a professional course of study on a college basis knew that still more books were necessary, books on a higher academic level. Therefore, Dr. Huebner planned and edited what became known as the "Appleton Series." Most of these volumes were available by the time the American College program was launched. With several from the "Harper Library," they were the core of life insurance study material recommended for the first C.L.U. candidates.

The "Appleton Series, Life Insurance, Its Economic and Social Relations," as it ultimately developed, was:

Huebner, S. S. *Economics of Life Insurance*, 1927.
Huebner, S. S., and McCahan, David. *Life Insurance as Investment*, 1933.
Huttinger, E. Paul. *The Law of Salesmanship*, 1927.
Loman, Harry J. *Life Insurance in Relation to Taxation*, 1928.
Madden, James L. *Wills, Trusts and Estates*, 1927.
Scully, C. Alison, and Ganse, Franklin W. *Business Life Insurance Trusts*, 1930.
Stevenson, John A. *Education and Philanthropy*, 1927.
Woods, Edward A. *The Sociology of Life Insurance*, 1928.

The Economics of Life Insurance by Dr. Huebner was the study of his life value concept. He had referred to the idea from the earliest days of his teaching, and in the *Textbook* in 1915 quoted the famous statement attributed to Benjamin Franklin:

It is a strange anomaly that men should be careful to insure their houses, their ships, their merchandise, and yet neglect to insure their lives, surely the most important of all to their families, and more subject to loss.

In 1924, he had made a comprehensive statement of his philosophy of life insurance based on the human life value concept in a talk before the National Association of Life Underwriters in Los Angeles. The speech made headlines in the next morning's *Los Angeles Times*. It revolutionized the thought and work of many life underwriters across the country. It lifted their sights and gave them what Dr. Huebner called "a track to run on" in the development of an economic philosophy. That philosophy provided a foundation for the professional concept of life underwriting as a calling. The idea was susceptible of dramatic illustration in those days. Because of the Florida real estate boom and the soaring stock market it was easy for people to think big. It did not frighten a man earning $20,000 a year to be told that he represented a capital value of several hundreds of thousands of dollars. Many were convinced by the logic or flattered by the suggestion, and the income tax situation was such that a person could quite comfortably manage to cover his life value with life insurance, if he so desired. The jumbo sales which resulted confirmed the underwriters' convictions about the soundness of the concept.

The life value idea naturally led to expanding relationships for the life insurance product and broadened the base for academic study. Some quotations from the famous Los Angeles speech will indicate how that could be.

In our economic life only two types of values exist, namely human life and property values. The life values consist of the character, industry, technical and managerial ability, power of initiative, and judgment of individuals. They have heretofore been regarded as intangible, economically indefinite, and difficult if not impossible of scientific treatment. The property values comprise land, buildings, machinery and equipment, raw materials, finished goods, and business goodwill. Being tangible in character, and thus more easily comprehended than the life values, these material things have for years been regarded as capable of scientific organization and management. They are therefore subjected to appraisal. Through the issue of stocks, bonds, warehouse receipts, bills of lading, and similar evidences of wealth, they are given perpetuity as working capital and fluidity as collateral for loans. They are also recognized as being subject to immediate or ultimate loss. Scientific use is therefore made, as a matter of ordinary business precaution, of the principles governing depreciation, sinking funds, and contracts of indemnity.

Without these practices, property values—like life values—would also be indefinite economically. But with the lessons so admirably

evolved for us in the field of property values and with this information to guide us, may we not ask why life values should not be
treated equally scientifically and be made equally tangible and
definite? Is it not ridiculous for a human being to make himself
more and more valuable all the time and then all of a sudden, just
when that value is greatest to his business and his family, have it
disappear entirely because of death or disability? Does it seem
reasonable that life values should be treated thus carelessly, especially since we owe a duty to others—to family and business associates—when the lessons of foresight, so fully prepared in connection
with property values, are before us for imitation?

The most important new development in economic thought will be
the recognition of the economic value of human life. I confidently
believe that the time is not far distant when, in wholesale fashion,
we shall apply to the economic organization, management, and conservation of life values the same scientific treatment that we now use
in connection with property. We shall do so to the extent of capital-
izing them with bonds to give them perpetuity as a working force
and fluidity as a source of credit, of subjecting them to the principles of depreciation, and of using the sinking-fund method to
assure realization of the contemplated object wherever man has a
future business or family obligation to fulfill that involves the hazard of uncertainty of the duration of the working life. I also believe
that Life Insurance alone affords the medium through which such
scientific treatment can be applied, and that it has no competitor.

Scientific treatment of life values is justified because of their mone-
tary importance in our economic affairs. Human life values—the
factors of personal skill, industry, judgment, and driving force,
that mean so much to business success—greatly exceed in importance all property values. These personal factors are after all the
real source of all other economic values. Were it not for them, there
would be no property values. Were I called upon to make an estimate of life values in the United States, based on the current earning capacity of our adult population, capitalized at an ordinary rate
of interest, I would place the total valuation at not less than six to
eight times the aggregate of the nation's material wealth. Surely,
such a predominating element in our national economic wealth
should be accorded scientific consideration when we have seen fit
to extend it for many years to the minor element. Instead, we have

from an economic standpoint largely ignored the creative force
that gives rise to property values. We have emphasized the effect
rather than the cause, the finished service rather than the performer
of the service, the temporary products rather than the permanent
producer of those products.

With respect to many classes of men, the life value constitutes practically all of their business worth. This is true of doctors, dentists,
teachers, clergymen, lawyers, engineers, architects, scientists, authors, actors, salesmen and innumerable other groups engaged in
professional or expert work. And the significant fact in this connection is that in many callings the greater the practitioner, the
greater his skill and compensation, the more complete the loss of the
business asset in the event of the passing of the life value involved.
The average doctor's practice, I am advised, can possibly be sold
for an amount equal to one year's income, a price appallingly small
when compared with the practitioner's earning capacity spread
over the normal working life. A great specialist, however, is irre-
placeable even to this small extent. In his case, because no substitute
exists, loss of the life value is equivalent to a total loss of the business asset. In many vocations—such as teaching, the ministry, the
stage, salesmanship, etc.—the loss of the life value, unless hedged
with insurance, almost invariably means a total loss of the capitalized business worth, irrespective of whether the practitioner is
great or mediocre. The same is also true of all persons working on
a salary, be they ordinary or expert.

Often the business under consideration is chiefly concerned with
contracts, the fulfillment of which involves great skill and managerial ability, much credit, and a considerable lapse of time. Here
the life value clearly exceeds the value of the equipment used. This
fact is attested to by the universal demand for adequate corporate
surety from the contractor. And surety companies, obligating themselves to complete the contract in the event of the contractor's
failure to do so for any reason, and knowing that completion of
the work is more dependent upon the personal ability of the contractor than upon his property assets, are always very careful to
inquire into his personal record of efficiency and the amount of Life
Insurance he carries.

Many types of business, although requiring some property for their
operation, have for their chief asset the good-will of clients, built

up in the course of years through close personal contact, confidence, and friendship. A prominent broker in securities, when asked by me to give an opinion concerning the value of his life to his business, replied after mature deliberation that in the event of his death probably fifty per cent of the good-will, which he had worked for years to create and hold and which was the main source of the current business income, would flow elsewhere within the course of a year. He expressed surprise at the inquiry, said he hadn't thought of things in that light before, and, knowing my general bent of thought, jovially expressed his belief that he ought to be a candidate for a substantial amount of Life Insurance indemnity.

In still another type of business, such as manufacturing and mercantile establishments, the property value seems to predominate. Yet even here, the most extreme type that we can select, a careful appraisal in the light of all attending circumstances will show that in the overwhelming mass of cases the directing life values in the business exceed in importance the property value actually owned by the concern. We are too apt to overlook the fact that most of the apparent property in such concerns is not owned out-right, but represents borrowed funds, and that the balance actually owned is largely non-liquid in character and is dependent for regular income producing value on a wisely shaped and well directed policy on the part of the owner.

Moreover, this balance of property actually owned, especially if it constitutes the major part of the owner's personal estate, as is usually the case, will in the event of his death likely suffer severe impairment through the payment of post-mortem taxes and other costs connected with the settlement of the estate, a possible curtailment of credit which, as already noted, often exceeds the actual property owned, and a diminution in earning capacity resulting from the loss of the directing life value itself. Where the business is in its formative stage, the loss of the life value, unless adequately hedged with Life Insurance, is often the cause of bankruptcy. By thus striking a net balance between the life and the property values, I am confident that the first will exceed the latter in the great majority of manufacturing and mercantile establishments.

Few appreciate the far-reaching economic importance of Life Insurance. It represents the application to human life values of the applied economic sciences, now so fully prepared and so generally taught with respect to property values....

A new philosophy of values is necessary to change our attitude of mind, and in turn, the trend of our text-books. Usually the subject of insurance is treated by economists in a single chapter, and often in the form of an appended one. To them, Life Insurance seems to be a problem difficult to weave into their discussion of production, exchange, distribution and consumption. Nevertheless, it is an important factor in all of these divisions of economics. Its universal and adequate use would radically alter for the better the character and amount of present consumption. Its vast accumulation of assets from the millions of our population, and its distribution of these assets by way of investment and payment of claims, are two of the most stupendous phases of modern exchange. It is also highly creative by increasing personal initiative through removal of the paralyzing effect of worry and fear, by enlarging greatly the available fund of working capital through systematic, compulsory, and profitable thrift, by increasing tremendously the amount of available business credit, and by indemnifying business against the loss of the personal factors that give it direction and force. Life values underlie all business enterprises. Where business property values exist, life values are inseparably interwoven with them. Since economics is the "science of business" and since life values greatly exceed in importance the property values and are fundamental to business success, it seems reasonable that much more space in our economic texts ought to be devoted to their business aspects and to their scientific treatment by means of Life Insurance.

In discussing life values in business, we are apt to forget that the family is also a business. We are inclined to overlook the fact that all Life Insurance is business insurance, even when effected solely for the purpose of family protection. The family should be every man's first and most important business. From the economic standpoint, it is a business partnership which, like any other partnership, is legally dissolved through the death of either partner. If business partnership insurance is desirable, and that is conceded, then certainly the breadwinning partner in the family, for the same fundamental reason, should also be insured for the benefit of the surviving dependent partners. The family should be organized and operated in accordance with business principles. Just like any other business enterprise, it should be safe-guarded against financial impairment or bankruptcy through the loss of its strategic life value.

All the principles already discussed with reference to life values in business are equally applicable to the family relationship. To permit the starting of a family partnership, when the only contributed capital is the native ability, good-will and current earning capacity of its head, is little short of a crime, unless adequate provision has been made for a guaranteed potential estate through the medium of Life Insurance.

In reviewing the *Economics of Life Insurance*, a contemporary life insurance journal appraised also the changing times which were producing a climate favorable to a major academic program for life insurance salesmen. The following quotations are significant.

Professor Huebner's book is valuable to every agent in the field who is trying sincerely to do his work in a professional spirit and with a professional outlook. Not one agent in ten has any conception of the benefits of life insurance such as are here presented. How could he have? Not even the most skilled agent can read it without gaining intellectual progress, which is bound to be reflected in greater financial returns. The broadened outlook alone that it will create would be well worth-while, but don't forget, that this new outlook itself cannot escape being translated, almost without one's knowing it, into larger ability and more satisfying success. . . .

The argument is built about the thought which is Professor Huebner's central contribution to the philosophy of life insurance,— namely, that the human life value, the predominating economic element in our business and family affairs, should be given the same scientific treatment that we now extend to property possessions. . . .

The publication of the books in this series provokes certain reflections on how times have changed. Imagine such a collection, written from their lofty standpoint of scholarship in general, and of knowledge of the most modern social sciences in particular, twenty-five years ago! The project would have beggared the imagination.

At the beginning of the present century the books of any value available on life insurance were practically confined to actuarial science. There, of course, the field was well represented. But whatever existed on the medical or legal or agency aspects of the subject was crude and limited and dry indeed.

As a matter of fact, the same was true of books dealing with business in general. Be it noted that this was before the days of business with a big "B." Yet look at the current book-lists of our leading publishers! The change is profound; it would be startling were we not so accustomed to it. The tremendous amount of work that has been done in the scientific study of the phenomena of business during the first quarter of this century is simply another revelation of what can be accomplished in any given field when, the time being ripe, it becomes desirable to turn on to that field the illumination that comes only from investigation conducted by competent men. . . .

At this point, let me interject a fuller statement of what science is and the way it works.

In science the facts bearing on a given problem are presented as completely as possible, and are classified with reference to their significant bearings upon the problem. . . .

Science is also a work of the imagination, and gives to the worker the same sense of satisfaction that is experienced by the creative artist. No better illustration of this could be found than Professor Huebner's book. In the working-out of a principle, and in the systematizing of many facts under a broad generalization, every scientist finds a creator's joy. He gives form and significance to the disordered materials of experience.

Ours is a generation of pioneers in this new faith. It has taken many years to create in men the understanding and the courage that will accept truth in any field,—but most of all perhaps in Life Insurance, —simply because it is the truth. And the direct influence on practical life of such a scientific study as Professor Huebner has here undertaken is enormous. The conception of life insurance that he builds up is bound to influence all his readers and followers, to the point of almost revolutionizing our conception of its social and business utilities. Such scientific work is both an instrument and a guaranty of progress, and will affect men's attitude toward experience, and thereby promote their material advance. . . .

In no part of the great field of American business has a work of larger significance been accomplished than in life insurance. In the first place, the gigantic growth of the institution is both the cause and the result of the study that men of vision and trained observation and sound reasoning have given to it. The life insurance of the era of the Armstrong investigation of 1905 holds much the same relation to the life insurance of today that the automobile of that vintage holds to the 1928 models of the best manufacturers. The distance both have come, in every detail of executive engineering and sales operations, is stupendous.

To prove this you have only to try to imagine the subject of this article, Professor Huebner's "Economics of Life Insurance," the foundation book of this new series, as having appeared in 1905.

In the first place, it could not have been written, for the reason that no one living had ever worked out anything resembling the philosophy of life insurance that it contains. In the second place, its message would have fallen flat on an uninterested insurance fraternity, because no person had the philosophical comprehension of the subject to form the necessary point of contact, so to speak, to mesh-in with its assumptions and ideas. And finally, so far as the public is concerned, it would have been considered, doubtless, as little more than the Utopia of a visionary, if not the empty gesture of an extravagant quixotism.

But a great change has come, and the insurance world is ready and willing to absorb broad interpretations of its service in the terms of Professor Huebner's philosophy. Reading his book is like drawing back a curtain that hangs in front of a window, looking out over a far-flung panorama of natural scenery, embracing every feature of a beautiful prospect. Here in one charming view is presented an extended vista of the serviceableness of life insurance—a vista that is as inspiring as it is novel and arresting.

At this period, life underwriters in Canada as well as those in the United States were trying to upgrade life insurance sales activities through an educational program. In 1924, the Life Underwriters Association of Canada was incorporated under a charter from Parliament. One of the powers granted was the right to conduct examinations and award to qualified candidates the right to use the title "Chartered Life Underwriter of Canada." Leaders in the Association started the program by authorizing, in 1925, a group of carefully selected honorary Chartered Life Underwriters. Only these forty-eight men ever have been thus honored.

The C.L.U. program in Canada from the beginning required the candidate's membership in the Association. Examinations at first were administered by the Association's Educational Committee, but in 1929 the Association was empowered to create a subsidiary organization, the Institute of Chartered Life Underwriters of Canada. The governing body of the Institute is appointed by the Association. Over the years, of course, there were developments in the study and examination programs. Now the C.L.U. curriculum, study classes, and examinations are directed by the Extension Department of the University of Toronto, but administered by the Institute. There has never been a general educational prerequisite for the C.L.U. program in Canada. The three-part examination now covers life insurance fundamentals and subjects related to professional life underwriting. The examinations appear to be somewhat less extensive in subject matter and possibly less advanced in academic level than those of the American College. Continued use of "the title," if won, is dependent on maintenance of Association membership. This requirement is carefully policed by local associations.

The beginning of the Canadian C.L.U. program, the production of an increasing number of life insurance books, and many other developments were forces converging during the 1920s to give impetus to the new project in the United States. The time was ripening to launch a national institutional program for preparing and recognizing professional life underwriters.

Chapter 6

THE AMERICAN COLLEGE IS BORN

When, in 1914, Dr. Huebner publicly suggested a national program of education and certification for life underwriters, the idea was warmly received. But no steam got into its promotion. World War I diverted people's thoughts. Other educational enterprises took the energies of leaders. Each year at the convention of the National Association of Life Underwriters there was a variety of reports by committees on educational standards, scientific salesmanship, and college courses in life insurance.

Then, in Los Angeles, Dr. Huebner presented his life value concept to the 1924 convention. He opened to the underwriters new visions of the limitless potentialities of their business. They got excited about themselves as the representatives of a titanic industry, underwriting multiplying billions of dollars of life value. Suddenly the climate was right for aggressive development of the idea of organized professional training for life underwriters on a national basis, at the college level.

Three years later, George Alder, president of the National Association of Life Underwriters, introduced for the first time a president of the American College of Life Underwriters. In his speech, he looked back to what happened at that Los Angeles meeting.

The Convention had been adjourned, the last thing on the program had been done and the ladies were waiting in the audience for their husbands to go out with them and play golf or something of that kind. Then up came a man* who had sponsored the thing [the American College idea] for years. We felt it had gone to the boards, but he rushed up to me and said we could do something. He said we could get Ed Woods to look at the thing.

He told the ladies to wait. I don't know what he gave them to do, but they did wait. Anyway, we got the thing going. We rehabilitated it. The American College of Life Underwriters was started on its way again. . . .

If you think we didn't work, if you think the thing hasn't gone on in a way that was just like wild fire all over the country, you don't know what I know, because I have been everywhere and people are waiting for it and they want it. They want a professionalized business for the men in it.

Today we have with us the man by whose grace we were able to reinstate the thing, Mr. Edward A. Woods, and he is going to talk to us as the President of the American College of Life Underwriters. Mr. Woods!

The record adds that after this impassioned introduction, "the audience arose, applauded and cheered!"

The road from 1924 to that happy moment had by no means been easy. Nor were the underwriters following the same route. Some were concerned primarily with establishing machinery for recognition of competent, experienced men who had a professional attitude toward life insurance selling. They wanted some way of publicly setting apart those underwriters from the policy peddlers, the "quick buck" salesmen, and the floaters in the busi-

---

*Several contemporaries agree that this was probably Ernest J. Clark. He and Edward A. Woods, with Dr. Huebner, had been constantly nursing the idea of an industry-sponsored educational project. Paul F. Clark commented that Mr. Alder, of Salt Lake City, far from the eastern centers of life insurance activity, was normally unaware of much that they had been doing. He might have thought "the thing" was dead, but it was merely dormant, waiting until the time was ripe for successful promotion. Thinking back to the Los Angeles convention in 1924, Paul Clark reminisced about what was involved then in attending a California N.A.L.U. meeting. He said: "A whole lot of us went out there together on the train. It took nearly a week. We had a wonderful trip. We stopped at the Grand Canyon going out and came back by the Canadian Rockies."

ness. The National Association had set up a Committee on No-
menclature to work out some means of certification and public
identification of qualified life underwriters. Guy MacLaughlin
was the hard-working chairman of that committee for several
years. Part of his project was to assemble a list of qualified life
underwriters nominated by individuals in the business, officials
of life insurance organizations, life insurance journalists, and
others. These were men and women judged by their peers to be
worthy of confidence and honor.

Mr. MacLaughlin and his associates, thinking of the distinguished American College of Surgeons, talked of an American
College of Life Underwriters. Some suggested that a fundamental
examination on life insurance principles and practices ought to
be part of this certification.

At the same time, the National Association was working for
a more extensive life insurance course of study in the curriculums
of liberal arts colleges and university business schools. In 1925,
Frank L. Jones, then chairman of the N.A.L.U. Education Committee, called a meeting in New York to consider the whole
question of an outline for such a course. Dr. Huebner was there,
as well as professors or deans from Columbia, University of
Pittsburgh, Carnegie Institute, and New York University. Winslow Russell, John A. Stevenson, Edward A. Woods, Frank L.
Jones and Griffin M. Lovelace also attended.

Consequently, Dr. Huebner prepared an outline for use by
Association members in missionary work with college and university authorities. Published the next year, "Outline of Collegiate Courses in the Functions, Principles and Practices of Life
Insurance" helped educators to visualize the content of a course,
and provided information about printed study material.

As National Association leaders talked and corresponded with
professional educators about the possibilities for life insurance
classes in colleges and universities, they sought advice, too, about
their own plans for establishing life insurance selling as a profession. That such an industry project should include an educa-

Blowup of 1924 newspaper report concerning the human life value concept, given to Dr. Huebner in 1957.

tional program was endorsed by the professors, provided the standards would meet the requirements of recognized, degree-granting institutions. This advice underscored a principle that Dr. Huebner had been advocating unceasingly.

In N.A.L.U., strong differences of opinion developed. The objectives were the same—to raise the standards of life underwriting and create a new image of the salesman in the public mind. However, many felt it was important to recognize experienced, ethical underwriters, worthy of public trust, while others were convinced that a major educational program integrated with college-level study was fundamental. The situation became deadlocked, and it was the developments at Los Angeles described by Mr. Alder which triggered new cooperation. Moreover, Mr.

Woods had such unusual prestige in the industry, and had for
so long been identified with educational programs and underwriter development, that it was possible for differing elements
to unite under his banner.

It was an historic action when in January, 1927, the trustees of
the National Association of Life Underwriters formally approved creation of the American College of Life Underwriters.
Ernest J. Clark had handled, in 1921, incorporation of the National Association under the laws of the District of Columbia, and
he was asked to serve again in this capacity for the new college.
At Mr. Clark's request, Edward S. Brashears, a Washington
lawyer, became "resident agent" to accept service on behalf of
the proposed College, in accordance with legal requirements.
Mr. Brashears was also a life underwriter, an agent of the Union
Central, and an active member of the National Association. On
March 22, 1927, a certificate of incorporation was issued for
the American College of Life Underwriters. Ernest J. Clark and
Edward S. Brashears personally signed the certificate in Washington on that day. Other incorporators signed at their first meeting, three days later.

The incorporators, also named the first directors, were:
George D. Alder, Franklin W. Ganse, Frank L. Jones, Hugh D.
Hart, Paul F. Clark, John Newton Russell, Ernest J. Clark, Edward S. Brashears, Edward A. Woods, J. Stanley Edwards, Guy
MacLaughlin, and Charles L. Scott. Several of these men, already introduced in this story, had a long-time interest in the
proposed college. Others were included because of their leadership in Association affairs, and as one reminiscing friend commented, "concerning educational things, did not know beans
when the bag was opened." A few of the men had not graduated
from high school, and so were antagonistic to the educational
prerequisites for the new examination program. Only three of
the incorporators won the designation. Six of the 12 had been
presidents of the National Association, and Paul F. Clark served
for 1928-29. The first bylaws provided that at least nine of the

directors should be, when elected, members of the Executive Committee of the National Association of Life Underwriters. Subsequently, the directorship was enlarged, representation was given to life insurance executives and educators, and the indirect tie to N.A.L.U. was eliminated.

Brief biographies of the incorporators indicate a variety of talents and experience, and show widespread geographical support for the program.

Guy MacLaughlin, of Houston, was a typical Texan. He was hard working and energetic in supporting what he believed to be "for the good of the cause." He was long an active member of N.A.L.U. and devoted to good salesmanship and ethical practices.

Charles L. Scott was a million-dollar salesman from Kansas City, a dependable worker and highly respected by his associates.

George D. Alder was then president of the National Association, and was referred to as the Grand Old Man of Salt Lake City. He loved the West, and refused promotions which would have taken him away. He and Dr. Huebner enjoyed trips together to the brilliant Cedar Breaks, Bryce Canyon, and other Rocky Mountain areas.

Hugh D. Hart was a young general agent from Little Rock, Arkansas, an excellent speaker, a man with a fine mind. He was soon to become agency vice president of Penn Mutual Life Insurance Company, and proved a good ambassador for the College in its early days.

Frank L. Jones has been mentioned in connection with the life insurance courses for servicemen in Europe and students in American colleges, and as president of the National Association. He had been a teacher and member of the Indiana State Board of Education before becoming a salesman for the Equitable Life of New York in Indianapolis. He was strongly committed to training for life underwriters, but differed from Dr. Huebner and others who believed an educational program should include economics, law, and finance, as well as specific life insurance material.

John Newton Russell, of Los Angeles, had been N.A.L.U. president for 1916-17. He was a highly successful general agent, a delightful personality, tall, well groomed, and a power on the West Coast. Some one remarked, "When he said yes to the idea of the American College, it was important." In his honor, the John Newton Russell Memorial Award has been given annually since 1942. Appropriately, Dr. Huebner was the first recipient.

J. Stanley Edwards entered the life insurance business as a student at the University of Denver, in his father's general agency for the Aetna Life. He later became his father's partner, and succeeded him, continuing with the company for over 50 years. He was a leading citizen of Denver. A life-long university sports booster, he enthusiastically followed the football team around the country. After his death, the *Eastern Underwriter* termed him "one of the group of early life insurance leaders credited with making N.A.L.U. the strong organization it is to-day." Over the years he had held all its offices and many important committee chairmanships. He was president for 1919-20. He won the John Newton Russell Award for 1944, and his invaluable service to the American College led to his election as life trustee in 1953. He was a rooter and booster for whatever he believed in, and his judgment was good. Dr. Huebner recalls that Mr. Edwards felt he did not know much about educational affairs, and kept still when academic questions were being discussed.

Franklin W. Ganse, a lawyer who lectured to life underwriters on inheritance taxes and similar subjects, became a life underwriter himself, and a pioneer in estate planning through life insurance. For many years he was chairman of the N.A.L.U. Committee on Cooperation with Trust Companies, and as such attended many trust conferences with the American Bankers Association. He did a tremendous service for the life insurance business in liaison with the bankers. Friends remember him as energetic, tactful, a magnetic personality, and a speaker of more than ordinary ability. Mr. Ganse was a member of Paul Clark's agency in Boston. He became the first treasurer of the American College, and ably handled the College's slim finances until 1939. Of the early days he said, "In its first year the College was very poor indeed, and if there were even a shoestring in its financial structure, I never discovered it." Mr. Ganse was one of the few incorporators who became a C.L.U. He took all the examinations in 1930, at the age of seventy. He was still young at that age, and played golf until he was eighty-two. Mr. Ganse became a life trustee of the College.

Paul F. Clark's early experience as a life insurance student has been mentioned. He progressed from work with his uncle in Baltimore to his own agency for the John Hancock Mutual in Boston. He built there an outstanding organization, the largest agency for his company in the nation and the largest in New England for any company. He became John Hancock's president in 1944, and was chairman of the Board from 1957 until his retirement in 1963. He continues to serve the company as a director. Mr. Clark was N.A.L.U. president for 1928-29. He became a C.L.U. in 1931. He took all the examinations at once, and said he could not use his hand for a week after. He served the American College continuously in many capacities, and now is chairman of the Board of Trustees. He received the John Newton Russell Memorial Award in 1945.

Paul Clark said, "I was devoted to my uncle." He recognizes Ernest J. Clark, Dr. Huebner, and Edward A. Woods as the real founders of the American College. It was Ernest Clark who, through the years, hammered out with Dr. Huebner the framework of the College. Under his auspices, Dr. Huebner first was introduced to the leading life underwriters in the United States. In the Clark agency, Dr. Huebner first voiced the concept of the American College. When Mr. Clark was president of N.A.L.U. in 1913-14, Dr. Huebner first appeared on the national convention platform. Ernest Clark served as the second president of the American College from 1928 to 1934, and was a life trustee.

Such were the men of ability, vision, and dedication who

founded the American College of Life Underwriters. The incorporating directors gathered for their organizational meeting at the Palmer House in Chicago on March 25, 1927. At that time, the following officers were elected: Edward A. Woods, president; Guy MacLaughlin, vice president; Ernest J. Clark, secretary; Franklin W. Ganse, treasurer; Solomon S. Huebner, dean; and Everett M. Ensign, registrar. Mr. Ensign was executive secretary of the National Association of Life Underwriters. Bylaws, which had been prepared by Ernest Clark and Dr. Huebner, were discussed and adopted.

The bylaws stated four objectives of the College:

1. To cooperate with colleges and universities in training students for the career of professional life underwriter.
2. To cooperate with educational institutions in general life insurance education.
3. To conduct, if occasion demands, its own institution for the training of resident students for the profession of life underwriting.
4. To recognize properly qualified life underwriters with a professional degree. [The term "degree" was changed later to "designation."]

The bylaws, generally broad in their terms, permitted immediate delegation of responsibility. The directors at this meeting, therefore, named an Executive Committee who, with the dean, would decide on standards and procedures and launch the College program promptly.

The Executive Committee included Edward A. Woods, Ernest J. Clark, Frank L. Jones, Guy MacLaughlin, and Franklin W. Ganse. They met at the Mayflower Hotel in Washington on May 3, 1927. The minutes of the meeting are pallid reading, but it was a fiery session, lasting all day and far into the night. A great variety of questions had to be decided, and on some matters there was bitter difference of opinion.

The first matter to be discussed was the name of the degree. Chartered Life Underwriter, the term used in Canada, had been

Early leaders of the American College, pictured as life trustees in 1954. *Left to right:* Ernest J. Clark, Dr. S. S. Huebner, Julian S. Myrick, J. Stanley Edwards, Paul F. Clark.

mentioned. "Certified" was offered as an alternate word, but it was pointed out that the public was familiar with certified milk, and that the English term "chartered" had more dignity. Nobody came to blows about that, and "Chartered Life Underwriter" was the designation adopted by common agreement.

The question of honorary degrees generated more heat. Some members of the committee felt that honorary degrees were desirable, not only for the people who would like to have them, but also for the empty treasury, which would be enriched by payments for the title. Dr. Huebner, Mr. Woods, and Mr. Clark fought hard against such degrees. They believed that only by strict enforcement of high academic standards could the College serve the institution of life insurance and win the respect of educational authorities. Granting honorary degrees would open the door to "diploma mill" operations and scuttle the whole program.

Another matter of academic importance was the educational background of the candidates. Dr. Huebner insisted that, as colleges required high school graduation or its equivalent for entrance, so the new college should have that prerequisite. Others charged that was undemocratic and unworthy of a business in which so many self-made men had won outstanding success. Dr. Huebner was supported, however, and the high school prerequisite was adopted.

Naturally, the scope of examination material was a subject for serious consideration. Dr. Huebner recommended a curriculum covering life insurance fundamentals and salesmanship, economics, taxation, commercial law, wills, trusts, corporation finance, commercial credit, banking, investments, English, and public speaking. He listed 23 books with 8,000 pages of text to implement the student's preparation. Such a program was vigorously opposed by some members of the committee. They urged an alternate, simplified plan which Dr. Huebner's supporters scornfully referred to as "a two-dollar package." In the heat of the argument some people walked out and slammed the door, but they came back and compromised. Eventually, most of Dr. Huebner's topics were covered, though the recommended reading was cut in half.

The machinery of the examination program also was crystallized at this meeting. It was decided that, if applications warranted, examinations would be held twice a year at central places in each state, and under the auspices of recognized educational institutions.

The Committee also faced its financial problems. The College had no money and any activity would involve expenses. There had been a tacit understanding that the National Association would underwrite the project until the College could stand on its own financial feet. Mr. Ganse, the new treasurer, was instructed to ask the Association for a loan of $1,000 at 6 per cent to get things started. That loan later was negotiated, and eventually was written off as a gift to the College.

All in all, that first meeting accomplished a great deal, and most of the decisions seemed well directed. Dr. Huebner was happy about progress, and felt at ease to begin a long-planned exchange professorship in the Orient. He left in June to be gone nearly a year. He soon was pursued by letters and cablegrams from Mr. Woods. Monkey wrenches were getting into the machinery. Dr. Huebner recalls that his own indignation over developments once inspired a $17 cabled reply.

When the National Association of Life Underwriters met in Memphis in September, 1927, Edward A. Woods presented the program of the American College, and particularly defended its high academic standards. He invited applications from candidates for examinations to be held in June, 1928, explaining how candidates must submit elaborate applications with detailed personal information to permit careful screening before the tests. The charge for the five examinations was $100. (This was changed to $50 before the first examinations took place.) In his general comments, Mr. Woods also emphasized how much the program owed to Dr. Huebner:

The first purpose of the American College of Life Underwriters is to give a degree similar to the degree of certified public accountants to those who come up to the required tests. The second purpose of this college, or the result of it, will be that colleges throughout the country will give courses on Life Underwriting. . . .

The giving of a college degree sounds like a simple proposition, but I wish you knew the patient work that your far-flung executive committee of the college, stretching from Houston, Texas, to Boston, has given to it. We are confronted at once with the proposition that a college degree has to mean something in the college world, and that if we give it to people on standards not recognized by the outstanding colleges, these colleges will put it aside as they put aside a proposal to call a man mortician rather than undertaker, or a realtor as compared with a real estate man. . . .

In conferring with the college deans as to what they felt was sufficient qualification for this degree, we ran up against the fact that this degree should be mighty hard to get. And I tell you frankly if we get fifty people in the United States to get the college degree the first year, we will be doing mighty well.

The colleges have looked askance at any proposition without a good educational background, high school or its equivalent. The colleges, of course, require a general knowledge of the subjects that underlie the work of the Life Underwriter, and we have been working under the leadership of Dr. Huebner, who ought to be put on the payroll of Life Insurance companies, who is doing all this work for nothing. We were up against the proposition of how it is going to be possible to give this degree widely and yet have the persons qualify for it by that study that all the college deans say is necessary. . . .

At the same time, my friends, we can't make this a cheap degree. If you are going to make it a cheap degree that college men will laugh at, you are going to ruin the whole thing. . . .

I want you to understand the difficulties under which your committee has been laboring in trying to accommodate the people who will deserve it, and who will be a credit to Life Underwriters, and in establishing a curriculum that will meet the standards of the great universities all over the country. . . .

I don't want you to think we have been unmindful of the difficulty of expecting business men to get the educational background. At the same time we have had to yield to the opinion of college deans and recognize its importance. You must remember there are only 140,000 physicians in the United States, and those men paid thousands of dollars, spent some four years in college and four years in medical school and two years of interneship, and then bought hundreds of dollars of equipment to begin to practice medicine. There are 50,000 more Life Underwriters than there are physicians in the country, and if these conditions seem hard to you, think of the lawyer or the physician or the architect or the trained nurse even. My gardener spent three years in Scotland to learn to plant flowers and vegetables, and many gardeners from Scotland and Ireland and England spend more time than that in apprenticeships. My last Scotch gardener got a shilling a week for the two years he learned gardening. . . .

I don't know a man who deserves as much thanks as Dr. Huebner for the inspiring effort he has given. Furthermore, Dr. Huebner's name has carried weight with every college we have corresponded with. If we had corresponded as Life Underwriters we wouldn't have anything like the position that is coming from Dr. Huebner's standing. His name carries weight that is of exceeding value to us, and the result of this effort, whereby courses will be given in colleges in places convenient to Life Underwriters, will be much greater than we could ever accomplish by setting up one college of our own where the people of Detroit or Seattle or Los Angeles or Miami would have to go.

If in college after college Life Underwriting will be made a subject of study, in order to give a man a professional standing, that will be one of the greatest benefits that can come from this college. We had to accommodate our views to the ideas not only of Dr. Huebner but to other college deans.

After the convention delegates had had a night to think over the ambitious C.L.U. program (and in many cases to develop criticisms and objections), Mr. Woods was introduced again to present a supplementary idea—the Accredited Life Underwriter plan. He stated frankly:

The National Life Underwriters Association realizes that there are a great many people who perhaps do not wish to take the [C.L.U.] course, that it is too difficult for them to take, that the degree is too difficult to secure. We hope it will be difficult. The way to success in this business, as in any other, is not easy.

He then proposed that, on payment of $50, a member of a local life underwriters association certified as outstanding in character and sales performance could apply to the American College for recognition. If he were rated acceptable by the College authorities, he would receive an attractive, leather-incased card reading: "The National Association of Life Underwriters certifies that [name] is an Accredited National Association Life Underwriter qualified to render professional Life Underwriting service." If the Accredited Life Underwriter later passed the C.L.U. examinations, his initial $50 payment would be applied against the $100 C.L.U. fee. This team of proposals seemed to satisfy everybody, and both plans were approved by the Association in convention.

During the next few months, work was completed in the preparation of application blanks, study lists, preliminary plans for examination centers, and so on. Mr. Woods brought in for the job Dr. Arthur M. Spalding, professor of marketing and selling at the University of Pittsburgh. He became the first salaried employee of the American College at the rather good rate of $100 a month. Dr. Spalding was a graduate of Des Moines University and the Harvard Graduate School of Business Administration. He also had become head of the School of Life Insurance Salesmanship, which had been transferred from Carnegie Institute to the University of Pittsburgh. In addition, he was educational adviser to the great Edward A. Woods agency.

Then, in November, 1927, Edward A. Woods died. The tribute in the *Eastern Underwriter* read:

One of the biggest creative brains that American business has ever known stopped working when Edward A. Woods died in Pittsburgh

last week following an attack of appendicitis and heart disease. He
was sixty-two years old.

The news of his death was a bombshell to life insurance men, especially to those who had seen him at the National Association convention in Memphis where he was as active, resourceful and inspiring as ever, and where he was devoting most of his time to seeing
that the new American College of Life Underwriters was safely
launched under the auspices of the National Association. The College, which is to sponsor examinations which will result in the
awarding of the degrees of Certified [*sic*] Life Underwriter, was
his latest baby, and he was president of the College. He took as
much interest in it as he did some years ago in promoting the Carnegie School of Life Insurance Salesmanship, the Life Insurance
Sales Research Bureau and other cooperative, educational and managerial movements in the business . . .

Most everybody in life insurance who is anybody knew and admired Edward A. Woods personally and thousands of other life men
had heard him make one or more of his extraordinary eloquent
and informative speeches. He made hundreds of addresses, rarely
spoke from notes and could talk on any subject as he was a man
of widest reading and culture . . .

He was not happy, however, unless there was something to occupy
his mind outside of the routine. When he got a new constructive
idea, the value of which he had convinced himself of by long
thought, he could not let it drop and started to make as many con-
verts as he could.

He was a born proselyter. Most men would have been satisfied to
have been the head of the largest general agency in the United
States but that was not enough for Mr. Woods. He was always doing some work on a book, or planning an educational campaign
or tying himself up with some philanthropy, or other public spirited
drive.

Mr. Woods was a life insurance salesman who took his own
medicine. He often showed friends a little black book, kept in his
pocket, wherein he listed a schedule of his personal insurance.

After his death, the total was reported at $1,002,000. He also held $150,000 of insurance on members of his family, and $250,000 on stockholders of the Edward A. Woods Company.

His personal insurance included substantial endowments with life-income provision for himself, an educational policy, a policy payable to Princeton University (which had given him an honorary degree), a policy to underwrite his subscriptions to the University of Pittsburgh and the Tuberculosis League of Pittsburgh, income policies for his children and sister, and a policy to provide each year a $100 Christmas present for his wife.

A later story revealed something of Mr. Woods' generosity while alive. From its inception, he had been making annual gifts of $7,000 to the Pittsburgh Tuberculosis League. He gave $500 a year to each of five or six Y.M.C.A. branches. He also spent thousands of dollars every year on his work for the National Association of Life Underwriters and in research for his books.

Edward A. Woods had given richly of his money. But he had given also of himself. The work he did so well for the American College launched it safely, and 10,000 graduates today pay him honor.

Chapter 7

THE FIRST C.L.U.s

Dr. Huebner returned to Philadelphia early in 1928. On his first day at the university, one of his associates handed him the announcement of the American College, prepared in accordance with the convention decisions, and including the Accredited Life Underwriter plan. The friend futilely recommended, "First sit down, then read this, but do keep calm."

Dr. Huebner had been warned of developments by Mr. Woods' cablegrams, but to see the plan actually presented in print was shocking. He grabbed the telephone and complained vehemently to Ernest Clark: "You've killed it! If you persist in this certification plan I will have nothing to do with the College. I am *through*." Mr. Clark was sympathetic and reiterated his personal opposition to anything but a high-grade, truly educational program. So Dr. Huebner agreed to stay on the team.

A month or so later, at the first possible meeting of the College directors, Dr. Huebner was elected to the Board, filling the place of Edward A. Woods. He was the first professional educator to be included. At that meeting, Hugh D. Hart, one of the incorporators, submitted his resignation as director, since he had become vice president of the Penn Mutual. The Board agreed that representation by home office officials was desirable, and voted unanimously to ask Mr. Hart to withdraw his resignation. This was done, and Mr. Hart continued as director until 1931. When the Board met in Philadelphia, the members enjoyed the hospitality of the Penn Mutual home office. In those days of no College headquarters and no expense accounts, such generosity was a matter of some consequence.

Professor Spalding had been acting as assistant to Mr. Woods and chairman of a one-man Board of Admissions. At the directors' meeting in the spring of 1928 he reported what he had done to promote the College through informational mailings to the presidents of all local life underwriter associations and the presidents of about fifty of the largest life insurance companies. He commented that reactions generally had been favorable and cooperative. He turned over to Dr. Huebner all relevant correspondence, and also a draft of questions for the first series of examinations which he had prepared. He continued as registrar, and did the bulk of the work of the Registration Board for many years.

On Dr. Huebner's recommendation, and after considerable discussion, the Board made a number of changes in previous decisions. It agreed to discontinue the proposed relationship between the Accredited Life Underwriter and C.L.U. programs. The accreditation fee would be an independent $50; the fee for the C.L.U. series of examinations would be lowered to $50. It decided that candidates might take the examinations in two different years, if desired: first, Parts I, II, and III; later, Parts IV and V.

The required five years of life insurance experience for eligibility to take the examinations was reduced to three. The Board also decided that college students might take the examinations without life insurance experience, but, if successful in the examinations, would not receive the C.L.U. until satisfactory experience had been achieved.

On recommendation by Dr. Huebner, it was agreed that no reading lists would be printed. A mimeographed list of textbooks suggested for examination preparation would be available on request. The Board felt that criticism would result from more definite sponsorship of a limited group of books.

A three-member Board of Admissions was established to deal

promptly with applications from candidates. Professor Spalding was named chairman, with Paul Clark and Hugh Hart as assisting members. The application forms were detailed in the information requested, and all candidates were screened carefully.

An important item of business at this April meeting was election of a successor to President Edward A. Woods. He had strongly supported Dr. Huebner in his concept of a highly professional program for the C.L.U. Not all members of the Board were yet in complete sympathy with this ideal. The choice of a new president, therefore, involved considerable conflict between the two factions. But in the end, Ernest J. Clark was elected by unanimous ballot. However, within a few months an unreconciled member resigned. William M. Duff, president of the Edward A. Woods Company, was elected to fill his place, bringing a strong friend to the College.

Also at this meeting, John Marshall Holcombe, Jr., was elected secretary of the College. Mr. Holcombe was then head of the Life Insurance Sales Research Bureau (later merged with the Association of Life Agency Officers to become the Life Insurance Agency Management Association), and an influential figure in life insurance agency affairs. Mr. Holcombe's father had been president of the Phoenix Mutual Life Insurance Company. Marshall had had some experience as a home office claim attorney. He had taught life insurance courses to the A.E.F. in France after World War I. When the Bureau was organized in 1922 with 13 member companies, he found the real opportunity for his talents. By 1928, he had built the membership to about 150 companies. He was by nature a salesman and a promoter. He had unbounded energy, a capacity for sustained enthusiasm, and a great talent for making and keeping a wide circle of friends. An associate wrote of him: "Nothing held Marshall Holcombe back very long, or dampened permanently his enthusiasm for the great goals he saw in the field of life insurance education for its own people especially, and for the general public. He acknowledged no impossibilities and saw few real difficulties." That was just the sort of ally the new College needed.

The directors set as the dates for the first series of examinations June 28, 29, and 30, 1928. To Dr. Huebner and Professor Spalding they left all details of administration, with power to act independently.

The C.L.U. application for the first year's examinations reflected the close relationship between the College and the National Association of Life Underwriters. The form was a four-page, letter-size folder. It called for information about age, family, education, business experience, and production records. In addition, it inquired about life insurance books read within the previous five years, and life insurance magazines read regularly. Most interesting, it asked about membership in a local life underwriters association, official responsibility therein, attendance at sales congresses within two years, and at any annual N.A.L.U. conventions. Finally, the applicant was asked to commit himself, "to uphold the standards of life insurance and adhere to the Code of Ethics adopted by the National Association of Life Underwriters."

Completed applications for the first series of examinations were received from 42 people. Several other applications with inadequate data could not be considered. Of the 42, three were rejected because the applicants could not show high school qualifications.

When the historic June dates arrived, 34 approved candidates sat for the examinations. Twenty candidates were university graduates. The examinations were scheduled for two and a half days, as at present. They were held in 1928 at 14 universities from California to Boston. Participating were: University of Washington (Seattle), University of Southern California, University of Minnesota, Oklahoma City University, University of Nebraska, Rice Institute (Houston, Texas), University of Cincinnati, Indiana University, Detroit University, Buffalo School of

Commerce, University of Pittsburgh, University of Pennsylvania, New York University, and Boston University.

The examination questions seem simple today. For instance, the following five questions comprised the first half of the examination on life insurance fundamentals.

1. Give seven (7) specific uses of life insurance for the individual policyholder.
2. What is a trust company? What are the beneficial results of trust company and life insurance company cooperation?
3. Explain the various ways in which life insurance proves helpful in connection with the settlement of estates.
4. State the economic advantages of life annuities.
5. Define so-called "partnership life insurance," and explain briefly the economic advantages derived therefrom.

The examination also included a mathematical calculation question, which was, then as today, an insurmountable hurdle to some people.

For interested readers, the entire first examination series is reproduced in the appendix. The questions should be read with a realization of the very limited study material available then, and the lack of aid in academic preparation for most life underwriters of that day. People who could pass these examinations were really above average, and the failure record was high.

Of the 34 approved candidates who sat for the examinations, only 21 passed. Failure was a considerable shock to some who had anticipated that as successful life underwriters they would surely pass.

An unusual story is connected with one set of papers. The question of eligibility to take the examinations had been hotly debated at the formative stages of the College program. The original bylaw article on this point was very broad. Termed "Admission," it read:

Admission to the College shall be restricted to those of such mature age and mind as to satisfy the Dean and the Board of Directors that the applicant for admission has mental development equal to that attained in a two-year College course or its equivalent and is possessed of such traits as will fit him to successfully discharge the obligations of the profession with credit to the College and himself.

Dr. Huebner felt strongly that graduation from an accredited high school or the equivalent should be a prerequisite. He said a college program, to be respected by educators, could have no less a foundation. Not all members of the College Board of Directors shared this view. One man, who did not himself have a high school diploma, protested vehemently that the C.P.A. program, which they were using in many ways as a model, allowed anybody to take examinations. Dr. Huebner declared that unbelievable. It proved to be true, however, in some states at that time. Dr. Huebner stuck by his principle in spite of losing that reinforcement, and by his administrative ruling, his standard was applied from the beginning.

His opponent was adamant too. When the first examinations were given, he brazenly appeared at the local examination center, overawed the proctor, and wrote his answers to the questions.

The end of this story so full of fireworks is hidden in a colorless item in the official minutes of the Board of Directors meeting the next month, which, significantly, he did not attend. It was unanimously voted that, "in all cases where examination papers are submitted by unqualified applicants, no official record be made with respect thereto, and that such examinations be treated as null and void."

At this same meeting, the Board adopted "a complete definition of the educational prerequisites required on the part of all candidates for the C.L.U. degree." These requirements were published in the next official information booklet.

Any man or woman over 21 years of age, with a certificate of graduation from a four year high school (or its equivalent as evidenced by proper credentials showing that the applicant has passed on the subject matter of a four year high school course under the supervision and direction of the principal of the school or of educational bodies, whose certificate would be accepted for admission to any standard college or university), and who has had at least 3 years of satisfactory life insurance experience, may apply for permission to take the C.L.U. examinations. Graduates of universities and colleges may make application to take the examinations at any scheduled date following their graduation, but, though successful, will not be granted the degree until the completion of three years of satisfactory life insurance experience. "Life insurance experience" relates to salesmanship, management activities, or such other life insurance pursuits as, in the opinion of the Board of Directors, have a vital bearing upon the dissemination of life insurance.

From the beginning, examination papers were handled according to best university practice. Each examination book was known to the grader only by number. A young University of Pennsylvania professor, David McCahan, was paid $200 to assist Dr. Huebner in the grading. Each examination part was marked separately, and the passing grade was 70. Fourteen candidates passed all five examinations with 70 or better. A second group of seven candidates "failed slightly" in one examination, but passed the other four, making an average well above 70. These 21 were recommended by Dr. Huebner as eligible to receive the C.L.U. degree, and that recommendation was sustained by the Board.

One man who passed all the examinations satisfactorily was a Wharton School student from China, Dr. Yien Düng of Shanghai, who had not yet had three years of satisfactory life insurance experience. The Board agreed that he should be approved to receive the degree on completion of the experience. Dr. Huebner kept in touch with him after he returned to China, but he never qualified for the C.L.U.

Two other people completed only the first instalment, Parts I, II, and III, and were eligible to finish the examinations later.

The candidates who passed two or three parts were given credit for those examinations; but those who passed only one were required to take all five again if they wished to continue. For the first group, re-examinations were granted at no expense. Later, however, $10 each was set as the fee.

The list of the first successful candidates, together with their home cities ·and life insurance connections, is interesting. Mr. Woods' enthusiastic leadership is reflected in the number of Equitable representatives. Noteworthy are the geographical spread of the candidates, the appearance of a woman (a Vassar College graduate in the Woods agency), and the inclusion of a number of men who later were outstanding in the College and the business. The list follows as it appears in the official report to the Board of Directors.

C. Vivian Anderson	Cincinnati	Provident Mutual Life Insurance Company
Irvin Bendiner	Philadelphia	New York Life Insurance Company
Lowell T. Boyd	Kokomo, Ind.	General Agent, Equitable Life Insurance Company of Iowa
Henry L. Choate	Washington, D.C.	General Agent, Mutual Benefit Life Insurance Company
M. B. Cohill	Pittsburgh	Assistant Manager, The Edward A. Woods Company of the Equitable Life Assurance Society
F. C. Dickson	Butler, Pa.	Equitable Life Assurance Society
Ted Dreyer	Los Angeles	Pacific Mutual Life Insurance Company
William McG. Duff	Pittsburgh	President, The Edward A. Woods Company of the Equitable Life Assurance Society
W. Rankin Furey	Pittsburgh	Berkshire Life Insurance Company
Lara P. Good	San Diego	Assistant Manager, Prudential Insurance Company
H. L. Harvey	Kalamazoo	Equitable Insurance Company of Iowa
Grant L. Hill	New York, N.Y.	Agency Superintendent, Guardian Life Insurance Company
Marguerite L. Snider	Uniontown, Pa.	Equitable Life Assurance Society
Lisle A. Spencer	Youngstown, O.	Equitable Life Assurance Society
F. J. Stevenson	Pittsburgh	Equitable Life Assurance Society

Maurice S. Tabor	Buffalo, N.Y.	Travelers Insurance Company
Leon A. Triggs	Minneapolis	Berkshire Life Insurance Company and President, Minneapolis Association of Life Underwriters
C. J. Westerman	Pittsburgh	Equitable Life Assurance Society
L. N. Whitelaw	New York, N.Y.	Equitable Life Assurance Society
Edward Wallis Woods	Pittsburgh	Equitable Life Assurance Society
Lawrence C. Woods, Jr.	Pittsburgh	Equitable Life Assurance Society

These 21 candidates recommended by Dean Huebner were approved by the College Board to receive the C.L.U. degree. Because the College was the child of the National Association of Life Underwriters, the Board decided on the national convention as the natural place for "graduation." The diploma form it chose cost $20 more than the alternate, but it was of "superior design." The expense for this item is detailed in the minutes as follows:

Steel plate	$270.00
21 Skin Diplomas @ $1.90	39.90
Engrossing @ $ .50 each	10.50
College Seal and Impressing on same	10.00
TOTAL	$330.40

The source of the College seal is not recorded beyond a note in the directors' minutes giving the Executive Committee authority to select it. Blue and gold were chosen as the College colors because Dr. Huebner said blue was the life insurance color. Diplomas were to be tied with blue and gold ribbon, and the diploma presentation was to be an impressive ceremony.

The first group of graduates was given careful instructions about the appropriate use of the C.L.U. Dr. Huebner especially urged that the degree not be used for "advertising purposes." He had told the Board: "If we don't do something about it, we will soon find this degree misused in a way that will hurt the College in the eyes of others." This concern for the professional use of the C.L.U. has been maintained constantly.

It was obvious, however, that public recognition of C.L.U.
holders was worthwhile. Paul F. Clark suggested wearing a key.
The Phi Beta Kappa key had an honored history older than the
nation. The Harvard School of Business Administration graduates also had an identifying key. So that idea was adopted.

Only six graduates were at the Detroit convention in September, 1928. President of the National Association Julian S. Myrick
welcomed them to the convention platform where President
Ernest Clark presented the diplomas. Mr. Myrick spoke enthusiastically:

The year of 1928 marks a new epoch, and it marks a new leadership. And we are here today to witness it. We are here today to
witness this newly formed College present the first diplomas that
they have issued, and in the years to come it will go down in history
to our credit.

I like to think that this new leadership will go down through the
ages, and I congratulate on your behalf each and every one of the
men who are going to receive the Degree.

Dr. Huebner gave the convention a brief report about the first
year's progress and the prospects of the College.

Thirty-five candidates, from 21 different cities and 12 states, took
the first examination, and of these 21 qualified for the degree of
chartered life underwriter. This is more than twice the number, we
are told, that qualified at the first certified public accountancy examination. The successful candidates are to be congratulated. But
so, also, should be the unsuccessful ones, who showed their spirit
and demonstrated their belief in a new order of things for the profession of life underwriting. The majority of the unsuccessful candidates have already said that they feel amply repaid through the
benefits derived from the course of study to which they have applied themselves, and nearly all have already signified their intention of trying again next December. That represents a fine spirit
and nothing has pleased me more. It is better to strive and fail in
a good cause, than not to try at all. Nearly one-half of the success-

ful candidates are associated with one company, and that company
has reason to feel proud. . . .

Inquiries thus far indicate that 125 candidates are now preparing
for the next two examinations, and the correspondence has been so
voluminous as to make your registrar and dean dizzy at times. Various universities and agency superintendents have also written that
they are urging their prepared personnel to take the test. Several companies, through their educational departments, by way of
printed literature or correspondence, are circularizing their personnel throughout the country. Nor must we overlook the activity
of certain life underwriters' associations. One has advised that it
expects to have 20 candidates take the examination in December,
and another 10. It should be stated, also, that the C.L.U. degree has
even a tendency to become international in character. . . .

For the coming December and June examinations correspondence
indicates at this date that we shall have three candidates, respectively from China, Madras and Prince Rupert. Foreign insurance
interests are vitally interested in our College. On my recent trip I
found the Japanese and Chinese anxious to know about it and its
aims. And I may add that one of the leading insurance educators
of Europe has requested the preparation of an article on "Life Insurance Education in America," with emphasis upon the American
College of Life Underwriters' movement, for publication in the official organ of one of the world's leading educational insurance organizations with a membership in 24 nations.

Wherever I traveled this summer, attending numerous company and
association conventions, I was struck by the genuine interest in the
American College of Life Underwriters and by the large number
who have personally assured me that they will strive for the C.L.U.
degree. Everything seems to point to a total of at least 100 taking
the next examination. I am now sure that the College has been successfully launched. I believe that the day is not far distant when
your National Association, since education is the key to the future
of successful life underwriting, will be convinced that the American
College of Life Underwriters is one of the greatest, if not the greatest
factor for good that it has ever initiated and fostered. . . .

Although we have only fairly started, general familiarity with the
College and its standards and purposes already exists throughout

educational circles. The correspondence shows whole-hearted interest, great enthusiasm, and is proceeding unabated. Twenty-five leading universities and colleges have already, through their deans or directors of their business schools, endorsed our College and its aims, and have given their assurance of co-operation and support.

About half a dozen of these institutions have signified their willingness to offer to their students in insurance the entire range of subjects outlined for the C.L.U. degree. Others indicated their willingness to do so as fast as conditions permit. Three leading universities have stated their intention to recognize the C.L.U. degree in their circulars in a manner similar to that accorded to the C.P.A. degree.

The College has had the fullest cooperation, without a single exception, from universities and colleges in the establishment of examination centers. In fact, a number that had not been approached about the matter because we had no candidates for the examination in those districts, offered their accommodations gratuitously.

The future of the college seems exceedingly bright. The dean, and the same is true of his colleagues, entered the service of the college because of a profound belief in the value of education. But we entered with a little fear and trembling. We wondered whether the time was just ripe, although we were sure of the correctness of the idea. We are now feeling much better.

The midwinter examinations to which Dr. Huebner referred were given December 27, 28, and 29, 1928. Fifty-three candidates were approved, but only 32 sat. They wrote their papers at most of the universities used in June, as well as State University of Iowa, University of Kansas, Columbia University, and Brown University. At five examination centers candidates did not appear—a critical matter of expense and of public relations. The costs were charged back to the delinquent students. The December experience indicated that midwinter was a bad time for examinations, and the decision was made to omit it in the future.

It was truly a time of adjustment. Professor Spalding reflected a serious problem when he said in nice academic phraseology:

"It would seem that underwriters often underestimate the knowledge and proficiency required in various subjects. The fact that an underwriter had been a successful producer does not necessarily mean that he is capable of passing a rigid examination on such subjects as economics, investments, money and credit or commercial law." Dr. Huebner spoke more bluntly and comprehensively when he said: "We have applicants coming up for the degree who apparently have no more idea of what it means than the man in the moon."

The examinations in December, 1928, were somewhat more difficult than the first tests. In releasing copies of the questions, an official statement was made:

> The questions used in the December examination were in many respects typical of those which will be used in the future, particularly in regard to character, comprehensiveness and form. This reflects the viewpoint of the officers of the College, who are of the opinion that the December questions approximate in a marked degree the standards which will ultimately take form.

The examination questions for December, 1928, also are given in the appendix.

Fifteen candidates were successful in the December examinations, and were qualified by experience to be granted the C.L.U. This made a total of 36 for the first year. The second group, with home city and business connection, is as follows:

Angelo Herbert Bennell	Youngstown, O.	Mutual Life of New York
Robert Ogden Bickel	Cedar Rapids, Ia.	District Manager, National Life of Vermont
Martin Patrick Coonan	St. Paul, Minn.	Special Agent, Northwestern Mutual Life Insurance Company
Isaac Milton Craig	Uniontown, Pa.	Equitable Life Assurance Society
Robert Franklin Freeman	Los Angeles, Cal.	Assistant Manager, Pacific Mutual Life Insurance Company

John Edwin Laird	Yakima, Wash.	Equitable Life Assurance Society
Corinne V. Loomis	Boston, Mass.	Sales Manager, Women's Department, Paul F. Clark Agency, John Hancock Mutual Life Insurance Company
Cramer A. Marsteller	Youngstown, O.	Equitable Life Assurance Society
Earle H. Schaeffer	Harrisburg, Pa.	Manager, Southern Pennsylvania, Fidelity Mutual Life Insurance Company
Herbert Lowe Smith	Harrisburg, Pa.	General Agent, Northwestern Mutual Life Insurance Company
Mildred F. Stone	Newark, N.J.	Agency Personnel Secretary, Mutual Benefit Life Insurance Company
Elsie Ullrich	Philadelphia, Pa.	Fidelity Mutual Life Insurance Company
Nelson M. Way	New York City	Canada Life Insurance Company
Denver Wharton	Cresson, Pa.	Equitable Life Assurance Society
Joseph Knox Wilson	Jersey City, N.J.	Equitable Life Assurance Society

The financial situation of the College in its first year was precarious, and the directors operated with strictest economy. On Dr. Huebner's return, the $100 salary previously paid to Professor Spalding became two honoraria, $50 a month for each. In spite of Dr. Huebner's vigorous disapproval of the Accredited Life Underwriter plan, the $50 fees paid by approved applicants made up a sizable part of the College budget for the few years before the plan was discontinued.

At the directors' meeting in September, 1928, the expenses of the College for 1928-29 were estimated at about $5,000. The treasurer hoped for 150 registrations from student applicants, which would balance the budget comfortably, but he also asked authority to borrow operating funds, if necessary.

With such financial pressure, some additional fund raising was inevitable. Friends of the College were feeling the loss of Edward A. Woods, their dynamic first president. The idea of a memorial fund in his honor, which also would aid financially the College

William M. Duff.

Robert Dechert.

he had helped to found, was a natural. The announcement, with the first appeal for contributions, was made at the 1928 N.A.L.U. convention. The response was immediate and generous. In the next few months, over $50,000 was pledged. This amount was somewhat increased subsequently, and the sum collected has been maintained as the College's first endowment fund.

It was in connection with the Edward A. Woods Foundation that Robert Dechert first served the American College. The Executive Committee, meeting at the home office of the Penn Mutual Life, was considering some technical problems related to the trust instrument. Mr. Hart called Mr. Dechert, then attorney for the Penn Mutual, to come to its assistance, and he was most helpful. Later, as Dr. Huebner realized that he would have frequent need for legal guidance in College affairs, he asked permission to retain Mr. Dechert as counsel on a permanent basis. He was given the green light with the caution to remember the state of the College finances.

When Mr. Dechert was approached, he readily agreed to serve the College, and expressed his willingness to work without a fee. Dr. Huebner did not believe that was fair, and urged him to name a modest amount. Mr. Dechert and the College directors agreed on $200 as an annual retainer, and thus an association of inestimable value to the College began officially in 1936. Mr. Dechert became a leading attorney in Philadelphia and nationally known in appointive service for the federal government, but he continued to serve the American College with devoted interest. He is currently counsel for the College, and in 1961 was elected a life trustee.

Financial problems and the practical tasks of administering the examination program were pressing. However, the College officials did not forget that one of their major purposes was to cooperate with colleges and universities to improve life insurance teaching in these institutions. On this subject, Dr. Huebner spoke to the directors:

One of the great problems in the college world is the finding of teachers. On the one hand we do a lot for teachers in placing them, and on the other we can cooperate a great deal with institutions in giving them teachers. We have promised cooperation in two of our declared purposes. Three universities have already asked us for teachers; I have placed one teacher with one of these institutions. . . .

Owing to the neglect of this subject in the past, and the sudden growth of this demand, they [the colleges] are up against it, and therefore, I suggest that our College cooperate by establishing a clearing house for teachers . . . but in recommending a teacher it is highly important that the right person be recommended. Most teachers hold a life position, and if we give a lemon to an institution, it is the worst kind of cooperation. So I would suggest probably the Dean's office, through correspondence and otherwise, accumulate a file of teachers, investigate their records, and do the utmost that we can do to help any educational institution that desires an instructional force.

This plan was approved by the directors. Thus, from the very beginning, the American College worked on a problem fundamental to practical improvement of life insurance teaching. This cooperation was probably the most important factor in meeting a basic need until the founding of the S. S. Huebner Foundation for Insurance Education in 1940.

Chapter 8

UP—IN SPITE OF DEPRESSION

With the successful first year safely behind them, the College directors consolidated their position and prepared for new victories. The directors, though themselves a representative group, realized that they could not be heard for the College all over the United States. Therefore, the idea of an Advisory Council was developed. The men and women chosen for this responsibility were carefully selected for their demonstrated interest in the College and their basic good judgment. Their duties were, "to work under the supervision and guidance of the Dean in approaching educational institutions for the purpose of installing the American College program, and such other cooperative work as may be requested by the executive officers of the College." President Ernest Clark voiced the opinion of the Board when he emphasized the necessity to give each Council member "specific instructions along certain standard lines, so he won't go off half cocked." Members of the first Advisory Council were announced early in 1929. These 30 ambassadors made a great contribution to the College in its beginning years. The following list is reproduced from the minutes of the Board of Directors.

Alfred C. Newell	Atlanta, Ga.	General Agent, Columbian National Life Insurance Company (Graduate of University of Georgia-1891)
John H. Outcalt	Birmingham, Ala.	General Agent, Penn Mutual Life Insurance Company (Graduate of West Point-1924)

Maurice S. Tabor, C.L.U.	Buffalo, N.Y.	Travelers Insurance Company
B. Scott Blanton	Charlotte, N.C.	Manager, Phoenix Mutual Life Insurance Company
J. W. Bishop	Chattanooga, Tenn.	General Agent, Volunteer State Life Insurance Company (Peabody College)
Seaborn T. Whatley	Chicago, Ill.	General Agent, Aetna Life Insurance Company (Graduate of University of Alabama)
C. Vivian Anderson, C.L.U.	Cincinnati, O.	Provident Mutual Life Insurance Company (Graduate of Miami University-1913)
Ralph W. Hoyer	Columbus, O.	General Agent, John Hancock Mutual Life Insurance Company (Graduate of Ohio State University-1906)
J. Max Spangler	Dallas, Texas	Assistant Manager, Kansas City Life Insurance Company
Harry S. Haskins	Des Moines, Ia.	State Agent, John Hancock Mutual Life Insurance Company (Graduate of Grinnell College and University of Minnesota)
John W. Yates	Detroit, Mich.	General Agent, Massachusetts Mutual Life Insurance Company
James W. Haughton	Fort Wayne, Ind.	General Agent, Connecticut General Life Insurance Company
Herbert L. Smith	Harrisburg, Pa.	General Agent, Northwestern Mutual Life Insurance Company (Graduate of West Virginia Wesleyan College-1911)
Richard H. Habbe	Indianapolis, Ind.	Massachusetts Mutual Life Insurance Company (Graduate of University of Illinois-1914)
Gordon H. Campbell	Little Rock, Ark.	General Agent, Aetna Life Insurance Company (Lake Forest and University of Chicago)
Henry J. Powell	Louisville, Ky.	Manager, Equitable Life Assurance Society
A. C. Larson	Madison, Wisconsin	State Agent, Central Life Insurance Company

R. Henry Lake	Memphis, Tenn.	General Agent, Equitable Life Assurance Society (University of Mississippi)
Leon A. Triggs, C.L.U.	Minneapolis, Minn.	General Agent, Berkshire Life Insurance Company (Graduate of University of Illinois-1914)
B. B. Macfarlane (Miss)	New Orleans, La.	Agency Supervisor, Pan American Life Insurance Company
Julian S. Myrick	New York, N.Y.	Manager, Mutual Life Insurance Company
C. Carroll Day	Oklahoma City, Okla.	General Agent, Pacific Mutual Life Insurance Company
Seth B. Thompson	Portland, Oregon	General Agent, Penn Mutual Life Insurance Company (Stanford University)
C. C. White	Providence, R.I.	Secretary, Puritan Life Insurance Company (Graduate of Brown University-1900)
Neil D. Sills	Richmond, Va.	General Agent, Sun Life Assurance Company
Lara P. Good, C.L.U.	San Diego, Calif.	Assistant Manager, Prudential Insurance Company (Indiana University)
C. W. Peterson	San Francisco, Calif.	Manager, Phoenix Mutual Life Insurance Company (Graduate of University of Washington-1920)
Marshall L. Baker	Seattle, Wash.	Northern Life Insurance Company (Graduate of Adrian College-1901)
Frank M. See	St. Louis, Mo.	Manager, Union Central Life Insurance Company (Graduate of Missouri State University-1911)
Pendleton E. Miller	Topeka, Kansas	District Manager, Equitable Life Assurance Society (Graduate of Washburn College-1913)

Dr. Huebner's February, 1929, report to the directors concerning study plans and prospective candidates for the June examinations reflects the effective service of the Advisory Council, and the vigorous interest in the new program across the country. High lights of this report follow:

All indications point to a large number of candidates next June. Not only are a considerable number of companies emphasizing the importance of the examinations to their personnel, but the College has now succeeded in establishing a close contact with local life underwriters' associations and educational institutions through its Advisory Council of thirty members. Each of these Councilors represents the College for his section of the country and was appointed to further its aims and purposes with the underwriters' associations as well as with the universities and colleges of his territory. Advices to date indicate that candidates are preparing to register for the June examinations in at least 41 cities, representing 23 different states. In 24 of these cities, study groups have been or are being organized for those qualified to take the examinations and in 11 of these instances the university or college of the center is cooperating in the educational work.

Thirty leading universities and colleges have given the American College of Life Underwriters assurances of their wholehearted cooperation, and stand ready to offer all or nearly all of the C.L.U. program just as soon as the matter can be properly arranged. They have expressed their belief in no uncertain terms in the correctness of the cause which the American College espouses. In many instances the business schools of these universities or colleges have taken the educational initiative in their respective communities and are waiting for an acceptance from the underwriters along practical lines....

The University of Baltimore stands ready to give our entire program ... The University of Pennsylvania will recognize the C.L.U. degree in its catalogue next year and a statement is inserted in Wharton School circular that all students are urged and expected to take the C.L.U. examination ... There will be about seventeen candidates in Philadelphia next June. The New York University Training School is going to run a review course for the graduates of the School.

Syracuse University is with us and will recognize the degree, but the life underwriters are very slow to grasp the hand that is extended by the University.

At Buffalo things are moving very well. Mr. Sheehan, President of the life underwriters association, teaches life insurance, and they have made arrangements with the University of Buffalo to give instruction in courses we require. Eight are now preparing for the C.L.U. degree.

Cleveland has a C.L.U. course of instruction now in progress. University of Cincinnati has recognized the degree. From Detroit, our Advisory Councilor, Mr. Yates, writes very enthusiastically. He happens to be President of the Managers Association and has secured consent of the local university to cooperate with the American College. There will be several candidates for the degree. At Flint, Grand Rapids, Kalamazoo, and Fort Wayne, several candidates are preparing for the C.L.U. examinations.

Our Advisory Councilor, Mr. Whatley, of Chicago, is a trustee of Northwestern University, and is attempting to get the ball rolling at that point. Madison and Milwaukee will furnish candidates for the C.L.U. degree, and Mr. A. C. Larson, member of the Advisory Council at Madison, is doing excellent work. At Minneapolis they have a study class, and our Advisory Councilor and alumnus, Mr. Triggs, is a most enthusiastic worker. The University of Minnesota is giving the American College course, and we are going to have a number of candidates from there.

Omaha probably has the largest class in the United States, totalling 103. The University of Omaha took the initiative, and through the Chamber of Commerce put it across. At Kansas City, Mr. Scott arranged a meeting with the General Agents and Managers on the occasion of my visit, and he has promised at least ten candidates for the June examinations from Kansas City.

At Oklahoma City, Advisory Councilor Day has taken hold of the matter and at least four candidates are coming up for examination. At Tulsa there is a study class of eight for the June examinations. Birmingham will have at least three.

William and Mary College at Williamsburg, Virginia, stands ready to give the work; the life underwriters, however, are a little slow in extending the desired cooperation. Harrisburg, Pittsburgh, Topeka, Kansas; Camden, New Jersey; Indianapolis, and Wilmington all report progress and prospective candidates for the June examinations. At Columbus, Ohio, a considerable number have made inquiry regarding the degree, and Mr. Hoyer, our member of the Advisory Council, is taking the question up with the Ohio State University.

At Davenport, Iowa, ten are studying for the degree. In the District of Columbia, at least three are preparing, and York, Pennsylvania, also has a study class.

There are 88 live inquiries for the coming examination and there are 56 additional inquiries for information which are not listed in the data referred to.

The enthusiastic prophecy for a good group of candidates was fulfilled. In fact, the number of successful examinees was about double that of the first year. Leaders of the American College shared the optimism of most of the country in that summer of 1929. Of the 68 men and women who passed all the 1929 examinations, 51 were college graduates, and several had advanced degrees. Six were insurance teachers, and 34 were said by Dr. Huebner to "hold positions of some importance" in the business.

Among members of this class who subsequently made important contributions to the College and the industry were: Howard H. Cammack, then general agent for the John Hancock in West Virginia, and later a president of the American Society of Chartered Life Underwriters; Paul W. Cook, agents' instructor in the Mutual Benefit Life agency in Chicago, chairman of the Million Dollar Round Table in 1951, and trustee of the College, 1944-56; Walter A. Craig, Mutual Benefit Life agent in Philadelphia, who gave incomparable service as first editor of the *Journal of the American Society of Chartered Life Underwriters;* H. Cochran Fisher, Aetna Life agent in Washington, D.C., who for the next generation was a leader in the National Association of Life Underwriters; Clarence B. Metzger, assistant to the president of the Edward A. Woods Company in Pittsburgh, now vice president of the Equitable Life Assurance Society, and College trustee since 1949; and David McCahan, assistant professor of insurance, University of Pennsylvania, and for the next 25 years a pillar of strength in the College and the Society.

Clarence B. Metzger. (*Bachrach*)

After reviewing the records of this class, the directors "declared them eligible for the degree," but could not authorize the award of the C.L.U. because of a development in educational affairs in Washington. In March, 1929, Congress passed a law requiring all degree-conferring institutions to be licensed by the Board of Education of the District of Columbia. The law forbade any such institutions, when organized in the District, to "use as its title in whole or in part, the words United States, Federal, American, National, Civil Service, or any other words which might reasonably imply an official connection with the Government of the United States or any of its departments." Being chartered in the District as a "college" and granting a "degree" the College was obliged to apply for a license. Of course, voluminous questionnaires were answered. President Clark and Dean Huebner went to Washington for extensive interviews. The directors were deeply concerned about a real threat to the program.

The authorities in Washington carefully investigated the academic procedures and standards of the College. In various ways they asked repeatedly, "Did you ever allow an unqualified person to take examinations?" "Did you ever grant your degree without examination?"

The College officers proudly gave a ringing "No" in answer to both questions. The investigators were probing for diploma mill operations, and Dr. Huebner presented meticulous records with supporting documents to show the unvarying high standards of the American College. His ability to produce such proof was justification for many battles he had fought, and a bulwark for others still to come.

Although satisfied about the quality of the College, the authorities still balked at licensing a college without buildings or faculty being empowered to grant a degree. Gradually it became apparent that one or the other term would have to be relinquished.

The directors felt that the College was truly an institution of higher learning. Its choice of program decentralization was deliberate. "Make it *national,* make it *national!*" was the repeated exhortation of Dr. Huebner's Wharton School mentor, Dr. Emory R. Johnson, in the pre-organizational years of the C.L.U. movement. Dr. Huebner considers his advice a major factor in the success and influence of the College. For its purposes, the College could best conduct its teaching and examination program through other institutions of higher learning all over the country. This decision had been basic in formulating plans for the College. In no other way could great numbers of working life underwriters have been expected to undertake the prolonged course of study.

President Clark spoke of this characteristic of the College at the life underwriters' national convention in 1931:

The Chartered Life Underwriter course is probably the only course of study in the world that has been so perfectly standardized. Whether given at the leading universities of America or in foreign countries, or under direction of trained study group teachers and leaders, all C.L.U. candidates must make the same preparation, submit to the same examinations, and have their examination papers graded by the same corps of graders, under the exacting rules and regulations as established by the American College. We have no record in the history of education of any other specialized course of study being established in this manner and its universal standardization so completely controlled; which fact gives to the C.L.U. designation a unique and outstanding distinction.

When the directors discussed the use of "degree" it was pointed out that the recognitions for the Certified Public Accountant and Fellow of the Actuarial Society, both reflecting extensive and college-grade work, were not technically degrees. The significance of a professional recognition depends more on the performance of those who hold it than on some arbitrary rating. Therefore, the American College directors agreed that henceforth the C.L.U. "degree" should become a "designation." They were thus able to retain the name American College of Life Underwriters with the blessing of the educational authorities in Washington.

In the first few years, the majority of candidates for the C.L.U. program were college graduates. Their preparation for the examinations was mainly a review of college courses. It was feasible for candidates to complete such review so that they could take all five parts of the examination in one year, or two at most. As the college-graduate cream of potential C.L.U.s was skimmed off, more study helps became necessary. In 1930, the College began to publish the "Topical Outline"—a detailed study outline to help students keep on the track and on schedule in preparation for their examinations. To assist in developing the "Outline," Dr. Huebner asked permission to enlist professional collaborators, even if it "cost a little money." The modest budget was stretched to pay $50 each to two specialists. One was Irvin Bendiner, C.L.U. (1928), and a member of the Pennsylvania

Bar. He worked on Part IV, which was then commercial law. He was a strong supporter of the American College, a C.L.U. teacher, and a valuable adviser to Dr. Huebner until his untimely death in 1946.

As C.L.U. examination preparation became a matter not merely of review, but of actual basic study, candidates needed more time. Early in the 1930s, the College began to urge taking examinations in installments of one, or not more than two, a year.

In spite of the increasing burden of study and the difficulties of the depression, activity was amazing. An insurance publication listed the West Coast classes for 1932. In Seattle, 10 men were reviewing for all examinations; 14 were working on the first three; and two other groups were studying other parts. In Portland, 14 men were preparing for three examinations. In San Francisco, 26 college and university graduates were enrolled in a review class preparing for the five examinations. In Los Angeles, the University of Southern California had 100 men studying with Verne Steward, C.L.U. There were also independent groups of eight men in Los Angeles with Lloyd Lafot, C.L.U. and 20 in San Diego with Lara P. Good, C.L.U.

Chicago developments in 1933 were outlined for members in the bulletin of the Chicago Association of Life Underwriters:

> Chicago now has 75 of the 702 C.L.U.'s in the nation. Twenty additional Chicago underwriters have completed one or more of the examinations.

> Chicago, New York, and Philadelphia have passed the pioneering stage and the movement, in these cities at least, is entering upon a second phase of its development. The educational program has to be revised to meet the new situation.

> Most cities in the earliest stages of the movement organized independent study groups and prepared for all five examinations in one year. This has been feasible because the men as a whole were thoroughly qualified by reason of college educations followed by self-

development and field experience. They could quickly review the material because they had taken courses in college covering Examinations III, IV and V, and there were enough men available and interested to successfully operate these groups.

The next development has been the affiliation with the leading universities and the organization of review courses preparing well qualified men for all examinations in one year.

The combination of the two above-mentioned methods produced a large nucleus of C.L.U.'s in Chicago and other cities. With approximately one out of every ten members of the Chicago Life Underwriters being C.L.U.'s or on the way, the prospective new candidates are fewer.

The movement in Chicago now definitely enters a second phase, wherein the educational and preparation courses are concentrated entirely on the installment plan of taking the examinations. Instead of a C.L.U. Review Course preparing for all five examinations, Northwestern University, with the endorsement and cooperation of the Chicago C.L.U. Chapter, is to offer a review course preparing underwriters for Examinations I, II and III.

At the N.A.L.U. convention in 1933, Dr. Huebner reported:

I wonder how many appreciate the fact that the active history of the American College of Life Underwriters almost coincides with the years of this dismal major business depression. The first year of real active functioning of the College was 1929. In that year 114 took the examinations. In October and November of that year the memorable stock market panic occurred, and thereafter the nation rapidly slid off into the never to be forgotten depression. Nineteen hundred and thirty was a bad year, but the number of candidates rose to 235, an increase of over 100%. Nineteen hundred and thirty-one was a still worse year, but the number of candidates taking examinations rose to 521, another increase of 120%. Nineteen hundred and thirty-two was a terrible year, but the number of examined candidates rose to 638. Nineteen hundred and thirty-three was an awful year, with every business activity sliding downward to an appalling extent, even including life insurance with its increased man-power. Frankly, I was fearful and ready for a 20% decline. But I was pleasantly surprised since the number of examinated candidates last June rose to 663, or the highest ever.

Plotted on a chart, the course of business was ever downward; while the number of examined C.L.U. candidates proceeded ever upward. I doubt whether there is any other educational movement in the nation which has experienced such a record in such a dismal period. At present there are 750 who have completed all of their examinations successfully, and another 665 who are on the way to their objective with a completion of the program in part, or in all a total of 1,415. This is a number in excess of 7% of the total membership of this National Association, and that result has been accomplished within five years, and four of the five being depression years. . . .

When the economic sun breaks clearly through the economic clouds of today, the momentum of the movement is bound to become even greater, and we shall become accustomed to speak of at least 1,000 examined candidates a year. I have never seen a finer C.L.U. spirit in the various cities I have visited than I have this summer. Everywhere the C.L.U. chapters are working with real enthusiasm. I have never seen any group of people anywhere, who work so unselfishly for a cause and for their fellow underwriters.

By this time, there were significant and enouraging reactions in at least some of the companies' home offices. The College officers publicized these favorable activities, hoping to make them more widespread. For instance, in the *Announcement* for 1932-33 they reported:

A substantial number of insurance companies have evidenced their interest in the C.L.U. movement by adopting various practical plans for inducing their representatives to pursue the necessary educational work. These vary considerably in nature.

Certain companies have, through general agents or managers, conventions and regional conferences, or home office publications, emphasized the benefits to be gained from following the C.L.U. course of study. Others have given special recognition in various ways to successful candidates, formulated educational programs of their own in line with that advocated by the American College, refunded

examination fees in whole or in part to their representatives successful in attaining the designation, promised reimbursement for the
cost of text books to successful candidates, supplied such books
through circulating libraries or arranged for purchasing them at
a discount. One company has announced a guarantee of $250 a
month for a period of one year to each representative of the company who earns the designation. Several companies are planning to
make educational surveys of their representatives in order more
effectively to meet the educational needs of such representatives as
are preparing for the C.L.U. examinations. Another significant evidence of support by home officials is the expression of a desire by
several of them to have the educational program extended to the
home office personnel.

President Ernest J. Clark spoke to the directors concerning
progress through the fall of 1933:

The progress made by the American College during the past year
has not only been highly satisfactory, but almost extraordinary, in
view of the adverse conditions with which we have had to contend
because of the economic condition, the moratorium, the continued
depression and the effect which the entire combination has had on
the life underwriters of the country. It is not only marvelous that the
College has made such excellent progress in the extension of its educational program, but also in conjunction with its finances. We have
balanced our budget and have no outstanding obligations.

The early C.L.U. candidates were plagued not only by the
major problems of their times, but by minor troubles in that
primitive day before air conditioning. Robert G. Richards, in
1929 agency secretary of the Atlantic Life, was one of the first
100 C.L.U.s in the nation. He wrote of his study and experiences
for the benefit of the field force, and included this vivid report:

There are some things in connection with the taking of the exams
that will always remain in my mind. There were four of us who
took them at the University of Richmond, during the hottest days
of June. The morning exams were taken under pleasant conditions,
but in the afternoon the sunshine and the flies poured in on us, and
the latter were a terrific nuisance. In order to work, I had to unroll

my sleeves to cover my arms to the wrists, and finally I placed a handkerchief over my head, which left very few exposed places. Even then I had to brush flies off the paper and ink.

A gratifying aspect of College progress in these years was the development of cooperation with colleges and universities across the country. Only 12 participated in 1929, but by 1933 there were 63. The practical assistance such institutions gave in examination preparation and provision of examination centers went hand in hand with an increase of insurance courses in their own curriculums. Dr. Huebner reported in 1933 that 99 colleges and universities were offering a general course in insurance. About half the course was a study of life insurance. Also, 52 institutions reported 65 special courses involving principles, practices, and economics of life insurance. Some 8,500 students were enrolled in these courses. Some students would become life insurance workers, but the majority would become business and professional people in other fields, the buyers and beneficiaries of life insurance. Their information about the product and its services would make them more creative participants in a buying situation.

As demands for insurance courses developed, university faculty members felt their need to exchange ideas and to work together on common teaching problems. In 1931, Frank G. Dickinson, assistant professor of insurance and statistics at the University of Illinois, promoted the idea of an insurance teachers' round-table program at the meeting of the American Economic Association. He persuaded Dr. Huebner to serve as chairman. The experience was so helpful that those present took steps which resulted the next year in the organization of the American Association of University Teachers of Insurance.

Not surprisingly, Dr. Huebner was made president; Dr. Ralph H. Blanchard, Columbia University, vice president; and Dr. Dickinson, secretary-treasurer. The three-member executive committee included A. H. Mowbray, University of California; S. H. Nerlove, University of Chicago; and Corliss L. Parry, Metropolitan Life Insurance Company.

The organization proposed to promote insurance teaching, research, and publications; to provide an open forum for the discussion of all kinds of insurance subjects; and to cooperate with other organizations with similar interests. The first annual meeting in 1933 illustrated how valuable this organization could be in bringing reality to the academic work of college teachers. Authorities from the life insurance business, as well as professors, spoke on such topics as the depression record of life insurance companies, the effects of inflation on life insurance, the public need for many life insurance companies, and the ways in which the life insurance business had been affected by the banking moratorium. To provide life insurance students throughout the country with pertinent information about these matters through their teachers' discussions with experts was a real service. The Association illustrated the accomplishment of part of the purpose of the American College of Life Underwriters: "to cooperate with educational institutions in general life insurance education."

The American Association of University Teachers of Insurance expanded its membership and usefulness over the years. Since 1960, to indicate its broader purposes, it has been called the American Risk and Insurance Association.

As president of A.A.U.T.I. for its first two years, Dr. Huebner was an ideal liaison between the professors and the business. He emphasized what might be called the liberal arts aspect of life underwriting. He gave the teachers "a track to run on," as he said, by presenting life insurance from an economic point of view through his life value concept. He preached the necessity to have life underwriting education organized according to highest academic standards.

The following quotation from one of Dr. Huebner's talks in the early 1930s shows how he emphasized the need of college-level education for life underwriters.

Relatively less and less shall we emphasize the purely death aspect of life insurance. More and more life insurance will be presented as a creative force in the fields of thrift, investment, credit, conservation of life, protection of the existing property estate, organized philanthropy, and fundamental usefulness in the current business affairs of the insured. The life underwriter must therefore know more than just the narrow technique of life insurance itself. He must be a business man, competent and confident in his knowledge of business, so that his mind may be on a full parity with that of the business man whom he is endeavoring to influence and to serve life insurance-wise. He therefore needs to have a good background of knowledge in the fields of economics, business law, private and corporate finance, banking and credit, and investments. These subjects are fundamental to an understanding and solution of the problems of any business.

Other business callings have long recognized this point of view. Some twenty-seven years ago accounting initiated its educational program leading to the designation of "Certified Public Accountant." The technique of accounting constitutes the backbone of the course, but the allied business subjects of a fundamental nature to all business are also included. An accountant is not an accountant when he knows only the narrow mechanical groove of accounting. He must know also the fundamentals and the problems of business if he is to apply his calling intelligently and creatively for business men.

Some twenty-seven years ago American banking established its American Institute of Banking course of study, extending over three years and operating in all the leading cities of America. The technique of banking constitutes the backbone of the course, but the allied business subjects of a fundamental nature to all business are again included. A banker is not a banker when he knows only the narrow mechanical groove of banking. He must also be a business man who understands the fundamentals and problems of business since he is obliged to deal with them daily in many ways. As William Feather has so well stated in his *A Business Man's Philosophy:* "Successful men in business are those who understand what is going on around them. Some men master only the details of the job. Others master the principles behind the job."

Chapter 9

THE MEN WHO BUILT

"The invaluable services of Dr. S. S. Huebner as dean and Dr. David McCahan as secretary and assistant dean—that combination is depression-proof." Such was President Clark's evaluation of the two men most responsible for the growth of the College in its early years.

No other life insurance educator in the world could have brought to the American College what Dr. Huebner did. He pioneered life insurance teaching from the economic point of view. He had built a department at the University of Pennsylvania's Wharton School which, in many circles, gave it more of a reputation as an *insurance* school than as a *business* school. He was known around the world through his exchange professorship in Japan and his world lecture trip through China, the Far East, and Germany.

He was already the author or editor of 16 volumes used widely among English-speaking students, and in translation by many others. He had given distinguished service to the United States Government in investigations and legislative studies relating to insurance and commerce.

He had been honored by the University of Pennsylvania for "what you have accomplished for mankind in one of the important economic fields and in recognition of what you have done in service of the University by holding before your students high standards of personal integrity and of social responsibility." That evaluation appeared in the citation when he was awarded

111

an honorary degree of Doctor of Science as part of the Wharton School's fiftieth anniversary observance.

With it all, he was voted the most popular professor in the University. The young men liked his happy disposition, his enthusiasm, his evident enjoyment of life and ideas. They respected him as a teacher, and responded to the mental stimulus of his stiff courses. They liked his characteristic red neckties, and cherished the memories of conferences while he rocked in his rocking chair behind his big desk long before a president of the United States dramatized the value of that exercise.*

Dr. Huebner was a crusader. He had strong convictions about the value of the C.L.U. program, and welcomed the opportunity to "sell" it to life underwriters. Like a good life insurance salesman, he studied the objections he most frequently encountered and prepared his answers. The following quotations are from his speech before the National Association of Life Underwriters 1931 convention in San Francisco.

In traveling about the country I find that certain fallacious views seem to militate against the C.L.U. program in certain quarters. Although ridiculous, these views are the result of misunderstanding and misinformation. Unfortunately, they are often held by well-meaning people who have others under their guidance. For ever so many the gross error of these views is only too apparent. Yet because of their prevalence I am prompted to state and answer them briefly. They are:

(1) The C.L.U. program takes too long and takes too much time. —This view is absolutely incorrect. The C.L.U. program, it is true, represents for the first time in life underwriting the long term course idea. We are deliberately advocating the four year program for those who have not previously had the benefit of the recommended work. We desire proper assimilation and not cramming, and feel that preparation over a four year period is most desirable.

---

*A complete biography of Dr. Huebner is available: Mildred F. Stone, *The Teacher Who Changed an Industry* (Homewood, Illinois: Richard D. Irwin, Inc., 1960).

We would sooner have fewer Chartered Life Underwriters in the earlier years with a view to having many more in the future. The Certified Public Accountancy, American Institute of Banking, and other professional courses extend over a similar period, and in certain instances over even longer periods. These professions do not shy at a four year program, under reasonable circumstances, and life underwriters should see the wisdom of adopting a similar course if they wish to continue to emphasize the title of "underwriter." . . .

(2) The program decreases production during the period of preparation.—This viewpoint is absolutely untrue. It might be so for those who have not had this work before and who prepare for all five examinations in a single year, manifestly an absurdity. But who ever advocated such an idea! Certainly not the educational officers of the College. We desire to have the work completed in annual installments over a four year period, each year involving weekly 2 or 3 evenings of consistent study. This will certainly not prove harmful to the health of any one. Nor will it interfere with any person's available time, because where is the underwriter or the teacher who does not waste 2 or 3 evenings a week? Moreover stimulation of the mind, in the way we are advocating, does not lead to a decrease in production. I have yet to hear of the first candidate, who came up for any of the C.L.U. examinations, and who did his work of preparation on the installment plan which we are recommending, who has complained that his production suffered. Instead they inform us that their best year to date was the very year in which they did this work, thereby stimulating their minds to greater initiative and activity. If any one should understand the benefits of the installment plan it is the life underwriter. He teaches daily that an investment estate should be created conveniently and surely through the installment method. Why in the world is it so hard for these same underwriters to understand the convenience and ease of accumulating an educational estate through that same installment method? The C.L.U. program may be made hard if the underwriter insists. But it is really easy, if pursued in a sensible way, i.e., on the installment method.

(3) The program is too expensive—That also is absolutely not so. If we have in mind five or ten dollar education only—the peanut view—then anything is too expensive. But if we take a comprehensive view of education, namely, as an investment which will increase

current annual earning capacity by at least one thousand dollars a year, as well as afford the other personal advantages already referred to, the expenditure annually of $50 to $100, and the devotion of 2 or 3 evenings of work a week for four years is certainly not asking too much. Failure to see this point certainly comes under the old adage of "Penny wise and pound foolish." Moreover, any underwriter worthy of this type of training should during every year of his preparation acquire ideas which, when currently translated into commissions, will pay for the entire outlay several times over before the examination is taken. In other words, there is really no expense at all for the worthwhile candidate. There is, instead, an immediate source of profit, contrary to what is the case in most other professional courses of preparation.

(4) We already have a life insurance course, and it covers the ground pretty thoroughly.—That view is certainly refreshing. Reference is usually made to the so-called short courses offered in many quarters. These courses are good as far as they go. They are not opposed by us in the slightest. They do a lot for the beginner, and should certainly whet the appetite for more. But to hold out the idea to the novice that completion of a few-weeks' or a few-months' course represents final graduation is a view so untenable that I doubt whether a single author of such courses would be willing to subscribe to such a refreshing idea . . .

(5) Too much education is not a good thing.—This attitude I am afraid represents the drummer's point of view. The view is interesting in that it reverses the old adage "A little learning is a dangerous thing" into "Substantial learning is dangerous and little learning is innocently safe." It is hardly worthwhile dwelling upon this phase, yet I am surprised at its prevalence. The C.L.U. program, let us frankly admit, by no means covers everything. It is, however, a program which covers the needs for mastery of subject matter as understood by leaders in the calling of life underwriting. . . .

(6) If the College can elevate the poor or mediocre salesman well and good, but the others in our Agency are fair producers and substantial earners of income and really need no further training.— This is probably the most shocking view of all. Yet I am surprised how frequently and sincerely it has been presented to me. Let me say that we do not wish to bother with those who are inherently dull, lazy, indifferent, or otherwise under average. We desire to deal with

those who are industrious, possess aptitude for their calling, have the mainspring of ambition and progress in their souls, and are animated by a desire for personal upbuilding through investment and work. In other words, we believe that a good man can be made better, but that a poor stick will continue to be a stick.

Dr. Huebner was certainly the peripatetic professor. For five years beginning in 1930—a particularly strategic period for the American College—he had an especially strenuous and valuable schedule, thanks to the Massachusetts Mutual Life Insurance Company. That company paid him a fee and expenses to visit its

Dr. Huebner on the steps of Logan Hall, 1960. (*Shaw*)

agencies all over the United States to discuss the life value concept and other fundamentals of life insurance education. Then, with the company's permission, he took an extra day at each city to promote the College with the life underwriters, speak to public audiences, visit colleges and universities, and generally advance the C.L.U. program.

During this early period the directors also took advantage of Dr. Huebner's services to sell the College to leaders of the life insurance business. Generally speaking, it was life underwriters in the field, rather than home office men, who promoted the American College in the beginning. Many companies were lukewarm or antagonistic to the College program, although there were a number of brilliant exceptions.

Life insurance home office men needed a lot of indoctrination. They were often far behind the American College in their concepts of life insurance education. Friends of the College opened doors wherever they could. Through Frank L. Jones, chairman of the Executive Committee of the Life Insurance Sales Research Bureau, and John Marshall Holcombe, Jr., Bureau manager, Dr. Huebner was invited, in the fall of 1929, to speak before the annual meeting of the Association of Life Agency Officers and the Life Insurance Sales Research Bureau (now combined as the Life Insurance Agency Management Association).

Later in the year, he addressed the Association of Life Insurance Presidents (now the Life Insurance Association of America). These groups represented about the top hundred companies in the business, and about 90 per cent of the nation's insurance in force.

Dr. Huebner delivered a strong message to these top executives and agency officials. His talks differed somewhat in approach for the two organizations, but stressed the same essentials.

Life insurance is a vocation of ideas and expert knowledge in the application of those ideas to the needs of clients. It involves service of a high order, and service is more than mere honesty and routine labor. Service means honesty plus knowledge. . . .

The American College of Life Underwriters is essentially a young man's movement. Many in the calling are older and well established, and are the survival of the fittest. They may not care to undergo the suggested program. But they should support the movement in the interest of the cause which they have represented for so many years. . . . If that is done, there can be no doubt that the movement must be regarded as a rich investment, both with respect to emolument as well as mental satisfaction. Everybody will be the gainer. As life underwriters do the right thing in the interest of public service, so the public will do the right thing to the underwriter. Such reciprocity is inevitable. But in every calling, the calling itself must take the initiative, and the public mind will then recognize and follow. . . .

The principal key to the future growth of life insurance is life insurance education through all of our educational channels. This is true with respect to both seller and buyer. . . .

More and more life insurance will seek as its field representatives persons who will want to be in position to know and to give more accurate advice, who will want to supplement their ordinary training and education with a higher degree of understanding of their calling, and who will want their minds to be on a parity with those of the educated business men whom he is seeking to influence and serve. Teaching individuals, as distinguished from solicitation based on ordinary appeal, will soon be the outstanding factor in efficient salesmanship. On the other hand, life insurance, just like many other services which have preceded it in this respect, will want more and more to gain a place in our educational system. The public will then be educated in life insurance, just as it now is in other important economic fields, and will cease to regard life insurance as an intangible and mysterious thing, the price of which is to be grudgingly borne. Through education the seller's mind and the buyer's mind will increasingly meet on common ground, and the calling of life underwriting will correspondingly rise in public esteem. But in this process of education it behooves the business of life insurance to lead instead of being led, and to insist upon proper fitness on the part of its representatives who aspire to underwrite business and professional men.

The American College of Life Underwriters fits intimately into every important phase of the educational program which life insurance ought to stress. Although founded and originally sponsored by the National Association of Life Underwriters, the College is a separate and distinct organization which is and which will remain absolutely independent of the Association in its management and in the pursuit of its educational policies. It is absolutely nonprofit-making in character and exists solely for the educational advancement of life insurance and life underwriting.

The College was designed to do for life underwriting what the C.P.A. movement has so well accomplished for accounting during the past quarter of a century. Its objects are to place life insurance adequately in our educational system, partly to foster training for the career of life underwriter and partly to cooperate with institutions of learning in general life insurance education, to make the public more conscious of the dignity and service value of life underwriting, and to set an educational objective towards which all salesmen may strive as best they can in the interest of themselves and the public they serve. The College was created to perform in a large way, comprehensively and nationally, the same kind of educational work which so many companies have seen fit to stress in recent years in one form or another. Those who complete successfully the entire program are awarded a professional recognition, just as is done in the field of accounting. But it is not the diploma, as such, which is emphasized. Instead it is the required study over a considerable period, the higher viewpoint of service which the student necessarily acquires concerning his calling because of such study, and the inevitable understanding which he obtains that his calling will require continued study, which constitute the heart of the matter.

Dr. Huebner constantly emphasized the personal economics involved in the C.L.U. program. Speaking to the National Association of Life Underwriters at its 1930 convention in Toronto, he said:

Business represents the judicious union of two kinds of capital, namely, property capital and human life value capital. In most callings, and especially in the professions, the property capital is relatively small and the life value capital is by far the more important. This is particularly true in the calling of life underwriting, which is and should be a profession of the highest order.

The life underwriter is not paid for length of toil or degree of perspiring effort. If that were the basis of compensation, the life underwriter would be a mere wage earner, chained to a desk with a watchful superintendent over him enforcing a contract of hire based on stipulated hours of mechanical toil. Professionally, the life underwriter is paid by the buyer of insurance. The compensation is earned not for the mere act of selling something, but for the rendering of sound advice based on knowledge of his subject.

Like the lawyer or surgeon, the life underwriter may earn his thousands of dollars in a few hours, and without any justified suggestion of a rebate from the client, if the proposition is large enough and the advisory counsel in connection therewith sound and practical. . . .

There is no such thing as final graduation in life underwriting, and extremely inappropriate is the frequently heard expression: "Young man come into life insurance; it requires no capital." That statement may be true if our concept is limited to property capital. Life underwriting, like nearly all the professions, requires little property for its conduct. But if we have in mind the life value asset, representing investment by way of education and training, life underwriting in its true sense requires a large amount of capital by way of study and time in the development of underwriter's mental equipment.

Reporting on the Toronto convention to the Chicago Life Underwriters Association, Gerard S. Brown wrote in its bulletin:

A salient note through out the gathering was constant reference to the growth of the *Chartered Life Underwriter* movement. The momentum which this idea has gained and the enthusiasm over it were amazing even to those who had worked hardest for it and who were most optimistic over its possibilities. It ran through talk in the lobby as well as in the convention hall. It is sweeping the life insurance world.

The Chartered Life Underwriter sees in that designation not so much an accomplished end as a challenge to continued and unremitting progress. Recognition of this kind imposes a responsibility to measure up to constantly more elevated standards in our great business. For life insurance, especially field practice, is dynamic, and we are keenly conscious of an obligation to keep pace with its growth.

Very early in the activities of the College, the burdens of administration mounted far beyond the capacity of Dr. Huebner and volunteer helpers. Dr. Huebner was besieged by requests for articles, invitations to speak, and letters of inquiry about the College program, in addition to his basic work of planning for examinations, developing contacts with teachers, and giving guidance to the Advisory Council and cooperating universities. Therefore, early in 1929, the directors made an important move.

The office of assistant dean was created, and Dr. David McCahan was appointed to the position at "the nominal honorarium of $50 a month." This, incidentally, was the same amount Dr. Huebner was receiving.

Dr. McCahan had been Dr. Huebner's student in the Wharton School. Son of a country banker in southern Pennsylvania, he made highest grades in school but got black marks for deportment. Such a record today indicates to pedagogues a brilliant mind not adequately challenged. Dr. McCahan's career demonstrated his remarkable intellectual endowments and his capacity for an immense amount of work. He worked his way through high school and university, chiefly by vacation jobs in his father's bank. He assumed he probably would end up as a banker, but became a statistics teacher at the Wharton School, and received his M.A. there in 1922. Soon he decided he did not want to spend his life on statistics, and accepted a job with the Insurance Department of the Chamber of Commerce of the United States. This work gave him a national viewpoint and contacts. He gained a wide personal acquaintance as he traveled during vacations to accumulate information for his doctoral thesis on state insurance. About this time, Dr. Huebner "got after him," urging his return to the University.

David McCahan had been attracted as a student by Dr. Huebner's teaching and personality. He admired the teacher's creativity in building the Insurance Department at the Wharton School. He liked the group of able men Dr. Huebner was drawing to himself, and recognized an opportunity for a personal career in a stimulating atmosphere where hard work would be given credit and rewarded. He therefore returned to Pennsylvania in 1926, and won his Ph.D. in 1928 teaching in Dr. Huebner's department. It was natural that Dr. Huebner should look to his newest assistant at the Wharton School as a possible reinforcement in the operations of the College.

Dr. Huebner and Dr. McCahan were a remarkable team. Someone has said that in a sense Dr. Huebner was the architect of the American College and Dr. McCahan was the builder. Dr. Huebner had the vision, provided the blueprint, but left the fine points of construction to others. Dr. Cahan was dedicated to Dr. Huebner and to his objectives. There were deep mutual respect and liking between the two. Both were extraordinarily hard workers. Dr. Huebner pushed mountains of work over to Dr. McCahan—the overwhelming paper work, enormous correspondence, organizational details, and office procedures. Somehow Dr. McCahan kept all the projects going. Their budget was pitiful, too. Dr. McCahan did many detailed jobs which others could have done had there been money to pay for such help.

Dr. McCahan brought not only a keen mind, sound education, and willing hands to the work of the College, but also an admirable character. He was a man of principle and the deepest personal integrity. A minor illustration of this occurred quite early in his work for the College. Candidates from the West Indies, Europe, and the Orient were participating in the program. One day he came to Dr. Huebner with a troubled face to report that he had just received a present from a Japanese candidate. He felt that in honor he should return it, for he wanted to be under no possible obligation to any candidate. Dr. Huebner, fresh from months in the Orient and experienced in the courteous ways of Japanese students at the Wharton School, reassured him. He might without hesitation accept the gift. To refuse would seriously offend a well-meaning friend whose national custom inspired a gift as a mark of personal esteem for a man he respected. It was in no sense a bribe.

Dr. McCahan stood as a rock with Dr. Huebner on several serious issues in the early days of the College. One was the matter of honorary C.L.U.s. Many successful old-timers, highly respected in the business, felt the academic requirements of the program quite beyond them. There was great pressure, constantly renewed, to make exceptions for them, either by awarding the designation without examination or waiving the educational prerequisites.

Today it is surprising to realize how many successful businessmen in all walks of life were literally self-educated, self-made men, a generation ago. The prerequisite of high school graduation as a qualification for taking C.L.U. examinations was a real hurdle to many ambitious life underwriters. But Dr. Huebner, Dr. McCahan, and others knew that acceptance of the C.L.U. program among educators depended on meeting established academic standards. If life underwriting education through the the American College were ever to become a part of the higher education system of the nation, it must follow the pattern. All colleges and universities of any reputation required high school graduation or its equivalent.

Various plans were worked out to establish that precious equivalency. If a candidate could, by examination or other means, satisfy the entrance requirements of a reputable college or university, and could produce evidence that he was acceptable there without condition as a regular member of the freshman class, the American College also would accept him. Columbia University and several others developed programs for correspondence study and examinations which led to high school equivalency credits. Night schools in many cities also enabled adults to earn high school diplomas. To their great credit, not a few life underwriters spent the time and money to do the basic study which in some way qualified them as candidates for C.L.U. work. After World War II, the G.E.D. (General Education Development) tests made it fairly easy to establish high school equivalency qualifications.

For many years, however, the requirement was a practical problem and/or a sore point, and American College leaders had constantly to defend this position. A portion of the official *Announcement* discussing this problem was written by Dr. Mc-Cahan, and reflects his human understanding of the candidates who feared losing face, as well as his professorial devotion to academic standards.

Among the older men in life underwriting are some who have attained a well-rounded education through self-study and who have achieved distinction for the fine character of the service they render but who cannot spare the time from the pressure of other duties to meet these eligibility requirements. Many of them, now well advanced in years, received their early schooling in a day when an eighth grade education was thought to be all the preparation needed for business life. Subsequently, they have witnessed a pronounced change in the public concept as to the scope of such an education, and being unable to pursue further studies in a regular educational institution, have developed themselves mentally by other means. Recognizing the inherent worth of such underwriters, many of whom have reached the top and are nationally known, the College authorities have devoted much time and thought to consideration of plans by which their desire to take the C.L.U. examinations might be met. For reasons mentioned above, however, experience has demonstrated the absolute necessity for maintaining the standards already established, and not a single exception has been made. It is hoped that for the good of the whole movement, such underwriters will continue to extend their loyal support and will encourage those with whom they have an influence to take the examinations. For their own individual benefit they may wish to follow the suggested program of study, as after all, the education contemplated by the C.L.U. designation is the real goal to be sought rather than the recognition itself.

Dr. Huebner explained to a life underwriters' convention:

We simply cannot waive this educational prerequisite. It is a universal American condition in educational circles. Were we to do otherwise, the cooperation of the colleges and universities would be withdrawn at once, and the C.L.U. designation would become a mere commercial badge without standing in the educational world. We would have died before birth, if the College had decided to operate in defiance of the universal custom.

The problems of the depression affected the attitudes of life underwriters toward the College program. With incomes down, they often felt they just didn't have the money. (Some checks sent in for fees came back to the College stamped "no funds.") Many salesmen, pressed by competition, wanted a tag to set them apart as better than their associates. There was renewed demand for "a short course."

Through all these pitfalls, Dr. Huebner, Dr. McCahan, and other College leaders steadily pursued their course. Dr. Huebner, the fighter, waded in and debated the issues. Dr. McCahan, having soberly studied the problems and come to his conclusions about what was right, let the storms of criticism beat on his unperturbed convictions. He answered questions patiently, endlessly, meticulously, taking any amount of time and trouble, trusting people would come around to his point of view if they knew the facts. In this, as in so many other ways, Dr. Huebner and Dr. McCahan marvelously complemented each other.

Concerning these formative years, Dr. McCahan wrote:

Scarcely had the College gotten under way with its broad program when major economic, political and social changes started to occur with startling rapidity. The uncertainties which these changes produced might well have deterred the College founders from initiating activities when they did, had the changes been foreseeable. And yet the changes themselves have had such a marked influence upon the financial problems of the professional and business classes as to intensify the need for the services of life underwriters educated in the subjects covered by C. L. U. examinations. Thus, the very forces which decreased the income of underwriters and increased the demands upon their time for conserving existent business and building new production concurrently generated the forces which emphasized the importance of investing time and money in education.

Establishment of high standards for award of the C.L.U. designation was doubly difficult against this background of conflicting trends. For certain underwriters viewed the designation only as a means of building prestige with the public, of gaining a competitive advantage over their fellows, or of commercializing their knowledge in some other manner. Any broadening of vision or training derived in the course of preparation for C.L.U. examinations was frequently regarded by such underwriters as of secondary importance. Educational prerequisites, experience requirements, comprehensive examination problems, and long time, thorough courses of instruction did not fit into their mental picture of the way in which the C.L.U. diploma might benefit them.

But the College was definitely committed to the maintenance of true professional standards. It was obliged to adopt principles and practices of operation in conformity with present day concepts as to the factors which characterize a profession. It could not compromise and still win the respect and cooperation of other professional groups or of leading educators. Fortunately for the success of the movement, many outstandingly able, broad visioned underwriters were either associated in the management of the College through membership on its Board of Directors or were among the early candidates for the designation. With their assistance, the College officials have not only succeeded in maintaining standards on a high level and applying them impartially but have also consistently striven to bring about a better understanding of the reasons for high standards, of the practical value to the underwriter in pursuing a C.L.U. education rather than a C.L.U. diploma as his goal, and of the desirability for developing adequate C.L.U. educational facilities on a permanent basis.

Foundations were being laid in the College's first decade. They had to go down deep and be sound in structure if the building which would later become evident to the insuring public were to be of enduring quality. Much of the effort expended in laying these foundations showed no immediate results. Activities designed to educate underwriters on the meaning of a professional concept and to help them get started on the right kind of educational program, or to assist colleges and universities in the broadening of curricula so that they might suitably meet the instructional needs of this new profession were not directly reflected in public recognition of the Chartered Life Underwriter. That was inevitable even if not relished by those who expected quick returns. The College's policy has always been to discourage any advertising of the designation and to encourage broad and intelligent application of the C.L.U. knowledge to the end that the holder of the designation might be known by his works and not his words.

Dr. McCahan, in this quotation, paid tribute to the Board of Directors and the C.L.U.s themselves. They too were important builders of the College in its early years. Many of the Board members were not high school graduates, and as they struggled with the problem of educational prerequisites, one suggested that he ought not to be holding his position. His associates hastened to remind him that all Board members did not serve the College in the same way. For instance, who could do what he had done recently in promoting a lecture by Dr. Huebner which had drawn a capacity audience of 1,800, with several hundred more turned away?

Most of the incorporators of the College never became C.L.U.s. Many Board members in the early years were chosen because of their influence and interest in the cause rather than their own C.L.U. aspirations.

The graduates did immeasurable service in advancing the C.L.U. program. The first C.L.U.s recognized their great opportunity as builders, and organized themselves immediately after the first conferments. C. Vivian Anderson, of Cincinnati, was the first president of this rather informal association. The next year, the larger group of graduates felt that a more formal organization would be desirable "to be of real assistance in promoting the welfare of the American College."

A committee for arrangements included E. J. Clark, S. S. Huebner, and David McCahan of the College, as well as C.L.U.s Harry McNamer (the 1929 president), Howard H. Cammack, and H. Lawrence Choate. The committee drafted a constitution

and bylaws, which were submitted by mail to all qualified
C.L.U.s for their ratification and acceptance.

As stated in the constitution, the objectives of the Alumni Association of the American College of Life Underwriters were:

> To advance in every legitimate way the higher education of those
> engaged in the profession of life insurance and students who con-
> template entering the career of professional life underwriter.

> To maintain at all times the dignity and high professional standards
> that properly attach to the Chartered Life Underwriter designa-
> tion.

> To co-operate with the American College of Life Underwriters in
> extending its influence and educational program among the uni-
> versities and colleges of America.

> To bring into social and friendly relations those engaged in the pro-
> fession of life insurance who have acquired the C.L.U. designation.

Later, when local C.L.U. groups were developing around the
country, and C.L.U.s were evolving their philosophy of purposeful professional cooperation, the national organization changed
its name to "National Chapter—Chartered Life Underwriters."
Then, in 1940, it became the present American Society of Chartered Life Underwriters. The concept of the group moved rather
quickly from any possible emphasis on social relationships, rem-
iniscent of college alumni with memories of a common campus
life, to concentration on common professional aims of the American College and its graduates.

Dr. McCahan became the secretary for the association. For
years he did all the careful record-keeping, and gave a continuity
of leadership that laid a foundation for the truly professional organization the Society has become. It might have been simply a
trade association for C.L.U.s. He guided it to concentration on
promoting the educational program and supporting the professional aims of the College.

Frederick W. Floyd.

Local C.L.U. groups were formed as quickly as reasonable numbers of graduates became eligible. By 1931, 10 had been organized in Baltimore, Chicago, Los Angeles, New York, Philadelphia, Pittsburgh, Portland, San Francisco, St. Louis, and Washington, D.C.

The C.L.U.s supplemented and then replaced the early advisory committee in relations with local colleges and universities. They helped organize formal classes and informal study groups. They prospected for worthy C.L.U. candidates, and did a good job—often a hard job—of selling men and women on the undertaking. They served as advance agents in setting up conferences and meetings for Dr. Huebner and Dr. McCahan across the country. As mentioned, Dr. Huebner traveled extensively during the first summers of the College's existence, and it was local C.L.U.s who often set the stage to make those trips and visits profitable.

An interesting project in those days was Dr. Huebner's public lectures on life insurance. He spoke on the life value concept, business life insurance, and living values of life insurance. These lectures drew enormous audiences. Hundreds and sometimes thousands crowded public auditoriums and hotel ballrooms to hear life insurance discussed in ways that were absolutely new to most of the listeners. Not only life underwriters but bankers, trust officers, accountants, lawyers, educators, and many policyholders came to hear this dynamic teacher. No wonder local C.L.U.s were proud of their dean.

A specific responsibility assumed and discharged by local C.L.U. groups in all states was the legal registration of the C.L.U. as a trade mark to protect it from unauthorized use. The College directors had registered the designation with the federal authorities, but could not afford the $900 cost of state procedures. This service was appreciated by the College.

The graduates helped defray expenses of the directory of C.L.U.s, which was printed annually in the early years. The list was considered an important recruiting tool, since it was studded with nationally recognized leaders among life underwriters. The chapters also made modest grants to help pay College administration costs.

Over the years, the graduates have shown a remarkable devotion to the purposes of the College in many practical ways. The unselfish, and in many cases anonymous, service rendered by C.L.U.s throughout the country is a marvel to observers from other businesses. It is surely one of the major factors in C.L.U. progress.

It is appropriate here to make permanent record, and recognize the great contributions to the College, of the staff executives of the Society: Frederick W. Floyd, executive secretary, 1946-50; Leroy G. Steinbeck, executive manager, 1950-57; and Paul

Front and reverse of C.L.U. key (*enlarged*), showing the seal of the College.

S. Mills, managing director, 1957 to present. To name all the
members of the Society who rendered great service would be impossible. Their representatives, listed in order of service, are the
outstanding men, and one woman, who were presidents of what
is now the American Society of Chartered Life Underwriters.

C. Vivian Anderson, Cincinnati, Ohio   (deceased)
Harry McNamer, Louisville, Kentucky   (deceased)
A. H. Bennell, Pittsburgh, Pennsylvania   (deceased)
Gerard S. Brown, Chicago, Illinois
William P. Stedman, Baltimore, Maryland
Lawrence C. Woods, Jr., Pittsburgh, Pennsylvania
Paul F. Clark, Boston, Massachusetts
Fred L. Cassidy, Seattle, Washington (deceased)
Alfred J. Johannsen, Chicago, Illinois
Kellogg Van Winkle, Beverly Hills, California
Joseph H. Reese, Sr., Philadelphia, Pennsylvania
Earle W. Brailey, Cleveland, Ohio
Benjamin Alk, New York City
John D. Moynahan, Chicago, Illinois
George E. Lackey, Detroit, Michigan   (deceased)
M. Luther Buchanan, Boston, Massachusetts
James Elton Bragg, New York City   (deceased)
Clifford H. Orr, Philadelphia, Pennsylvania

Roland D. Hinkle, Chicago, Illinois (deceased)
William S. Leighton, Minneapolis, Minnesota (deceased)
Martin I. Scott, Los Angeles, California
Karl K. Krogue, Spokane, Washington
Howard H. Cammack, Albany, New York
Carl M. Spero, New York City
James W. Smither, Jr., New Orleans, Louisiana (deceased)
Gerald W. Page, Los Angeles, California
Frank Cooper, Fort Worth, Texas (deceased)
George Neitlich, Boston, Massachusetts
Fitzhugh Traylor, Indianapolis, Indiana (deceased)
Eugene C. DeVol, Philadelphia, Pennsylvania
William H. Andrews, Jr., Greensboro, North Carolina
Robert L. Woods, Los Angeles, California
Lillian G. Hogue, Detroit, Michigan
Herbert W. Florer, Boston, Massachusetts
James P. Poole, Atlanta, Georgia

Chapter 10

ESTABLISHING PATTERNS

When the first examinations were a current event, a friendly life insurance publication editorialized on the C.L.U. movement. Reference was made to "the energetic idealism of the leading field men" who were responsible for raising standards of life insurance service to the public. The writer continued in florid style:

An exceedingly notable fruition of this strenuous gospel of the true aspect of life insurance has been the establishment of the American College of Life Underwriters through which the degree of Certified [*sic*] Life Underwriter can be obtained by those measuring up to the requirements. It is vividly significant that this institution of life insurance learning has been established and is supported by the contributions of the agents who during all these past years have been insisting upon the professional character of their vocation. We understand that the companies do not contribute a dollar toward the maintenance of the College, although we cannot perceive any good reason for them to refrain from doing so, except that the agents may not wish it. . . .

The dream of the recognition of the life underwriter as a professional man will be realized. Then, the small and mean and unqualified muddiers of the life insurance stream will by necessity turn their petty competitive and unfair practices to some other activity. The high vocation of life insurance will gradually but surely become cleared of the undesirable hangers-on and side line practitioners. The quacks will disappear into the limbo where quacks ultimately go.

The reference to the independence of the American College from the beginning is essentially correct. The leaders were field men prominently identified with the National Association of Life Underwriters, and the first year's C.L.U. examination applications asked for evidence of N.A.L.U. membership and activity. That did not mean membership was a requirement for eligibility, however, and the next year the questions were removed.

Originally, all directors were N.A.L.U. members. But in 1930, the Board was enlarged to 21 members in order to add men who were home office executives or leaders in other life insurance organizations.

The first C.L.U. conferments were made at a regular session of the N.A.L.U. annual convention. For many years, Dr. Huebner and President Clark spoke on the regular convention program, or reported to the Executive Committee of N.A.L.U. When the number of C.L.U. graduates became large, the conferments were made at a special session of the convention, which continues to be the practice. For many years, and through 1961, the C.L.U. was given a place in the general convention program—the American College Hour session. Most recent newcomers have not been aware of the historic background of these convention habits.

By necessity, the College was at first somewhat dependent on the N.A.L.U. for "seed money." The few thousand dollars advanced to the College eventually was written off as a gift, but the N.A.L.U. never attempted to control the College. It recognized from the beginning that an educational institution must be independent of any direction by a trade association.

Office space was provided at first by courtesy of other organizations, as shown by the directory in the early bulletins. The registrar was Arthur M. Spalding, first in Pittsburgh with the E. A. Woods Company, then at the home office of the Equitable Society in New York. The dean and assistant dean were listed at Logan Hall of the University of Pennsylvania. The makeshift space and volunteer work continued for several years, involving, as President Clark said, "herculean efforts" from all who carried on the routine work of the College. Finally, in 1931, the directors stated that they "could no longer presume on the Wharton School for accommodations," and fortunately saw their way clear to renting two small rooms in an office building near Logan Hall. There a full-time secretary was installed at $125 a month, more than Dr. Huebner and Dr. McCahan were drawing together. She soon needed help to keep up with the work. By 1933, the office annually received 5,000 first-class letters and sent out 14-15,000, of which some 5,000 were dictated personally by the dean or assistant dean. These statistics, officially reported to the directors, seem incredible. Dr. Huebner now wonders how they ever lived through it. They worked at their individual responsibilities, and met over lunch to discuss problems. Seldom knowing what they ate, they made decisions and laid out plans.

About this time, the Finance Committee recommended that "as soon as practicable" the College should, for its protection, buy insurance on the lives of Dr. Huebner ($100,000) and Dr. McCahan ($25,000). Dr. Huebner successfully opposed the idea, although he and Dr. McCahan both appreciated the disposition of the directors. Dr. Huebner thought the College did not have the money even for term insurance. Moreover, he felt that business insurance was a wonderful idea when replacement was impossible or difficult. His view was that Dr. McCahan could have replaced him, and that others who were at the Wharton School or who had gone on from his department also could pick up the responsibilities, if necessary.

During these years, many patterns of College activity were crystallizing. Dr. McCahan was beginning the public relations program of the College. Each year he sent out to home-town newspapers press releases for each new graduate. He notified each home office of successful candidates in its company, with suggestions for recognition of the new C.L.U.s from company officers and in company publications. He sent several dozen news stories to insurance publications during the year. He planned and supervised the production of information booklets distributed to candidates. The insurance press was very cooperative, and a number of trade papers ran the C.L.U. examination questions with typical answers annually for many years.

At first, College officials were loath to recommend specific books for C.L.U. study. When they did yield to entreaties for such help, they sent out a mimeographed list, almost apologetically, not wanting to add the dignity of print. A list of suggested books gradually became an accepted guide, although the College always emphasized that mastery of subject matter through any source was the important thing. The College never published books. Like the plan to operate through established institutions rather than conduct separate classes or examination centers, this was a basic preliminary decision. It will be recalled, however, that before the College started, Dr. Huebner cooperated with D. Appleton and Company in planning and editing the "Appleton Series" which furnished a valuable part of the C.L.U. study material in the early years. Other college-level textbooks in the areas studied were not yet available.

The C.L.U. pledge was written by Dr. Huebner very early in the College history. It gave brief expression to the basic ideals of professional life underwriters, including not only the spirit of the golden rule, but the concept of the other man's point of view. To give someone what you would like is not necessarily good service, for you and he may have different purposes.

The pledge has become a traditional part of the conferment exercises for new C.L.U.s. The solemn ceremony not only emphasizes standards for professional service in life underwriting, but also provides motivation for achievement of the ideals.

The charge to new C.L.U.s, heard each year at the national conferment and in local ceremonies across the country, also had its roots in the early days. In 1931, President Clark addressed the graduates in part as follows. Many of his phrases are familiar to new C.L.U.s of recent years.

Every Chartered Life Underwriter should conduct himself or herself at all times with honor and dignity, inflexibly avoiding practices that will bring dishonor or reproach on the life underwriting profession or the C.L.U. designation. You should carefully refrain from what might appear to be a commercializing or misuse of the designation, or an attitude indicating a "superiority complex," and especially toward other life underwriters. Strive to help the other fellow whenever circumstances permit and give generously of your ability not only to your clients and your company, but to improving of methods and conditions of the life underwriting fraternity. In this respect, you can be a power in your community and your local life underwriters' association.

Let me also urge each of you as an alumnus of the American College to lend your co-operation at all times to the advancement of the Chartered Life Underwriter movement, and if called upon by the College to render some service that will be helpful, give generously of your time and ability as the circumstances involved may dictate.

The first examination questions were prepared by Dr. Huebner, with some specialized help from two other people. This obviously was not the best system for various reasons. In the summer of 1928, the Executive Committee of the Board took steps to formalize examination procedure. The examinations henceforth were to be written in standard examination books like those used at the University of Pennsylvania. An Examination Board of five men particularly qualified in each area assisted in preparing examination questions and wrote typical answers. Each man received a $50 fee. The minutes added:

In this way a great deal of trouble for the graders may be avoided. It is no easy task for the graders to set forth detailed answers to all the questions covered during fifteen hours of examinations.

In asking the full Board of Directors for confirmation of the plan for the Examination Board, Dr. Huebner said:

The first set I got up personally, and I took every criticism too hard I guess. It was a one-man affair, and I don't think these examinations ought to be a one-man affair. I should like five minds at least.

Last December I had three fellows working rather hard on the job, and I am sure the questions were better as a result.

From the beginning, poor papers were given a failing mark only if at least two graders concurred. Defending the decisions of the graders was a difficult responsibility for Dr. Huebner and Dr. McCahan. Whenever they traveled, somebody in almost every city took them aside after a meeting, or even appeared when their train pulled into the station, to demand an explanation of why so-and-so did not pass.

The Examination Board "took the heat off" the dean's office, and was invaluable to the College in its early form. In 1944, it was enlarged. Irvin Bendiner was the first chairman, and meetings were held week ends at his summer home on the New Jersey

Examinations Questions Committee, 1955. *Back row, left to right:* Davis W. Gregg, Edwin H. White, J. Carlton Smith, Herbert C. Graebner, William M. Howard. *Middle row:* Arthur W. Mason, Jr., Harold W. Gardiner, Dan M. McGill, S. S. Huebner, Earle W. Brailey. *Front:* James Elton Bragg.

shore. Dr. Huebner recalls that, being an early riser, he was about the house before most of the others, and Mr. Bendiner's little daughter delighted in entertaining him in the kitchen, demonstrating her skill in frying eggs and flipping pancakes.

The first year, a few home office people involved in sales training and sales promotion took the C.L.U. examinations and were judged eligible to receive the C.L.U. In general, however, the program was rather jealously guarded as a course for field representatives. As interest on the part of other home office candidates developed, the directors moved to open the examinations to any who were otherwise qualified, and to award to them, not the C.L.U. designation, but a "certificate of proficiency." The life underwriting experience requirement for eligibility to receive the C.L.U. designation was defined as selling life insurance, teaching life insurance and managing or supervising those engaged in selling life insurance. The *Announcement* for 1932-33 explained:

> The C.L.U. designation itself is not awarded without the selling, teaching or managerial experience because the particular significance of the designation is that it denotes to laymen that the holder is a life underwriter, as well as that he has acquired a broad education and is competent to render a sound insurance service.

Trust officers soon became interested in C.L.U. recognition, and caused heated discussion among the Board. There was strong feeling that only life insurance people should be so honored. It was finally agreed, however, that trust officers might qualify for the certificate of proficiency.

Interest in recognition for academic preparation in management developed early. At their meeting in 1930, the directors approved the idea of a sixth examination in management for those who already had achieved the C.L.U. designation. Success in this examination would be recognized only by a certificate. It became apparent that appropriate study material was scarce, and the program, slow to get under way at all, was hampered for many years.

The management examinations were given first in 1933. The Life Insurance Sales Research Bureau (now the Life Insurance Agency Management Association), with the special assistance of John Marshall Holcombe, Jr., and H. G. Kenagy, was very helpful in outlining the scope of these examinations.

Concerning this new project, Dr. Huebner spoke to the N.A.L.U. convention in 1933:

> But standardization educationally is also needed from the other standpoint, namely production and management. Here there has been much the same happy-go-lucky procedure which has prevailed among personal producers themselves. All sorts of personal viewpoints and approaches seem to prevail. Some emphasize high-powered methods, whereas others follow a program of laissez faire. Some emphasize careful selection, whereas others use it mildly or practically ignore the idea. All sorts of personal management and development plans are also in use. Great variation exists with respect to organization from the standpoints of office, financial and statistical methods, financial management and the interpretation of accounts, sales management, the management of sales personnel, sales promotion, and business correspondence. Broadly speaking, with due respect to certain exceptions, there has been no definite scientific approach, no standardization in the light of the knowledge which has developed in that field of activity during recent years. . . .

The course of study comprises two installments with two examinations on "business administration" and "sales administration" respectively. The American College will do its full share to further this program and have it properly reflected in due course in our higher institutions of learning, just as it has furthered the C.L.U. program itself. The program is based on the fact that, to a large extent, the work of general agents and managers involves a knowledge of subjects not necessarily associated with the preparation of the personal producer. The first examinations were held last June with 32 general agents and managers taking the test.

The 23 successful candidates who received the first management certificates in 1933 were from all parts of the country and Shanghai, China. The list, as it was submitted to the directors, follows:

Bendiner, Irvin CLU	Philadelphia, Pa.	Underwriter, New York Life Insurance Co.
Boyce, William L., CLU	Syracuse, New York	Agency Manager, Equitable Life Assurance Society of the United States
Boyd, Daniel H., CLU	Paterson, New Jersey	Branch Manager, Equitable Life Assurance Society of the U.S.
Brayton, Howard C., CLU	Portland, Oregon	Underwriter, Mutual Life Insurance Co. of N.Y.
Brewer, Charles E., CLU	New York City, N.Y.	Instructor of Agents, Mutual Benefit Life Insurance Company
Chang, Tuh-Yui, CLU	Shanghai, China	Associate Actuary and Agency Supervisor, China United Assurance Society, Ltd.
Choate, Henry L., CLU	Washington, D.C.	General Agent, Mutual Benefit Life Ins. Co.
Emerson, Ralph W., CLU	St. Louis, Mo.	Agency Supervisor, Northwestern Mutual Life Insurance Company
Good, Lara P., CLU	San Diego, Calif.	Manager, Ordinary Dept., Prudential Insurance Co. of America
Herman, Maurice D., CLU	Minneapolis, Minn.	Underwriter, Equitable Life Assurance Society of the U.S.
Leavitt, Erasmus D., CLU	Los Angeles, Calif.	Underwriter, Penn Mutual Life Insurance Co.
Link, George, CLU	Washington, D.C.	Ass't Secretary, Policyholders Service Dept., Acacia Mutual Life Insurance Company
Litz, Arthur W., CLU	Nashville, Tenn.	Manager, Great Southern Life Insurance Co. of Houston, Texas
McGiveran, Ben S., CLU	Eau Claire, Wis.	General Agent, Northwestern Mutual Life Insurance Co.
McMillin, Joseph L., CLU	Baltimore, Md.	Underwriter, Mutual Life Insurance Co.
Reese, Joseph H., CLU	Philadelphia, Pa.	Manager, Penn Mutual Life Insurance Co.

Smith, Norvin, E., CLU	Los Angeles, Calif.	President, Guaranteed Estates Company, Ltd.
Smith, Warren H., CLU	Cleveland, Ohio	Agency Supervisor, State Mutual Life Assurance Company
Steward, Verne, CLU	Los Angeles, Calif.	Underwriter, Penn Mutual Life Insurance Co.
Stone, Paul D., CLU	Portland, Ore.	Supervisor, Mutual Benefit Life Insurance Co.
Strong, Ricks, CLU	Columbus, Ohio	Manager, Missouri State Life Insurance Co.
Walter, Richard F., CLU	Boston, Mass.	Underwriter, Equitable Life Assurance Society of the U.S.
White, Edwin, H., CLU	New York City, N.Y.	Estate Planning Manager, Aetna Life Insurance Co.

The progress of the College program and an increase of students were accompanied by progress in financial affairs. A review of the slow but steady advance inspires admiration for the faith of those early leaders. When the College was two years old the president reported:

> At the present time we are spending about $250 a month which is a disgracefully small amount for the tremendous amount of work which the American College is doing. The reason it is small is because Dean Huebner and Assistant Dean McCahan, Registrar Spalding and the President's office are doing a colossal amount of gratis work....

> The major portion of the examination fees from candidates is consumed in the handling of the examinations, the grading of papers, in the postage that is involved. This averages about $40 and the excess of $10 out of the $50 fee is left to go into the treasury of the College for expenses....

> The treasurer tells us that we have enough money to last us five months. Then we will have no further revenue until receipts from the June examinations of next year.

The directors coped with this situation in various ways. At one point, Vice President William Duff contributed $500 for general expenses. The price of the first edition of the little blue information booklet, which appeared annually for many years, was $310 for 5,000 copies. This cost was defrayed by gifts from E. J. Clark, Paul Clark, Arthur Spalding, John McNamara, Julian Myrick, S. T. Whatley, and Franklin Ganse, who were at the meeting when the bill was presented.

Julian Myrick was elected director in 1929. He had been a friend of the College from the beginning, and was president of N.A.L.U. the year of the College's first conferment exercises. He was close to men of means, and was responsible for gifts for current expenses running around $1,000 annually for several years. Eventually, the Edward A. Woods Foundation produced several thousand dollars of annual income.

At this period, there was a general appeal to N.A.L.U. members for gifts in support of the College, with the suggestion that five dollars each would be acceptable. The number of friends who responded to this call for help was encouraging, though the amount raised was hardly significant. Some old-timers today, who are not C.L.U.s, speak with pride about being contributors in those early days. They believed in the cause, though the designation was beyond them.

It also became routine about midwinter for Mr. Ganse and Paul Clark to borrow from a bank in Boston to carry the College over until spring. The directors and officers of the College pinched every penny, took every honorable means of getting services gratis or at reduced prices, and each year managed to balance the budget. Gradually, Mr. Ganse's annual reports advanced from "all bills paid and $14 balance" to "$22 balance" then to more comfortable amounts.

The College was started without financial support from the life insurance companies, but naturally the directors began looking their way quite soon. President Ernest Clark first went to his own home office, as he reported in his brief article sketching the history of the College at its twentieth anniversary.

Many life insurance executives were initially cold to the Chartered Life Underwriter program of the American College. There was a general feeling that it was too academic to succeed. This was illustrated in a personal interview I had with the late Walton L. Crocker, then President of the John Hancock Mutual Life Insurance Company. I outlined to Mr. Crocker the plan in detail and requested him, on behalf of the Company, to establish five annual scholarships at $100 each, to be awarded to the five John Hancock agents who made the best grades in a written examination. The idea was that the College would refund to the five candidates their examination fees and retain in the College treasury the balance of the $500 contribution each year to be used toward expenses. I wanted the Company with which I had been associated for many years, to become the leader among the life insurance companies of America in financially cooperating with the American College in this or a similar manner.

Mr. Crocker's response was: "E. J., I think you and Dr. Huebner are attempting a utopian proposition. Ideal? Yes, but in magnitude of objective, utopian. However, I am going to go along with you and will grant your request."

My response was: "Mr. Crocker, in the combined judgment of those of us who have thus far advanced this higher educational movement in life insurance education, it is not utopian, but a most practical solution of the problem and we have every reason to believe in its ultimate success." He said, "I hope that turns out to be so!"

When the Edward A. Woods Foundation was organized, an appeal to the companies was received with varying degrees of warmth. The first executive to respond was O. J. Arnold, president of the Northwestern National, with $1,000. In the first year, similar amounts were subscribed by the Guardian Life of New York, the Pacific Mutual, and the Union Central.

The John Hancock scholarship plan for subsidizing the College through an overpayment of fees for its candidates was followed by others. Soon several companies were cooperating by reimbursing their agents for examination fees. In 1932, Dr.

Huebner reported, "about fifty companies have already taken steps to support and encourage the C.L.U. movement in one way or another."

As early as 1932, the clipping files at the American College contained many items from *The Field* (Phoenix Mutual), *Agency Items* (Equitable of New York), *The Pelican* (Mutual Benefit Life), *Provident Notes* (Provident Mutual Life), *The Signature* (John Hancock), *Fidelity Field Man* (Fidelity Mutual), *Life Aetna-Izer* (Aetna Life), *The News Letter* (Penn Mutual), and *The Radiator* (Massachusetts Mutual). These publicity aids were current news of successful candidates, statistics and promotional articles about the College often written by the company's C.L.U.s, and examination questions with typical answers.

The cooperative attitude was far from unanimous, and many executives were definitely hostile. Dr. Huebner remembers one company president who literally laughed with scorn at the idea of educating life insurance agents, and told him, "You'll never get up to the first limb of that tree."

Another protested to the distinguished professor, "I can't understand why you have cast in your lot with the scum of our business." To which Dr. Huebner hotly rejoined, "Is that what you think of the men who give you your reason for being—who keep the life insurance business alive?"

Some companies seemed uncooperative, but really were not. Dr. Huebner remembers an early conversation with Henry North, vice president of the Metropolitan. Mr. North said: "You must think we're against you. We haven't done anything yet, but don't be discouraged. We're big. It takes time to get us moving." The promise implied was well fulfilled. Within a few years, the Metropolitan was giving help of great significance to the whole College program.

Officially, the Northwestern Mutual was slow in supporting the C.L.U. movement, but the company's agents ran with the ball themselves. They organized the first company association of

Dr. Huebner at his desk in Logan Hall, about 1930.

alumni, and carried on a very successful promotion until the home office caught their conviction.

In 1934-35, the directory of graduates showed the Northwestern Mutual with the largest number of C.L.U.s in any company. Not surprisingly, the Equitable of New York had almost as many because of the impetus given in the earliest years by members of the E. A. Woods Company. The Massachusetts Mutual was next, reflecting Dr. Huebner's personal promotion. He had selected some thirty general agents of that company as his best prospects, and concentrated on them during his summer work with the company. Within a few years, a dozen of them had qualified and were stirring up interest among their agents. The Mutual Benefit Life had the fourth largest group. Oliver Thurman, the agency vice president, was one of the first home office executives to be a director of the College. The fifth largest number was in the Penn Mutual, the company of Hugh Hart and Dr. John Stevenson, who gave the College strong support even before it began operations.

By 1934, there were 904 C.L.U.s, representing 39 states, the District of Columbia, China, Hawaii, and India, and activity also was beginning in Japan. Some seventy accredited colleges and universities were cooperating as examination centers and in preparatory work. Financial problems were less critical, if not easy. Company cooperation was growing constantly in financial matters and in promotion of the program among agents.

President Clark felt that the objectives he had set for himself when he accepted the presidency in 1928 had been achieved. The vision which he had first glimpsed some twenty years before was more than fulfilled. Moreover, Mr. Clark had long been hard of hearing. This was a great practical handicap. Although his deafness increased, his pride made him loath to use a hearing aid, even when his disability became acute. He admitted the difficulty, and took in good spirit the humorous protests of his friends, who delighted in trying to prove to him that he needed help. One reported that he would test him in all sorts of ways to see how far he was guided by facial expressions rather than hearing. One day the friend met Mr. Clark and greeted him, smiling: "Hello, E. J., was that you I saw going down Charles Street this morning with a beautiful lady?" He was not at all surprised to have Mr. Clark reply, "Yes, it is a beautiful day, isn't it?"

The directors were not unprepared to have Mr. Clark decline renomination at the annual meeting in 1934. He said:

It was twenty years ago, just about now, that Dr. Huebner and I first began to discuss the question of a life underwriters' college. That was at the conclusion of the Cincinnati convention in 1914.

It took thirteen years for that seed which was planted then to sprout into the organization of this College. That was in 1927; the College was organized, as you will recall, in March, 1927, seven and one-half years ago.

During all that time, Dr. Huebner and I have worked together just about as harmoniously as any two men could possibly work. I don't recall that we ever had a difference of opinion on any policy or anything pertaining to the conduct of the American College. It has been some twenty years of just about the most pleasant experience any man could possibly have.

Dr. Huebner said most feelingly in after years: "How fortunate we were to have him at that time when everything was starting." Mr. Clark was a fine gentleman. He was meticulous in his dress and manner—outward symbols for those who knew him to be of ordered mind and devoted to principle. For him, standards were not relative; things were right or wrong. He had a determined desire for things to be right with the American College. Dr. Huebner said he never went back on a promise or compromised on a matter of conviction.

E. J. Clark's double purpose for the new college was expressed in a message to his associates in the John Hancock when he wrote:

The American College of Life Underwriters does not exist merely to award C.L.U. recognitions to persons who have attained to certain academic standards. It is striving primarily to place the entire vocation of life underwriting upon a higher educational and professional plane and provide the most far-reaching and complete preparation for this vocation that has ever been given to the life insurance world.

Appraising his beloved uncle's ambitions to establish life insurance as a part of the nation's educational system, Paul F. Clark said: "He got it in. Bless his heart!"

Chapter 11

HOW FAR HAVE THEY GONE?
AN APPRAISAL

By 1934, the American College and the C.L.U. program were a going movement. The foundation had been laid in a number of basic decisions about operations.

First was independence. The College would not be financially dependent on trade organizations or life insurance companies in any way that would affect its freedom of operation. There would be no organizational association with or control by any life insurance institution.

Second was academic standards. The College committed itself definitely to follow the best college academic practice in educational prerequisites for candidates and in administration of examinations. The C.L.U. would be a designation earned by a uniform and universal examination procedure, the same in every part of the country and throughout the world. There would be no honorary C.L.U.s.

Third was the scope of the educational program. The College would not follow an educational "package" philosophy. The aim was a broad-based educational approach to make a C.L.U. not only a skilled life insurance technician, but also an adviser understanding the problems of business, sociology, and human relationships.

Fourth was method of operation. The College determined to carry on its program through established, qualified educational institutions. Thus, expansion could come quickly as interest developed almost anywhere in this country or abroad. The College decided not to publish its own books, but to use standard college textbooks already available, and to encourage the creation of textbooks useful not only in its program but also in any college insurance education.

By 1934, progress was indicated by an increase of C.L.U.s with representation among the recognized leaders of the industry; by established relationships with outstanding educational institutions in all parts of the country; by acceptance on the part of an encouraging number of home offices.

The next era was to see the accomplishment of plans for permanent, adequate financial support, and the strengthening of the educational program to meet expanding demands.

Chapter 12

EXPANDING THE PROGRAM

When Ernest Clark declined re-election as president of the American College in 1934, there was a revision of the College bylaws and a number of changes in titles and positions. Mr. Clark became chairman of the Board of Directors with responsibility for financing the College, and William M. Duff, who had been vice president, became vice chairman of the Board.

The president was chief educational officer of the College, and Dr. Huebner was elected to that office. Dr. McCahan, who had been assistant dean and secretary, became dean. Dr. John A. Stevenson took his place as secretary.

Dr. Huebner, in his new position of leadership, almost immediately challenged his associates on the College Board with the need for a new vision. He saw that the College had gone as far as volunteers could take it with only two dedicated, salaried officers and break-even financing. Further expansion would require more staff and more money. In this problem, as in many during the years, the Board turned to one of its own members, John Marshall Holcombe, Jr. Mr. Holcombe was then head of the Life Insurance Sales Research Bureau, and close to its parent organization, the Association of Life Agency Officers.

As a result of his suggestion, the Life Agency Officers appointed a "Committee for the American College of Life Underwriters," with Henry E. North, vice president of the Metropolitan Life, as chairman. Mr. North brought to the Committee as his staff assistant one of his company associates, Earl R. Trangmar. Mr. Trangmar's experience in fund raising and promotion and his sympathetic understanding of the purposes of the College made him a tremendous asset to the Committee. He subsequently became a staunch friend of the College on his own account, and gave outstanding service which led to his being named a life trustee in 1961, a few months before his sudden death.

The Life Agency Officers committee began functioning in 1936. The members, in addition to Mr. North, were: O. J. Arnold, Northwestern National Life; Joseph C. Behan, Massachusetts

Earl R. Trangmar.

Mutual; Grant L. Hill, Northwestern Mutual; W. W. Klingman, Equitable Life of New York; James A. McLain, Guardian Life; John A. Stevenson, Penn Mutual; and Henry B. Sutphen, Prudential. They first made a careful study of the current work of the College, its immediate needs, and its future opportunities. They reviewed the prodigious activities of Dr. Huebner and Dr. McCahan at headquarters, and in their far-flung travels. Each visited 30 to 50 cities a year to inspire candidates, to spread information about the College program among life underwriters and home office men, and to establish connections with colleges and universities.

They listened to Dr. Huebner and Dr. McCahan describe the great need for increased helps for students. The failure ratio in the 1934 examinations had been the highest in the experience of the College, and 1935 was only slightly more favorable. It was evident that the College program was broadening its base and attracting candidates with less experience and capacity to prepare for examinations without more help. The ambitious candidates were trying to help themselves. The College *Announcement* for 1936–37 carried an interesting report of activity.

> In some cities underwriters have organized their own study groups with a Chartered Life Underwriter or another of their number in charge. In certain places these groups have been created because no other educational facilities are available. These groups are sometimes sponsored by an underwriters' association or a particular agency but may consist of a group of underwriters with common interests who band themselves together for mutual benefit in studying for the examinations. Fourteen such groups had been reported to the American College by the fall of 1929 and twenty-nine a year later, but the latter number has since then been greatly increased. Groups reported to the College as actively functioning during the year preceding the 1936 examinations were located in the following cities.

Phoenix, Ariz.	Albany, N.Y.
Little Rock, Ark.	Buffalo, N.Y.
Los Angeles, Calif.	New York, N.Y.

Oakland, Calif.	Rochester, N.Y.
Denver, Colo.	Utica, N.Y.
Hartford, Conn.	Cincinnati, Ohio
New Haven, Conn.	Cleveland, Ohio
Washington, D.C.	Columbus, Ohio
Jacksonville, Fla.	Warren, Ohio
Tampa, Fla.	Youngstown, Ohio
Atlanta, Ga.	Muskogee, Okla.
Chicago, Ill.	Oklahoma City, Okla.
Bloomington, Ind.	Tulsa, Okla.
Indianapolis, Ind.	Portland, Ore.
South Bend, Ind.	Philadelphia, Pa.
Cedar Rapids, Iowa	Pittsburgh, Pa.
Wichita, Kans.	Charleston, S.C.
Louisville, Ky.	Nashville, Tenn.
Portland, Maine	Dallas, Texas
Baltimore, Md.	Houston, Texas
Boston, Mass.	San Antonio, Texas
Springfield, Mass.	Richmond, Va.
Detroit, Mich.	Roanoke, Va.
Flint, Mich.	Tacoma, Wash.
St. Paul, Minn.	Yakima, Wash.
Kansas City, Mo.	Eau Claire, Wis.
St. Joseph, Mo.	Milwaukee, Wis.
St. Louis, Mo.	Oshkosh, Wis.

These groups doubtless represent but a transitory phase of the life underwriting educational movement, for the most successful are those which have been organized to provide a well directed review for underwriters who have already received organized and thorough instruction in most of the subjects contemplated by C.L.U. standards. Accordingly, as the better educated underwriters qualify for their designations, it is quite likely that the educational work will pass very largely into the hands of colleges and universities which are equipped to give adequate and thorough instruction over an extended period of time. This has been the experience in other professions.

The study groups were not only helpful to the candidates, but in at least one case made a direct financial contribution to the College. In 1938, the Board acknowledged with thanks the receipt of $22.72 from John W. Yates, of Los Angeles. This gift was a surplus in the funds of a local C.L.U. study class.

The College officers also pointed out that informational and promotional work was needed in more cities and with more colleges. For example, the C.L.U. program was going well in Kansas City and Seattle. In Kansas City, Oliver J. Neibel was doing a tremendous volunteer job, but could hardly cover the opportunities in Topeka, St. Joseph, and Joplin. Similarly, Fred L. Cassidy was giving splendid leadership in Seattle, but nothing was happening in places like Tacoma, Bellingham, Yakima, and Spokane.

C.L.U. volunteers like those men and the College officers had done an amazing amount of work not only with candidates but also with educational institutions. By that time, there were 332 insurance courses of all kinds with some 8,600 students in 143 colleges and universities across the country. Most of these courses had been introduced in the past decade, largely due to the activities of the American College, Dr. McCahan stated in his summary of the survey which provided these statistics.

Dr. Huebner outlined to the Committee of the Life Agency Officers how greatly additional staff help would strengthen College contacts with the educational institutions and enable the College to stimulate additional university work in insurance. For the assistance necessary, Dr. Huebner described his candidate:

> We need a man well educated. We need a man whose personality is such that he can meet with presidents and deans; we need a man who can make a good speech, and we need a man who can confer with the underwriters. A man who isn't just right is worse than nothing. We have to get the right kind of a man, and I don't see how you can get a man like that and pull him away from somewhere else unless we give him a contract, say at least of five years' standing, and I think an annual compensation of $7,500 as a minimum.

After the weeks of careful study, the Committee reported:

As a result of this inquiry it was ascertained that the College would require at least $30,000 additional income annually if present and prospective demands were to be adequately met. It was, as a matter of fact, something of a mystery to the Committee as to how the College had been able to accomplish what it has accomplished with the limited and uncertain revenues upon which it has heretofore depended. Certainly the annual balancing of the budget, and the 10-year record of no deficits could not have been achieved except by unsparing sacrifices in time and labor by the administrative officers of the College, and members of the College Board.

To raise $30,000 from the companies, not only once but annually, suggested to Earl Trangmar the need for a pattern and big thinking. He outlined to Mr. North the idea of a formula for each company's gift that, hopefully, would yield the desired total, and would be the foundation for the future. The formula worked out to six or seven thousand dollars for the Metropolitan. Mr. North was appalled. He said: "I have Lincoln [President Leroy Lincoln of the Metropolitan] committed to give $500. Now you say we ought to ask for more than ten times as much." To which Mr. Trangmar replied: "Give Lincoln a chance at it. He's a statesman and will appreciate what we're doing."

Mr. Trangmar urged all the Committee members to go directly to the top with their appeals to the companies. The mid-1930s was a difficult time, and many agency vice presidents were afraid to bring up any major financial request for a new project. Most were delighted to have the Committee go over their heads on this matter.

The Committee not only asked for the money. It did a wonderful job of selling the College. After its campaign, few company presidents had to ask, "What does C.L.U. mean?" "Does all this study for life insurance agents do any good?"

The specific plan the Committee devised envisioned yearly gifts, based on a formula, from the companies, and offered credit certificates to C.L.U. candidates representing cooperating com-

Henry E. North, retiring trustee, receives Resolution of Appreciation presented by Cecil J. North on behalf of the Board of Trustees, 1959.

panies. The plan became known as the Cooperative Fund for Underwriter Training.

The Committee recommended doubling the amount of the C.L.U. examination fee, from \$50 to \$100 for the five parts, and the College took that action. Candidates paid \$50 if they were members of cooperating companies. The balance was made up through credit certificates issued by their companies drawing on the Cooperative Fund. To simplify operations, a company could issue an unlimited number of credit certificates if it had contributed its full gift according to the formula of 50 cents per million of insurance in force (less group and reinsurance from other companies).

The Committee did a tremendous task in personally approaching hundreds of home office executives. In three months, it had its

$30,000, representing nearly 100 per cent response from the top 110 life insurance companies in the United States, and scattered participation by others. The Metropolitan Life not only encouraged the leadership of Mr. North and Mr. Trangmar in this enterprise, but also assumed the full expense of the considerable correspondence and printing involved in the initial campaign. The Committee's report for the first year was triumphant.

> The first-year response has approached the unanimous more nearly than in any cooperative enterprise thus far sponsored by the companies...
>
> It is desirable in any cooperative appeal for funds to reduce the project to the simplest possible elements, so that demands upon the energy and time of the Committee can be kept within reasonable bounds. The companies were therefore asked for a direct contribution solely on the grounds that the work of the College is in the interest of the public and is a definite contribution to life insurance service, aside from any question as to the number of underwriters representing a given company who may have availed themselves of the facilities of the College.
>
> That the subscriptions were tendered as direct subscriptions to the College in response to that appeal, and to that appeal alone, is a splendid commentary on the broad views of life insurance executives...
>
> The Committee [raising the money] will be strictly a committee of the Association of Life Agency Officers, wholly independent of the College and having no part in management. It will act simply in the role of sponsor for the fund, of which fund the College will become the beneficiary.

The response of the business to this fund-raising project was not only a commentary on the wide interest of the companies in an educational program. It was also a testimony to the general confidence of the companies in the program being developed by the American College.

The Cooperative Fund, so vigorously launched by Henry North, Mr. Trangmar, and the Life Agency Officers Committee, has continued to be a major source of income for the College. With the growth of the business, gifts to the Fund grew also, keeping pace with the increasing fees for C.L.U. examinations. The program now is handled by a committee of the College which includes many prominent company presidents. In 1962–63, 223 companies contributed a total of $217,984 to the project, named in 1960 the Cooperative Fund for Underwriter Education.

With the new resources from the Cooperative Fund, the College promptly embarked on the expansion program. An Educational Advisory Department was established. As director, the Board named Professor John P. Williams, of Davidson College, North Carolina, who already had been doing excellent work locally to promote the C.L.U. program. He joined the staff in September, 1937. In a very real sense, John P. Williams was the first full-time employee of the American College. Over the next 14 years, he traveled the country from border to border and coast to coast, encouraging life insurance men and women to undertake the C.L.U. program, helping persons interested in organizing C.L.U. classes, and working with C.L.U. teachers. The first educational conferences of the College were organized under his direction. These conferences helped open the lines of communication between the College and the teachers and students. Tall and distinguished looking, and known affectionately as "Shorty" Williams by his many friends in life insurance and education, John P. Williams deserves much credit for building interest in the C.L.U. during the period of his service.

In the Educational Advisory Department, Birchard E. Wyatt was employed as educational counselor. He had been a student of Dr. Huebner and Dr. McCahan at the University of Pennsylvania. These new field representatives of the College received annual salaries of $10,000 and $6,000 respectively.

Even before they were on the job, the promise of help inspired agents in the field to new enthusiasm for C.L.U. study. The fact that companies were committed to financial support of the C.L.U. program probably resulted in considerable home office stimulation of agents. There was a 40 per cent increase in local study groups, so that the number around the country preparing for the 1938 examinations totaled 123, with an estimated enrollment of three thousand. By the next year, there were 68 additional groups.

First recipients of the 25-year C.L.U. Teacher Award, 1959. *Left to right:* George L. Buck of Seattle; Dr. S. S. Huebner; Albert J. Schick of Newark, New Jersey.

The number of candidates actually taking examinations more than doubled in the five years after establishment of the Cooperative Fund and its financing of the expanded College preparatory program. In 1940, there were 1,735 candidates from 340 cities and towns in 43 states, the District of Columbia, and Hawaii. They represented 88 different companies.

The new Educational Advisory Department conducted regional conferences for C.L.U. study group leaders. It prepared a teachers' manual and study supplements for the students. These provided an outline which kept students up to date and assured complete coverage of the material included in the examinations. The ratio of passing in 1940 was 62.3 per cent, the best for three years, and indicated a reversal of a discouraging trend.

A reference library was established at the College in 1937,

and the Board appointed a Committee on Library and Publications to develop this area. In 1940, the Department of Educational Publications was created, with Dr. Clyde M. Kahler as director.

By that time, field work activities had developed successfully. Seven regional conferences had been held in 1940 from New York to San Francisco, covering all 43 states involved in C.L.U. work. The conferences brought together nearly two hundred men representing 121 study groups and university classes. The conferees included 21 college teachers, as well as C.L.U.s and other underwriters active in the study program. The Educational Advisory Department also developed contacts with home office men charged with responsibilities for education and training. The College *Announcement* at this time described the work of the Educational Advisory Department:

> The main purposes of the new Department are to cooperate with university and college teachers, study group leaders, educational committees of C.L.U. Chapters or Life Underwriter Associations, and other educational leaders, in the development and strengthening of instructional facilities for persons engaged in, or contemplating life underwriting as a career; to stimulate life underwriters, and others engaged in life insurance activities, to study for examinations offered by the College; to develop sound methods of educational procedure, and foster their use by candidates; and to assist individual candidates to find solutions to their educational problems.
>
> In addition to cooperating in the preparation of new educational material, such as that to which reference has been made, members of the Educational Advisory Department staff will spend a substantial portion of their time in field work, visiting each year as many centers of C.L.U. instruction as time will permit.

In the early days when finances were a constant burden for every one who felt responsible for the College, every detail was carefully watched by many people. There was no money for such luxury as an auditor, and apparently little need to fear the misuse of a dime. However, by 1935 the annual budget was about $30,000. Although the treasurer was bonded, he suggested there also should be an audit. He reminded the Board: "My books have never been examined, or my reports checked at all. I think you ought at least find out if I have the money in the bank that I report on hand." There was a suggestion that Paul Clark and Julian Myrick be an auditing committee. Mr. Clark objected: "I assure you any audit I would make wouldn't be worth the paper it is written on. I don't know about Myrick." The final decision was to get a C.P.A. to do the job "for $25 or $50," if possible, although E. J. Clark still thought they should save the money.

The next year it was possible to increase the honoraria for Dr. Huebner and Dr. McCahan to $5,600 each annually. Mr. Dechert, the counsel, received a yearly retainer of $200.

In 1937, the treasurer's bond was increased to $50,000, and the College was big business. Dr. Huebner and Dr. McCahan each were paid $1,000 a month for their full-time work in the summer during the University vacation.

The Board was concerned not only about fair salaries but also about a retirement plan. A Pension Committee, consisting of Paul Clark, Dr. John A. Stevenson, and Mr. Myrick as chairman, investigated plans used in leading educational institutions. The program adopted was based on matching contributions from the College and the employee of 5 per cent each of the 1939–40 salary. These funds were used to purchase individual annuities for each eligible employee in the company of his choice. Over the years, the employee benefits plan has been changed and expanded. Life insurance benefits were included for the first time in 1955. Provision is made now for a pension of approximately half salary at sixty-five, together with death benefits, long-term disability benefits, travel accident coverage, and medical expense coverage. All parts of the program except the last are on a noncontributory basis.

Chapter 13

PROVING ITS WORTH

Although the College was expanding its program and gaining more financial and moral support from the home offices, there was still a necessity to convince the entire industry of the importance of the C.L.U. movement. Good friends of the College took a major part in this campaign.

Grant L. Hill, then Northwestern Mutual agencies director and a director of the College, conducted a survey among C.L.U.s to get facts about what the C.L.U. meant to them and the public. He made a persuasive presentation of the results to the National Association of Life Underwriters at its 1934 convention. At that time, the C.L.U. conferment exercises were still an integral part of the N.A.L.U. convention program, reflecting the continued parental interest of N.A.L.U. in its stalwart offspring. The occasion was scheduled during a regular morning session attended by delegates generally. Speaking of the value of the C.L.U. movement to the public, Mr. Hill said in part:

> What is the value of our movement to the public? It gives through the instrument of the C.L.U. designation a measuring stick as to experience, ability and dependability that can be applied uniformly in any section of the country.

> Very well, is this measuring stick being used today? There are many examples that it is. Probably the best is the fact that for several years the Consumers Research Bureau has advised its subscribers definitely and flatly that protection against incompetent agents is assured by going to a C.L.U.

Mr. Hill then quoted the verbatim report of a salesman to whom a prospect had given a very cold reception with an unexpected reversal. The salesman wrote:

Then, suddenly, he wheeled about as though he had had a bright idea and asked, "Are you a C.L.U.?" I replied: "I am." Then his guard came down, he smiled and said: "The deuce you are" and invited me into his office where we had an excellent discussion of his life insurance problems. I asked him what he knew about the C.L.U. designation. He said he and his wife read the Consumers Research from cover to cover and he knew they recommended anyone interested in life insurance to get in touch with a C.L.U.

Mr. Hill added the story of another experience with a corporation executive, again in the salesman's own words:

During the conversation he [the prospect] looked at my C.L.U. key. . . . I told him it was an insignia denoting that the wearer had qualified for it by completing a course covering not only life insurance but many of the subjects in the realm of business, law, economics, and so forth, with which a well-posted life insurance man should be familiar in order to be able to properly advise his clients. My prospect expressed considerable interest in this information and . . . asked me if I could attribute any increase in my business to having qualified as a C.L.U., to which I replied I had found the study beneficial but that I could not attribute a single definite case directly on account of the designation.

"Well," he said, "maybe you cannot say that a week from now." He then told me the directors of his corporation were considering corporation insurance and that several insurance men had discussed the idea with them but none had been able to answer several questions to his satisfaction . . . Two days later I secured his application for $100,000 payable to the corporation, which was promptly issued and paid for. I have since insured two other executives of this corporation, using the president as a reference, and the total premiums on the three cases amounted to about $6,000.

As a third illustration of what C.L.U. field men actually were experiencing, Mr. Hill quoted a man from Los Angeles:

I had been in competition on a case for over two weeks and I realized that it would be necessary for me to build in my prospect's mind additional confidence in my company and myself if I were to win the case. Sitting in his office a few days ago, I noticed hanging on his wall a framed certificate issued by the American Institute of Accountants. In answer to my question as to why he had taken the examinations which had resulted in the issuing of this certificate, he replied: "Because I knew it would give me prestige with the people to whom I was talking."

My chance had come, and in a few moments I had explained to him what the Chartered Life Underwriter designation represented in the life insurance fraternity. Monday of this week I received a call giving me this business. It was a small case, but there was more pleasure in having written it than in having placed a larger case without competition.

In summary, Mr. Hill continued:

Actual examples such as I have given are legion and I think prove conclusively that while the public generally may not know of the C.L.U. movement, when its significance is pointed out to them, they value it highly and are ready and willing to accept it. In fact, occasionally a member of the insurance buying public has expressed surprise that a business of such importance as ours, and 100 years old, has not taken this step long ago....

Please do not misunderstand the point I wish to make. You know as do I, that there are plenty of able and well-informed life insurance agents who do a splendid volume of business and conduct themselves in a high class professional manner without the aid of the C.L.U. award. Moreover, you know that will continue to be true. Just as we know there are a number of auditors who are extremely competent and know as much about accounting as do many C.P.A.'s. However, today it is extremely difficult for the auditor to prove that ability to the satisfaction of the public because of the ready acceptance of the C.P.A. idea.

And if any of you have time for a little research reading, I would suggest that you delve into the beginning and growth of the Ameri-

Grant L. Hill.

Dr. Huebner as many students remember him.

can Institute of Accountants, Actuarial Society of America, American Bar Association and the American Medical Association if you want to appreciate the tremendous strides made by the C.L.U. movement in seven short years, and the way in which the founders of the American College have benefited by the experience of these four organizations.

Mr. Hill reported that he had asked C.L.U.s specific questions about the value of C.L.U. work. Asked whether the C.L.U. educational program had increased production, 94.4 per cent answered yes. Asked whether the study had affected the persistency of their business, 86 per cent said it had effected an increase. Asked about the value of the study in regard to quality of service, 99.8 per cent of the personal producers replied it had enabled them to give better service to clients, while 100 per cent of those C.L.U.s with management duties gave the same answer.

Mr. Hill quoted facts about C.L.U. production leadership in two companies:

An extremely interesting and impressive statement has just been issued by the Equitable Life Assurance Society to the effect that its C.L.U.'s in personal production amount to less than ½ of 1 per cent of the company's active underwriters, yet 8 per cent of the honor roll for the first seven months of this year consists of C.L.U.'s. Of the 100 leading producers for that period, C.L.U.'s held the following rank: 1st, 5th, 22nd, 33rd, 53rd, 56th, 63rd and 83rd. The company further added that of its leading agencies, 20 per cent were in charge of C.L.U.'s or have C.L.U.'s on their managerial staffs.

On checking over the 100 C.L.U.'s with the Northwestern Mutual, I find 71 are devoting all their time to personal production and 13 of this number are to be found among our 100 leading agents in the past company club ending this June. In other words, 1 out of every 6 of our C.L.U. personal producers made the "100 leading agents" group in the past club year.

I am sure some of you have heard the thought expressed "if you want to ruin a good producer, have him prepare for the C.L.U. designation." Certainly the figures of the Equitable and of these other companies belie that.

An interesting report made by the 25 agents in Los Angeles who took the examinations in June showed that 23 of the 25 made marked increases this year over their paid-for business last year— an increase decidedly in excess of that which could be attributed to a betterment of business conditions.

The depression years gave a special setting for study of the value of C.L.U. work. Mr. Hill compared the performance of his company's C.L.U.s with the average company production:

The average production of our C.L.U.'s the past four years—figuring June to June—was in excess of the average production of our agents devoting their full time to life insurance by the following proportions:

> 1930–1931..................126 per cent in excess
> 1931–1932..................176 per cent in excess
> 1932–1933..................142 per cent in excess
> 1933–1934..................194 per cent in excess

This certainly proves that the average man with a C.L.U. designation is not only very much above average in personal production but maintained that production at a much higher level during the depression years than the average agent of the company.

To me these are not only interesting figures but are the basis for a conclusion that the American College movement has a definite measurable asset value, one to which agency management and companies can give very serious thought.

In 1936, Paul F. Clark, then enjoying great prestige as general agent of the largest life insurance agency in New England, presented a study of C.L.U. statistics "from the general agent's point of view." Those statistics were developed from a comprehensive survey of 82 agencies with two or more C.L.U.s in 39 cities, representing 18 companies, and covering 303 C.L.U.s.

Mr. Clark's questions and the answers received in his survey gave strong evidence of the value of the C.L.U. program.

Question: Is the C.L.U. movement helpful in recruiting? Answer from 73 per cent, yes.

Question: Is the C.L.U. program useful in training? General agents felt that the C.L.U. was invaluable for advanced training.

Question: What effect does C.L.U. work have on production? The statistics almost invariably showed an increase in production, even during the study years. Specifically, the C.L.U.s studied showed a 23 per cent increase for 1935 over 1934. Of the agencies in the survey, 71 per cent reported that C.L.U.s on the average wrote larger cases which tended to be more profitable for the general agent than ones and twos.

Question: Does the business of C.L.U.s have better persistency? Answer from 67 per cent of the agencies, yes.

Question: Does the C.L.U. stay in the business? Over half the agencies believed the agency turnover was favorably affected, and, in fact, only nine C.L.U. losses were reported in all the questionnaires.

The questionnaire replies also indicated overwhelmingly that the C.L.U.s brought prestige to the agency, and that, in general, the individual C.L.U. was particularly cooperative and constructive as a member of the group.

This survey, widely publicized, helped build appreciation of C.L.U.s in the industry. As Mr. Clark said, it was a thought-provoking answer to "the doubts and fears expressed from time to time by certain general agents as to the effect of the C.L.U. movement upon the immediate sales of their agents and the profits of the agency."

The prestige of the C.L.U. program was enhanced by the testimony of its friends, but the College felt intrinsic values that would speak for themselves also were important. There was constant effort on the part of College officials to maintain scrupulous fairness and professional standards in administering the examinations. Some of the problems reflected in the records are a bit startling. For example, the Board recommended that steps be taken to prevent a substitute from sitting for a candidate in the examinations.

Examination questions required great advance secrecy, of

Paul F. Clark.

course, and only in most unusual cases were any examinations allowed at times other than those specified. In Knoxville, Tennessee, one year, Part III examinations for 11 candidates were not received. The proctor and the College telegraphed and telephoned back and forth. Hasty search was made in the city and university post offices. Finally, Dr. McCahan dictated the questions over the telephone to the proctor, and the examination was given several hours late. Unfortunately, none of these candidates passed. The original examination questions were found later, carefully locked in the university safe. The College allowed the candidates to take the examinations again the next year at no additional cost.

The records reflect a charitable disposition on the part of the College in regard to refunds of fees, as well as enforcement of deadlines, late penalties, etc. The records are full of special cases considered by the Executive Committee. Requests for refunds were accompanied by reports of broken bones and new babies. One candidate was called from the examination to take his wife to the hospital; another who did not get to the examination had babysitter complications with big sister while mother was in the hospital with little sister; still another, in the excitement of having a son, forgot the C.L.U. deadline.

C.L.U. qualifications other than passing the examinations were a frequent cause of difficulty. The College took the matter of ethical standards very seriously. Retail credit reports on candidates were studied, and recommendations from personal sources were required. In 1936, the application blank was changed to emphasize the complete standards for qualification and to strengthen the College position in the face of threatened suits by disappointed candidates.

In the depression years, notes in the minutes of the Executive Committee refer to the withholding of certain designations until all stipulated bills were settled by the candidate. There were problems related to checks on closed banks, or just plain rubber checks that had been mailed to meet a deadline.

Economic history of the era is reflected in the new contract made with the jeweler who manufactured the C.L.U. keys. With the change in the price of gold, the cost of the key increased from $6.50 to $8.15.

Requests for special rulings on experience qualifications were frequent then as today. Brokers often could not measure production records so exactly as the typical personal producer. Qualifications for insurance teachers were based on the courses they taught over a period of years. Trust officers were repeatedly refused the C.L.U. designation at this period, although they were readily granted the certificate of proficiency, if they were properly qualified. After 1938, trust officers who could prove more than 50 per cent of their time was directly associated with life insurance trust work for a three-year period were granted the C.L.U.

Distinction between the Canadian C.L.U. and that granted by the American College was a frequent matter of discussion. The educational standards of the two designations were not the same. Finally, in 1937, an agreement was reached that qualified Canadian Chartered Life Underwriters coming to the United States should use C.L.U. (Canada); American College C.L.U.s going to Canada should use C.L.U. (U.S.).

From the beginning, the College had imposed strict limitations on the use of the C.L.U. designation in publicity. The administration did not want to antagonize underwriters who were not C.L.U.s. It also was sensitive to the possibility of offense to other professional men if "undignified publicity" were given to Chartered Life Underwriters. College prohibitions meant a practical problem for the salesmen. Successful candidates felt strongly that if the C.L.U. were to be meaningful to the public, they ought to be able to talk about it. They urged the College to give them some sort of official statement which could be used. Reluctantly, Dr. McCahan recommended that course to the Board, admitting that in spite of rules, C.L.U.s were using their own definitions, which were "awkward, lame and even inaccurate." In 1937, however, the Board reaffirmed its position and authorized the distribution of an official statement of policy, as follows:

The C.L.U. designation is protected under the laws of all states and of the Federal government. No person is permitted to use it until after his C.L.U. diploma has been officially conferred by the American College of Life Underwriters.

The designation Chartered Life Underwriter or its abbreviation "C.L.U." may be used in a dignified manner just as similar recognitions are employed in accounting, medicine and other professions. Either the full expression or the initials may be used after the name on business cards, stationery, office advertising or signed articles, but always in a way compatible with maintaining the dignity of the College that conferred the recognition.

To avoid any appearance of commercialization in promotion of the Chartered Life Underwriter (C.L.U.) program, the Board of Directors of the American College of Life Underwriters has adopted the policy, repeatedly confirmed on numerous occasions, of banning any efforts on the part of the individual holders of the designation to acquaint the insuring public with its significance and has reserved to the College itself the right of issuing any publicity or other material for that purpose. Such publicity efforts may be effected only through College publications, newspaper and insurance journal releases, addresses, and such other means as may be specifically approved by the Board of Directors of the College.

Individual holders of the C.L.U. designation should note that adoption of the policy outlined above does not permit announcements to their prospects that the C.L.U. designation has been awarded nor does it permit the use of circulars or other material attempting to explain the significance of attaining the designation. Use of the C.L.U. designation by its holders is literally restricted to the methods outlined in the second paragraph above for the purpose of (1) avoiding unethical practices, (2) preventing unfair comparisons with able and well-established life underwriters who do not happen to be C.L.U.'s, and (3) emphasizing the importance of C.L.U.'s being recognized for the quality of the service they render.

It is hoped that every person who holds the designation will appreciate the significance of the College's policy and will cooperate fully in complying with it.

When the American College approached its tenth anniversary, there naturally came the idea of celebration. Again Dr. Huebner voiced the attitude of the College toward publicity:

> Only one disturbing factor appears, namely a disposition to use the occasion for advertising with the public over the radio and probably other means. I fear this would be a mistake. Let us not forget the other underwriters and their feelings. After all, with the public it is the number of C.L.U.'s and the quality of their work which constitutes the best advertising. Aside from that we should not go beyond what members are already permitted to do in using their designation.

The tenth examination series completed a period of achievement that surely merited celebration. In June, 1936, 980 candidates took examinations. This, like each year before it, marked an advance over previous records. The candidates were from 200 communities in 41 states, the District of Columbia, and Hawaii, and represented 85 life insurance companies. The 107 completers of 1936 brought the full number of C.L.U.s to 1,116.

As previously mentioned, C.L.U.s had organized themselves promptly after the first examinations in 1928. Graduates had been a tremendous strength to the College throughout its existence. However, the membership was quite scattered. Their 1936 president, Fred L. Cassidy, of Seattle, commented that some members apparently "didn't know what the National Chapter existed for." Under the leadership of Thomas G. Murrell, of New York, a vigorous membership campaign was organized with splendid results—nearly 75 per cent of the potential actually was realized in membership. Mr. Cassidy reported:

> We have found that the C.L.U. can be sold just the same as life insurance can be sold by some one man taking responsibility and working for it. For instance, Lawrence Choate of Washington has

stirred up considerable interest in some who were hard nuts to crack as far as the C.L.U. is concerned and has done an exceptionally good piece of work.

The increased enthusiasm of C.L.U.s at this strategic time made them the natural channel for the dignified observance desired for the tenth anniversary of the College. The National Chapter sponsored the preparation of a brief history of the College, and shared the expense of publication and distribution. The book was *The First Decade*, by Lawrence C. Woods, Jr., nephew of Edward A. Woods.

President Alfred J. Johannsen also reported for the National Chapter:

> We are a little bit proud of the work we did in carrying out plans for celebrating the Tenth Anniversary of the founding of the American College of Life Underwriters. Thirty-nine dinners were held in the principal cities of the United States. Nearly every dinner was held on the night of March 22nd and ranged from modest sized groups to one of over 600 people. The calibre of the speakers, the subjects, the character and dignity of the meetings were such that we feel the anniversary was fittingly observed. The widespread publicity the dinners received in the insurance press was gratifying to all of us.

The First Decade included interesting directories of the College and of the National Chapter in the tenth anniversary year. It is impressive to see the outstanding names in life insurance history which appear in these rosters.

OFFICERS OF THE AMERICAN COLLEGE OF LIFE UNDERWRITERS

Chairman of the Board	*Ernest J. Clark
President	Dr. S. S. Huebner
Vice President	William M. Duff
Dean	Dr. David McCahan
Secretary	Dr. John A. Stevenson
Treasurer	Franklin W. Ganse
Counsel	Robert Dechert

*Former president of the National Association of Life Underwriters.

DIRECTORS

O. J. Arnold, President
 Northwestern National Life Insurance Company
 Minneapolis, Minn.

*Ernest J. Clark, State Agent
 John Hancock Mutual Life Insurance Company
 Baltimore, Md.

*Paul F. Clark, General Agent
 John Hancock Mutual Life Insurance Company
 Boston, Mass.

Michael J. Cleary, President
 Northwestern Mutual Life Insurance Company
 Milwaukee, Wis.

O. Sam Cummings, Manager
 Kansas City Life Insurance Company
 Dallas, Texas

William M. Duff, President and Manager
 Edward A. Woods Company
 Pittsburgh, Pa.

*J. Stanley Edwards, General Agent
 Aetna Life Insurance Company
 Denver, Colo.

Franklin W. Ganse
 Ganse-King Estate Service
 Boston, Mass.

Grant L. Hill, Director of Agencies
 Northwestern Mutual Life Insurance Company
 Milwaukee, Wis.

John Marshall Holcombe, Jr., Manager
 Life Insurance Sales Research Bureau
 Hartford, Conn.

Dr. S. S. Huebner, Professor of Insurance and Commerce
 Wharton School of Finance and Commerce
 University of Pennsylvania
 Philadelphia, Pa.

*George E. Lackey, General Agent
 Massachusetts Mutual Life Insurance Company
 Detroit, Mich.

---

*Former president of the National Association of Life Underwriters.

Dr. David McCahan, Professor of Insurance
　　Wharton School of Finance and Commerce
　　University of Pennsylvania
　　Philadelphia, Pa.
*Julian S. Myrick, Manager
　　Mutual Life Insurance Company of New York
　　New York, N.Y.
Henry E. North, Vice President
　　Metropolitan Life Insurance Company
　　New York, N.Y.
*Theodore M. Riehle, Associate Manager
　　Equitable Life Assurance Society of the United States
　　New York, N.Y.
*John Newton Russell, Manager
　　Pacific Mutual Insurance Company
　　Los Angeles, Calif.
Charles L. Scott, General Agent
　　Massachusetts Mutual Life Insurance Company
　　Kansas City, Mo.
Dr. John A. Stevenson, Executive Vice President
　　Penn Mutual Life Insurance Company
　　Philadelphia, Pa.
Oliver M. Thurman, Vice President
　　Mutual Benefit Life Insurance Company
　　Newark, N.J.
*S. T. Whatley, Vice President
　　Aetna Life Insurance Company
　　Hartford, Conn.

NATIONAL CHAPTER
CHARTERED LIFE UNDERWRITERS
OFFICERS

President . . . . Alfred J. Johannsen
Vice President . . . . Kellogg VanWinkle
Treasurer . . . . Charles L. Post
Secretary . . . . David McCahan

DIRECTORS

Benjamin Alk . . . . New York, N.Y.
Earle W. Brailey . . . . Cleveland, Ohio

---

*Former president of the National Association of Life Underwriters.

George J. Brown .... Lafayette, Ind.
Frederick Bruchholz .... Chicago, Ill.
Fred L. Cassidy .... Seattle, Wash.
H. L. Choate .... Washington, D.C.
Paul F. Clark .... Boston, Mass.
Glenn B. Dorr .... Hartford, Conn.
Harold W. Dougher .... Los Angeles, Calif.
Freeman Essex .... Portland, Ore.
Homer G. Hewitt .... Houston, Texas
Oliver J. Neibel .... Kansas City, Mo.
Millard R. Orr .... Philadelphia, Pa.

LOCAL CHAPTERS—C.L.U.
(Listed in the order of their organization*)

CHAPTER	PRESIDENT IN 1937
Chicago, Ill.	L. Mortimer Buckley
Philadelphia, Pa.	Paul B. Banks
Baltimore, Md.	Urquhart S. Dowell
Los Angeles, Calif.	Harold W. Dougher
Portland, Ore.	Freeman Essex
San Francisco, Calif.	James H. Wood
St. Louis, Mo.	Ray E. Flint
Washington, D.C.	James A. DeForce
New York, N.Y.	Leroy N. Whitelaw
Cincinnati, Ohio	C. Rigdon Robb
Seattle, Wash.	Joseph P. Mulder
Cleveland, Ohio	Ethel M. Wood
Pittsburgh, Pa.	R. Maxwell Stevenson
Syracuse, N.Y.	Henry B. Mertens
Boston, Mass.	Corinne V. Loomis
Indianapolis, Ind.	Francis D. Brosnan
Peoria, Ill.	John H. Roth, Jr.

*The current files on the American Society, based on new research with the help of all available documents, give a slightly different order for the organization of the first twenty chapters. The official record now shows: Chicago, Illinois; Philadelphia, Pennsylvania; Washington, D.C. (now known as District of Columbia); St. Louis, Missouri; Baltimore, Maryland; Los Angeles, California; San Francisco, California; New York City; Cincinnati, Ohio; Seattle, Washington; Cleveland, Ohio; Pittsburgh, Pennsylvania; Syracuse, New York; Boston, Massachusetts; Indianapolis, Indiana; Tulsa, Oklahoma; Buffalo, New York; Peoria, Illinois; Portland, Oregon; Rochester, New York.

Buffalo, N.Y. ....Austin H. Feltus
Tulsa, Okla. ....William T. Scott
Rochester, N.Y. ....Ellen M. Putnam
Kansas City, Mo. ....Dix Teachenor
Wichita, Kan. ....Clayton Mammel
Detroit, Mich. ....Floyd A. McCartney
Milwaukee, Wis. ....T. Westley Tuttle
Minneapolis-St. Paul, Minn. ....John O. Todd
Denver, Colo. ....C. E. Eddleblute
Hartford, Conn. ....Wilbur S. Pratt
Louisville, Ky. ....Charles T. Cravens
Omaha, Neb. ....Dave Noble
Houston, Texas ....Sam R. Hay, Jr.
Charlotte, N.C. ....Harry J. Spencer
Oklahoma City, Okla. ....Theo. M. Green
Little Rock, Ark. ....Fred Poe
Dallas, Texas ....Rudolph E. Fried
Davenport, Iowa ....Dick LeBuhn

The increasing appreciation felt by the College for the alumni was indicated by a bylaw change in 1937, providing that the president of the National Chapter should be an ex officio member of the College Board. In 1940, the National Chapter changed its name, and became the American Society of Chartered Life Underwriters.

During the strategic 1930s, C.L.U.s were important to the College as individuals as well as a group. Benjamin N. Woodson emphasized this fact as he reminisced about those years. He had entered the life insurance business in 1926 as a $16-a-week stenographer for a little company in Omaha. Soon he felt the pull of field work, became a salesman, and was writing an application a week. As a youngster in the business, he began to hear about the C.L.U. For a while it seemed out of his class, although in 1933 and 1934, in Seattle, he helped the pioneer teacher, George Buck, with some of the study groups. By 1937, when young Woodson joined the staff of the Life Insurance Sales Research Bureau in Hartford, he recognized that the leaders in the business whom he admired were C.L.U.s.

These men, who were the young men's heroes of the time, as

he said, gave prestige to the C.L.U. before the C.L.U. gave prestige to them. Such men were Irvin Bendiner, of Philadelphia, creative, articulate, widely sought as a speaker; Paul W. Cook, of Chicago, brilliant, witty, persuasive; J. Harry Wood, of Hartford, keen, dynamic, an innovator; George Lackey, of Detroit, a vigorous, colorful figure making history in his big agency; James Elton Bragg, with tremendous prestige in the industry because of his life insurance educational work at New York University and other centers around the country; Grant Hill, popular agency vice president of one of the leading companies, inspiring its agency force to pre-eminent C.L.U. achievements; and many others.

Seeing men like this in all areas of life insurance sales leadership proud to qualify as C.L.U.s made young men all over the country feel that not only was it an honor to be a C.L.U. but it was a shame *not* to be. After many good intentions, Mr. Woodson finally followed through, passed his five examinations in two years, and became a C.L.U. in 1940.

He became one of the most helpful and vigorous supporters of the College. Through the years, he has assumed personal responsibility for recruiting and nurturing C.L.U. candidates. He has presented (*not*, he says, via company expense account) more than 50 C.L.U. keys to the graduates he encouraged and sponsored. He, too, has radiated his own prestige on the C.L.U. movement. Since 1958, Mr. Woodson has been a trustee of the College. Incidentally, Mr. Woodson has been widely quoted, in the years since he earned his designation, to the effect that, "It is always easier to take C.L.U. examinations next year than it is to take them this year!"

The life insurance press gave constant support to the C.L.U. program during the 1930s. *Life Association News* carried a regular C.L.U. page. This important service to the College as well as to the readers was another evidence of the sympathetic bond between the National Association of Life Underwriters and the College.

In 1935, *Life Insurance Selling* had three successive issues dedicated to C.L.U.s. On the cover of the first issue this statement appeared.

> This issue of *Life Insurance Selling* is dedicated to the American College of Life Underwriters and to the more than 900 Chartered Life Underwriters whose standards of life insurance salesmanship are causing the public to have a fuller appreciation of life insurance.

An editorial in the same issue said in part:

> So far as we are able to determine, this is the first time that a national life insurance magazine such as *Life Insurance Selling* has devoted an entire magazine to the Chartered Life Underwriter movement.

> Because *Life Insurance Selling* believes that the C.L.U. movement is making for a higher standard of life insurance salesmanship, we are glad to endorse the American College of Life Underwriters, and the C.L.U. work generally by devoting this issue to it. At the same time we congratulate the 900 holders of the C.L.U. designation and the sponsors of the movement for the rapid strides of progress they are making toward a higher, cleaner, more proficient type of salesmanship and life insurance counsel.

Such appraisals from an independent source increased the industry's respect for the C.L.U. program and publicized its progress.

For several years successively, the January *New York Journal of Commerce* published double-column, page-long stories by Dr. McCahan concerning the American College. He discussed the purposes and program of the College with its nationwide organization of study classes and university cooperation. He reported statistics of progress, and thus presented the College to an important segment of the business and financial world.

In 1938, Ernest J. Clark retired as chairman of the Board. As director, president, and chairman, he had given devoted and effective leadership to the College through the difficult period of its

birth and what Dr. Huebner referred to as "the pioneering decade." In a unanimous desire to honor him and two other associates, the Board, meeting in September, 1938, named three life
trustees,* Ernest J. Clark, Franklin W. Ganse, and Solomon S.
Huebner. These men were cited for "outstanding, constructive
and devoted service to the College."

Mr. Clark continued his helpful interest in the College and
attendance at Board meetings until his death, at eighty-six, in
1958. Mr. Ganse had been treasurer of the College from the beginning. He performed the increasingly responsible job in Boston. He was succeeded in 1939 by Sewell W. Hodge, then treasurer of the Provident Mutual in Philadelphia, who has served
since. Dr. Huebner in the late 1930s was in poor health. It had
been necessary for him to limit his traveling, so he missed several
Board meetings. His friends felt great concern about his future.

To succeed Mr. Clark as chairman, the Board chose Julian S.
Myrick. Mr. Myrick had been a director since 1929, and already
had proved his unique value to the College. Mr. Trangmar, who
worked closely with the College and Mr. Myrick for more than
25 years, commented shortly before his death that Mr. Myrick's
election as chairman was one of the most fortunate things that
ever happened to the College. He has unusual talent in bringing
people together and inspiring enthusiasm for a common task.

Mr. Myrick has had great prestige in the industry and in American life generally. His acceptance of leadership in the College
brought many fringe benefits to the C.L.U. movement. In 1960,
when Mr. Myrick celebrated his eightieth birthday, his career
was featured in the New York daily newspapers, *The New York-
er,* and *Time Magazine,* as well as in the insurance press.

The *Time* story is typical, and gives an interesting picture of
the man who is one of the greats in the American College history.

---

*In December, 1937, the College adopted new bylaws, enlarging the Board and
replacing the term "director" with "trustee." Provision was made for three types of
trustees: term trustees, 21, elected in three classes, each for a term of three years;
life trustees, not to exceed five; and ex officio trustees, namely the counsel of the
College and the president of the National Chapter.

Julian S. Myrick.

The grand old man of U.S. life insurance turned 80 last week, took time out to enjoy a birthday dinner at Manhattan's Union Club and to admire the hundreds of cards that festooned the bottle-green walls of his office in the Empire State Building. But otherwise, it was another working day to Julian S. Myrick. One of the best salesmen in the business, he has sold more than a million dollars' worth of insurance a year for the past two years to qualify for the Million Dollar Round Table, the profession's highest honor, attained last year only by 2,688 of the nation's 250,000 fulltime life-insurance salesmen.

To keep in selling trim, Myrick begins each day with a 45-minute workout with 2-lb. dumbbells and Indian clubs, plays tennis three times a week. He gave up smoking cigars in 1924, quit chewing them in 1959, and hardly ever takes a drink until sundown. Then he drinks up to five martinis, often takes wine with the main course and brandy afterward.

Aside from his own success, Myrick has pioneered some important changes in the insurance business. In 1910 he helped found the first training school for agents, later, initiated the concept of estate planning. He helped set up the American College of Life Underwriters, the degree-granting agency for life-insurance salesmen, and has served as the college's board chairman for the past 20 years.

Julian Myrick started out in the insurance business as a $25-a-week applications clerk in 1898, soon struck up a friendship with another clerk, an athlete, organist and composer from Yale named Charles Ives. In 1907 they established their own office, soon were selling nearly $2,000,000 a year. . . .

Myrick became president of the U.S. Lawn Tennis Association in the early '20s, also headed the Davis Cup Committee whose teams won the cup six years in a row. Once when touring with the 1924 Olympic team, Myrick flattered the Queen of Spain into a doubles match (Queen Victoria, with Vincent Richards, beat Hazel Hotchkiss Wightman and Myrick).

At one time Myrick, who is married and has four daughters and a son, actually retired from the insurance business. In 1949 he stepped down from a vice-presidency of the Mutual of New York to help

Herbert Hoover, an old friend, enlist public support for the Hoover Commission's recommendations for organizational changes in the Federal Government. When that job was finished, Myrick longed for something else to do, decided to go back to his old sales agency as a consultant. "But," says Myrick, "nobody consults you about insurance. You have to go out and consult them."

Mr. Myrick was elected a life trustee in 1939, and served as Board chairman until 1960, when he became chairman emeritus. He was succeeded by Paul F. Clark.

Testimony to the worth of the C.L.U. program came through that most sincere praise, imitation. In 1942, the American Institute of Property and Liability Underwriters was organized to do for property and casualty people what the American College was doing for persons in life and health insurance. The impetus for the organization came through the American Association of University Teachers of Insurance, of which Dr. Huebner was first president and Dr. McCahan the 1941 president. A committee from A.A.U.T.I. presented to representatives of leading property and casualty insurance organizations a comprehensive story of the history and methods of the American College. They outlined the development of life insurance courses in colleges and universities, and the success of hundreds of life insurance men and women in achieving the C.L.U. designation. They reviewed many problems the College had met and solved, and suggested the opportunity for a new property insurance organization to build on the C.L.U. experience.

The Institute was chartered in Pennsylvania with headquarters in Philadelphia. Dr. Huebner was named chairman of the Board, and his University of Pennsylvania associate, Dr. Harry J. Loman, became dean. From the beginning, the Institute benefited greatly from the pioneering experience of the College. With the College, the Institute has always used the same university centers and proctors for its examinations. The program of the Institute is patterned closely after the College in that it has no resident classes, but works through established colleges and universities and local study groups. The designation awarded by the Institute is Chartered Property and Casualty Underwriter (C.P.C.U.).

Through the years, the College and the Institute have developed joint programs and services to the great advantage of the insurance industry and cooperating educators. The Institute occupied part of the College building at 3924 Walnut Street in Philadelphia, and continues at Bryn Mawr as co-occupant of Huebner Hall on a "share the expense" basis.

Chapter 14

THE S. S. HUEBNER FOUNDATION
FOR INSURANCE EDUCATION

Because the American College had adopted the principle of using existing local educational facilities throughout the country to support its program, the extent and quality of such facilities were very important to the College. Also, the expansion of insurance education in colleges and universities was an objective of the College from its earliest years.

In 1936, the College published a study by Dr. Huebner and Dr. McCahan which reported the kind and amount of insurance instruction being given on the college level in American institutions in 1935-36. Dr. Huebner had made a similar study in 1906 at the beginning of his own life insurance teaching, one in 1927, and another, with Dr. McCahan, in 1932.

Dr. Huebner and Dr. McCahan in the 1935-36 study reported "phenomenal growth" in insurance education, with 143 colleges and universities offering a total of 332 courses. Most of the instructors involved were professional teachers, but only 24 out of 137 were giving as much as half-time to insurance work. One of the greatest hurdles to further expansion was the dearth of competent teachers. In fact, a considerable number of institutions could not set up courses because they did not have an adequately prepared instructor—a deplorable situation to the promoters of insurance education.

Dr. Huebner and Dr. McCahan ascribed a large part of the recent progress to the demand for educational facilities for life un-

186

derwriters preparing for C.L.U. examinations. The need was turning teachers' attention to the field, and administrators were actively seeking qualified instructors from beyond the campus.

Commenting informally about this situation to the trustees, Dr. Huebner reported:

It is also interesting to note how many institutions of learning are taking C.L.U.s on the faculty. Our problem of university cooperation is not in connection with the last three examinations. Nearly every institution of learning can furnish instruction in those subjects. The problem seems to be in life insurance. For example, within the past two weeks at the University of Washington, the president said: "We can give everything except life insurance. But this is what I will do. If the life underwriters can nominate a C.L.U. who they believe can teach the subject-matter of the first two examinations, I'll take him on my faculty." Likewise, President Jardine in Wichita made exactly the same statement: "Furnish me a man who knows his subject. If you can find the right C.L.U. I will put him on the faculty." So in a great many instances the institutions of learning have the disposition to take our C.L.U.s on the faculty to teach the insurance matter.

With this great need for teachers to implement the C.L.U. program, with Dr. Huebner's personal interest in the matter, it was most logical that this area became the object of a new enterprise. Dr. Huebner had been seriously ill. Many people feared that the days of his personal contribution to the cause of life insurance education were coming to an end. Throughout the industry there was an urgent desire to pay him honor—to give tangible tribute to his unique service to the industry. Many recognized that he had been a key force in the transformation of life insurance selling from policy peddling to a professional calling.

As life insurance leaders discussed the matter, several guiding principles emerged. First, the project attempted should be intrinsically valuable and interesting to all the business. Second, it should be so logically associated with Dr. Huebner that there would be real motivation in having his name attached to it. Third, it must be so important and worthwhile that having his name connected with it would be a distinct honor for Dr. Huebner.

As they talked, the leaders considered what might be done in connection with the C.L.U. movement. They thought about Dr. Huebner's life work in college teaching and his keen desire to see growth in the college program of insurance education. They all knew that for the C.L.U., and for college teaching generally, the great obstacle to progress was the lack of qualified insurance teachers.

From the midst of discussion, an idea crystallized. Surely Dr. McCahan had a major role in it. Joseph H. Reese helped. Holgar J. Johnson and Thomas I. Parkinson also were among the leaders, but there were many others too.

Soon the life insurance business united, through the Life Insurance Association of America, the American Life Convention, and the Institute of Life Insurance, to honor Dr. Huebner by raising a fund to advance insurance education. On an experimental basis for five years, the cooperating life insurance companies undertook to provide $25,000 a year for a Huebner Educational Fund, to be used to further insurance teacher training.

The annual American College conferment dinner, held during the 1940 convention of the National Association of Life Underwriters in Philadelphia, was chosen as the time for announcement of the new program. It was planned as a great testimonial occasion honoring Dr. Huebner.

On the historic evening of September 26, 1940, the grand ballroom of the Bellevue Stratford Hotel was crowded to overflowing with 1,200 guests. Dr. Huebner had been in the care of two doctors all day. He was crippled with arthritis, but he told the physicians to do anything—just get him in shape to do and say what would be appropriate for the evening. He arrived in a wheelchair to take his place at the head table. Then his great willpower, aided by the doctors' drugs, asserted itself, and he was a most adequate guest of honor.

Julian S. Myrick, chairman of the American College Board,

was toastmaster. He said in his opening remarks: "It is a privilege to preside over this great meeting tonight which has been brought together to do honor to Dr. Solomon Stephen Huebner. ... It is the first time in all the years that I have ever known the Institution of Life Insurance to gather in such a representative way." Then he referred to the list in the souvenir program of the sponsoring organizations with their representative members. These, indeed, represented the whole life insurance industry. The men named were of such outstanding caliber that most are known even today, though many are long since dead.

The Association of Life Insurance Presidents
  Vincent P. Whitsitt, Manager
  Major Thomas I. Parkinson, Committee Chairman

The Institute of Life Insurance
  M. Albert Linton, Chairman of the Board
  Holgar J. Johnson, President
  John A. Stevenson, Committee Chairman

American Life Convention
  Cornelius A. Craig, President
  Colonel C. B. Robbins, Manager
  Edward E. Rhodes, Committee Chairman

The Association of Life Agency Officers
  Alexander E. Patterson, Chairman
  Grant L. Hill, Committee Chairman

The National Association of Life Underwriters
  Charles J. Zimmerman, President
  Roger B. Hull, Manager
  Theodore M. Riehle, Committee Chairman

The American College of Life Underwriters
  Julian S. Myrick, Chairman of the Board
  Paul F. Clark, Committee Chairman

The American Society of Chartered Life Underwriters
  Earle W. Brailey, President
  Benjamin Alk, Committee Chairman

American Association of University Teachers of Insurance
Dr. David McCahan, President

Association of Life Insurance Medical Directors
Dr. Harold M. Frost, President

Home Office Life Underwriters Association
Leigh Cruess, President

The Life Advertisers Association
Karl Ljung, President
Cyrus T. Steven, Committee Chairman

The Life Insurance Sales Research Bureau
Vincent B. Coffin, Chairman of the Board
John Marshall Holcombe, Jr., Manager

Dr. Huebner gave the conferment address. Charles J. Zimmerman, president of the National Association of Life Underwriters, paid tribute to Dr. Huebner on behalf of the field forces of America, and presented their beautiful gifts of silver services and Spode china to Dr. and Mrs. Huebner. Dr. Paul Musser, vice president, spoke in honor of Dr. Huebner on behalf of the University of Pennsylvania.

Finally, as the climax of the evening, came the introduction of Major Thomas I. Parkinson, president of the Equitable Life Assurance Society of New York and chairman of the Cooperative Industry Committee. Speaking with appreciation and affection, he announced to Dr. Huebner the fund which had been provided in his honor to advance the training of insurance teachers.

Nobody who attended that dinner ever will forget it. Dr. Huebner's response was brief. The friends there were nearly as moved as the man whom they so gladly honored. One of the guests called the occasion "as great a tribute as the life insurance business could offer a man."

The S. S. Huebner Foundation took concrete form through a formal declaration on December 18, 1940. The declaration was signed by three representatives each of the American Life Convention, the Institute of Life Insurance, and the Life Insurance

Organization meeting for the Huebner testimonial project which became the S. S. Huebner Foundation, Major Parkinson, host. *Left to right:* Sterling Pierson, counsel of the Equitable Life of New York; David McCahan, dean of the American College of Life Underwriters; Frank Jones, vice president of the Equitable Life of New York; John A. Stevenson, president of the Penn Mutual Life; Joseph H. Reese, chairman of the Huebner testimonial meeting which was held at the N.A.L.U. annual convention; Paul F. Clark, president of the John Hancock Mutual Life; Holgar J. Johnson, president of the Institute of Life Insurance; Thomas J. Parkinson, president of the Equitable of New York; Julian S. Myrick, chairman of the Board of the American College; Theodore H. Riehle, general agent, Equitable Life of New York; Grant Hill, vice president of the Northwestern Mutual Life; William Graham, vice president of the Equitable Life of New York; Benjamin Alk, president of the Life Underwriters Association of New York City; Ray D. Murphy, vice president and actuary of the Equitable Life of New York; Arthur P. Carroll, assistant secretary of the Equitable Life of New York.

Association of America. Those nine men also became the first official Cooperating Committee of the Foundation. They were H. H. Armstrong, O. J. Arnold, Leroy A. Lincoln, M. Albert Linton, E. E. Rhodes, A. A. Rydgren, John A. Stevenson, Frank C. Weidenborner, and Thomas I. Parkinson. More than sixty companies were first-year donors to the Foundation. It seemed wise to have the money-raising operations separated from the educational program. So it was decided to delegate the latter to a university. Not surprisingly, the University of Pennsylvania was designated, at least for the beginning.

The University named Dr. David McCahan executive director for the program, and appointed an Administrative Board to supervise the general operations. The first Administrative Board was:

> Honorary Chairman: S. S. Huebner, professor of insurance and commerce, Wharton School of Finance and Commerce, University of Pennsylvania, and president of the American College of Life Underwriters.
>
> Chairman: Harry J. Loman, professor of insurance and director of the graduate division of the Wharton School of Finance and Commerce, University of Pennsylvania.
>
> Executive Director: David McCahan, professor of insurance, Wharton School of Finance and Commerce, University of Pennsylvania, and dean of the American College of Life Underwriters.
>
> Ralph H. Blanchard, professor of insurance, School of Business, Columbia University.
>
> Edison L. Bowers, associate professor of economics, School of Commerce, The Ohio State University.
>
> Paul H. Musser, administrative vice president, University of Pennsylvania.
>
> Edwin B. Williams, dean of the Graduate School of Arts and Sciences, University of Pennsylvania.

The first *Announcement* of the Foundation outlined the need for the work being undertaken, set forth the plan which was to be followed, and commented about the advantages of Pennsylvania as the designated university.

The colleges and universities of the country have not, for the most part, been adequately staffed with experienced insurance teachers. . . . This is indeed not surprising when it is realized that, outside of courses in insurance law and actuarial science primarily designed for prospective lawyers and actuaries, courses in insurance are comparatively late arrivals in the curricula of our higher educational institutions, being entirely a development of the Twentieth Century. Thus, out of 584 courses reported by 235 institutions in a recent survey made by the American College of Life Underwriters, more than one-half have been introduced within the past fifteen years. It is further significant to note that of the 384 teachers reported as conducting these 584 courses, 88 are part-time teachers whose principal vocation is not teaching. Two hundred and fifty-eight are full-time teachers who devote more than half of their teaching time to subjects other than insurance. Only 38 are full-time teachers with at least half of their teaching load in the field of insurance.

Since the quality and effectiveness of a teacher grow with his years of research and continued study, the logical method for helping to strengthen education in insurance is to strengthen the individual teacher by giving him the opportunity and the means to broaden his own understanding of the subject. To that end . . . a foundation which would provide:

1. Fellowships for graduate study available to teachers now in accredited colleges or universities who desire to study for a Doctor's degree, and who now hold at least a Bachelor's degree.

2. Scholarships for graduate study available to recent graduates of accredited colleges or universities who desire to prepare for an insurance teaching career by studying for either a Master's or Doctor's degree.

3. Scholarships for graduate study available to graduates of accredited colleges or universities now associated with insurance companies who desire to prepare for educational work within their own companies by studying for either a Master's or Doctor's degree, such scholarships to be financed by specific contributions for the purpose unless the funds available from the foundation are more than sufficient to meet the need for fellowships and scholarships among persons preparing for the teaching profession as a life career.

4. For building up and maintaining a central research library in insurance books and other source material which would be available through circulating privileges to teachers in accredited colleges and universities desirous of conducting research in insurance subjects.

5. For publishing research theses and other studies which constitute a distinct contribution directly or indirectly to insurance knowledge. . . .

Selection of the University of Pennsylvania for initial administration of the funds received by this foundation was also prompted by the hope that many future teachers would thereby have an opportunity during the years to come of sharing the vision and inspiration of Dr. Huebner's teaching as well as by the fact that Dr. Huebner has gathered about him a staff of twelve experienced full-time teachers who have acquired an understanding of their subject which can come only with research, continued study and maturity. Five of his associates in Pennsylvania's Insurance Department are full professors, one is an associate professor, four are assistant professors and two are intructors. Except the two instructors, all have taught insurance at the University of Pennsylvania for at least fifteen years. Many contributions to insurance literature have been made by these associates and numerous are the constructive services which they have rendered in a great variety of responsible private and public positions.

Moreover a broad range of graduate courses is now being offered by the University of Pennsylvania which enables the institution to meet the needs of all types of students. Included therein are seven full-year courses in different divisions of the insurance field as well as courses in all of the other business subjects closely related thereto. These courses have been developed over a period of time after exhaustive study and intelligent experimentation. They are designed especially for graduate work and are not open to undergraduate or special students.

Dr. Huebner's department at the University of Pennsylvania is a unit of Pennsylvania's Wharton School of Finance and Commerce, a veritable laboratory of the social sciences, affording a unique opportunity for the study of modern social and economic problems by insurance experts and the coordinated research efforts of experts in all of the social sciences toward application of insurance principles to the needs of the American public.

The S. S. Huebner Foundation was established as a tribute to Dr. Huebner. Many observers agree that it is also a monument to David McCahan. As executive director, Dr. McCahan immediately got the program under way. His superb organizing ability was evident in the prompt and effective attention to the machinery of operation. In the first year, he had prepared the necessary literature and articles for college publication which brought the

Dr. Dan M. McGill and Dr. Huebner before the Alfred Jonniaux portrait (1952) which was the gift of Wharton School students who had specialized in insurance and which hangs in the library of the S. S. Huebner Foundation. (*Shaw*)

Foundation program to the attention of prospective fellows and scholars. He investigated suggested projects and outlined opportunities for research. He laid plans for the development of a research service center.

Dr. McCahan also began the long series of interviews to screen applicants for fellowships and scholarships. With unusual discernment and judgment, he studied the men asking for grants. He appraised the individual's personality and his qualifications, mental and otherwise, for success in college-level teaching. He sought to weigh the strength of each applicant's desire to devote himself to a lifetime career in insurance teaching. He evaluated the candidate's practical opportunities for placement and progress.

The great success of the Huebner Foundation undoubtedly owes much to the caliber of the men Dr. McCahan chose. The first awards were granted for 1941-42. There were four scholarships and five fellowships. One fellow was Dan M. McGill, of Maryville, Tennessee. For him, as for others, studies were interrupted by war service. The Foundation grants necessarily were withheld for lack of applicants, but Dr. McCahan continued other activities. Major Dan McGill, Army Air Corps, returned promptly after the war, attained his Ph.D. in 1947, and became director of the Foundation in 1954. Another fellow for 1946-47 was Lt. Davis W. Gregg, United States Navy, who had been a graduate student at the University of Pennsylvania before the war. In the same 1946-47 group of fellows was Herbert C. Graebner, who had been a professor of economics and business at Westminster College. Dr. McCahan had no crystal ball to help him select as Huebner fellows the future executive director of the Foundation as well as the future president and the future dean of the American College, but his skill in seeing student potential enabled him to pick these and others who have built outstanding careers in insurance education.

The Huebner Foundation fulfilled its objectives so effectively, even with the war interruptions, that in 1952 the cooperating companies established a permanent organization.

The S. S. Huebner Foundation for Insurance Education is without time limit and independent of the three industry organizations which were its original Cooperating Committee. It also is established permanently in its relationship with the University of Pennsylvania. The Foundation headquarters and research library are a part of the Insurance Center in Dietrich Hall.

For 1961-62, the Foundation's twentieth year, about $90,000 was contributed by 123 life insurance companies for the support of the Foundation and its program. Over the years, some 85,000 copies of 20 Huebner Foundation books have been put into use around the world. During the two decades, 103 individuals aspiring to an insurance teaching career at the college level have been given grants. Of this group, but not including those still in residence at the Foundation, 71 are engaged currently in insurance education. These men are affiliated with 47 educational institutions in 25 states, Puerto Rico, and Pakistan, and they constitute more than a quarter of the full-time teachers of risk and insurance at the college level.

The Huebner Foundation developed not only as an instrument of recognition for Dr. Huebner, but as a direct result of the need for professional insurance teachers reflected in the experience of the American College over its first 15 years. This Foundation, functioning independently from the beginning, has made a great contribution to the furthering of insurance education and research and the strengthening of the American College program.

Chapter 15

THE WAR YEARS

In its first decade, the College had made tremendous progress in numbers of graduates and candidates, in prestige, in organization, and in financing. In 1939, 1,746 candidates sat for 3,125 examinations, the largest totals to date. But it would be many years before such records would be matched again. The turmoil in Europe was reflected first in College affairs by difficulties in establishing the educational prerequisite for candidates educated abroad. Dr. McCahan reported to the Board of Trustees in 1940:

> . . . The war situation had made it difficult during the past year to secure satisfactory educational credentials for some foreign-born candidates, and with the destruction of records and changes in government which appear inevitable, it is highly probable that similar difficulties will be experienced for many years to come. This naturally raises a question as to what the College should regard as satisfactory educational credentials under such circumstances. In fairness to the candidates who are involved, some flexibility is essential, but at the same time the educational prerequisite must be safeguarded.

It was decided that credentials, evidence, or sworn statements concerning courses taken and graduation from a foreign school would be reviewed. The name of the school would be submitted to the Division of Comparative Education in Washington to determine whether the education reflected by such credentials should be considered the equivalent of graduation from an accredited American high school. Thus, in spite of difficulties, the College steadfastly maintained the educational prerequisite that meant so much in its academic reputation.

The declaration of war in Europe made it harder for young people in the United States to set long-term goals. Life underwriters shared the tendency to concentrate on today, or at most on a near tomorrow. The value of education for life underwriters was a well-sold idea, but more men were asking for a short course, strong in features that would pay off quickly. This popular sentiment grew with the pressures of war, and was nourished by criticisms of and dissatisfactions with what was felt to be an inflexible College program.

To meet the needs of the industry, determined after wide consultation with field men and home office educational officers, the Insurance Research and Review Service published an excellent series of books by Paul Speicher and his staff. The material was simple, brief, specifically vocation-directed, and written with Mr. Speicher's unique motivation and color. In three volumes, the student had a course including fundamentals, programing, and sales techniques. Using this material, local life underwriter associations organized study classes on what became known as "the St. Louis plan," after the association which gave the idea original publicity. In 1940, there were 31 such courses with a total enrollment of 3,651. This response to the St. Louis plan indicated that it was meeting a real need, particularly in view of the psychology of the times. The course was so much easier and shorter than the C.L.U. program. It was open to anyone, since associations did not need educational prerequisites as did the College. People who felt they should study considered the C.L.U. course with its heavy academic demands over several years, and often would conclude: "I think I'll take the association class."

The local associations promoted their classes with enthusiasm and good salesmanship. They had the practical appeal of a study plan geared directly to helping men improve their sales. The number of St. Louis plan students went up, and C.L.U. enrollments went down. The American College naturally was concerned. Dr.

McCahan and Mr. Williams went to Hartford to consult with John Marshall Holcombe, Jr., a trustee of the College. During the summer and fall of 1939, several meetings were held, with Dr. Huebner, Earl Trangmar, Irvin Bendiner, Julian S. Myrick, and B. N. Woodson also attending. Their thoughtful analysis was that there was indeed a legitimate demand for a course less academic than the C.L.U., on an intermediate level and with more emphasis on sales techniques.

In 1940, the Executive Committee of the American College appointed a Technical Committee composed of Mr. Bendiner, Mr. Trangmar, and Mr. Woodson, with Dr. Huebner, Dr. McCahan, and Mr. Williams. Dean McCahan was asked to make a survey of the current educational needs of the industry as a basis for study and recommendations by the Technical Committee. It recommended that an intermediate course—between the elementary company courses and the C.L.U. program—be organized on an institutional basis with skilled teaching. The course should have industry supervision and recognition. It should emphasize practical salesmanship. The Committee further recommended that the College *not* attempt to organize such a course, but offer to cooperate with any industry groups which might want to do so.

The Association of Life Agency Officers took leadership in the new enterprise through its Committee on Training, of which Chester O. Fischer, vice president of the Massachusetts Mutual, was then chairman. Benjamin N. Woodson was secretary. This Committee and its various subcommittees, which included Dr. Huebner, Dr. McCahan, and Mr. Williams, met repeatedly, and made specific progress in the development of proposals for a Life Underwriters' Service Training Program. Areas of content, text material, and teaching plans were agreed on. The Life Agency Officers approved the plan at their 1941 meeting in November, and it looked as though the launching were near. The Committee set Monday, December 8, 1941, for its next meeting, at the Waldorf in New York City. They did indeed meet that morning, but they sat in silence to listen by radio to the voice of Franklin D. Roosevelt asking the Congress of the United States to declare war on Japan.

Clearly this was no time for a new life insurance education program. Plans were shelved "for the duration" and the Life Underwriter Training Council did not become a reality until 1947.

The discussions concerning an intermediate course helped the American College officers analyze their own program. They decided to modify the examination schedule somewhat, the first real change from the beginning. The old Examination II was merged with a new Part E, which was a fifth examination to test the application of material covered by the first four parts. This new examination was first given in 1942. Instead of Parts I, II, III, IV, and V the examinations now became Parts A, B, C, D, and E. The material covered was still generally the same: life insurance fundamentals; economics, government, and sociology; law, trusts, and taxes; corporation finance, banking and credit, and investments.

Following the high point of 1,746 candidates in 1939, the number taking C.L.U. examinations declined, slightly in 1940, but with increasing rapidity to the low of 706 in 1944. President Huebner's comments in the 1942 *Annual Report* recall conditions which many readers remember only too well.

Many of our younger candidates for the C.L.U. designation entered military or naval service, while many others were doubtful as to their military status and could not be prevailed upon to begin, or to continue their study program, in view of the anticipated calling into the Service. College and university courses throughout the country, related to the C.L.U. subjects of study, were also greatly decimated as regards student attendance, and in ever so many instances were abandoned, and the customary substantial quota of C.L.U. candidates from this source was, therefore, not available this year to the American College. A considerable number of study groups (outside of College circles) also could not be started, or had to be abandoned if they had been started, because of difficulty in securing new teachers and holding those who had formerly taken charge of the work of instruction. Moreover, there was also a con-

siderable demoralization of college faculties everywhere because
of the entrance of teachers into the Government service, or because
of the necessity of teachers seeking temporary employment elsewhere, owing to depletion of student personnel.

The College applied itself vigorously to keeping in touch with
candidates, whether on the job or in service. Concerning the 1944
examinations, Dr. Huebner wrote:

In spite of war conditions, 706 candidates took C.L.U. examinations
on June 7, 8, and 9, at ninety-seven educational institutions, four
Army camps or Naval bases, and one German prison camp. The 102
examination centers, to meet the convenience of candidates under
present adverse conditions, represented an unusually wide geo-
graphic distribution, there being at least one center for nearly every
state of the United States, and three outside of continental borders.

The examinations in a German prison camp were taken by a
thirty-one-year-old representative of the Metropolitan Life at Easton, Pennsylvania, who, as a lieutenant colonel, had been among
the first American troops ashore in French Morocco. He was cap-
tured in the Tunisia campaign. His examinations were arranged
through the War Prisoners Aid of the Y.M.C.A. That organization
also provided him with the necessary study materials. The examinations were proctored properly by the educational officer in the
prison camp.

During these years, over a thousand C.L.U.s and C.L.U. candidates were known to be in the armed services. The College made
every effort to keep in touch to prepare them for return to life underwriting, or to encourage continuance of C.L.U. studies. There
was much individual correspondence, as well as a number of
blanket mailings. The *Annual Report* of the College was sent to
C.L.U.s in service to keep them informed of progress. Study supplements were offered free to servicemen on request.

These dislocated life underwriters expressed great interest in
"refresher material." To meet that need, the College prepared
four "Significant Developments" monographs in the areas of the

first four C.L.U. examinations. These publications averaged about 125 pages, and covered such things as the new C.S.O. Table of Mortality and Guertin Committee legislation, pension plans, new taxes, restrictions on business and trade, developments in social security—a great variety of current events. The information was extremely valuable, and well received. The booklets were supplied free on request to servicemen, and were used widely by other C.L.U. students.

In 1945 there was a real reversal of the downtrend in C.L.U. candidates. In spite of the great numbers of young men still in service, 952 candidates, a 34 per cent increase over the previous year, took examinations in nearly every state and in England, France, Germany, Hawaii, India, Puerto Rico, and the South Pacific.

What C.L.U. activity among servicemen was like in terms of individuals can be glimpsed from an article in the Mutual Benefit Life agents' magazine, *The Pelican,* May, 1945.

Study for a professional career in life underwriting seems very unlikely for a person on active duty in the country's armed forces. One hardly associates it with bomber piloting, the operation of a naval vessel or an infantry invasion. Yet during the past year the American College of Life Underwriters has received literally hundreds of letters pertaining to such study from men in the Army, Navy and Marine Corps scattered all over the globe. Some have already earned their designation. Most had been registered as approved candidates before entry into war service and are now attempting to complete the program of study and examinations which had been interrupted. But a substantial number, growing rather rapidly, are former life underwriters who had never previously shown any interest in the C.L.U. program.

It is interesting to note that one C.L.U. study group, consisting exclusively of sixteen Navy men, is in operation. It is located at the U.S. Naval Training Center at Farragut, Idaho. The members come from nine different states. Fourteen of them had previously been in life insurance, representing ten different life insurance companies. For most persons, however, a regularly organized study group is

out of the question. There have been cases of two or three persons
in the same unit preparing together, as two young gunnery officers
who had by chance been assigned to the same merchant vessel, but
generally each man is working "on his own" and is subject to all
the handicaps which that entails.

The College was laying the foundation for enlarged operations
as soon as the war was over. In 1944, two very important steps
were taken.

One was the creation of a new and more widely representative
College Examination Board. The area of examinations was one
in which there had been considerable dissatisfaction and criticism. The charge of "too academic" had been highlighted during
discussions of the intermediate course before the war. Field men
often felt decisions by the College administrators were arbitrary
and inflexible. It seemed highly desirable to bring more field men
and educators into this phase of College responsibility. Dr. Huebner described the situation:

> Selection of the most advantageous and most valuable study ma-
> terial for each of the five areas of the C.L.U. study program, the
> planning and preparation of Study Supplements, preparation of
> the questions for each of the five C.L.U. examinations, arrange-
> ment of numerous examination centers throughout the nation, dis-
> tribution of the examination questions and their protection during
> the distribution, arrangement for the efficient proctoring of the ex-
> aminations at so many widely scattered examination centers, the
> appointment of graders, the standardization of a grading system on
> a fair and efficient basis, the reporting of the grades, and the wise
> handling of disgruntled examinees, are all problems of such diffi-
> culty as to tax human ingenuity to the uttermost. They all consti-
> tute problems requiring judgment and much labor, patience and
> tact. They are also controversial in many respects, and often bitterly
> so. Perfection, suitable to all, will never be reached in this particular
> area. The most that can be hoped for is substantial equality and
> equity, with gradual improvement in the course of time through a
> combined judgment of numerous informed minds working coopera-
> tively.

Thus far the task of exercising judgment with respect to all of the aforementioned factors has devolved essentially upon the officers of the College. They have always sought the cooperative help of outside authorities, and have had the active and valued cooperation of many persons. But it is questionable whether the responsibility for such important matters should rest solely with the officers of the College. Such is not the case in other institutions of higher learning. Rather it would seem that the officers should have the guidance of a representative group of informed persons to whom perplexing questions of policy may be submitted for consideration and decision, so that the officers may obtain a cross section of various views on the policies and procedures to be administered.

A committee of C.L.U.s appointed to study the situation included: Joseph H. Reese, chairman; Lawrence C. Woods, Jr., James Elton Bragg, Irvin Bendiner, and Hampton H. Irwin. They worked for months, then submitted recommendations to the Board of Trustees which led, in September, 1944, to the creation of the Examination Board of the American College of Life Underwriters, representing C.L.U.s, educators, home offices, and the American College. The 1945 Board, with Irvin Bendiner as chairman, was:

Representing active life underwriters
    Irvin Bendiner, C.L.U.
    James Elton Bragg, C.L.U.
    Lawrence C. Woods, Jr., C.L.U.
Representing a university or college
    Laurence J. Ackerman
Representing life insurance companies
    Ben H. Williams, C.L.U.
    Earl R. Trangmar
Representing the American College of Life Underwriters
    S. S. Huebner
    David McCahan, C.L.U.
    John P. Williams, C.L.U.

The Board promptly attacked its problems with the organization of subcommittees as follows:

Subcommittee on the Aims and Objectives of the College:
> Earl R. Trangmar, Chairman

Irvin Bendiner   John P. Williams

Subcommittee on Scope of the C.L.U. Program, the C.L.U. Reading List, and Study Materials:
> Earl R. Trangmar, Chairman

Laurence J. Ackerman   David McCahan
James Elton Bragg   John P. Williams

Subcommittee on Examination Questions:
> James Elton Bragg, Chairman

Laurence J. Ackerman   Earl R. Trangmar
David McCahan   Ben H. Williams

Subcommittee on Grading Procedures and Notification of Results:
> Lawrence C. Woods, Jr., Chairman

David McCahan   Earl R. Trangmar
> John P. Williams

Subcommittee on Complaints:
> Irvin Bendiner, Chairman

S. S. Huebner   David McCahan

(The president of the College was made an ex officio member of all of the aforementioned subcommittees.)

The committees accomplished a prodigious amount of work during the next few months—analysis, discussion, formulation of conclusions—for which the College must still be deeply indebted. The 22 recommendations of the Examination Board went to the root of a number of operational problems which had been troublesome. They established procedures for review and revision of study materials, and control of the scope of the examinations. All recommendations were adopted by the Board, and thus the foundation was laid for greater cooperation and understanding between the College and its students.

One Examination Board recommendation looked to the possibility of textbook preparation by the College. Therefore, on July 19, 1945, the Executive Committee voted, and the trustees subsequently approved, a fifth objective for the College.

To promote research and the preparation and publication of text books and other material deemed essential to the fullest realization of this College's program of study in all of the fields of knowledge with which a life underwriter should be acquainted.

As chairman, Irvin Bendiner gave wise and dynamic leadership to the Examination Board in its first years. It was a tragic loss when he died at forty-six in November, 1946, following a heart attack. From his hospital bed, Mr. Bendiner sent a message to the Phoenix Mutual Life Insurance Company's convention, which he had been scheduled to address. "Four White Walls and a Ceiling" became a classic among life underwriters, a stirring human document, a message to life insurance salesmen about their service. In introduction he said:

My first conscious recollection, as my head came out from the oxygen tent, was to send for a copy of my will, my life insurance policies, my wife's black book, and, of course, my wife. The result, some hours later, was to bring to me the most complete peace of mind that an individual man could have, particularly in relationship to the material well-being of his dependents.

Then he reviewed in some detail the complications and limitations of his property other than life insurance, and concluded:

I had always known that life insurance was my principal asset. I had always known that it had taken the largest portion of my earnings. I had always known theoretically that it could accomplish many things in a person's estate. I had thought, taught and preached about its intangible quality in bringing peace of mind and developing credit and character, but I had never had to meet it face to face as an important factor in my own well-being. As I reviewed a brief lifetime of accomplishment, as measured by material accumulations, I found that my life insurance was the basis for whatever peace of mind I could find in my picture.

Life underwriters all over the country honored the memory of Irvin Bendiner, and were inspired professionally and personally by his example. The story he told emphasized the need for life underwriters with broad-based education—the C.L.U. ideal.

Countless individuals had special reasons to remember Mr. Bendiner with gratitude. He had interested himself actively in helping other people achieve the C.L.U. A typical story with an unusual setting was told in *Life Association News* by George N. Quigley, Jr.

A young college boy with one more year of school to finish climbed on the train in Denver one hot August day in 1931, to take the short trip to Pueblo, Colorado. As he took a seat in the observation car he found that the only other occupant of the car was a gentleman of rather unusual appearance. The man was dressed in black; black suit, black socks, black shoes, black knit necktie and on the luggage rack above him was a black Homburg hat. To complete the picture, he wore dark horn-rimmed glasses and had black hair.

As the train started on its slow journey from Denver to Colorado Springs, some seventy-five miles away, the boy noticed the older man's enjoyment of the view from the windows of the observation car. Soon they were engaged in conversation. It developed that the man was an Easterner who had never been west of Philadelphia. He was en route to the meeting of the Top Club of the New York Life Insurance Company being held at Colorado Springs. He reveled in the scenery unfolding as the train approached the majestic range of mountains ringing the Springs.

When the Easterner learned that the college boy was contemplating a life insurance career, he launched immediately into an earnest plea that the young man, as soon as he graduated from college, must begin to study for the C.L.U. designation. The boy had never heard of C.L.U., but the Easterner enthusiastically related the dream of Dr. Huebner and the story of the American College of Life Underwriters. He proudly showed the boy his own C.L.U. key, won in 1928, the first year that C.L.U. examinations were given. He painted a vision of the future of the life insurance business and the part which the C.L.U. movement would play in it. This vision caught the boy's imagination—it gave substance and life to a professional concept of the life insurance business such as he had never heard before. Before they parted, the Easterner had kindled a spark in the western boy's mind and heart convincing him of the absolute necessity of becoming a C.L.U. just as quickly as possible after entering the insurance business. He took the boy's name and address, found out exactly when he would be graduating from the University of Colorado and the company the young man intended to represent. It was a different company from his own but he was no less eager to make sure the young man would enter the life insurance business and qualify himself as a professional than if the boy had been his own son.

Nearly a year later, on the day the boy graduated from the university, a letter arrived reminding him of the train conversation and urging him once again to start immediately on his C.L.U. studies. The Easterner also informed the boy that he had asked Dr. David McCahan, then Dean of the American College, to send information on courses of study, texts and other pertinent data to the young man.

Companies had little in the way of training courses at that time and C.L.U. study took the place of sales training. There were no formal classes; it was necessary to pursue a course of home study, getting text books from the library or buying them as required. Getting started in a new business at age 21, in the depths of the depression, was not easy. There were many times when the young man was discouraged to the point of giving up the life insurance business. But it seemed that every time he found himself in that mood, another letter would arrive from the Easterner—no longer a stranger now; through correspondence he had become a valued counselor and friend. These periodic letters were sent to check up on the young man, to see whether he was diligently pursuing his C.L.U. studies, to offer assistance and encourage him to keep it up even though the going was rough. The personal interest of the stranger strengthened the young man's resolution; he persisted and the following June took and passed three of the examinations. No sooner had the results been released than he received a very heartwarming letter from his friend offering congratulations and urging him to complete his studies. A year later the final examinations were completed. It was hard to know who was more delighted—the young man who had just completed the course or his long-distance sponsor back in Philadelphia!

As you may have guessed by now, I was that young man. The stranger from Philadelphia whose name meant nothing to me when I first met him was the late Irvin Bendiner, C.L.U., multi-million dollar producer, perennial company leader, and author of some of the finest life insurance literature ever turned out in this country.

Irvin Bendiner was at the pinnacle of his career. He was one of the busiest men in the entire insurance world.

To lead the important Examination Board after Mr. Bendiner's death, James Elton Bragg was named chairman. Mr. Bragg had

Irvin Bendiner. (*Blank & Stoller*)

become a C.L.U. in 1933. He was president of the American Society in 1944-45, and was elected a trustee of the College in 1945. For many years he was a professor of life insurance at the New York University School of Commerce, Accounts, and Finance. He rendered a tremendous service to the life insurance industry through his university courses and his many summer courses at various places about the country. He was a prolific writer, contributing to insurance trade and technical journals, and a very popular speaker in great demand among university and life underwriter audiences. Long associated, as manager, with the Guardian Life of New York, he also served the Union Central and the Manhattan Life. He was always active in life underwriter association affairs. This kind of experience in education and life insurance made Mr. Bragg a logical choice for the Examination Board leadership. His devotion to the C.L.U. idea, his judicious temperament, and his warm personality enabled him to give unusual service in this capacity until his death in 1957. Dr. Huebner said of him:

> Elton Bragg, in his quiet and effective manner, was a key figure in the implementation of major educational policy decisions regarding the College in the period of his service as chairman of the Examination Board and as a trustee. In his quiet but forceful way he accomplished an immense amount of good on behalf of the C.L.U. program in his service to the College and to the American Society.

James Elton Bragg was one of the half dozen most valuable men in the first 30 years of C.L.U. history, in the opinion of Howard H. Cammack, C.L.U. (1929) and president of the American Society of Chartered Life Underwriters, 1950-51. Mr. Cammack worked closely with him in C.L.U. affairs for many years. He said Mr. Bragg had a real gift for negotiation. He could act as a buffer between discordant elements in a group, having somehow the ability to take the sting from opposing positions. Mr. Cammack recalled that often at the end of a meeting full of conflict and apparently without progress, Mr. Bragg would summarize

James Elton Bragg.

and introduce unifying factors. He stated things in a nonrigid way that did not arouse antagonism, and "somehow you got somewhere."

M. Luther Buchanan, of Boston, president of the American Society in 1943-44, is credited by many with vitalizing the Society. He got out among C.L.U.s all over the country, asking questions, seeking strengths, probing for weaknesses, and crystallizing a vision of what the Society might become. As president the next year, Mr. Bragg built on this foundation. He unified the Society, and forged it into a tool for the strong support of the College educational program. The graduates had from the beginning been the strength of the College, but he helped harness that strength and guide it along a track which led to high goals.

In 1944, the public relations committees of the College and the Society met jointly. They were: Joseph H. Reese, chairman; Julian S. Myrick and Earl R. Trangmar for the College; Charles E. Brewer, Jr., chairman; Walter A. Craig and Benjamin Alk for the Society. They discussed all phases of communication problems for the two organizations—how to build the image of the College program for the industry, for members, and for the public; how to promote the educational programs of the College and the Society. The immediate result was a booklet, *C.L.U. on the March*, a well-organized statement of what the C.L.U. movement is and what it accomplishes. In the first year, 17,000 copies were distributed. It crystallized common objectives for all friends of the C.L.U. movement, and brought the two organizations into a new phase of team work. The deliberations of the joint committee demonstrated again the value of understanding and cooperation between the College and the Society through their official representatives. The College, therefore, added the Society's vice president ex officio to its Board (as the Society's president had been for some time), and the Society in 1945 made the College president and dean ex officio members of the Society Board of Directors. Thus, in various ways, a wonderful foundation was created for expanded programs after the war.

Chapter 16

THREE GREAT TESTS:
A RECORD OF ACHIEVEMENT

From the great depression through World War II, the American College met three great tests. Could it survive financially? Could it maintain its academic standards and concept of broadbased education for life underwriters, and at the same time attract constantly increasing numbers of candidates? Could it pursue its course during the war without ruinous setbacks or deflections?

Each test was passed successfully, if not without stress. The establishment of the Cooperative Fund for Underwriter Training, through the leadership of the Association of Life Agency Officers, united the life insurance companies of the country to give permanent financial support to the College by financial aid to their own candidates. The Fund was planned so that it has grown naturally through the years with the growth of the business and the needs of increasing numbers of C.L.U. students. The Fund has given the College financial resources for a broad program of field supervision of C.L.U. studies in colleges and universities and in local groups. It has provided the means for publications necessary to candidates' effective preparation for the C.L.U. examinations.

The American College also successfully met the challenge and competition of study courses on a less academic level. The Board conclusively reaffirmed its commitment to the college-level, broad-based program. It accepted criticisms of its operations and worked out plans for strengthening procedures while maintaining

214

flexibility and realistic adjustment to the needs of those served by it. Coming to grips with this situation was rewarded by success in recruiting increasing numbers of new candidates, even before the end of the war.

In fact, the war seemed to prove the vitality of the American College. It was a great testimony to the program that many classes did continue during the period in spite of travel difficulties, pressures of "home front" responsibilities, the emotional distractions of the times, and the interruptions in leadership as young men everywhere were called into service. The follow-up program of the College with servicemen was a morale builder. It had a real part in channeling career-minded life underwriters back to the job promptly. During the war the College crystallized its own plans for aggressive expansion. The progress of College affairs was undoubtedly slowed down by the war, but the course was steadily forward toward established objectives.

In all these tests, the C.L.U.s themselves were a strong reinforcement. Their records of accomplishments as C.L.U.s influenced the companies in providing important financial support to C.L.U. students as well as to the College. Their prestige and commitment to the highest objectives for the College made possible the reaffirmation of College standards. Their willingness to sell the idea and their recruitment of candidates meant continued growth of the movement which was essential to its continued life. Through the war years, C.L.U.s all over the country were particularly valuable in maintaining classes and building for the future. In the midst of the war, the leaders of the American Society did particularly creative work in their own organization and in co-operation with the College.

It was in this period that the Society developed as a real partner in the College program. The final page of *C.L.U. on the March* summarized achievements and looked to the future:

. . . All that has been presented in this booklet is at best merely a partial record—only a preview of the possibilities in the profession of Chartered Life Underwriter. The recognition enjoyed by physicians, lawyers, architects, certified public accountants, and by members of many other distinguished professions, has not been achieved in a day, or a decade; it is the result rather of the labors of many men through many generations. The remarkable fact about the Chartered Life Underwriter program is that so much has been accomplished in so short a time. . . . Few if any of the professions can show such progress in a comparable period, and this, perhaps more than anything else, testifies to the soundness of the concept on which the American College of Life Underwriters, the American Society, and the C.L.U. have built. The American Society has come to enjoy the respect of other recognized professional societies; the College enjoys this equal respect among educational institutions; and the individual C.L.U. is, according to his merit, winning like recognition in cities and towns everywhere throughout the nation. . . . These first years have been pioneering years, years of blazing trails and clearing the way. The man now undertaking to become a C.L.U. is the beneficiary of the large work that already has been done. . . . The interests of the College, of the American Society, of the local chapter, and of the individual C.L.U., are mutual and interdependent. Each can go forward only if all go forward as one. Nor should any doubt that this can be done. The future is certified by the great work already accomplished. Let us, then, assure that certainty by going forward *together* and by so doing make this certainty doubly certain.

C.L.U. is, in truth, on the march!

Chapter 17

THE GIs COME HOME

Some important C.L.U. projects were waiting for the war to end, and were launched within a year after V-J Day. Even before the end of the war, Howard H. Cammack got planning underway for a postgraduate summer session. He was the chairman of the committee which, with Laurence J. Ackerman as dean, enrolled 39 C.L.U.s for the first Institute of the American Society of Chartered Life Underwriters at the University of Connecticut in June, 1946. The Storrs experiment was a great success, and in each subsequent summer, other Institutes have been held on university campuses across the country. C.L.U.s recognize their professional obligation for continuous study, and hundreds of life underwriters over the years have benefited greatly from these sessions.

A second project of major significance was publication of *The Journal of the American Society of Chartered Life Underwriters*, long a dream of the College and C.L.U. leaders. The first year's editorial board was James Elton Bragg, Karl K. Krogue, William S. Leighton, and Martin I. Scott, with Walter A. Craig, chairman. All these men were devoted, enthusiastic workers in the cause, but Walter Craig's services as editor were valuable beyond measure. He was a graduate of the University of Pennsylvania, where he had played football and was editor-in-chief of the *Red and Blue*. He had been a life underwriter since 1923, a C.L.U. since 1929, and an active member of local, state, and national life underwriter and C.L.U. organizations. In 1946, he was awarded the President's Cup of the Philadelphia Association of Life Underwriters. As the name indicated, the *Journal* was a project of the

Society, but the College guaranteed early financial support. *Journal* subscriptions were offered to the public as well as to C.L.U.s, and from the beginning the publication had a wide audience among trust officers, attorneys, accountants, bankers, and educators.

The titles of articles and authors in the first issue, for September, 1946, indicate the quality standards the quarterly has maintained consistently through the years.

New Horizons in Life Insurance—S. S. Huebner, Ph.D., Sc.D., Professor of Insurance, University of Pennsylvania

The Creation of Estate Plans—Mayo Adams Shattuck, Attorney, Boston

Life Insurance and Rising Prices—M. Albert Linton, President, Provident Mutual Life Insurance Company

Valuation of Business Interests—Deane C. Davis, Vice President and General Counsel, National Life Insurance Company of Vermont

The Search for Economic Security—Marcus Nadler, Ph.D., Professor of Banking and Finance, New York University

Collateral Assignments of Life Insurance Policies—John V. Bloys, Assistant General Counsel, Life Insurance Association of America

The Insured and Beneficiary in Common Disaster—Warner F. Haldeman, Associate Counsel, Penn Mutual Life Insurance Company

The Spendthrift Clause in Life Insurance—John Barker, Jr., Counsel, New England Mutual Life Insurance Company

The homecoming of thousands of GIs stimulated C.L.U. activities throughout the country. The *Annual Report* for 1947 carried the jubilant headline: "A Year of Full Recovery—Results Surpass the Prewar High Record of 1939." Up from the 1944 low point, 2,564 candidates took examinations in 1947 (compared to 706), and 1,655 new candidates were enrolled (compared with 260). Statistically, it was by all odds the banner year in College history.

In this twentieth anniversary year, the College proudly reported that 2,999 candidates had completed the entire series of examinations, 2,801 holding the C.L.U. designation and 78 the certificate of proficiency. The balance had not yet completed experience requirements. Another 4,496 candidates had completed part of the examinations. One hundred-eighty-seven study groups had been active during the year with 4,517 students enrolled. The national scope of activities is indicated by the annotated map in the Appendix.

The twentieth anniversary of the College was recognized in celebrations across the country. Joseph H. Reese had been named chairman of a special committee to arrange a dignified observance of this important milestone in College history. C.L.U.s frequently cooperated with local life underwriter associations in meetings where a College officer or trustee was the speaker. Naturally, the theme of the talks usually was the development of the concept of professional life underwriting, and the history of the progress of the College. During the spring of 1947, the insurance magazines were full of news:

> . . . Atlanta was the first to stage an event recognizing the twentieth anniversary of the founding of the American College of Life Underwriters . . . In observance of the anniversary of the American College the St. Louis Chapter of the American Society presented Mayo Adams Shattuck before a joint meeting of the Chapter, the Corporate Fiduciaries Association and the Life and Trust Council . . . the Indianapolis Chapter held its long-planned anniversary luncheon with 150 guests . . . the Detroit Chapter enjoyed a most successful twentieth anniversary meeting . . . the Richmond Association of Life Underwriters and the Richmond Chapter held an outstanding meeting . . . the Baltimore Chapter had a notable gathering of the city's leading life underwriters and many prominent citizens to commemorate the founding of the American College . . . the Grand Rapids Association held a special anniversary celebration for the American College and the Grand Rapids Chapter of the Society was formally instituted.

These high lights suggest the way C.L.U.s all over the country took advantage of the anniversary occasion. The events emphasized the cordial relations between C.L.U.s and underwriters generally, and presented to the public the concept of the professional life insurance salesman.

Through the activities of Cecil North and Earl Trangmar, the Life Insurance Agency Management Association inspired cooperation among the companies in time devoted to the C.L.U. program at company conventions, in company publications, and in other special promotion.

Joseph H. Reese. (*Bachrach*)

The National Association of Life Underwriters not only cooperated through local associations, but also dedicated the March issue of *Life Association News* to the C.L.U. The C.L.U. conferment dinner at the N.A.L.U. annual convention in Boston naturally featured College history. At the American College Hour session of the convention, Trygve Lie, secretary general of the United Nations, was the speaker. His acceptance of the College's invitation was an honor which measured the stature the College had attained in its two decades.

Incidentally, a practical mark of commendation was given the College about this time. The Insurance Commissioner of Pennsylvania issued a directive waiving the written examination for license in the case of Chartered Life Underwriters desiring to do business in the State.

The Journal of the American Society of Chartered Life Underwriters also dedicated its March, 1947, issue to the anniversary. Special historical articles were written by Walter Craig, Ernest J. Clark, Dr. Huebner, and Dr. McCahan.

With the end of the war, it had been possible to step up publishing activities. In 1945, an Examination Board subcommittee, with James Elton Bragg as chairman, made a detailed and thoughtful study of the need for new and more adequate study material for examination preparation. Dr. John A. Stevenson was named editor-in-chief in 1946, and over the next several years gave leadership and expert advice in the development of books and brochures. Representative are Gilbert T. Stephenson's *Estates and Trusts*, published by Appleton-Century-Crofts, Incorporated, in 1949, and the seven new brochures listed in the *Annual Report* for 1948. The titles indicate the contemporary changes professional underwriters were seeking to recognize and understand.

Needs and the Life Underwriter
Fundamentals of Federal Old Age and Survivor's Insurance
Fundamentals of Government Life Insurance and Related Benefits
Changing Patterns in the Distribution of the National Income

Inflationary Versus Deflationary Factors in Our Post War Economy
Investments of Life Insurance Companies—Their Changing Fron-
tiers
Developments in Governmental Supervision of Insurance

In the reassessment of study material and scope of examinations, general field comment was invited to contribute to the
thought of committees and subcommittees. Many C.L.U. students
will smile to know that a question raised frequently concerned
inclusion of the mathematics of rates and reserves in the examination for the first Part. Many candidates through the years have
come to grief on those questions. Generally, the passing ratio for
the first examination has been poorer than any of the others. At
last there was so much talk on the subject that the Examination
Board felt constrained to make a strong and formal statement:

> . . . a study of the mathematical principles is essential to an under-
> standing of the soundness and equity of the methods used by life
> insurance companies in sharing risks. It is their strong belief [of
> the Subcommittee on Examination Questions] that such a knowl-
> edge is essential to comprehending the heart and soul of the legal
> reserve life insurance system. This point of view was endorsed by
> the Examination Board as a whole . . . in continuing the use of a
> question regarding the mathematics of life insurance.

The College also continued its high standard for determining
a candidate's eligibility for examinations. In 1947, the trustees
voted to adopt the General Educational Development tests as a
measure of high school education equivalence. This was a great
help to many candidates who had not completed high school, or
who had no school records available in the United States.

When the College was faced with the news that its office space,
which had become inadequate anyway, would not be re-leased in
1949, a committee to locate new quarters was appointed. It included Joseph H. Reese, chairman, with John A. Stevenson and
Sewell W. Hodge. Preliminary reports of its considerations led
the trustees to suggest a permanent home for the College and So-

Walter A. Craig.

ciety, financed in part by funds of the Edward A. Woods Foundation. With this new objective, the Quarters Committee, and especially Mr. Reese, resumed their efforts with enthusiasm. By personally canvassing the University of Pennsylvania neighborhood,
which had been tentatively selected as the desirable location, Mr.
Reese discovered a handsome old brick and stucco residence that
had possibilities. This was purchased and remodeled to provide
comfortable accommodations for the American College, the
American Society, the S. S. Huebner Foundation, the American
Institute for Property and Liability Underwriters, and the Society
of Chartered Property and Casualty Underwriters.

In this project, the Penn Mutual Life Insurance Company was
especially helpful. Dr. Stevenson, the company's president, was
a member of the committee. Mr. Dechert, counsel for the College,

also had been a staff member of the company's law department. LeRoy E. Varner, A. Barton Lewis, and Harry L. Baker, Jr., of the company's engineering department, gave helpful advice and practical aid. Last, but by no means least, a 20-year, 4 per cent mortgage for $55,000 was arranged with the Penn Mutual. Without it, the purchase would have been impossible. The trustees commented in official minutes that "few can realize the enormous amount of work" done by the Quarters Committee who "surveyed the whole problem, ascertained the needs of the College and Society, found and selected the premises, negotiated an advantageous purchase, supervised the alterations and repairs, arranged a sound and satisfactory plan of financing."

The dedication of 3924 Walnut Street in 1948 established "the first permanent national center of insurance education on the collegiate and professional level," the insurance press reported. The occasion brought together insurance producers, company executives, and educators to pay tribute to the founding fathers and current leaders of the American College.

The Philadelphia Chapter of the American Society, Eugene C. DeVol, president, sponsored the dedication luncheon attended by some 250 people. Julian S. Myrick was the toastmaster. Leroy A. Lincoln, president of the Metropolitan Life and the Life Insurance Association of America, and Clifford H. Orr, president of the National Association of Life Underwriters, spoke for the industry. Harold E. Stassen, president of the University of Pennsylvania, made the principal address. He referred to the fact that 20 years earlier there were only 21 C.L.U.s, and now there were over three thousand, with 125 in Philadelphia alone. He stated that our American free economy could not function without the insurance principle freely applied so that the risks inherent in our system could be spread widely. Then he continued:

> Three things determine the future of life insurance. First, if beneficiaries and policyholders feel that the programs arranged for them have been soundly conceived; second, if the investments of life insurance companies prove sound, both from the company viewpoint

and from the broad viewpoint of their benefit to society; and third, if the story of the benefits of insurance is effectively carried to the free people of a free nation. Only if these three tests are met will the institution of life insurance flourish.

Another guest whose presence gave special pleasure to Dr. Huebner on this significant day was Dr. Emory R. Johnson. Mr.

Sewall W. Hodge.

Myrick introduced him as "Dr. Huebner's mentor" and stated that "although unheralded and unsung he did much in early days to help urge the realization of the College objective" and especially "always emphasized a national pattern." Dr. Johnson was the University of Pennsylvania department head under whom Dr. Huebner first taught. He had unselfishly promoted the separation of the insurance courses so that Dr. Huebner might become head of his own department. He also wisely and sympathetically encouraged and guided Dr. Huebner in the strategic formative years of the College, using frequently words which Dr. Huebner still quotes: "Make it national!"

The day of the dedication there was a special meeting of the trustees, chiefly to express thanksgiving and mutual congratulations for all that the new building symbolized. Trustees present were: Julian S. Myrick, S.S. Huebner, David McCahan, Sewell W. Hodge, Ernest J. Clark, James Elton Bragg, Chester O. Fischer, John Marshall Holcombe, Jr., J. Roger Hull, George L. Hunt, Joseph H. Reese, and Harold M. Stewart. Guests were: Alexander C. Robinson, IV, grandson of Edward A. Woods; Ross M. Trump, assistant dean; Earl Trangmar; John P. Williams; and representatives of the American Society, Walter A. Craig, Frederick W. Floyd, Carl M. Spero, Harry Hoffman, Raymond C. Johnson, Douglas S. Perry, Alice E. Roché.

Dr. Harry J. Loman with Dr. Huebner at the doorway of 3924 Walnut Street, Philadelphia. (*Shaw*)

The new headquarters offered an appropriate opportunity for tributes and memorials. The board room was furnished in honor of Julian S. Myrick by the trustees of the College and the directors of the Society. His company, the Mutual Life of New York, gave a fine portrait of Mr. Myrick to be hung in the room. The presentation was made by Roger Hull, a College trustee and then vice president of the company. Mr. Myrick had been a friend of the College from the beginning, and chairman of the trustees since 1938. Dr. Huebner characterized his service: "He has been a most efficient chairman of our Board, always on the job, and never letting things wait—a patient, diplomatic force in the solution of difficult problems."

John Henry Russell furnished the reception room in memory of his father, John Newton Russell, one of the four key men Ernest J. Clark had committed to the vision which resulted in the American College, and one of the incorporators and directors of the College.

Mrs. Marjory Woods Robinson, daughter of Edward A. Woods, gave the College a portrait of her father and a valuable collection of ivories which had been one of his personal pleasures. Mrs. Robinson suggested that the College might keep certain designated items and sell whatever else they wished. The attractive display, long admired in the reception room of 3924 Walnut, is now in the library of Huebner Hall.

Ernest J. Clark, one of the founders and long the president of the College, provided his own portrait for the headquarters collection.

C.L.U.s all over the world contributed to the purchase of a portrait of Dr. Huebner by Alice Kent Stoddard. The painting was presented by Howard H. Cammack on behalf of the members of the American Society, of which he was then president, at a dramatic unveiling at the N.A.L.U. 1950 convention in Washington. This portrait hung in the reception room of 3924 Walnut Street until it was transferred to the place of honor in the College library in Bryn Mawr.

The College had been founded and supported by young men,

Garden view of the 3924 Walnut Street Headquarters building. (*Shaw*)

and the continuity in the ranks of its leaders had been quite remarkable. Now, after 20 years, death seemed to hit often. In
1948, George E. Lackey died. He had contributed greatly to the
cause as an early C.L.U., a director, and for many years a member of the Executive Committee. He was well known as the successful general agent in Detroit for the Massachusetts Mutual,
a vigorous and popular speaker, N.A.L.U. president for 1930-31,
prominent in the American Society, and its 1942-43 president.

In 1949, the College lost one of its stalwart supporters in the ranks of home office executives. O. J. Arnold was president and chairman of the board of the Northwestern National Life Insurance Company. Mr. Arnold had given his company's help to the College from the early days, and had served as director.

Within a few months, William M. Duff also died. Mr. Duff was a pioneer C.L.U. in the class of 1928. He became a director the same year, and served all his life. He was secretary of the College for several years, vice president later, for 16 years a member of the Registration Board, chairman of the original committee for the Edward A. Woods Foundation, and long a member of the difficult Committee on Irregular Cases. He was a real pillar of the College structure.

The Committee on Irregular Cases handled chiefly the sensitive matters of moral qualifications of C.L.U. candidates. "A good moral character" was from the beginning a prerequisite for granting the C.L.U. designation, and the College took this qualification very seriously. For some years, confidential inspection reports were received for all candidates. Later, confidential

Reception room at 3924 Walnut Street.

statements from companies, managers, and others were used. Mr. Duff was for years chairman of this Committee, and with Counsel Robert Dechert gave much attention to these delicate problems. For instance, it was reported circumspectly that "there was considerable unhappiness" as to "the possible awarding of the designation" to a candidate who was known to show "extraordinary violence and unjustifiable abuse" to local life underwriters. He had been expelled from the association, and in turn was suing the association. Another candidate, who was a lawyer as well as a life underwriter, had made away with some $20,000 of clients' funds.

Another great loss, also in 1949, came in the death of Dr. John A. Stevenson. The trustees paid "tribute to a distinguished friend and leader" for "his unusually significant contribution to the progress and welfare of the College." He had been a director and member of the Executive Committee since 1934, chairman of the Registration Board 1933–43, member of the Agency Management Examination Committee since 1931, editor-in-chief of new publications after the war, and, of course, a most valuable worker in the new headquarters building project. The trustees' resolution said in part:

Beginning his professional career in the ranks of education and winning distinction therein for originality, creative spirit and dynamic personality, which characterized him as a writer, teacher and educational administrator, he entered the business arena, where his talents were rapidly recognized by his advancement to the high executive post which he attained in becoming president of the Penn Mutual Life Insurance Company. . . . John Stevenson was a stanch believer in the broad economic and social mission of life insurance and in the essential worth of the life underwriter through whom it would find practical adaptation to the individual needs. He was an ardent supporter of professional standards on a high plane, and a long-time proponent of educational principles which blended the practical with the theoretical. All of these found expression in the aims and activities of the College, and in the promotion thereof he was especially fitted to serve the College exceptionally well.

In the summer of 1950, the cause of the C.L.U. suffered another blow in the sudden death of Walter A. Craig, editor of *The Journal of the American Society of Chartered Life Underwriters.* He had had the cooperation of two superbly qualified associate editors since early 1947, in place of the original Editorial Board. These associates were Harry Krueger, whose entire business life had been in life insurance with the Northwestern Mutual, and who was then its general agent in New York City; and Leland T. Waggoner, who also was a life insurance man from the beginning of his business career, and was at that time in Boston as manager of Mutual Life of New York's leading agency. These three men had worked together most effectively, making the *Journal* in four years what Raymond C. Johnson, then chairman of the College-Society Public Relations Committee, called "the greatest public relations activity" of the period for both organizations. The *Journal* had about equal circulation among C.L.U.s and non-C.L.U.s who were largely professional people outside the industry. It was giving the professional life underwriter a highly favorable image among the associated professions.

In the midst of the great losses to the College in the years immediately after the war were the new recruits in the crusade for professional life underwriting. One of these, a young man returned from service, was Davis W. Gregg, a Huebner fellow who became assistant dean in October, 1949. In reporting his appointment, the trustees spoke of his scholastic attainments and his effective work at The Ohio State University and with the life underwriters in Columbus. They concluded, "From the standpoint of personality, ability, interest and initiative, Dr. Gregg should become a real asset to the College."

Chapter 18

NEW BLOOD

The exciting progress of the College in the years immediately after the war could not hide disturbing undercurrents of criticism and discontent. Many people—far too many—were speaking out about personal disappointments in their C.L.U. experiences: these examinations were too hard; the work was too academic; they were not honored as C.L.U.s as they expected to be, and so on. Tensions were building up. Misunderstandings were multiplying. Clearly the College must again project a vision of its objectives. It must establish channels of communication with industry leaders and the average field man.

One of Dr. Gregg's first assignments was a study of these problems. With Leroy G. Steinbeck, newly appointed executive manager of the Society, he made a comprehensive analysis of what he called the "audiences" of the College. These were divided into 11 classes such as C.L.U.s, underwriters not C.L.U.s, home office agency executives, university teachers, and others. The action suggested for these audiences included eight research studies, 10 new publications, field visits, group conferences, and various other activities. The study, submitted to the trustees as a 21-page report, was warmly received. The Board voted a special fund of $15,000 to implement the recommendations.

A factor in the situation probably was that the Life Underwriter Training Council program had created some confusion in the minds of field men and in home offices. Urged to support both C.L.U. and L.U.T.C., home offices felt that the differences in their functions should be clarified. There was some discussion of the feasibility of permitting credit in the C.L.U. program for candidates who had successfully completed L.U.T.C. courses. Such a proposal overlooked the fact that the American College had established high professional standards which had to be maintained. If the College were to surrender any aspect of its examination of candidates, the effect on the significance of the C.L.U. designation would be disastrous. Especially for this reason, a new presentation of the distinctive character and the objectives of the College was called for.

There also came a decline in the number of new C.L.U. candidates and graduates. The international situation naturally had its part in these difficulties. The developments in the Korean "police action" were reflected in general college and university enrollments, and many young people were "disposed for the present to avoid the undertaking of a long-range program."

A major first step toward improving conditions was to make clear the unique purposes of the C.L.U. program. The College and the Life Underwriter Training Council named a joint committee to help clarify the situation so far as those two organizations were concerned. The members were James Elton Bragg, Earl Trangmar, Raymond C. Johnson, Orville E. Beal, Hubert E. Davis, and Edward L. Reiley, chairman. Their considerations paved the way to a new program of cooperation. Reporting for the committee to the College trustees, Mr. Reiley said:

At the outset the Committee agreed that the promotion of L.U.T.C. should emphasize the development of skill in the use of basic insurance information and principles; that emphasis in the promotion of C.L.U. should be on the acquisition of knowledge, the breadth and depth of which provides a basis of professional activity. Both courses should emphasize in their promotion the attitudes and ideals of an underwriter. . . .

It was further agreed that promotion material and particularly that which is released by the National Association of Life Underwriters should emphasize the correlation of the two programs as integral parts of a broad institutional movement, and also the fact that the life underwriter who first completes the L.U.T.C. course should continue his personal development by following the C.L.U. program.

With united effort to differentiate the purposes and scope of the C.L.U. and L.U.T.C. programs, the College stressing the *acquisition* of knowledge and the Council the development of skill in the *use* of knowledge, appreciation of both increased. Cooperation between the organizations ripened into the cordial and mutually helpful relationship which exists today.

From the beginning, a constant hazard to good public relations between the College and life underwriters generally was the great number of candidates who failed examinations. In spite of ample publicity concerning the high standards of the College, many poorly prepared people came to sit for the examinations. The fault was sometimes in the student who underestimated the requirements. Sometimes the lack of adequate preparatory resources was the reason. The Educational Advisory Department, which meant almost solely John P. Williams, had been making strenuous efforts to remedy the situation. In 1948–49, for instance, the Department conducted three regional conferences in Dallas, Atlanta, and Columbus, Ohio, for study group teachers and key local C.L.U.s, and visited C.L.U.s in 71 cities of 26 states in an effort to promote understanding of requirements and improve preparation.

Southern Methodist University developed a correspondence study course based on effective work done by J. Carlton Smith, Southwestern Life Insurance Company educational director, in his carefully supervised and well motivated plan for his own company. The University of Wisconsin and Washington State University also experimented with correspondence courses. The College approved of these plans and encouraged them, but felt they were not really an adequate substitute for personal group study.

Following the recommendations of the Gregg report, the College stepped up its program of revision and expansion of study supplements and brochures, and published a greatly enlarged teacher's manual for each study part. It started the monthly publication *Teacher Topics*, which gave teachers and group leaders a clearing house for ideas on teaching techniques and motivation, and brought practical help to those working in a new field.

Considerable publicity was given to the Examination Board. Emphasis was placed on its function in determining the scope of C.L.U. study, its part in formulating the examination questions, and particularly its membership of five practical life insurance men and four people professionally engaged in life insurance education.

A number of eminent professors at the University of Pennsylvania made up the majority of the Board of Graders in the early years of the College. As the required number of graders increased, representatives from other institutions of higher learning served on the Board. Now the geographical distribution of members covers the entire country. In addition to the professional educators, successful businessmen and C.L.U.s also have been invited regularly to round out the Board membership. Among those who played a prominent part in the grading process for many years were: John R. Abersold, Edward M. Aiken, George L. Amrhein, William T. Beadles, Edward W. Carter, Bernard F. Cataldo, James J. Gallagher, Jr., Benjamin M. Gaston, John F. Jeremiah, Clyde M. Kahler, Richard deR. Kip, Chester A. Kline, Dan M. McGill, J. C. Phillips, Charles A. Rohlfing, David T. Rowlands, Karl W. H. Scholz, Donald Scoles, Leroy B. Scott, Herbert E. Sim, Carl Stern, Arthur I. Sternhell, F. J. Stevenson, W. E. Warrington, and Charles M. Weber.

Throughout the years, the educational officers of the College played an active role in grading. In addition to the present officers, consisting of Messrs. Crowe, Dotterweich, Graebner, Gregg, Hallman, Horn, and Keir, others who have served while officers are: Arthur W. Mason; Albert H. Clark, assistant director of examinations, 1959–60; William M. Howard, director of educational publications, 1953–54; Daniel P. Kedzie, director of management education, 1960–61; Thomas J. Luck, director of management education, 1956–58; Ross M. Trump, assistant dean, 1947–49; and James R. Young, director of publications, 1952.

Members of the Board of Graders contributed not only their experience and knowledge to this important task, but also contributed to other educational matters of the College. A complete listing of Board members who served five years or more is found in Appendix E.

The process of grading according to accepted academic standards was publicized repeatedly. Many disappointed candidates were interested to learn—but not really comforted—that papers which appeared near or below passing always were graded a second time by another person. Then borderline examinations had a further appraisal by a Review Panel. Of course, graders never knew whose examination was being marked, since each was identified only by number. The whole procedure was as error-proof as any ever devised, and the graders were competent and specially briefed for the task.

A special effort was made to have candidates understand the group judgment involved in grading. The College described in detail how the grading panel sat at the same time the examinations were being taken, and, in effect, took the examinations orally. The graders individually and collectively contributed the answer to each question, while a secretary made careful notes. They itemized factors which should be required in a correct answer, and decided on answers that would be rejected as incorrect. Then, as a group they decided how the 10 points of credit for the question should be distributed among the factors which would make up a complete answer. Following this basic work, each grader graded approximately 20 books, using the key. Then they again compared notes as a group to see how their original basis for grading had worked out in practice. They agreed on any additional answers that would be accepted, any additional points that would be rejected, and changes, if any, that should be made in distribution of the 10 points of credit. This group consideration of what constituted acceptable answers increased the candidate's faith in the examination process. Essentially the same procedure is followed still for the essay questions.

The increased supporting activity of the College strained the budget. Examination fees were raised in 1951 to $30 for each part, $15 from the student and $15 through a credit certificate backed by the Cooperative Fund for Underwriter Training. The first great increase in financial resources for the College had come when the Fund was organized under the auspices of the Association of Life Agency Officers. At that time, the credit certificate idea was adopted, and the Fund matched the $10-per part fee paid by the student. The Fund has continued to match a candidate's fees with contributions from the Cooperative Fund, if the student's company is a Fund participator.

In 1950, the American College gave major support to a collateral educational activity of great significance. The Graduate Workshop in Family Financial Security Education was carried on, under a grant from the Institute of Life Insurance, by a national committee of which Dr. McCahan was a member. Thirty-three teachers and educational supervisors from high school systems throughout the country came together for summer sessions at the University of Pennsylvania. They received regular graduate credit for their work. They studied various subject matter having to do with family financial security, and converted the material into teaching units for use in secondary schools. A substantial amount of time was given to life insurance, and Dr. Huebner was scheduled for several lectures. This project was a definite success. The whole program has grown over the years, and recently similar workshops have been held each summer at about a dozen university campuses from California to Connecticut. The formal university courses have enrolled about 6,000 teachers and administrators from cities and towns all over the country. At home, these educators have participated in local programs of in-service training and workshops which have reached 8,000 others. In addition to Dr. Huebner and Dr. McCahan, Dr.

Gregg and Dean Graebner have had important parts in this activity.

In the midst of these great pressures and the need to expand services, the College rather suddenly received several crippling blows. Dr. McCahan had a serious heart attack early in 1951. Mr. Williams became ill and left the College in June. Edmond H. Curcuru, the new director of promotional services who had begun important work, was called back to the army due to the Korean action.

During this period, four outstanding educators made major contributions to the welfare of the College. They were Dr. Dan M. McGill, Professor William T. Beadles, Professor Herbert C. Graebner, and J. Carlton Smith. These men took responsibility for special projects, served as consultants, and generally gave their support to the whole College program. Without them, progress at this time could not have been accomplished.

The need for this help, so well supplied, resulted largely from the fact that the College still had only part-time leadership. Dr. Huebner and Dr. McCahan were members of the faculty at the University of Pennsylvania as they had been throughout their association with the College, and they carried many other responsibilities. The work of the College had grown so fast, and Dr. Huebner and Dr. McCahan had extended themselves so vigorously to meet the demands of the situation, that the trustees did not realize how greatly the College needed full-time service at the officers' level. Up to this time, with the exception of Ross Trump's short tenure and John Williams' longer service, no other persons devoted their entire effort to the American College on the executive level.

Mr. Myrick told the trustees squarely that the College had been understaffed for years, that he believed Dr. McCahan's health had been broken because of the tremendous load he had carried, and that the College "must under no circumstances permit the situation to exist in the future." He emphasized that it would "be cheaper in the long run to have the executive staff of the College carry a normal load, that they could be more creative and that the College would gain from the standpoint of not losing people due to health reasons."

That summer of 1951 Dr. McCahan was named executive vice president to assist the president and work with the dean. Dr. Gregg was promoted to the office of dean. Dr. Gregg with Dr. Huebner shouldered the work of the Educational Advisory Department, and traveled widely, visiting colleges and life underwriter groups. In the fall, Walter B. Wheeler was added to the staff as director of field services, and Arthur W. Mason, Jr., became director of college relations. They divided between them the work of the Educational Advisory Department.

Dr. Gregg and Leroy Steinbeck undertook that year to rekindle the enthusiasm of C.L.U.s across the country. In a series of carefully planned meetings, they sought to restore understanding and unity, and bring the creative force of C.L.U.s again to building the College program. They aimed to establish two-way communication. With criticisms and questions freely voiced, these young leaders endeavored to give the information and interpretation that would reawaken devotion to the College and its aims.

An important meeting was held in Chicago. There, Lorraine S. Sinton was currently president of what Dr. Huebner said at the time was "just about the best C.L.U. chapter we have anywhere in the country." The chapter membership included John O. Todd and Paul W. Cook and many other members of the Million Dollar Round Table. The aggressive activity of this chapter showed up the dissatisfactions that existed in Chicago as well as in other parts of the country. Many Chicago agencies refused to cooperate with the chapter's candidate recruiting and study programs; and many C.L.U.s refused to join the chapter.

The meeting, called by Miss Sinton, proved historic. It was attended by Dr. Gregg and Mr. Steinbeck, and by more than 20 Chicagoans, half of whom were members of the Million Dollar Round Table. Every effort was made to get full expression of opinion. Notes of the discussions, as well as the memories of those who were there, suggest that it was a cathartic session. One man, who had been a million dollar producer for many years, had earned his C.L.U. for the purpose of being qualified to criticize. The record says:

> He prefaced his remarks by saying that he did not want to attend the meeting but Miss Sinton had insisted that he come and express his thoughts. He stated that ever since his acquaintance with C.L.U. began that his reaction was summarized by the word "disappointment." He said that he feels that the program has definitely retrogressed rather than moved forward, that the entire program is entirely too pedantic and that he has never known anyone who gained any sales advantage from C.L.U. He bitterly criticized the classes he attended at Northwestern and stated that he would not have completed his C.L.U. work had not a close personal friend requested he do so. He said the designation had meant nothing to him and he did not intend to use it. He stated that the present meeting itself indicated that C.L.U. was on the defensive and obviously there was much fundamental weakness in the program.

This was a minority opinion at the meeting, but undoubtedly reflected the feelings of many people around the country. The points raised by the speaker were discussed at length. Pros and cons of a variety of matters were presented, and many negative attitudes were brought out into the healing air of new information and interpretation. The consensus afterward was that this meeting had a tremendous influence in building unity among discordant elements in Chicago, and the effect was wholesome as the news spread elsewhere.

Through 1951, Dr. Gregg, on behalf of the College, was cooperating vigorously with the American Society to promote a "Huebner Class" of new candidates for the 1952 examinations. The New Candidate Committee of the Society had been created to do the vital job of recruiting for growth. James W. Smither, Jr., vice president of the Society, was the chairman. He named five regional chairmen—Hugh S. Bell for the West, William H. Andrews, Jr., for the South, Chester T. Wardwell for the Mid-

Leroy G. Steinbeck.

William H. Andrews, Jr.

west, William B. Hoyer for the Middle East, and C. Lamont Post for the East. The Committee selected C.L.U. leaders in 100 cities across the country to lead in systematizing recruitment and in local promotion. Seven conferences were held in Philadelphia, Atlanta, Dallas, San Francisco, Chicago, Pittsburgh, and Albany. There, plans for the nationwide program were formulated and forces were rallied to enroll a sharply increased number of new students. It was natural to designate this group as the Huebner Class, in honor of the man who had for so long been a key figure in the work, and whose retirement was planned for 1952.

The New Candidate Committee launched its drive with a big luncheon in Philadelphia, attended by many notables and the life insurance press. Nominations of possible candidates were solicited from about the top hundred life insurance companies of the country, and more than ten thousand names were suggested. These were followed up locally, and in 1952, 1,240 new candidates sat for examinations, an increase of 34 per cent over the previous year. The number has gone up every year since, and in 1962 was over four thousand.

One of the truths which emerged from the period of tension and dissension was that any professional movement essentially grows slowly. Progress may seem spectacular, as in the case of the American College in its first 25 years. However, the group of C.L.U.s was really small in comparison with the great army of life underwriters. Public understanding of the designation and its meaning was very limited. The letters C.L.U. had no magic power to transform the man who used them or revolutionize the attitude of the buying public.

A strong group of C.L.U.s in any locality has more influence there than any national advertising or public relations efforts. They are the key people in creating the local image of the C.L.U. They are the most effective proponents of the high professional standards of the academic program. They are the strongest magnets for drawing qualified new candidates into C.L.U. work.

Out of the experiences of the postwar years, the Society came to accept its key responsibility in recruiting, and in the last decade has given incalculable service to the College in this regard. The Joint New Candidate Committee was organized in 1952, with Gerald W. Page, second vice president of the Society, as chairman. There were six other members—two home office men, two field managers and two salesmen. This committee has proved its great value in continuing activities which are among the Society's greatest services to the American College.

Chapter 19

THE SILVER JUBILEE

The year 1952 brought the twenty-fifth anniversary of the College. The Joint Committee on Public Relations of the College and Society named a Subcommittee on the Silver Anniversary which included David B. Fluegelman, Donald E. Lynch, Earl R. Trangmar, and Donald F. Barnes, chairman. These men inspired recognition for the College and its program in a variety of ways. The whole life insurance business became conscious of what the C.L.U. meant and what C.L.U.s were doing.

At regularly scheduled industry functions, the American College and C.L.U.s were featured. For example, the Northwestern Mutual observed the Silver Anniversary at its annual convention. The session was called to order with the ringing of silver bells. Following a dramatic scenario written by Harold W. Gardiner, then educational director for the company, Ben S. McGiveran, first president of the Northwestern Mutual C.L.U. Society, gave a capsule history of the College. Grant L. Hill reviewed the history of the C.L.U. in the Northwestern. Reference was made to Louis A. Walker, Rockland, Maine, the Northwestern agent who took and passed his first C.L.U. examination at the age of seventy-six. Various class groups of C.L.U.s among Northwestern graduates were saluted, and the presentation closed with all C.L.U.s repeating together the C.L.U. pledge.

The regular C.L.U. conferment dinner, held during the National Association of Life Underwriters September convention in Atlantic City, was the occasion for special recognition of the Anniversary. Carl M. Spero, president of the American Society, presided; Dr. Robert L. Johnson, president of Temple University, gave the address; and members of the first graduating class were honored at a special guest table on the platform. In the archives

Portrait of Dr. Huebner by Alice Kent Stoddard (1950).

of the College is a silver-covered dinner program autographed by those members of the class of 1928: L. N. Whitelaw, Grant L. Hill, H. L. Harvey, Lawrence C. Woods, Jr., C. Vivian Anderson, F. J. Stevenson, W. Rankin Furey, Lisle A. Spencer, Maurice S. Tabor, and H. Lawrence Choate.

Later in the fall, the fellowship lunch of the Life Insurance Agency Management Association annual meeting honored the American College, and particularly Dr. Huebner on his retirement as president. A volume presented to Dr. Huebner contained personal letters from presidents of more than two hundred life insurance companies. Likewise, the annual dinner of the Life Managers Association of New York City saluted Dr. Huebner as its guest of honor.

The June, 1952, issue of the C.L.U. *Journal* was a unique tribute to Dr. Huebner in its content, and also to the College in the date of its appearance. The preface to the issue was written by Harold E. Stassen, president of the University of Pennsylvania. He brought into sharp focus the high lights of Dr. Huebner's career with its significance to the University of Pennsylvania and to the American College. His brief historical statement and tribute are repeated here.

Rarely does one find in the life of a university—particularly a university as old as this one—an individual who has made the total contribution to it and to life outside that Dr. Solomon S. Huebner has made in his almost 50 years of service at the University of Pennsylvania. I consider it a great pleasure and privilege to have this opportunity to pay tribute to him and through tribute to him, to join in commemorating the 25th anniversary of the American College of Life Underwriters which he was instrumental in founding and of which he was the first dean.

Dr. Huebner came to the University of Pennsylvania in the fall of 1903 as the recipient of the Harrison Fellowship in Economics to complete his work for his Ph.D. He had already received from the university of his native state—Wisconsin—the Bachelor of Letters in 1902 and the Master of Letters in 1903. It was his master's thesis in *Railway Age* and other journals which was primarily responsible for his being awarded the Harrison Fellowship. Typical of his quest for adventure and his thirst for knowledge, Dr. Huebner was on a bicycle tour of Europe when he received notice of the award. During the next two years, he completed his doctoral thesis on Marine Insurance and received his Ph.D. in Economics in 1905.

At this time the Wharton School of Finance and Commerce of the University of Pennsylvania was one of three collegiate schools of business in the United States and it was the oldest—having been founded in 1881. Courses in applied economics were viewed somewhat with disdain by the classical economists of most universities. An understanding of an important business such as insurance was considered to be outside the tradition of scholarship of a university. But Dr. Huebner thought differently and one morning, after scanning the insurance company reports of the New York Journal of Commerce and being impressed with the fact that the leading business school offered no course to help future business men in this field, he took it upon himself to convey to Provost C. C. Harrison his idea regarding the establishment of a course in insurance. Provost Harrison, himself a man of broad vision and of action, readily saw the merit of the idea and Solomon S. Huebner became the first instructor of insurance at a salary of $500 a year.

Promotion was rapid. In 1906, Dr. Huebner was appointed Assistant Professor of Insurance and Commerce; in 1908, he was made Professor; and in 1913, when it was decided to make Insurance a separate department, he became the Chairman of the Insurance Department. In 1908 he edited the first of a series of books—titled *Insurance*—for the American Academy of Political and Social Science. He had to start his insurance course from nothing. He had to organize the course, write the textbook, and train the teachers who were to become his associates. In 1911 his first book, *Property Insurance*, was published and received immediate recognition in the insurance field. Since then he has been the author of numerous books and articles on all phases of insurance. He has edited the six-volume Appleton *Life Insurance Series* and the American Academy series on insurance and the commodity markets. Frequently voted the most popular professor on campus, recognized by the University with the honorary degree of Doctor of Science in 1931, and elected as a faculty member to the honorary societies of Beta Gamma Sigma and Pi Gamma Mu, Dr. Huebner is a much beloved and greatly respected member of our university family. His idealism and his constructive personal philosophy have been an inspiration to many thousands of students who have had the privilege of his guidance over the years.

Not only has Dr. Huebner been an outstanding teacher and thinker in his field but he approximates the Greek ideal of a man who combines deep knowledge with the successful practical application of that knowledge. As an adviser to a Congressional Committee from 1912 to 1923, he was responsible for the creation of the U.S. Shipping Board and for the formation of the American Marine Insurance Syndicates. His development and popularization of the professional concept of insurance writing resulted in 1927 in the establishment of the American College of Life Underwriters and it was he who developed the now widely used theory of "life value." In 1927-28 he made an around-the-world lecture tour, visiting Japan, China, Philippines, Malaya, Ceylon, India, Egypt and ending with two weeks at the University of Berlin. He has spoken before large audiences in Cuba, Mexico, West Indies, Alaska, and Hawaii and lectured in practically every city in the United States and Canada. On my trip to Japan and Korea in 1950, I received several inquiries about Dr. Huebner from his former students and from persons whom he had met in 1927, which fact bore eloquent testimony to the affectionate regard they held for him and to the remarkable impress he had made upon them. Since drafting the Marine Insurance Act in 1922, Dr. Huebner has served on numerous occasions in an advisory capacity to various government agencies. From 1941 to 1945 he was a member of the War Department's Advisory Committee on Insurance.

In June of this year, Dr. Huebner will retire from his position as Chairman of the Department of Insurance—a post he has held since its inception 39 years ago. Fortunately for the university, he will continue to carry on his teaching. It is altogether fitting that *The Journal* of the American Society of Chartered Life Underwriters pay tribute to Dr. Huebner at the time when the institution of which he was a founder—the American College of Life Underwriters—is commemorating its 25th anniversary. "Sunny Sol"—as he is affectionately known to the thousands of his students—is a pioneer in the formulation and application of insurance principles; he is the dean of insurance teachers in America; he is the founder of the business college insurance courses; and he is considered by the University of Pennsylvania as one of the greatest teachers in its two century history. Education and the life insurance business owe him a debt that can never be repaid.

The articles in this issue of *The Journal* were written by men who had been Dr. Huebner's students. The titles of the articles are interesting in their scope, and the names and identification of the authors are impressive.

"A Collection of Huebnerian Philosophy"
by David McCahan, C.L.U., and Davis W. Gregg, C.L.U., the Executive Vice President and the Dean, The American College of Life Underwriters.

"Traits—Common and Different"
by Paul F. Clark, C.L.U., President, John Hancock Mutual Life Insurance Company.

"The Distribution of Surplus"
by Valentine Howell, Executive Vice President and Actuary, The Prudential Insurance Company of America.

"Life Insurance: A Tool in Estate Planning"
by Robert Irwin Mehr, Professor of Economics, University of Illinois.

"Current Problems on Pension Plans"
by Meyer M. Goldstein, C.L.U., Executive Director, Pension Planning Company.

"Arbitration: A Facet of Pension Planning and Pension Administration"
by Laurence J. Ackerman, Dean, School of Business Administration, University of Connecticut.

"The Agency Executive"
by Lewis W. S. Chapman, C.L.U., Director of Company Relations, Life Insurance Agency Management Association.

"Social Insurance and Private—Contrasts and Similarities"
by C. A. Kulp, Professor of Insurance, Wharton School of Commerce and Finance, University of Pennsylvania.

"Significant Contrasts and Comparisons between Life Insurance and the Various Property and Casualty Insurance Fields"
by Milton W. Mays, Insurance Executives Association.

"Cooperative Endeavor in the Accident and Health Field"
by J. F. Follmann, Jr., General Manager, Bureau of Accident and
Health Underwriters.

The editors of *The Journal* added their tribute in presenting
the Huebner Issue:

> All who have participated in the planning and execution of this spe-
> cial project have taken great satisfaction in paying this unique
> tribute to a man whose contribution to life insurance education has
> been unparalleled and whose influence will continue to grow, as the
> years go on, through the lives of the many who have sat at his feet.

The September, 1952, issue of *Life Association News* was devoted to the C.L.U. It contained articles about the College and
its history, items about prominent C.L.U.s, tributes from educators, and so on.

The Anniversary Committee requested life insurance companies to highlight the C.L.U. movement in some way in their trade
press advertisements in the summer of 1952. Practically every
prominent company did so, and thus was started a practice which
is still generally followed.

The John Hancock Mutual Life had developed an advertising
series for national magazines featuring famous Americans, such
diverse and interesting characters as Paul Revere, Abraham Lincoln, Stephen Foster, Johnny Appleseed, and Theodore Roosevelt. Now, in life insurance magazines, in the familiar format,
the company honored Dr. Huebner and the American College.
Under his picture and the heading, "He ably led, we gladly followed," was the stirring tribute:

> He's past seventy now. But time hasn't touched him inwardly.
> The old energy is still there, and the strong sense of calling,
> and the clear-eyed vision of the goal. He looks the part he's
> always played—a great teacher, a moulder of men.
>
> Talking to him now, you know why Dr. Solomon S. Huebner
> played such a hero's role in the building of today's
> multi-billion dollar life insurance business.

He never sold a dollar's worth of life insurance himself. But he
shaped the minds and inspired the men who have made the
great life insurance sales records of today. He gave us a sense of
our mission as handlers of dreams and hopes, not of dollars
and cents. Physicians, in their moments of self-searching, think
of Hippocrates. We think—or should—of Dr. Huebner.

It was half a century ago when young Solomon Huebner
saw the great need for *trained* young men in business. The
men were available; the training was not. He resolved
to change all that.

He started from scratch. There were few business schools
then, few textbooks, fewer teachers. So, when the
Wharton School announced a course in life insurance, with
Dr. Huebner as its guiding spirit, a new era had quietly
begun, though not many people realized it.

Teacher and students often learned together in
those pioneering days. The textbooks got written;
many he had to write himself. Eventually the
whole country and the nations of the world
began to feel the influence of Solomon S. Huebner. Some of
his students became important in the business world. Some
went out to teach to others what they had learned from him.

That would have been enough for most men. But
Dr. Huebner had just begun.

For fourteen years, he had nourished a dream that was
finally realized with the chartering of the American College
of Life Underwriters. Now all young men who wished to
qualify for the profession of life insurance could be tested
for aptitude, integrity, and willingness to work. Here they
could be trained in mind and heart for better service to
themselves, their clients, their companies, and their country.

Many of us have climbed to success on the ladder which
S. S. Huebner built for us. To show our gratitude, we have
offered him every honor at our disposal. He accepts them
graciously, but being the man he is, we think he finds
ample reward in knowing that his work has made thousands

of other careers possible. And perhaps his greatest reward
comes when he walks down a street in any American
town, and sees the self-respecting families in their
self-respecting houses, and knows what a part life insurance
has played in the confident rhythm of their lives.

Another feature of the Anniversary observance was the Silver
Anniversary Survey. What were the characteristics of the men
and women who had won the C.L.U. in its first 25 years? Questionnaires were sent to the more than four thousand C.L.U.s, and
85 per cent were returned. They revealed the gratifying fact that,
excluding those who had died, about 94 per cent of C.L.U. graduates were still active in the business—a remarkable record of
persistency.

The composite picture developed from the questionnaire
showed that in 1952 the typical C.L.U. was 45.5 years old, male,
married with one or two children, owned $50,000 of life insur-
ance, attended religious services, and was a member of the American Society and the National Association of Life Underwriters.
He attended two service clubs or other organizations quite regularly, within five years had held office in two or three organizations, and came into the business because of opportunity for increased earnings.

Most of the C.L.U.s at that time were writers of ordinary business or employed in field management. More than half were in
the larger companies with more than $1.5 billions of assets.

Asked specifically whether C.L.U. study cut income, the majority said no. On the contrary, 23.5 per cent reported a great
increase of income during C.L.U. study, and nearly 60 per cent
more reported some increase.

Questioned about motivation for study, about 50 per cent said
they took the C.L.U. work because they believed it was almost a
necessity for the future of the career underwriter. One-third replied they took the work to gain knowledge, and about 20 per cent
said they wanted the prestige.

Relating to the difficulty of the work, over one-third reported they had had to repeat at least one examination. The consensus was that Examination D on finance was the most difficult. Examination B on economics, government, and social problems was judged least practical, but nevertheless was said to have contributed most to rounding out the professional background of the candidates. Examination C on law, trusts, and taxes was rated unanimously most interesting and most valuable in increasing both the candidate's ability to give professional service and his income.

The majority of C.L.U.s replying said attainment of the designation had made them better life insurance men. This rating recalls some wise advice given by J. Carlton Smith, a well-known C.L.U. leader, a life-long educator, and then educational director of the Southwestern Life of Dallas. There was some sensitivity in the industry on the part of good life underwriters who were not C.L.U.s. The American College frequently felt called on to remind graduates of the virtue of humility. Writing in the Silver Anniversary issue of *Life Association News*, Mr. Smith said:

> No C.L.U. should ever be guilty of telling a layman that because he is a C.L.U. he is more capable of handling the layman's life insurance affairs than is a non-C.L.U. In the first place, it is no more ethical to say that than it is to run down another life insurance company. In the second place, it may not be true. I personally know some non-C.L.U.'s who do a better job of life underwriting than is performed by some C.L.U.'s whom I also know personally. It is not the purpose of C.L.U. study to make a person a better underwriter than some other underwriter. The purpose of C.L.U. study is to make *you* a better life underwriter than *you* were before you began that study. Suppose a C.L.U. is asked this question by a layman: "Is a C.L.U. a better life insurance man than other life insurance men?" I think his answer should be this: "Not necessarily so. All I can say is that I believe C.L.U. study made *me* a better underwriter than *I* was before I began it." That is a logical, sound, and ethical statement. I think it would be hard to improve upon. The American College of Life Underwriters and the American Society of Chartered Life Underwriters do not approve or countenance statements made by C.L.U.'s which cast aspersions on non-C.L.U.'s.

I do not mean by this that a C.L.U. should hide his light under a bushel. A C.L.U. *cannot* keep his light under a bushel, even if he attempts to do so. The public is very rapidly noticing more and more that there is such a class of underwriters as C.L.U.'s. And the public will notice it to an increasing extent in the future, as the number of C.L.U.'s increase. There is nothing the C.L.U.'s can do to minimize the pressure that the public will place to an increasing extent on non-C.L.U.'s as the years pass. The pressure is there, but the only thing the C.L.U. had to do with it was his action in becoming a C.L.U. and being recognized as such. It is my opinion that the best thing the non-C.L.U. can do about the situation is to become a C.L.U. In the future, the public will confer more and more of its favors upon the C.L.U.—just as it now confers the lion's share of its favors upon the CPA. It is the inevitable thing that happens when a profession raises its standards. It is merely a historical repetition of the same thing that has happened in every other profession during the process of raising educational and professional standards.

The Silver Anniversary Survey proved to be of major significance in the acceptance of the C.L.U. idea among life insurance leaders. Facts were substituted for subjective opinions. The implications of the value of C.L.U. education to the insuring public, to the individuals involved, and to the industry became clear.

Much credit for the success of the survey goes to Dr. Arthur W. Mason, Jr., then new to the staff of the American College as director of college relations. He tackled the survey research job with enthusiasm as one of his first assignments and, with other volunteer help, saw the project through to its successful conclusion. Dr. Mason's four years of full-time service came at a period when the College was still sadly understaffed, and his capable help was particularly appreciated. He is now associate dean of the School of Business and Public Administration of Washington University, St. Louis, but continues to serve the College as an educational consultant.

The activities and evaluations of the Silver Jubilee year revealed a need for an officer to take special responsibility for public relations. Howard D. Shaw was added to the staff in 1953 as director of public relations for the American College and the American Society, and served until 1959. He brought unusual talents to this position, and greatly increased the effectiveness of College and Society communication with their various audiences. Mr. Shaw had had extensive experience in public relations, sales promotion, and direct-mail advertising with the life insurance industry, and had been a key figure in promotion of the C.L.U. *Journal* as a consultant to the American Society. His talents and his deep devotion to the progress of the C.L.U. idea resulted in a period of intensely creative development of C.L.U. public relations. Further, he selected as an assistant in that formative time Marie DeGeorge Melone, who also made an outstanding contribution to the public relations program during her six years of service.

Chapter 20

DAVID McCAHAN

Dr. David McCahan, who had been associated with the College almost from its beginning, was named president in 1952, when Dr. Huebner retired and became president emeritus. Dr. McCahan took office in an atmosphere of optimism. He had had so great a part in the College's growth and development that no interruption to progress was seen in the transition. New staff members were becoming effective in an expanded program.

The College headquarters at 3924 Walnut Street, Philadelphia, was enlarged. When the building was purchased, the American Institute for Property and Liability Underwriters also was housed there with the idea that the arrangement would be temporary. However, it proved an efficient and useful situation. The Institute and the College have a common philosophy for college insurance education. Their close physical association proved practically convenient in the development of curriculums and study materials, in the cooperation with colleges, and for the convenience of academic visitors to officers of both organizations. There were also other reasons of efficiency and economy. Therefore, in building for the increased needs of the College, space was provided also for the Institute. At this time, the S. S. Huebner Foundation offices, which from the beginning had been with the College, were moved to the new Insurance Center in Dietrich Hall at the University of Pennsylvania.

For some time, the College officers and trustees, and especially the Registration Board, had been concerned about recognition for those whose experience record did not clearly qualify them for the C.L.U. The certificate of proficiency was considered definitely second class by many, and candidates were dissatisfied, especially since the same examinations were taken by all. Borderline cases required constant debate. On the other hand, there was a strong feeling that only salesmen and those experienced in sales work, teaching, and management should be eligible for the C.L.U. Therefore, a new designation, C.L.U. Associate, was adopted, and was awarded to 19 candidates in 1953.

The standard announced attempted to be very clear. The C.L.U. designation would be awarded to "persons engaged in life insurance sales and service, to persons managing, training or supervising those engaged in life insurance sales and service, and to college and university teachers of insurance." The C.L.U. Associate designation would be awarded to "persons engaged in all other life insurance activities." Of course, there were rules regarding length of service and character of work for both designations.

At this time, modifications concerning industrial agents were adopted, providing that 50 per cent of the production requirement for them might be in industrial business, though half must be ordinary. For salesmen specializing in accident and sickness business, 25 per cent of the minimum requirement might be represented by that type of coverage. Provision also was made for certificate of proficiency holders to exchange that for the C.L.U. Associate diploma. A news item stated:

> The C.L.U. Associate designation was created following a full year of intensive study and investigation of the need for a new designation by the Registration Board of the College, composed of Clarence B. Metzger, C.L.U., chairman of the Registration Board, and second vice president of the Equitable Life Assurance Society of the United States; Charles W. Campbell, C.L.U., newly appointed vice president of the Prudential Insurance Company of America and formerly manager of the Newark Agency of the same company; J. Roger Hull, C.L.U., executive vice president of the Mutual Life Insurance Company of New York; Joseph H. Reese, C.L.U., general agent in Philadelphia for the Penn Mutual Life Insurance Com-

David McCahan.

pany; and Davis W. Gregg, C.L.U., dean of the American College
of Life Underwriters.

Up to 1950, only about one hundred people had qualified for
the American College Certificate in Life Insurance Agency Management, although the program had started in 1933. At this
period, thoughtful work was being done, especially by Dr. Mc-
Cahan and Charles J. Zimmerman, who comprised a special committee. They consulted with advisers representing the Life Insurance Agency Management Association and the National
Association of Life Underwriters as well as the College. The following principles were reaffirmed:

1. The management program should conform to the American
   College principles in general, setting educational standards
   for academic knowledge and accrediting by examination.
2. Emphasis should be placed on the long-run acquisition of
   fundamental knowledge related to agency management
   rather than on the short-run development of skills.
3. The qualifications as to age, character, and accredited high
   school education should be the same as the C.L.U.
4. The two parts of the examinations should be:
   I. Business administration, from the point of view of under-
      standing principles—covering business organization and
      management, human relations and leadership, account-
      ing and agency finance, and business statistics.
   II. Sales and office administration in their functional as-
      pects—covering sales management, market research, and
      office management.

The program was revised substantially with the introduction
of more stimulating and practical study material. Under Wm.
Eugene Hays, chairman of the Management Examination Committee, pilot study groups were promoted vigorously in Philadelphia, Boston, New York, and Seattle. However, they were
still fairly small, and study material and teachers were still felt
to be inadequate. Nevertheless, the efforts resulted in 30 new

management graduates in 1953, and supporters of the program felt they were making progress. Real vitality did not come to the program until it had a full-time staff director several years later. The management program was not the only phase of College activity being hindered by budget limitations. The trustees recognized that they should take a hard look at the whole C.L.U. program to analyze its value, assess its cost on an adequate basis, and

C.L.U. conferment dinner, 1946. *Left to right:* Edward A. Krueger, Roland D. Hinkle, Mayo Adams Shattuck, Clifford H. Orr, Dr. McCahan, Dr. Huebner, James Elton Bragg, and Julian S. Myrick.

determine how additional funds could be raised, if necessary. Mr. Myrick therefore appointed a Special Committee on Financial Welfare to handle this broad responsibility. The Committee was: Harold M. Stewart, chairman; Dudley Dowell, W. Eugene Hays, Roger Hull, Cecil J. North, Charles J. Zimmerman, Earl R. Trangmar, secretary; and President McCahan, ex officio.

With the cooperation of College officers, a great mass of reports, financial summaries, statistics, and organization charts was brought together and studied carefully. The Committee wanted to answer first of all the question: Is the College of value to the life insurance business—to the companies, the agents, and the policyholders?

The evidence was strongly affirmative. The College was not only administering examinations to thousands of candidates and granting designations. Two or three times as many candidates were studying in C.L.U. classes and benefiting even without official recognition. The College was taking a leading part in expanding college courses in life insurance. Over a hundred C.L.U. study groups had been established, with direct college or university teaching or sponsorship. About 150 institutions were serving as examination centers. All this close cooperation with professional teachers was producing favorable educational results for the life insurance industry so far as colleges and universities were concerned. The College had made a tremendous contribution, directly and indirectly, to life insurance literature and the improvement of training procedures in individual companies and the business generally. The C.L.U. program had raised the sights of underwriters and the public in regard to professional service in life insurance selling.

The Special Committee assayed the crippling effect of inflation on College operations. Costs of materials, printing, travel, and communications of all kinds had increased sharply and constantly. Even though salaries to staff and payments for professional services in connection with examinations had advanced at a much slower rate, the College was sorely pinched.

The Special Committee outlined a broad program for improvement in field services to candidates and C.L.U. leaders through staff services and publications, for promotion and public relations, for activity with colleges and universities, and for upgrading College administrative procedures. They itemized the new

Harold M. Stewart.

manpower that would be needed and estimated other budget increases. The whole package carried an additional price tag of $70,000 a year.

On May 1, 1953, the College committee met with a special committee of the Society appointed to cooperate in its study. The Society committee included Howard H. Cammack, Benjamin M. Gaston, Harry Krueger, Gerald W. Page, and Carl M. Spero, chairman. After thorough discussions, the Society committee reached general agreement with the College committee, and added its weight to the recommendations.

The Special Committee on Financial Welfare recommended unanimously that the expanded program be adopted, and that steps be taken to raise the necessary money. The trustees, with the cooperation of the American Society in connection with promotion of new candidates and a constructive public relations program, immediately started down the road toward the goals which had been set forth. The charge for each C.L.U. examination was increased from $30 to $50 (one half payable through a credit certificate from contributors to the Cooperative Fund for Underwriter Training) beginning in 1955. This produced a substantial increase of funds quickly. The foundation was laid for increasing the formula for company contributions to the Fund, and for other action which greatly strengthened the financial position of the College. The Special Committee on Financial Welfare, or the Stewart Committee as it was frequently called because of the effective leadership of its chairman, was a vital factor in enabling the College to embrace the opportunities of the postwar era.

In June, 1954, a record-breaking 3,177 candidates took 4,142 C.L.U. examinations at 140 examination centers, and in the fall, 397 new designations were awarded. The College prepared to serve the broadening field of life underwriting by announcing that the next year's Examination A also would cover accident and sickness insurance. Philosophically, health insurance is a real part of life value protection.

With the College moving forward in numbers of candidates, in national influence, and in the scope of its program, President David McCahan died. He had had heart warnings previously, but lifetime habits of intense activity did not allow him to go slowly at the age of fifty-seven. The memorial resolution adopted by the trustees gave a significant review of his life and service.

The Board of Trustees of the American College of Life Underwriters record with deep sorrow the death on June 28, 1954, of their esteemed associate and co-worker, Dr. David McCahan. They wish also to express their grateful appreciation for his invaluable contribution to the sound development and growth of the American College and the Chartered Life Underwriter professional movement, during his long official connection with the College, as Assistant Dean from 1929 to 1934, as Secretary from 1930 to 1934, as Dean from 1934 to 1951, as a member of the Board of Trustees of the College from 1934 until his death, as Executive Vice President from 1951 to 1952, and as President from 1952 until his death.

Furthermore, the Board of Trustees wish to record their deep appreciation for Dr. McCahan's outstanding contributions in connection with the following:

As the principal organizer of the American Society of Chartered Life Underwriters (then called the National Chapter) and as Secretary of that organization from 1930 to 1945.

As Executive Director of the S. S. Huebner Foundation for Insurance Education from its inception in 1941 until his death, and as one of those most instrumental in shaping and organizing that Foundation.

As President of the American Association of University Teachers of Insurance from 1940 to 1941, when that Association and its Standing Committee on Professional Standards in Life, Property, and Casualty Insurance finally succeeded in inducing the property and casualty divisions of insurance to emulate the professional standards and procedures already pursued by the American College.

As Chairman of the Committee on Curriculum and Educational Procedure which prepared the program of study for the C.P.C.U.

examinations, given under the auspices of the American Institute for Property & Liability Underwriters, Inc., and as a member of the Board of Trustees of the Institute from the time of its incorporation until his death.

As a member of the National Committee on Family Financial Security Education and as one of those most instrumental in shaping and organizing the first "Graduate Workshop in Family Financial Security Education," conducted under this important plan of high school education for the public welfare.

All of the afore-mentioned organizations have been closely associated, and will continue to be so ever-increasingly, with the welfare, growing progress, and better public understanding of the American College. The American Society of Chartered Life Underwriters is now the effective motivating organization among C.L.U.s to further the professional concept in life underwriting; the Foundation exists to prepare well-qualified insurance teachers in universities and colleges, who will aid the cause of proper C.L.U. instruction and will become centers of influence for the College; the American Association of University Teachers of Insurance helps to spread, elevate, and unify American College efforts in American institutions of higher learning; the American Institute for Property and Liability Underwriters can and should cooperate with the American College and can help the College, just as the College can aid the Institute; and the Family Financial Security Education Program does much to further insurance education on the secondary level and thus tends to enlarge the public understanding of life insurance and professional life underwriting. So, when Dr. McCahan served these organizations with devotion, indefatigable industry, and outstanding wisdom, he was also serving the American College with corresponding devotion, industry, and wisdom. Dr. McCahan's viewpoint as Dean and President of the American College reached much beyond the fulfillment of immediate current official duties. He saw, as every Dean and President of the College should, the great force for good which allied educational organizations, if properly motivated, can give to the American College. This Board of Trustees, therefore, wish to record their deep appreciation for Dr. McCahan's active, highly intelligent, and American College-viewpoint participation in the welfare of the aforementioned educational organizations.

Dr. McCahan's working life was dedicated to education, and in particular to insurance education. From 1926 to 1934, he served as Assistant Professor of Insurance at the University of Pennsylvania, as Associate Professor of Insurance from 1934 to 1936, and as Professor of Insurance from 1936 until his death. During his teaching career, he wrote much about, as well as for, the American College; advised many students, teachers and underwriters about the nature and merits of the C.L.U. program; influenced ever so many to undertake the mastery of that program; and often advised other university and college authorities in their establishment of an adequate insurance educational curriculum, including the C.L.U. program, in the procuring of qualified insurance teachers, and in furthering their desire to cooperate with the American College for the benefit of the insurance industry and their communities. As well as being a teacher, Dr. McCahan was also a voluminous author and editor. He was also a meticulously able administrator. He loved research and careful analysis. He had a wide acquaintance with nearly every angle of the insurance industry and was ever hungry to garner in more and more data for useful educational purposes. In all of his many educational activities, we can think of Dr. McCahan always as sincere, industrious, and creative. To him, work appealed as if it were play; and he played hard, yes, sometimes, we felt, beyond his physical strength.

Last, but by no means least, we must also admire Dr. McCahan for his devotion to his family, to his church, to his community's educational welfare, and to his many friends.

Now that Dr. McCahan has departed from our midst, we realize what a great loss the insurance industry and insurance education have suffered. We think of his life's work as a rich legacy, as a living monument. His teaching and other achievements will continue to be a creative influence. The wonderful example he set for us will also continue to be a challenge.

With the death of Dr. McCahan, the American College lost not only its president, but a great creative force. Dr. McCahan had been an unusual complement to Dr. Huebner in the two-man years of the College. He had laid the groundwork organizationally for the College structure. He had done the desk work and

the detail while Dr. Huebner carried the banners. He had supported Dr. Huebner stalwartly in his standards for a professional
program. By nature he put others in the limelight. This was true
in his relationship not only with Dr. Huebner and the College but
also the leaders of the Society and its projects. Dr. McCahan had
a big part in creating the vision of the C.L.U. Institutes and the
Journal, which are popularly associated with other people. He
worked devotedly to make these projects important factors in
professionalizing the work of life underwriters.

An intimate observer commented that a secret of Dr. Mc-
Cahan's strength was his conviction about the importance of
education. He believed absolutely that what a man thinks matters, that a man's mental equipment determines the course of his
life. That was one reason for his dedicated work on the school
board of his home town of Swarthmore, and to his leadership of
the Presbyterian Sunday School there. To both these services he
gave himself unstintingly for many years, despite his heavy
schedule at the University and with the College. To him, education for life and for one's vocation mattered supremely. Because
he put that value on what he was doing, he brought to the work
an ingredient of worth that made it intrinsically more effective.
His personal integrity and his unwavering devotion to the highest
ideals for the College left their indelible stamp on the
organization.

Chapter 21

NEW FOUNDATIONS

In September, 1954, Dr. Davis Weinert Gregg was named president of the American College. Born in Austin, Texas, he was educated there in the public schools and was graduated from the University of Texas in 1939. From the Wharton School of the University of Pennsylvania, he received an M.B.A. degree in 1940. He was associated with the Aetna Life and Affiliated Companies in Hartford and Dallas for two years before being called to active duty with the U.S. Navy. He served as commanding officer of convoy escort vessels, and for one year taught Naval R.O.T.C. at the University of Minnesota. On release from the Navy, after four years, he was awarded a Huebner Foundation fellowship, and received his Ph.D. in economics from the University of Pennsylvania in 1948. Brief experience as an insurance professor at The Ohio State University and the Graduate School of Business of Stanford University preceded his appointment as assistant dean of the American College in 1949. As a student, then associate, of Dr. Huebner and Dr. McCahan, Dr. Gregg had had opportunity to become acquainted with the heritage of the College and the ideals of those who had been its builders over the years as well as to evaluate his own interest and capacity to carry on the work. The trustees felt they were putting the College in good hands.

To step into the deanship they chose Herbert C. Graebner, who held degrees from Valparaiso University and Northwestern University and had done additional graduate work at the University of Pennsylvania as a Huebner Foundation fellow. He was a member of the faculties of Valparaiso University, Westminster

College, and Butler University. Most recently, Professor Graebner had been dean of the College of Business Administration at
Butler University. He was a C.L.U., and had taught many
C.L.U. courses. He had served as an examination grader for the
College, and as a consultant on educational matters. In him, the
trustees recognized a "strong and devoted educational leader to
serve life insurance and collegiate insurance education."

With the two top officers at last given full-time appointments,
the College entered a new era. Dr. Huebner's retirement from the
University, Mr. Williams' retirement from the College, and the
death of Dr. McCahan had brought the trustees face to face with
the absolute necessity for building a full-time career staff in the
College to meet growing demands for creative and administrative
talent. The Stewart Special Committee on Financial Welfare
called these needs to the attention of the trustees, and the Committee's recommendations also led to the financial resources
which made it possible to start building a full-time officer staff.

At this time, Paul F. Clark was elected a life trustee. He was
an incorporator of the College, it will be recalled, and had served
on the Board from the beginning. He was also a founder of the
Million Dollar Round Table and a past president of the National
Association of Life Underwriters. His direct participation in the
affairs of the College, together with the influence of his leadership, made him an outstanding factor in College history. His
citation mentioned that he had "continuously and proudly identified himself with the growth and progress of the movement on
a local and national level" and concluded:

> His devotion and special service to the American College for more
> than a quarter of a century, his many and varied life insurance in-
> stitutional contributions, and his leadership as President of his
> great Company, all make him an outstanding choice for election
> as a Life Trustee of the College.

The next year, 1955, Mr. Clark was elected vice chairman of
the Board of Trustees.

Herbert C. Graebner. (*Bachrach*)

In 1957, Paul S. Mills was appointed managing director of the American Society, succeeding Leroy G. Steinbeck, who resigned in June of that year to become vice president of the Life Insurance Company of North America. Mr. Mills had a unique combination of successful experience as a life insurance salesman, manager, C.L.U. teacher, and college teacher. Following graduation from Indiana State Teachers College, graduate study at Harvard and Indiana Universities, and teaching at Michigan State, Indiana, and Butler Universities, Mr. Mills had a decade of successful work as a life insurance salesman and manager in the Middle West. He had been active in the Columbus, Ohio, Life Underwriters Association, and the C.L.U. chapter, and president of the General Agents and Managers Association.

Another new leader in College affairs was Dr. Jack C. Keir, who became head of the Educational Services Department in September, 1957, having served two years as director of educational publications. He was named assistant dean in 1958. Dr. Keir took degrees at Middlebury and Tufts Colleges, and received his Ph.D. from the University of Pennsylvania, where he studied as an S. S. Huebner Foundation fellow. He had been a university teacher of economics and finance, and head of the department of business administration at Kansas State College.

Succeeding Dr. Keir as director of educational publications in September, 1957, was W. W. Dotterweich. He is a graduate of Upsala College, and also was a Huebner fellow at the University of Pennsylvania where he took his M.A. and completed course work for a Ph.D. He taught insurance there and at Butler University, and was engaged for a time as an economist for the Prudential Insurance Company.

One of the first major enterprises to claim the attention of these new leaders in 1954 was a complete revision of the educational program of the College. Health insurance had been added to the curriculum a few years before, so there was need to develop that area to meet current demands. In this phase, Edwin J. Faulkner was very helpful. He was elected a trustee of the College in

Edwin J. Faulkner.

1959, and has served as chairman of the Committee on Health Insurance Education since 1961.

Curriculum changes also were required because of the great developments in group insurance, pensions, business coverages, and estate planning. The growth of social security and increased federal taxation were new factors in family financial programs. No major curriculum change had been made in over a decade. The Examination Board and the staff studied the matter devotedly for more than a year, consulting with teachers, company authorities, training specialists, and especially the new Council of Educational Advisers.

This group, initiated in 1955, was a careful selection of nine outstanding educators, with Dr. Leslie J. Buchan as chairman. Dr. Buchan was distinguished service professor of administration, School of Business and Public Administration, Washington University, St. Louis. The Council serves as an advisory group to the College and Institute officers in the study of special problems and policy matters related both to C.L.U. and C.P.C.U. programs. The Council evaluates educational objectives and progress, considers the extent and types of examinations, studies the relationships of undergraduate and graduate insurance courses, and analyzes problems peculiar to professional education for adults.

The Council of Educational Advisers always has been composed of outstanding American educators. Members of the first Council were: Dr. Buchan, chairman; Laurence J. Ackerman, dean of the School of Business Administration, University of Connecticut; Leonard H. Axe, dean of the School of Business, University of Kansas; Edison L. Bowers, professor and chairman of the department of economics of the College of Commerce and Administration, The Ohio State University; Horace B. Brown, Jr., dean of the College of Business Administration, University of Oklahoma; Delbert J. Duncan, dean of the School of Business, University of Colorado; Gordon Siefkin, dean of the School of Business Administration, Emory University; Stanley F. Teele, dean of the Graduate School of Business Administration, Harvard University; and Stephen W. Vasquez, dean of the School of Commerce, and Finance, St. Louis University. Others who have served on the Council include Paul Garner, dean of the School of Commerce and Business Administration, University of Alabama; Ossian R. MacKenzie, dean of the College of Business Administration, Pennsylvania State University; Thomas L. Norton, former dean of the School of Commerce, New York University; George W. Robbins, associate dean of the School of Business Administration, University of California at Los Angeles; James R. Surface, vice chancellor, University of Kansas; Miller Upton, president, Beloit College; and Arthur M. Weimer, dean of the School of Business, Indiana University.

Among the major matters discussed by the Council in the years of its existence have been the applicability of programed learning to professional education in insurance; possible research to determine insurance industry needs for college-trained manpower; college curriculum changes and effect on professional careers in insurance; criteria for determining professional competency for persons engaged in business; educational objectives of collegiate schools of business and evening divisions of college schools of business; an appraisal of the teaching-learning process; and specific curriculum problems for career insurance personnel in accounting, economics, business ethics, psychology, and human motivation.

The revised curriculum went into effect for the school year 1956-57. Five courses with a four-hour examination in each was still the pattern. The course designations were changed from Parts A, B, etc., to I, II, etc. Proper credit was allowed for completed work on the old basis. In announcing the new curriculum the College stated:

> The 1956 revised C.L.U. curriculum is designed to fit the modern environment in which the Chartered Life Underwriter works. Changes and adjustments are those which will equip the professionally-minded life insurance counselor to serve more competently the needs of the client of today. Some subjects have been reduced or eliminated; others increased in scope. The revised program embraces more on business life insurance, pensions, group insurance, taxation, annuities, and personal and family finance. It includes some fundamentals of accounting and the study of motivational psychology. It is beamed intensively to the requirements of the modern-day career life underwriter to give him thorough grounding in every phase of his specialty that helps him solve the financial security problems of his client community. . . .

> The equipment required to provide useful service of a professional quality obviously changes as conditions of modern life change. And in recent times, these conditions in every branch of business and family life have changed fast. Possession of a thorough understanding of all the implications of life insurance and related aspects of financial security is essential to true professional service; and helping the life underwriter to gain that understanding is a function of the American College.

Council of Educational Advisers, 1955. *Standing, left to right:* Laurence J. Ackerman, dean, School of Business Administration, University of Connecticut; Gordon Siefkin, dean, School of Business Administration, Emory University; Cecil Puckett, former dean, College of Business Administration, University of Denver; Stanley F. Teele, dean, Graduate School of Business Administration, Harvard University; Edison L. Bowers, chairman, Department of Economics, College of Commerce and Administration, The Ohio State University; and Horace B. Brown, Jr., dean, College of Business Administration, University of Oklahoma. *Seated:* Leonard H. Axe, dean, School of Business, University of Kansas; Leslie J. Buchan (chairman of the Council), professor of accounting, School of Business and Public Administration, Washington University; and Stephen W. Vasquez, dean, School of Commerce and Finance, St. Louis University.

With the new curriculum well established, the College proceeded to refine further its examination techniques. From the beginning, essay-type examinations had been used. As the number of examinations written increased (they nearly tripled in the decade after 1950), the pressure in grading became critical. The apparent solution was to use more graders and to have each person grade more papers. This seemed like a simple answer. However, it could be expected that in such conditions the reliability of grading would be reduced.

As early as 1951, objective testing with machine scoring had been discussed, but that did not then seem advisable for the College. However, as the burden of grading became greater, improvements in objective testing were developed, special research in insurance testing was done, and a new decision was reached. On recommendations of the officers, the Board of Trustees approved the appointment of Educational Testing Service, Princeton, New Jersey, as examination consultants for the College. Robert J. Solomon, an eminent authority in the field of testing, was assigned as program director of this project by the Educational Testing Service. For three years, he met with College committees and guided the officers in making the transition from an entirely essay to a combination objective and essay examination program. When Dr. Solomon was promoted within the E.T.S. organization, Dr. John A. Winterbottom succeeded him as program director. Assisting both Dr. Solomon and Dr. Winterbottom was Dr. Elisabeth Kimball.

Beginning with the 1959 examinations, the College adopted a plan combining the long-proven advantages of essay questions and the efficiency of objective procedures. Dean Graebner wrote an extensive article about the new plan of the College which included an interesting explanation of the decision.

One of the inherent weaknesses of relying completely on essay testing is the inability to examine the candidate over a wide area of studied materials. Each C.L.U. Part, for example, has 30 assignments. Obviously, in any one year it was necessary to omit certain assignments from the examination. Also, since the College annually publishes the essay questions and complete answers to the questions, there developed among some individuals and groups attempts to guess the sections of the course in which the questions would be asked each year. As a matter of fact, each year the College would get excellent answers to previous examination questions even though they did not fit as answers to the current examination questions!

By retaining the essay test on a reduced basis, the fundamental strengths of essay testing are retained. These strengths are that essay tests are especially suited to measure the candidate's ability to organize data, to think clearly, to write clearly and to use learning creatively.

Another very significant result brought about by essay testing is that of fostering sound and thorough study habits since the candidate knows he will be called upon to give evidence in his own organized answer that he understands and can integrate large areas of subject matter.

The coupling of the objective test with the essay test enables the candidate to give evidence of having an understanding of all of the assignments. The 100 objective items are selected in such a way as to have three items from each of 20 assignments and four from each of 10 assignments. In this way the entire examination affords the candidate the opportunity to present evidence of his breadth of knowledge over all 30 assignments and also his depth of understanding in certain selected areas.

From the candidates' standpoint, it is believed that the factor of physical endurance is less important with the new plan. The problem of fatigue associated with writing for four consecutive hours proved to be a real stumbling block for some C.L.U. candidates, especially the older persons long out of school and out of writing practice. The new format should measurably help these persons.

The combination examination is judged to be better balanced and fairer to the average candidate than the old essay type. In the four-hour examination period, the objective questions are given one and three-quarter hours and the essay questions two hours. The parts at first did not have equal value—the objective questions counted 40 per cent and the essay questions 60 per cent in the final score. Beginning in 1963, each part counted equally.

The change in curriculum involved an enormous burden for the Educational Publications Department of the College. There was complete revision or new production of 16 major publications including study guides and teachers' manuals, and brochures covering subjects not adequately treated in textbooks. *Teacher Topics* continued to be published regularly, and *Student Topics* began with three issues in 1957-58.

The new Joint Public Relations office, with Howard D. Shaw as director, shared in announcing and interpreting the new program through news releases and magazine articles. The *C.L.U. Annual Review*, which had been started in 1954 as a joint project of the College and the Society, also carried the story to the public.

Of course, effective work was done by personal contact. The regional educational conferences initiated several years previously were repeated and increased in number, bringing together teachers of C.L.U. groups, professional insurance educators, and life insurance leaders especially concerned with educational problems for specific discussion of plans and developments.

Incidentally, these teacher conferences, which are now conducted regionally each year throughout the United States, have become one of the most valuable phases of the work of the College. They focus on teaching methods and motivation for learning, and have greatly increased the effectiveness of C.L.U. study classes. About one-third of all C.L.U. classes are taught by full-time university insurance teachers. The need for teachers for the remaining classes has been met primarily by C.L.U.s chosen because of their knowledge and interest in assisting others to attain the C.L.U. designation. The conferences bring together these C.L.U. teachers and many university insurance teachers not currently teaching C.L.U. classes. The interchange of ideas and discussion of teaching and learning problems and techniques at these conferences have proven of great benefit and inspiration. The attendance of insurance company educators and other executives at these meetings also is mutually helpful.

To introduce the new curriculum, seven regional conferences were held for educational chairmen of local C.L.U. chapters representing 127 cities. About two hundred people attended the conferences in San Francisco, Dallas, Philadelphia, Chicago, Cleveland, Hartford, and Atlanta. The meetings made possible broad dissemination of information about the new curriculum, and provided a good appraisal of the grass roots reaction to it, which generally was very favorable.

The next year a new type of conference was held for "C.L.U. key men" in home offices. These meetings brought together in New York, Chicago, and Los Angeles representatives of nearly thirty companies for discussion of what was being done and what could be done to promote the C.L.U. program with the field forces of individual companies.

All these enlarged publication programs, public relations activities, staff field visits, and various College conferences were made possible through increasing financial support of the College. The money-raising responsibility of the Cooperative Fund for Underwriter Training had become a permanent part of the American College by change of bylaws in 1953. Paul F. Clark was named chairman of the committee for the Fund; Morton Boyd, vice chairman; Earl R. Trangmar, secretary; and 18 chief executives of life companies, members. This committee increased the number of companies participating in the Fund until it now represents about 95 per cent of all life insurance in force in this country. Annual contributions amount to more than $200,000. The increased numbers of candidates for examinations also increased College income, but it was still a hand-to-mouth existence even with a nearly half-million-dollar budget. The total annual investment in the C.L.U. educational program now is estimated to be several million dollars a year, including the annual budgets of the College and Society, C.L.U. departments in many home offices, funds from the companies and underwriters in fees, study class tuition, textbooks, and so on.

With the increase in College income and activities, there was, of course, an increase in its overall financial operations. The College was fortunate in securing the services of Sewell W. Hodge as treasurer of the College in 1939, and he has served in this capacity continuously since that time. Until his retirement as secretary-treasurer of the Provident Mutual Life Insurance Company, Mr. Hodge devoted much "after hours" time to College budgetary and financial operations. Since his retirement, he continues to serve on a part-time basis, and gives strong leadership to the Board in the College's expanded financial and investment operations.

The College and the Society continued joint efforts in recruiting new candidates. Dr. Huebner was active in this endeavor. His many speaking engagements throughout the country continued to draw big and enthusiastic audiences, and he was still an effective salesman of the C.L.U. idea. In 1953, soon after his retirement, he had made an extensive trip to South America, speaking to working insurance salesmen and university audiences in seven countries. In 1958, at the request of the State Department of the United States, he and Mrs. Huebner again made a trip abroad. This time they went to Japan, the Philippines, New Zealand, and Australia. He spoke everywhere to students, educators, and men in the insurance industry, expounding not only his life value concept and practical matters about insurance coverage, but also the importance of professional training for insurance sales activity. In Japan, Dr. Huebner had the almost unique honor of receiving from the Emperor the Order of the Sacred Treasure for his contribution to the welfare of the Japanese insurance industry.

Recognition abroad for this beloved C.L.U. leader and the American College added interest to the enterprise at home. Since Dr. Huebner had become such a symbol of professionalism in

Above: **Dr. Huebner holding the decoration of the Order of the Sacred Treasure.** *Below:* **Dr. Huebner displaying the scroll citation of the Order of the Sacred Treasure.** (*Shaw*)

life insurance selling and service, the College and Society enlisted him as chairman of the Committee of 1000, a group of C.L.U.s united in pledges to recruit at least one new candidate apiece for C.L.U. work. The Committee, initiated in 1959, started well, and has continued with profitable results. It is estimated that in four years the Committee has sponsored 1,800 new candidates. Dr. Huebner's eightieth birthday party in March, 1962, at the Union League in Philadelphia, included a huge three-tier birthday cake. It was decorated with hundreds of little red can-

Dr. and Mrs. Huebner at the Kyoto Royal Palace in Japan with President Gen Hirose of the Nippon Life, and his niece.

dles, each representing a new candidate sponsored in 1962 by the Committee of 1000.

The idea of personal sponsorship of candidates is not new. Dr. Huebner did it from the beginning. In the very early days, when he was doing summer work for the Massachusetts Mutual agencies, he began a program of promotion with a selected group of general agents whom he considered good C.L.U. material. In his five years of special work with that company, he had the satisfaction of seeing more than half of his 30 prospects qualify as C.L.U.s and go on to inspire their associates to do likewise. At that period, the Massachusetts Mutual was the outstanding company in C.L.U. accomplishment proportionate to size. Dr. Huebner has continued to preach the philosophy that every C.L.U. should assume responsibility for encouraging others to win the designation. Particularly in the early days, he was concerned by the limited vision of many salesmen interested in the C.L.U.

Dr. Huebner's 80th birthday cake decorated with candidate candles by the Committee of 1000.

program. They wanted the designation to set themselves apart as professionally qualified life underwriters, but most of them did not yet have a clear concept of the value of raising the standard of the industry as a whole.

To say, "There are only 16 C.L.U.s in our state, and I am one of them," may give an underwriter a sense of personal superiority. However, the designation cannot have real meaning in an area until there is a recognized group of underwriters performing according to its high professional standards.

Dr. Huebner gives not only his titular sponsorship to the Committee of 1000, but constant, enthusiastic cooperation. He writes countless letters to sponsors and candidates. The Committee presents his autographed picture to a sponsor when his candidate takes the first C.L.U. examination. When the candidate qualifies as a C.L.U., his sponsor receives a copy of Dr. Huebner's biography, *The Teacher Who Changed an Industry*.

Throughout the history of the C.L.U. movement, the local study group leader and university teacher of C.L.U. classes were key men in the progress of the College. To recognize their part in the great success of the enterprise, a new honor was inaugurated in 1959. This was the award of the Philadelphia Bowl—a sterling silver replica of a distinctively designed bowl in the Philadelphia Art Museum, with an engraved citation of appreciation "for dedicated C.L.U. teaching." At the 1959 C.L.U. conferment exercises in Philadelphia, bowls were awarded to three men who had taught C.L.U. classes for 25 years. These teachers were Dr. Huebner, Albert J. Schick, Newark, New Jersey, and George L. Buck, Seattle, Washington. In 1962, J. Russell Townsend, Jr., Indianapolis, Indiana, received the award.

The College was conscious of the need to honor its friends and supporters while they could enjoy the recognition. During these years, it lost in 1955 J. Stanley Edwards, incorporator of the College and life trustee; in 1957 James Elton Bragg, who had given outstanding leadership to the Examination Board; and in 1958 Ernest J. Clark, incorporator, past president, past chairman of the Board and life trustee.

For many years, the management examination program of the College had been a disappointment. Study materials were inadequate, and interest on the part of candidates was low. In spite of the vigorous efforts of volunteer chairmen from time to time, the program did not progress. It was apparent that special full-

Mr. Smith sponsors a C.L.U. candidate —a story in pictures, widely distributed. These shots show *(right)* Mr. Smith hanging an autographed photograph of Dr. Huebner which he received when his candidate took his first examination; *(below)* Mr. Smith entertaining his candidate and wife after successful completion of five examinations; *(bottom)* Mr. Smith's candidate receiving his C.L.U. diploma from Dr. Huebner. "Mr. Smith" is Benjamin M. Gaston, C.L.U., 1936; the candidate, B. M. Gaston, Jr., C.L.U. 1959 ˙nd his wife, Leslie.

time professional leadership was necessary. Therefore, after a long search, the trustees in 1956 appointed Dr. Thomas J. Luck director of management education. Dr. Luck was a specialist in the management field, and had been head of the department of business administration at the College of William and Mary, in Virginia. Dr. Luck laid a sound foundation for the revived program by a thorough review of the existing courses and exploratory development of new work, doing teaching himself in several pilot classes.

The new program was worked out with the cooperation of the Life Insurance Agency Management Association and the General Agents and Managers Conference of the National Association of Life Underwriters. It was a complete revision and modernization of the twenty-five-year-old course of studies for general agents, managers, and home office executives. The curriculum was built on the foundation of three basic parts interchangeable with C.L.U. examination Parts I, II, and IV; with two additional specialized parts covering human relations, management principles, and sales and financial management. Qualifying candidates were awarded diplomas in Agency Management.

At first it was thought best to withhold promotion of the new program until it was well tested. Formal introduction of the revised curriculum was made in the spring of 1958. The plan was to restrict activity to about a dozen cities so that Dr. Luck could work closely with study group leaders and students. Demand was so insistent, however, that there were 24 study classes with 394 students in 22 cities. In 1959, there were 88 completers, 10 times the number for the low year of 1955. The program has been constantly reappraised and improved. It has won steadily increasing approval, and 145 received the diploma in Agency Management at the 1962 conferment.

Another important educational development was the David McCahan Foundation. Following Dr. McCahan's death, Dr. Huebner, James Elton Bragg, and Charles J. Zimmerman were appointed a committee to plan a suitable memorial. They arranged for appropriate resolutions and a portrait of Dr. Mc-

Cahan for the College, with colored photographs for members of his family and the library of the Huebner Foundation. The committee then proposed an additional permanent memorial in the form of an educational foundation.

This idea was warmly approved. Grant L. Hill became chairman of the David McCahan Memorial Fund Committee to raise the necessary money, and the cause was supported generously by C.L.U.s all over the country. In 1956, through an appropriate bylaw, the David McCahan Foundation was established as an integral part of the College under the direction of a Governing Committee whose first chairman was Harold M. Stewart. He was succeeded by Holgar J. Johnson.

The initial objective of the Foundation was to finance an annual original lecture to be presented and discussed before an important university or industry group. The lecture would be distributed in printed form as "a contribution of unusual significance to life insurance and the insuring community." Provision also was made that this purpose might be varied somewhat as changing conditions or opportunities might suggest. The aim was to provide a "forum for creative thinking." The introduction to the first printed lecture stated:

> Annually, the Committee selects a distinguished authority known for his capacity for applying creative thinking to a problem and whose training equips him to penetrate beneath the obvious. The David McCahan Lectures, by analysing broad environmental issues on a scholarly plane, should suggest new avenues of opportunity to life insurance in its quest for better ways to serve. Conceivably they may also act as stimulants to other authorities for further exploration.

The first McCahan Foundation lecture was presented on May 21, 1957, as a high light of the two-day International Insurance Conference sponsored by the University of Pennsylvania. The Conference celebrated the seventy-fifth anniversary of the Wharton School of Finance and Commerce, and attracted outstanding insurance executives from the United States and abroad. Dr. Gregg was codirector of the Conference.

Dr. John Sloan Dickey, president of Dartmouth College, was the first McCahan Foundation lecturer on this historic occasion. His subject was, "The American Design: *E. Pluribus Unum,* But Still Many." He emphasized as America's strength our double urges to independence and social cooperation, creating a kind of tension that is stimulating and leads to achievement.

In his discussion following Dr. Dickey's address, Dr. Huebner pointed out how the American family illustrates this diversity— the individual strives for independence, but still feels a strong desire to build his own family community in the next generation. Life insurance is the financial tool most effective in helping attain objectives of independence and community within the family.

Thus, Dr. Dickey made the first contribution to the American family theme which is the focus of study under the McCahan Foundation. Subsequently, Dr. William Fielding Ogburn, late eminent sociologist of the University of Chicago, prepared a paper on "The Family in Our Changing Society" for the 1958 meeting of the American Life Convention in Chicago. The next year Dr. James H. S. Bossard, internationally known sociologist-economist of the University of Pennsylvania, presented a paper at the University of Connecticut on "Large and Small Families— A Study in Contrasts."

As perspective developed in the study of family life and life insurance, it became obvious that a practical need was to create college-level educational material which might give C.L.U. students a greater insight into family life. The Governing Committee referred to the American family as "the philosophical heart of life insurance," and commissioned Dr. Bossard to prepare a textbook on "The Life Cycle of the American Family." Dr. Bossard, recently retired, was intensely interested in the project, and held great hope for the contribution the new text could make to general education as well as to the American College program. Tragically, creation of the text was interrupted by his death after he had written the first chapter, "The Concept of the Family Cycle." A discussion of the concept of the whole volume had been planned for a seminar at the University of Texas in May, 1960. After Dr. Bossard's death, Dr. Gregg continued the seminar with a University of Texas faculty group interested in the subject.

In 1962, Dr. John W. Riley, Jr., on behalf of the McCahan Foundation, took direction of additional research leading to the creation of the textbook. Dr. Riley is second vice president and director of social research for the Equitable Life of New York, and formerly head of the department of sociology at Rutgers University. In 1963, the College Development Study Commission appointed a committee to look into expansion of basic research by the American College, including research in the area of the American family.

The American College is interested in insurance education on both the domestic and foreign levels. Dr. Huebner personally and through his books has had a great influence on insurance education abroad. In recent years, many overseas educators have turned to the American College for advice and information.

Periodically the American College made studies of insurance education in the colleges and universities of the United States. Never, however, had a comprehensive survey been made of world insurance courses and professors. In 1960, the American College published a study of world insurance education made by Dr. Gregg. The survey, "Insurance Courses in Colleges and Universities Outside the United States," was in six languages—French, Spanish, German, Italian, and Portuguese as well as English. Dr. Gregg was assisted initially by his secretary, Mechthild K. Longo, and subsequently by Helen L. Schmidt. A review of the work in the *Journal of Insurance*, published by the American Association of University Teachers of Insurance, characterized it as "the most ambitious and the most significant piece of international insurance research ever undertaken by any of the national insurance organizations." The review continued:

> It can and should lead to major results in the development of insurance education, and the exchange of information among insurance teachers, and in allowing persons all over the world with a serious interest in insurance education, to become acquainted with one

another. The authors and the American College of Life Underwriters have earned the gratitude of everyone who is really interested in furthering the progress of insurance.

Mrs. Schmidt's contribution to this study is illustrative of her many specialized services since coming to the College in 1949. She was administrative assistant to the dean, where she was closely concerned with the executive problems of registration and examination operations. In recent years, she has served as secretary to the president. In that post, her long experience, her great capacity for taking on administrative responsibilities, and her effective work in editorial tasks have relieved the College's administrative officers of many burdens.

Another woman with longer service who has made an outstanding contribution to the College is Esther M. Horr. Miss Horr received her baccalaureate from the University of Pennsylvania, and in 1937 joined the College staff as assistant to the dean. From the beginning, her responsibilities included supervision of the accounting and budgetary operations of the College. In 1960, she was appointed to the official position of assistant treasurer. On her twenty-fifth anniversary with the College, in 1962, Dr. Huebner said: "Twenty-five years with the American College is a long time—a quarter of a century extending over five-sevenths of the entire operational history of the organization. I am personally very grateful to Miss Horr for her loyal service and I know all my colleagues feel likewise. My hope is that she may continue to serve the College for many more years and that those years will be filled with health, happiness and contentment."

Over the years, the College has been fortunate in having the services of dedicated and devoted personnel in secretarial and clerical positions. Among those who had served five years or longer before leaving the employ of the College are: Mrs. Jane M. Grimes, Miss Anna M. Kelly, Mrs. Anna E. Kost, Mrs. Agnes Lang, Mrs. Frances McMaster, Mrs. Marie DeGeorge Melone, Miss Catherine S. Morton, and Mrs. Ruth P. Novastis.

A dozen other men and women have served five years or longer and continue in the employ of the College. Their effective work day by day makes possible the successful operation of the College. These people are: Mrs. Pearl Blake, Mrs. Virginia Eisenberger, Miss Elizabeth Horr, Miss Lenore Matthias, Mrs. Elsie Miller, Mrs. Loretta Reidenger, Mrs. Rose Shawcross, Mrs. Agnes Simonsen, Mrs. Margaret T. Simpson, Mr. J. Michael Casey, Mr. Peter Ranieri, and Mr. Owen Splain.

In addition, mention should be made of three persons whose tenure with the College was less than five years, but who served on special assignments. They are: Edmond H. Curcuru, director of public relations from February through May, 1951; Robert D. Wallingford, assistant to the dean from February through October, 1953; and Peter E. Camp, registrar from March, 1961, to September, 1963.

Richard T. McFalls has been business manager of the College since 1960. He worked for the College on a part-time basis while attending the Wharton School, and became a full-time staff member in 1957. As business manager, he has the responsibility for clerical personnel, purchasing, and building operation. He was of inestimable service to the College Building Committee during the construction of Huebner Hall.

In October, 1959, the College and Society were most fortunate in obtaining James A. Ballew to fill the vacancy created by the resignation of Howard Shaw. As director of public relations, Mr. Ballew brought to the job a rich educational background, having received his baccalaureate from Yale in 1948. His previous experience included editorial work on home office magazines of the Travelers Insurance Company and the Aetna, as well as publications of the Life Insurance Agency Management Association.

Chapter 22

FOR AN EXPANDING FUTURE

Each year since the Silver Anniversary of the College, a 25-year class of graduates has been honored at the C.L.U. conferment dinner. In 1961, Benjamin M. Gaston, a member of the class of 1936, was impressed to think of the sweeping changes which had occurred since he received his designation. He commented that if the class of 1936 had gone immediately into hibernation, and had emerged alongside the class of 1961, what changes they would have found, and how poorly they would have been equipped to serve the current life insurance market. Inspired by these thoughts, he wrote an article which was published in the C.L.U. *Journal*, summarizing the changes of the past quarter-century which affected life underwriters.

Mr. Gaston pointed out that in 1936 the United States was still deep in the great depression, and that World War II and the Korean conflict were in the future. From those cataclysmic national experiences came many of the developments of the next 25 years. In 1936, the government's problem was deflation, not inflation. Unions were weak. The Social Security Act had just been passed. National Service Life Insurance was yet to come. Interest rates were going down to the lowest point in years. Income taxes were relatively small and limited in their impact on the population generally.

Then he reviewed the changes—not only social security and veterans' benefits, but also the huge growth of the business; development of group insurance, pensions, profit-sharing plans, business insurance, and estate planning; reinsurance; the change

292

in relative importance of industrial insurance; the many plans for financing premiums by loans, pretax dollars, split-dollar arrangements, and other ways. He pointed out the exciting developments in medicine with resulting changes in underwriting standards, the increase of limits, the technical changes in life insurance operations actuarially and under the law. Truly, life underwriting in 1961 was very different from life underwriting in 1936.

Any successful educational institution must adapt to changing needs of its constituency. Contemplating the panorama of innovations in American business and society which Mr. Gaston reviewed, it is easy to see why the American College of the sixties must be different from the American College of the thirties.

The trustees constantly had been sensitive to the need to develop and adjust to changing conditions and opportunities. Important decisions were crystallized in 1960. The bylaws of the College were completely rewritten to include health insurance under the life value concept, to provide recognition for all qualified workers in the life and health insurance business, and to construct a College organization adequate for an expanding future.

The statement in Article I of the aims and objectives of the College was expanded appropriately, as quoted in the current College *Catalogue:*

It is the broad purpose of the American College of Life Underwriters to serve as an institution of higher learning for those persons who participate in the process of insuring human life values.

Specifically, the aims and objectives of the College are:

(1) To establish standards of education in the field of life and health insurance and in collateral fields.

(2) To cooperate with colleges and universities in preparing students for careers in life and health insurance.

(3) To cooperate with educational institutions in life and health insurance education for students in other fields.

(4) To promote research and the preparation and publication of textbooks and other material deemed essential to the fullest realization of the College's educational program.

(5) To recognize properly qualified persons with a professional designation and such other diplomas and certificates as are deemed appropriate.

(6) To establish, if occasion demands, its own resident institution, in which event the entrance qualifications of such institution shall conform to those of other accredited colleges and universities.

(7) To provide, in cooperation with the American Society of Chartered Life Underwriters, a program of continuing education for those who have attained the C.L.U. designation to help them better serve the life-value needs of the public.

Before this historic decision to concentrate on one all-inclusive C.L.U. designation was reached, serious consideration was given to the possibility of initiating a designation of Chartered Life Manager (C.L.M.). This led to additional proposals of other designations: C.H.U. for Chartered Health Underwriter, C.P.U. for Chartered Pension Underwriter, C.G.U. for Chartered Group Underwriter, C.E.P. for Chartered Estate Planner, and the like. Speaking later of this matter, Dr. Gregg said:

After lengthy investigation and discussion, it was concluded that public recognition of multiple designations in life and health insurance was highly unlikely, and that multiple designations would lead only to confusion and probable rejection by the public of the meaningfulness of all. Therefore, it was agreed that every effort should be made to have everyone in life and health insurance accept the C.L.U. as the one professional designation of specific significance to the life and health insurance-buying public (with C.P.C.U. as its counterpart in property insurance), and that every effort should continue to be made to build the meaning of this designation with the general public.

Then, too, it was reasoned that the fine academic acceptance of "C.L.U." as a designation comparable to "C.P.A." might be jeopardized by a multiplicity of awards. Finally, and perhaps most important, it seemed entirely appropriate that persons in health insurance should be permitted to earn the coveted C.L.U. since over the years it has tended to connote the broader concept of Chartered "Life Value" Underwriter.

Thus, the American College became a national college of life and health insurance, and its educational services are available to health insurance personnel on the same basis as life insurance people. Experience requirements were changed so that health insurance personnel could qualify fully for the C.L.U. designation, which now has the broader connotation of Chartered "Human Life Value" Underwriter. This move pleased Dr. Huebner greatly. From the beginning of his teaching he had urged the logic of considering health and disability protection as a part of the complete service of life underwriters. To explain the thinking of the trustees in their decision, Dr. Gregg stated:

> Several factors seem to explain the logic and the timing of the decision that the College should accept the responsibility of providing collegiate level education for health insurance personnel. In the first place, life and health insurance are allies in the sense that both provide protection for human life risks. The human life is exposed basically to the economic risks of premature death, disability, and retirement. Each results in economic loss. Hence, it can be said that life and health insurance are truly partners in serving the human life value insurance needs of the American public . . . perhaps it would be appropriate to use some supergeneric term such as "life value insurance" to describe the overall field of life and health insurance.

> A second factor is related to the rapid growth of health insurance in America in recent years. As the industry has expanded and assumed greater economic and social responsibility, it has inevitably felt the need for collegiate-level professional-type education. Life insurance went through this stage about three decades ago; the time for educational maturity for health insurance is now here.

> Also a factor is the greatly increased interest of the life insurance industry in health insurance in recent years. Many companies have

American College administrative officers in 1960. *Left to right:* Davis W. Gregg, James A. Ballew, Daniel P. Kedzie, G. Victor Hallman, Dr. Huebner, Albert H. Clark, Esther M. Horr, W. W. Dotterweich, Jack C. Keir, Walter B. Wheeler, Herbert C. Graebner.

expanded this area of their operations. This, in turn, has led to a strongly felt need for greater understanding of health insurance by life insurance field and home office personnel.

A fourth factor is the increasing sophistication of the public with reference to health insurance. Inevitably, this has created a need for better educated personnel within the industry. The day of the $10-annual premium accident policy is passing, and the day of diagnostic selling and programing to protect against disability, loss of income, and heavy medical expenses is now at hand.

A final factor is that as health insurance personnel are upgraded, inevitably they seek professional level recognition along with their professional level education. In the same way that the industry and its personnel need the education in order to serve the public effectively, the public needs some yardstick by which it can measure the competence of the health insurance personnel which serve it. This criterion is available only through a professional designation properly administered through an independent educational institution.

Another historic decision in this area was the re-definition of the broad inclusiveness of the American College as an institution of higher learning in life and health insurance. From the beginning, the C.L.U. had been granted not only to life insurance salesmen, but also to management in the home office and field and to insurance teachers. Still questions arose about eligibility qualifications.

A special committee considered this matter from all points of view, and sought the judgment of all groups in College and Society affairs. The agreement was that C.L.U. was the appropriate recognition not only for the field underwriter, but also for most life and health insurance personnel as well as teachers, regulators, brokers, and others involved in the process of insuring human life values. As stated, from the very early years most of these persons had been eligible and had received the C.L.U. on completing all the requirements. The efforts of the committee led to a specific clarification of who would be eligible, and to the agreement that, among others, full-time health insurance personnel should be permitted to earn the C.L.U.

This decision opened the door for those in responsible positions throughout life and health insurance companies. It encouraged them to strive for full understanding of the economic and social aspects of life and health insurance, thus broadly benefiting the companies, the field forces, and the public.

Through the years, the College standards as to who is eligible to sit for examinations, and the type of designation to be awarded, have been administered firmly by the Registration Board. The integrity and careful judgment these men bring to their responsibility are a very great assistance to the College officers in complex situations. Each year, several dozen cases involving special conditions are referred to the Board. Clarence B. Metzger has been chairman since 1951, succeeding John Marshall Holcombe, Jr.

Another major development of the C.L.U. program which the College adopted in 1960 was a series of certificate courses in specialized areas. The purpose of these courses is to provide education on the college level for specialized groups in life and health insurance. The Certificate Course in Agency Management, beginning with the 1962-63 academic year, replaces the Diploma in Agency Management with its five parts, three identical to regular C.L.U. examinations. Candidates now take two management examinations only (like the former M-3 and M-5), and receive a Certificate in Agency Management.

Two experimental certificate classes were conducted in the 1961-62 school year. Each comprised the first part of two new courses—company management and health insurance. It was contemplated that on successful completion of each course eligible candidates would receive respectively the American College Certificate in Company Management and Certificate in Health Insurance.

The pilot program showed that for the long range the health insurance course might better be designed for 30 sessions in one year, and that has been adopted as the standard plan. The course is designed for people in all segments of the life and health insurance business, and is organized at the college level. Similarly, the company management course is academically oriented.

The certificate courses generally will be more flexible in level, length, and content than the C.L.U. diploma program. However, each will have written examinations and will be administered on the same basis as C.L.U. examinations. The certificate courses will be open to C.L.U.s and non-C.L.U.s, except for advanced underwriting courses of a post-C.L.U. nature. Persons receiving certificates will not be permitted to indicate this on letterheads, business cards, insurance proposals, or advertising, so that there may be no public confusion with the established C.L.U. designation. Certificate courses are planned in group insurance, estate planning, and pensions.

A third area of the educational program of the College was re-defined in 1960 by establishment, with the American Society, of the Department of Continuing Education. One of the requirements of a profession is that its practitioners be regularly and persistently involved in continuing their education. The College and Society in the fall of 1956 had named a Joint Committee on Continuing Education to discuss the whole idea of the need and possible avenues of continuing education. Members of that preliminary group were: Chairman, Paul A. Norton*, H. C. Graebner*, Fitzhugh Traylor, George B. Byrnes*, Lantz L. Mackey, Loran E. Powell, Charles K. Reid II, Jack C. Windsor, Leslie J. Buchan, L. G. Steinbeck*, D. W. Gregg*, James Elton Bragg*, Coy G. Eklund, Ben S. McGiveran, Joseph H. Reese, Hilbert Rust*, Hal L. Nutt, John O. Todd, and Howard D. Shaw. Subsequently, a permanent committee was organized which comprised those starred in the foregoing list and Dr. Edmund L. Zalinski. This committee had several meetings in the spring of 1957, and agreed in recommending the creation of the joint department. It was determined that financing of the department would be shared equally by the Society and College. Although the Society's Institutes are a major avenue of continuing education, they were not

Raymond C. Johnson.
(*Bachrach*)

Paul A. Norton.

Charles W. Campbell.

Edmund L. Zalinski.

administratively a part of the responsibility of the joint department. Ideas for the program shifted back and forth considerably
over the next few years, and it was necessary to proceed slowly,
especially in the choice of leadership for the program.

Dr. Joseph M. Belth was appointed assistant director of continuing education in April, 1961, and made creative contributions at the beginning of certain aspects of the department's work.
Unfortunately, the College and Society lost his services to Indiana University within a year after he initiated this activity. Paul
S. Mills, managing director of the Society, served as director of
continuing education with Dr. Belth, and continued this responsibility until May, 1963, when Fred J. Dopheide assumed the directorship. Mr. Dopheide earned an LL.D. from the University
of Chicago Law School, and practiced law for a year after his
graduation. He came to the College and Society from a position
as brokerage manager for the Prudential Insurance Company of
America.

Although much of the program is still in the developmental
stage, considerable progress has been made in cosponsoring
with selected C.L.U. chapters one-day regional educational seminars for C.L.U.s throughout the country, and in preparing two
discussion outlines, "The Case of Dr. Smith" and "Stock Redemption." In 1962 and 1963 the discussion outlines were used
by 47 chapters—"The Case of Dr. Smith" in 32, and "Stock
Redemption" in 15.

C.L.U. seminars had their beginning with the first national
seminar in Philadelphia in September, 1959. The all-day program immediately preceding the National Association of Life
Underwriters convention was held on the University of Pennsylvania campus with more than seven hundred men and women
attending. The stated purpose was to provide "a forum for the
best thinking on vital questions concerning the meaning of life
insurance in today's economy." The speakers and their subjects
indicate the scope of that historic event. The papers presented

were published and widely distributed in the fall issue of *The Journal of the American Society of Chartered Life Underwriters.*

"Continuing Education" by Paul A. Norton.

"A New Quest for Security" by Karl R. Bopp, president of the Federal Reserve Bank of Philadelphia.

"A Modern Look at the Economics of Life Insurance" by S. S. Huebner.

"Life Insurance as an Investment Today" by Herbert C. Graebner.

"Meeting Our Responsibilities to the Public" by Benjamin N. Woodson.

"Some Practical Uses of Life Insurance in Modern Business" by Charles B. McCaffrey, of the Wharton School.

The second national seminar was held in Philadelphia on June 2, 1961, in connection with the dedication of Huebner Hall in Bryn Mawr. There were simultaneous separate sessions for home office executives and field people. Required "homework" for each was the study of transcripts of interviews.

The session for home office executives was based on a hypothetical case study by Abram T. Collier, senior vice president and general counsel of the John Hancock Mutual Life Insurance Company. The study script, "Decision at Zenith Life," brought out in recorded interviews the strengths and weaknesses of four senior executives being considered for the presidency of Zenith Life, a hypothetical large life insurance company. At the seminar, a panel of four distinguished leaders in business education debated the qualifications of the candidates, bringing out various psychological, leadership, and management principles. These panel members were: Edward C. Bursk, editor of the *Harvard Business Review;* Dr. Howard W. Johnson, dean of the School of Industrial Management, Massachusetts Institute of Technology; Dr. Harold J. Leavitt, professor of industrial administration and psychology in the Graduate School of Industrial Administration, Carnegie Institute of Technology; and Dr. Willis J. Winn, dean

of the Wharton School, University of Pennsylvania. Mr. Collier
was the moderator. Both the homework and the seminar session
proved thought provoking to those who participated. There was
strong difference of opinion in the audience, and when the vote
for Zenith president was announced, Dr. Winn proposed to the
audience: "Return to another national seminar two years from
now, which will be titled, 'Crisis at Zenith Life.' "

The seminar for field underwriters was, "Profiles of Excellence, A Dramatic Case Study of Life Underwriting." The homework was interviews with four fictitious candidates, written by
Leroy G. Steinbeck. The publicity for the session indicated questions the audience would consider:

> If there were an award for America's outstanding life underwriter,
> what sort of person should receive it? Would he be a life and qualify-
> ing member of MDRT . . . a consistent NQA qualifier . . . a "spe-
> cialist" . . . a "general practitioner" . . . a C.L.U. . . . or what? While
> no real award exists, there will be a real debate on this topic in
> Philadelphia on June 2 and it promises to be one of the truly memor-
> able programs put on anywhere in the life insurance business in
> recent years. In an unusual and dramatic setting (you've never seen
> a seminar staged like this one!), a panel of distinguished and forth-
> right agents and management people will examine the qualifications
> of four fictitious agents who have been nominated for the "1961
> Huebner Award" (also fictitious) as America's Outstanding Life
> Underwriter. In the course of spirited discussion, they will bring
> out those characteristics which are vital to a person's success in
> life insurance selling . . . drawing upon their own experiences and
> backgrounds for the benefit of the audience.

Roy Steinbeck was moderator for the underwriters' session.
The panel members were: Howard D. Goldman, general agent
for Northwestern Mutual, Richmond, Virginia; Arthur F. Priebe,
representative for Penn Mutual, Rockford, Illinois; E. Price
Ripley, representative for National Life of Vermont, Roanoke,
Virginia; and Bernard H. Zais, representative for Connecticut
Mutual, Rutland, Vermont.

Wm. Eugene Hays. (*Bachrach*)

Paul S. Mills.

In addition to the two national seminars, the Department of Continuing Education began a series of one-day seminars co-sponsored with individual chapters or, in a number of cases, groups of chapters in a certain geographical area. During 1962–63, one-day seminars were held in cooperation with the following chapters:

Milwaukee	Rocky	Pittsburgh
Seattle	Mountain	Buffalo
Miami	Richmond	Rochester
San Francisco	Cincinnati	Dallas
Oakland	Evansville	Fort Worth
San Jose	Indianapolis	Atlanta
Sacramento	Kentucky	New Orleans
Cleveland	Minneapolis	Baltimore
	St. Paul	

These one-day seminars followed a common pattern, with morning and afternoon sessions and a midday lunch. Recognized authorities in fields of advanced life insurance problems who had demonstrated effectiveness in communicating ideas to life underwriters in the summer C.L.U. Institutes discussed such broad subjects as profit-sharing plans, business interests in estates, and charitable giving in estate planning. In most instances, these one-day seminars were held on college campuses.

A large number of C.L.U.s sincerely want a plan for continuing their professional education. The College accepts its share of the responsibility to meet this need in the provision of materials and methods, and in cooperation with local groups in planning practical programs. There is also the long-range vision of continuing education programs on the Bryn Mawr campus.

An important development of the educational program of the College, indicated in the 1960 statement of objectives, is the extension of activities to students in other areas of learning. Some five hundred colleges and universities now have insurance courses. Increasingly over the years, College officers have worked with the faculties of many of these schools in planning survey insurance courses that appeal to the general student. This consultation service has been particularly effective in introducing creative concepts and in gaining adequate course time for life insurance coverage. Moreover, for students who never will be able to spare the class hours for such work, life insurance may be made a part of other standard courses. College consultants are working with professional schools—engineering, dental, medical, theological, educational, pharmaceutical—to incorporate or expand in courses already offered material on family financial planning, including life insurance. For example, courses on Economics for Engineers, Medical Civics, and Pastoral Counseling are strengthened by such material. The dean of one theological school commented that more than a quarter of a minister's time today may be spent in family counseling, often about financial problems. Beginning in 1962–63, the College's Lecture Bureau offered liberal arts colleges a lecture series. Qualified speakers are carrying the story of life insurance, presented as a special event in connection with courses in economics, mathematics, sociology, or other fields. Such education for the consumer will enable him to use life insurance more effectively in meeting personal needs.

In 1962–63, part-time educational consultants were added to the staff in order to meet the need for continued close contact with the growing number of C.L.U. students and teachers. These were: William T. Beadles, Illinois Wesleyan University, Bloomington, Illinois; Kenneth W. Herrick, Texas Christian University, Fort Worth; David A. Ivry, University of Connecticut, Storrs; and Arthur W. Mason, Jr., Washington University, St. Louis. These men are college professors and experienced C.L.U. teachers who are being assigned for visits to C.L.U. study groups in their respective local areas.

The College aims constantly to cooperate with local institutions and C.L.U. groups to improve teaching in C.L.U. classes. Each year, records of individual class teachers are studied, and help is given to correct any apparent weaknesses.

New teaching techniques are watched carefully. The College

currently has an appropriation of $15,000 to develop and experiment with the use of programed study material.

As in the past, new materials are being created to meet special needs. The expansion of Part V to a full-blown, individual section of the course, rather than a comprehensive examination, required new materials. Among the significant volumes developed by the College over the years for use in Part V is the book, *Human Behavior and Life Insurance,* authored by G. Hugh Russell and Kenneth Black, Jr., and published in 1963 by Prentice-Hall, Inc.

The College cannot stand still in its program. As it continues to serve the needs of the industry and the public, it is anticipated that in the next decade alone the number of students in organized C.L.U. classes might well be 25,000.

Chapter 23

MONEY AND MEN

As in the early history of the College, the expanding program brought need for more money, and especially for a broader base of permanent income. In 1958, a Special Committee on Financial Welfare had been appointed by the trustees. The operations of 1957–58 had shown a modest surplus, but the 1958–59 budget omitted many desirable items and still indicated a budgeted deficit of over $40,000. The decision had been made to move College headquarters to a suburban location, and to erect a building which necessarily would mean increased financial responsibility. Charles J. Zimmerman was named chairman of a new committee, which was charged to make a "thorough study of the College's present and future finances." The trustees agreed that the College must have a satisfactory reserve position that would assure future financial stability. This was not only important for the peace of mind of trustees and officers, but essential in recruiting outstanding men for the staff. Men of promise, such as the College needed, must see in the organization assurance of its continuation and growth.

Moreover, the student body was burgeoning. The number taking C.L.U. examinations in 1958 was 5,396, up from the postwar 1951 low point of 2,310; and the completers totaled 641, compared with the low of 367 in 1952. Such growth made it highly desirable to have adequate funds for research, teacher training, and other essential development activities.

The current $450,000 operational budget came principally from registration and examination fees, including the credit cer-

309

Charles J. Zimmerman.

tificates drawn on the Cooperative Fund for Underwriter Training. Good businessmen realized that this was not an adequate financial structure.

Joseph H. Reese was named vice chairman of the new Special Committee on Financial Welfare; Dr. Gregg, secretary; and members Orville E. Beal, Roger Hull, Raymond C. Johnson, Cecil J. North, Earl R. Trangmar, and William H. Andrews. The committee made a deep and comprehensive study during the next year. It re-evaluated the current program of the College, analyzed the probable or possible developments of the near future, studied available sources of income, and prepared far-reaching recommendations.

One outgrowth of this activity was appointment of a Special Committee on Aims and Objectives of the College. Raymond C. Johnson was chairman, and members were William H. Andrews, Orville E. Beal, Charles W. Campbell, Stanton G. Hale, S. S. Huebner, Gerald W. Page, James P. Poole, Gordon K. Smith, Earl R. Trangmar, Robert L. Woods, and Benjamin N. Woodson. The deliberations of this committee led to adoption of the official new statement of objectives described previously.

The Zimmerman Committee pointed out the magnitude of College operations in a picture few supporters of the College had visualized. For example, in 1958 the officers were supervising 555 people (including 446 university personnel—proctors and graders) working 23,000 man-hours. In connection simply with the professional examinations, for instance, these responsibilities in 1958 included:

1. Determining eligibility of 2,350 new candidates.
2. Preparing examination questions for seven different C.L.U. and management four-hour examinations.
3. Administering examinations at 169 regional centers in the United States and three places abroad.
4. Grading examinations—11,234 individual gradings by 66 graders.
5. Evaluating experience credentials for 760 completers.

Roger Hull.

6. Maintaining records on 12,000 candidates.
7. Awarding diplomas to 667 people.
8. Disseminating information to individuals, companies, and
   the press on the progress of active candidates—5,512 taking examinations that year.

The Zimmerman Committee helped the trustees to see the College of today and tomorrow with new perspective and understanding. It did an incomparable service in its thorough work of analysis, evaluation, and recommendation.

A major result of Committee studies was creation of two funds.
The first objective was a million-dollar Permanent Endowment
Fund. Roger Hull, president of the Mutual Life of New York,
accepted the chairmanship of the fund-raising committee. His
associates were top executives from a dozen leading companies.
They made an enthusiastic appeal to the life and health insurance
companies, asking for gifts in specific amounts based on company
size. Mr. Hull said: "The companies responded magnificently.
On the first go-around not a major company was out." In fact,
almost $850,000 of the million-dollar goal was pledged in a phe-
nomenal two-month period. Contributions are being paid over a
five-year period, and more than the million dollars now is assured from more than 150 companies. This is permanent endowment. The income will undergird other current revenue in the
general operation of the College, and provide the means for creative work in line with the broad purposes of the College.

The initial objective for the second fund, the C.L.U. Development Fund, was also a million dollars. The major part of this
money was intended to pay for the new College home in Bryn
Mawr; the remainder would support the program of continuing
education for C.L.U.s.

A National C.L.U. Development Council was set up with William H. Andrews, Jr., chairman. The Council included some 130
C.L.U.s representing every American Society chapter across the
country. They organized a nationwide drive to solicit contributions from C.L.U.s and friends of C.L.U. The kickoff dinner in

Philadelphia, October 21, 1960, was attended by nearly all members of the Council. Charles J. Zimmerman talked on a most appropriate subject, "We Make No Small Plans."

The Insurance Field in a major editorial concerning the project concluded:

> This exciting project, which is certain to capture the imagination of all Society members, is further evidence of what monumental thinkers and workers are trying to accomplish in major areas of vast importance to C.L.U.'s, and therefore to all life underwriters and the whole business of life insurance.

The drive was set up with Council members as key men in their respective communities. Donors who pledged $1,000 over a 10-year period would be enrolled as members of the Golden Key Society, with their names inscribed in the Golden Key Book at headquarters. They also would receive a specially designed golden key tie-clasp or lapel pin, and a framed golden key for the office. Further, a Golden Key Society luncheon at the annual meeting has become traditional.

Emphasis was placed on capital giving as well as gifts from current income. An attractive brochure describing a number of capital gift ideas was supplied for use of interested donors. Giving through life insurance policies also was encouraged. More than one hundred gifts were made in this way, and it may well be that life underwriters who made this kind of sale to themselves were strengthened in selling the idea of bequests through life insurance to others.

The results of the Development Fund campaign were impressive. Success was assured from the beginning, and by July 15, 1963, more than $921,000 had been pledged by 2,904 persons, of whom 607 were Golden Key Society members. Pledges and gifts have continued to come in, and College and Society leaders now visualize the Development Fund augmented without limit by current and testamentary gifts.

The C.L.U. Development Fund of the American College is

maintained as a separate fund with separate accounting, but is merged with other College funds for investment. A nine-man Board of Overseers makes recommendations to the College's Board of Trustees regarding allocation of Development Fund resources.

The Zimmerman Committee also emphasized the continuing importance of annual support from the life and health companies through the Cooperative Fund. The Fund is essentially a method whereby the companies provide financial assistance to their own personnel. Subscribers to the Fund are entitled to an unlimited number of C.L.U. examination credit certificates which their representatives may use to pay one-half of any C.L.U. or certificate examination fee. Subscriptions to the Cooperative Fund are based on a formula. Following the Zimmerman Committee recommendation, the formula has been changed in recent years to provide a minimum subscription of $100 annually, and a graduated increase beyond the former $11,250 maximum for the largest companies. The name of the Fund was changed in 1960 to the Cooperative Fund for Underwriter Education.

To co-ordinate the educational activities of the College on its several expanding fronts, the 1960 bylaws established the Educational Policy Board. It is composed of the dean, 12 members, and the chairman of the Committee on Continuing Education as an ex officio member. The Board is charged with general supervision of the educational policy of the College. Subcommittees have special responsibility for various phases of the work, such as the basic C.L.U. courses, management education, health insurance education, examination procedures, and so on.

In all, 15 standing committees were specified in the 1960 bylaws, and more than one hundred volunteers with specialized experience strengthen the official staff of the College. The majority, but not all, of the committee members are C.L.U.s. The bylaws provide that age seventy is the limit of service for trustees and committee members except those designated "life" or "emeritus." Typically, the men and women who have achieved the C.L.U. themselves are strong boosters for the cause. They are glad to give time, money, and influence for an expanding program to benefit individual underwriters, the life insurance industry, and the insuring public.

Through the years, new strands of strength were being woven into the rope of American College leadership. In 1960, Julian S. Myrick celebrated his eightieth birthday. He had made an outstanding contribution not only to the life insurance business, but to the world of sport through his interest in international tennis, and to the nation through his work with the Hoover Commission. With his service to the American College still at a high point of effectiveness, he chose to retire as chairman of the Board of Trustees. He had held that office for 22 years, and as chairman emeritus he continues to make important contributions to the progress of the College. In 1963, Mr. Myrick had the unusual distinction of being elected to two halls of fame; after being honored by election to the Insurance Hall of Fame at The Ohio State University, he was later named to the National Lawn Tennis Hall of Fame.

At the thirty-third annual C.L.U. conferment dinner, Mr. Myrick made the conferment address. He announced that Paul F. Clark had succeeded him as chairman of the American College, just as Clark had succeeded him in 1928 as president of the National Association of Life Underwriters. He reviewed the historic principles of the American College, the important changes that had just been adopted (as reported in this and the preceding chapter) and then turned to the future with these words of prophecy:

What will C.L.U. be like thirty-three years from now? Long-term prophecy is foolish, but will you permit the following suggestions?

The basic principles which have guided the College in the past will continue to prevail; the standards for earning the C.L.U. designation will be even higher than today.

Most field men and a substantial proportion of home office executives will hold the C.L.U. or some other diploma awarded by the College.

The American Society of C.L.U. will have a membership of 100,000.

Many other branches of American industry, business and finance will have educational programs modeled after the American College and leading to a professional designation.

C.L.U.s will have won recognition with the public, and the public will ask for, will expect, and will pay for professional service.

The College cannot measure the extent of its indebtedness to Julian Myrick. Not only did he give his own time, money, and influence to the cause of C.L.U., but he also was the magnet that drew many others into key positions in the work. Paul Clark said of him:

Julian Myrick's tireless energy, quick perception and generous understanding have inspired the loyalty and affection of all his associates in the development of the American College. He has always manifested that devotion to its interests without regard to self, which marks the truly professional man.

With Mr. Clark's election as chairman of the Board, Charles J. Zimmerman, long a helpful supporter of the College, was named vice chairman.

The next year Mr. Zimmerman and three others were named life trustees. The title honors men who have given outstanding service to the College for many years, and opens places among the term trustees for new leaders. The other new life trustees were: Robert Dechert, counsel of the College since 1936, whose sound judgment and broad experience had led the College safely through the mazes of many problems; Joseph H. Reese, Sr.,

secretary of the College since 1949, and the hardest-working
member of the building committees for two headquarters buildings; and Earl R. Trangmar, long a trustee and the man who
had made unusual contributions to the College through his part
in the creation and administration of the Cooperative Fund for
Underwriter Education. Mr. Trangmar was in good health at the
National Association of Life Underwriters convention where he
was first honored as a life trustee, but, to the sorrow of his many
friends, died hardly a month later.

Life Trustees, 1961. *Standing, left to right:* **Earl R. Trangmar, Robert
Dechert, Joseph H. Reese, Charles J. Zimmerman.** *Seated:* **Julian S. Myrick,
Dr. Huebner, Paul F. Clark.**

The 1960 bylaws named an enlarged list of College officials,
and provided for internal reorganization of departments for effective handling of the expanded program. In May, 1962, the
educational functions of the College were reorganized for greater
effectiveness. The work of the Department of Management Education was divided on a functional basis among the Departments
of Educational Services, Field Services, Educational Publica-

tions, and Examinations. Dr. Keir, as assistant dean, accepted responsibility for the Departments of Educational Publications and Examinations, and the office of the registrar. Mr. Dotterweich was appointed assistant dean, and assumed the overall responsibility of the Departments of Educational Services and Field Services.

As director of educational publications, G. Victor Hallman joined the official family in August, 1960. He had received his B.S. and M.A. at the Wharton School of Finance and Commerce, and had completed course work for his doctorate. He taught at Upsala and Rider Colleges as an assistant professor of insurance before coming to the American College. Mr. Hallman has proven an effective administrator in dealing with the exacting problems of the teaching and learning tools prepared by the College or recommended to the students by the College.

Dr. Robert M. Crowe joined the staff as director of examinations in September, 1961. After earning his baccalaureate at Boston College, he completed graduate work at the University of Pennsylvania. He taught insurance at Northeastern and Boston Universities before joining the College. With the expanding examination program, Dr. Crowe assumed responsibility for preparing and grading examinations in both the C.L.U. and certificate programs of the College.

As previously indicated, Walter B. Wheeler joined the College staff as director of field services in October, 1951. He earned his baccalaureate at the University of Georgia, then entered the life insurance business as an underwriter for the Equitable of New York. He joined the Northwestern Mutual, and in addition to his regular duties taught L.U.T.C. courses. Over the years, Mr. Wheeler has devoted himself in an energetic manner to becoming acquainted with C.L.U. and educational leaders throughout the country. Under his direction, the number of organized classes and study groups has grown steadily.

In June, 1963, Dr. Ronald C. Horn joined the American College staff as director of educational services. Dr. Horn received

Orville E. Beal. (*Bachrach*)

his doctorate at the University of Pennsylvania, and was assistant professor of insurance at Syracuse University before joining the American College. With additional new staff members, it is believed that now, for the first time in its history, the College is organized so that educational personnel can devote more of their time to creative research and writing. A vital college must, of course, *teach*, but it must also *learn*. Chairman Paul Clark quoted, during discussions concerning this fundamental concept, a statement by the head of the famous Massachusetts Institute of Technology. He said that is a great school because its faculty devote 75 per cent of their time to research; 25 per cent to teaching. A college must not only transmit existing knowledge to its students; it must create new knowledge.

Initiated by the trustees in 1962 was the College Development Study Commission. Orville E. Beal is chairman. The basic purpose of the Commission is "to study and evaluate the development of the College over the next decade, estimate the resource needs growing out of this development, and make appropriate recommendations to the Board of Trustees."

Among the major committees of the Commission working to accomplish this objective is a Committee on Growth Projection and Resource Needs, with Roger Hull as chairman; a Committee on Graduate School for Chartered Life Underwriters, with Charles J. Zimmerman as chairman; a Committee on Center for Advanced Studies in Risk and Insurance, with Orville E. Beal as chairman; a Committee on College's Future Role in Enforcing C.L.U. Professional Standards, with Ben S. McGiveran as chairman; and a Committee on Cooperation with the American Institute for Property and Liability Underwriters with Relation to Utilization of and Acquisition of Physical Facilities, with Davis W. Gregg as chairman.

At the request of the Beal Commission, the American Society of Chartered Life Underwriters appointed a similar commission to study the Society's future needs.

Dr. Gregg has a vision of the College in the future as a research center. It will have experimental laboratories for testing new teaching techniques and developing new materials. It will offer graduate study opportunities. It will be a research center for investigation into many phases of life and health insurance coverage as well as social and economic subjects. For example, much needs to be learned about careers in life and health insurance for college-trained people—what are the opportunities in companies, what specific education is prerequisite, what guidance and motivation can lead young people into such work? The whole question of the impact of life and health insurance on bank credit is another area for study. The American family in all its aspects is a research field already being explored by the McCahan Foundation.

Pure research in all these fields may be expected to have large and very tangible benefits to the insurance industry, as research in the physical sciences has benefited other kinds of business. Such investigation may become one of the important services of the American College in the future.

A calling which is based on well-organized academic training in a recognized area of knowledge, and which seeks constant adaptation to changing public needs through research has a claim on the good name of "profession." A college can work toward that end, as the American College has. In addition, to become a profession a calling needs a recognized code of ethics and means of enforcing its standard. The American Society had been working definitely in that direction over a number of years. The committee charged with the development of an appropriate standard was Frank E. Brennan, Elmer F. Davy, Lloyd Lafot, Robert K. Powers, George N. Quigley, Jr., Jack White, and Gerald W. Page, chairman, with Robert L. Woods and Paul S. Mills, ex officio. The committee was launched by order of the directors in 1958. The members were unanimous in their feeling that, to be effective, a code should be representative of the beliefs and practices of a majority of the Society. When it started work on the code, the committee sought suggestions from the membership for points to be included. The next year it submitted a proposed statement to Society members for comment and suggestions for changes and additions. Finally, in 1960, the code was adopted by the Board of Directors of the Society, and subsequently ratified by mail by a majority of the members. The code as adopted has two parts: guidance to professional conduct and rules of professional conduct. The official statement of this basis for professional service is given below.

THE CODE OF ETHICS
subscribed to by all members of the
American Society of
Chartered Life Underwriters

Because it is the desire of the members of the American Society of Chartered Life Underwriters to serve the insuring public in accordance with the purposes set forth in the Society's Bylaws;

And because members recognize and accept collective and individual responsibility for professional conduct in their relationships with the public, clients, fellow underwriters and companies;

Therefore, the members pledge themselves to the Code of Ethics, consisting of Guides to Professional Conduct and Rules of Professional Conduct, as set forth below:

I. GUIDES TO PROFESSIONAL CONDUCT

1. I shall, in the light of all the circumstances surrounding my client, which I shall make every conscientious effort to ascertain and to understand, give him that service which, had I been in the same circumstances, I would have applied to myself.

2. I shall place the welfare and interests of my clients above my own interests.

3. I shall render continuing service and counsel to my clients.

4. I shall continue to study and to improve my technical competency.

5. I shall keep abreast of changing conditions and legislation which may affect the financial plans of the insuring public and keep my clients informed of such changes as relate to them.

6. I shall accord the same courtesy and consideration to others engaged in related professions as I would wish to receive from them.

7. I shall refrain from engaging in any activity which, if practiced by a substantial number of members, would bring discredit to the institution of life insurance in general and to the American Society of Chartered Life Underwriters in particular.

8. I shall encourage others with the proper qualifications to earn the C.L.U. designation in the belief that this is in the best interests of the insuring public.

II. RULES OF PROFESSIONAL CONDUCT

1. A member shall obey all applicable laws governing life and health insurance.

2. A member shall conduct his personal and business affairs in such a manner as to avoid discrediting his reputation and impairing the public regard for life underwriting as a profession.

3. A member shall respect the confidential nature of the relationship existing between himself and his client.

4. A member shall respect the agent/principal relationship existing between himself and the company he represents.

5. A member shall avoid impairing the reputation or practice of another life underwriter.

6. Advertising the C.L.U. designation or its significance shall be done only in a manner approved by the American Society of Chartered Life Underwriters and the American College of Life Underwriters.

Chapter 24

THE CAMPUS AT BRYN MAWR

After thirty years of identification with Philadelphia and the University of Pennsylvania neighborhood, the trustees decided that plans for future growth of the College demanded extensive property financially possible only in the suburbs. Their eyes turned westward to other college communities. Joseph H. Reese, whose devotion and wisdom had made headquarters ownership at 3924 Walnut Street so satisfactory, was named chairman of a new building committee. Other members were: Orville E. Beal, then executive vice president of the Prudential Insurance Company; Eugene C. DeVol, past president of the American Society and Philadelphia general agent for the National Life of Vermont; Charles J. Zimmerman, president of the Connecticut Mutual; and Dr. Gregg.

The search for property was not easy. After some months, in June, 1959, the College purchased 10 acres of a beautiful old estate in Bryn Mawr, on the Pennsylvania Main Line. The property had been called Glenbrook, and while largely level, slopes gently toward a little stream and pond. The grounds are well wooded with big trees—maple, horse chestnut, and white pine, as well as rhododendron, azalea, and dogwood. The location chosen for the College building, where the old house had stood, is close to three especially beautiful specimen trees—a linden, said to be one of the largest and most shapely in the country, a huge Kentucky coffee tree, and a magnificent English beech.

Ground-breaking ceremonies for the new building were held on September 21, 1959, during the National Association of Life

Underwriters convention in Philadelphia. Many friends of the College journeyed in chartered buses the dozen miles from the shadow of William Penn to the new property. This was the first visit for most of them. The afternoon was warm and sunny, quite perfect for the ceremony under the shade of the bright-green-striped marquee. With silver shovels, Dr. Huebner, Mr. Reese, and others dug the ceremonial dirt. It was a thrilling occasion, the first of a series which followed with increasing drama.

The time capsule ceremony was held a year later, on October 20, 1960. It had been hoped that the roof would be on the building by that time, but a hurricane earlier in the fall had delayed construction so that the spectators still saw just the shell of what would be their magnificent new headquarters. Scaffolding, bulldozers, and raw materials were all a part of the picture.

Again the program took place in a tent on the lawn. The ceremony was symbolic of the broad outreach of the College and its associated organizations, and of the future they were dedicated to serve. The majority of the audience was members of the National C.L.U. Development Council who were assembled in Philadelphia to launch their million-dollar drive. In addition, there were College officers, trustees, staff and families, and representatives of 20 important insurance organizations. The man of the day was Dr. Huebner, for announcement had just been made that the building was to be named Huebner Hall, in his honor.

Paul F. Clark, chairman of the American College Board of Trustees and presiding officer at the ceremonies, said:

> It is appropriate that this building should help perpetuate the name of that great teacher who has given so much of himself to education and to insurance. His writing, teaching and inspirational leadership are symbolized by the beauty and dignity of this building which bears his name.

The time capsule is a cylindrical copper container about two feet high and a foot in diameter. Its cover is visible now in the floor of the reception foyer of Huebner Hall where the whole capsule is embedded.

Ground-breaking for Huebner Hall, Dr. Huebner digging. *Left to right:* Herbert P. Stellwagen, Robert Dechert, Joseph H. Reese.

After an invocation by Dr. Lester O. Schriver, executive vice president of the National Association of Life Underwriters, Mr. Clark invited representatives of insurance organizations to deposit their documents in the capsule. He explained the plans:

Located in the reception area of the new building is a cavity in solid concrete which will contain the copper capsule you see before you.

Time capsule in the floor of Huebner Hall. *Left to right:* S. S. Huebner, Paul F. Clark, Julian S. Myrick.

Within the capsule will be placed the documents we will present to our children and children's children. The bronze cap for the time capsule—which also is displayed before you—carries the inscription which is found on the front of your program.

The inscription indicates that this building shall be known as "Huebner Hall"—for our beloved Dr. S. S. Huebner who led the way in establishing this educational enterprise.

The inscription also indicates that this time capsule is to be opened fifty years from now, in the year 2010. At that time the world will have changed greatly, insurance will have changed, education will have changed. Hence, our imaginations are not stretched too much to picture a great educational institution on this site, the first building of which is Huebner Hall.

A number of distinguished guests have joined us today to present documents for deposit in the time capsule and for delivery to those who will open this capsule in 2010. I would like now to present them.

Dr. Huebner responded:

Mr. Clark and ladies and gentlemen, it is a great honor for me to represent the American College of Life Underwriters on this occasion and, assisted by Miss Gregg [Cindy, daughter of President Gregg] and Miss Graebner [Jane, daughter of Dean Graebner] who will, I hope, be invited back at the time the capsule is opened in the year 2010, deposit a copy of our current American College *Catalogue* and our 1959 *Annual Report*. I would say to you also at this time that the decision of the trustees to give this building my name is the greatest honor ever bestowed upon me, and is much appreciated by myself, Mrs. Huebner, and our entire family.

Another representative of special interest was Lillian G. Hogue, president of the American Society and field underwriter in Detroit for the New York Life. In responding to her invitation to come forward, Miss Hogue said:

It is a great honor for me to represent the American Society of Chartered Life Underwriters on this occasion. We in the American Society are extremely proud of our relationship with the American College. Symbolic of those bonds which enable us to achieve together what we could not achieve separately, I have asked Bill Gregg, son of Dave Gregg, president of the American College, and Marsha Mills, daughter of Paul Mills, managing director of the American Society, to assist me.

Marsha will deposit a copy of the summer issue of the C.L.U. *Journal*. Bill will deposit a copy of *Working Together for Professional Growth*.

On behalf of the Special Building Committee, Joseph H. Reese made a presentation. His grandson, Daniel, acted for him in placing the records in the capsule. It is possible that Daniel may follow his father and grandfather to become a third-generation C.L.U. and be present at the opening of the capsule in 2010.

It is a great pleasure on behalf of the committee to deposit in the time capsule a collection of colored photographs which tell the story of this property from the date it was purchased and which show the stages of construction of our new building from the day the ground was broken. We believe that this photographic record will be of great interest to those who follow us.

The largest deposit was made by William H. Andrews, chairman of the National C.L.U. Development Council. He said:

I am greatly honored to represent the C.L.U. Development Fund Committee and the National Development Council in presenting this rather large item for deposit in the time capsule. What I hold in my hand is a collection of newspaper pages from every city represented by a National Development Council member. These pages carry October, 1960 dates and, in many cases, relate news about life insurance in the particular community. It must be obvious to you that this portfolio will not fit into the time capsule. We are aware of this and it is our plan that each page will carry the name of the National Development Council member who presented it, and each page will be microfilmed for deposit in the capsule.

Mr. Clark, it is a pleasure to present this most interesting collection of newspaper pages from throughout the length and breadth of the United States.

Others who participated in the symbolic deposit of their historic documents were:

Dr. Davis W. Gregg, acting as first vice president of the American Association of University Teachers of Insurance.

Dr. Richard deR. Kip, director of examinations of the American Institute for Property and Liability Underwriters, Incorporated.

Ralph H. Kastner, associate general counsel of the American Life Convention.

Nelson M. Knowlton, president of the American Mutual Insurance Alliance and of Holyoke Mutual Fire Insurance Company.

Participants in time capsule ceremony. *Above, left to right:* Davis W. Gregg,
S. S. Huebner, Paul F. Clark, Paul S. Mills. *Below, back row:* Jane D.
Graebner, S. S. Huebner, Richard P. Mills; *front row:* Mary Cynthia Gregg,
Daniel Reese, Davis William Gregg, Marsha Jo Mills.

J. Dewey Dorsett, general manager of the Association of Casualty and Surety Companies.

Robert R. Neal, general manager of the Health Insurance Association of America.

John H. Dillard, president of the Insurance Institute of America and vice president of the Firemen's Fund Insurance Company.

Holgar J. Johnson, president of the Institute of Life Insurance.

William P. Lynch, member of the Board of Directors of the Life Insurance Agency Management Association and vice president of the Prudential Insurance Company of America.

Henry R. Glenn, general counsel and treasurer of the Life Insurance Association of America.

Alexander Hutchinson, president of the Life Underwriter Training Council and vice president of the Metropolitan Life Insurance Company.

Adon N. Smith, immediate past chairman of the Million Dollar Round Table and special agent in Charlotte for the Northwestern Mutual Life Insurance Company.

William E. North, president of the National Association of Life Underwriters and general manager in Evanston for the New York Life Insurance Company.

H. A. Coumbe, assistant general manager of the National Board of Fire Underwriters.

Dr. Harry J. Loman, chairman of the Administrative Board of the S. S. Huebner Foundation for Insurance Education.

Robert O. Young, president of the Society of Chartered Property and Casualty Underwriters, Incorporated, and an assistant secretary of the Insurance Company of North America.

Following the ceremony, the audience avoided ladders, ropes, and excavations as they inspected the building and grounds, and rejoiced together in the assurance of what was soon to be. Under the leadership of the architect, Mitchell and Giurgola, of Philadelphia, and with the cooperation of the labor unions and the weather, the building was completed so that the move from Philadelphia could be made in March, 1961.

Five organizations occupied the new home which took the generic title, "American Center for Insurance Education." The five organizations include: for life and health insurance, the American College and the American Society; for general insurance, the American Institute for Property and Liability Underwriters, Incorporated, the Society of Chartered Property and Casualty Underwriters, and the Insurance Institute of America. Total personnel was about seventy at that time. The American College owns the property. Maintenance and operating expenses are allocated in proportion to use—about 50 per cent to the College, 22 per cent to the American Society, and the balance to the C.P.C.U. organizations.

The cost for land, building, furnishings and equipment was approximately $850,000. The building, of brick and precast concrete panels, contains about 29,000 square feet. It contains reception area, library, board and conference rooms, and storage, machinery, and mail rooms. There are four general office areas, 31 private offices, and an attractively furnished lunchroom. Already it is apparent that the building will not long be adequate for the needs of the growing organizations. In fact, the Society of C.P.C.U. took other quarters in the summer of 1962.

Before the furniture was settled and boxes unpacked, the College entertained an important group of visitors. The Japanese Life Insurance Study Team spent a day discussing professional education in life and health insurance and inspecting the new quarters. The program included talks by Dr. Huebner and Dr. Gregg about the philosophy and activities of the College; an explanation of the financial side of the program by Sewell W.

Dr. Huebner in his Huebner Hall office.

Huebner Hall.

Hodge, treasurer of the College; and a discussion of plans for continuing education by Paul S. Mills, managing director of the American Society. Eight members of the visiting team were presidents, two were actuaries, one was assistant manager of research, and one director of general affairs, of their respective companies. This visit represents one of the important services of a national insurance center such as has been established at Bryn Mawr.

The College has long been regarded as one of the most unusual educational institutions in the United States. More than a dozen major industries, vocations, and businesses in recent years have sought discussions with College officials. They are trying to determine whether it would be feasible for their own industry or business to develop a plan of educational standards and to recognize professional attainment. They look to the American College of Life Underwriters as a possible pattern. For example, a past president of the American Bankers Association, speaking about education for trust officers, referred to the American College program:

> Estate planning has made great strides through the cooperation of a team of specialists. They consist of the lawyer with his special qualifications and Bachelor of Laws degree, the life insurance man who can become a Chartered Life Underwriter, the accountant who can qualify as a Certified Public Accountant, and the trustman.

> The time may be near when we should think seriously about some degree or designation for trustmen who have been graduated from one of our trust schools or have otherwise met exacting standards of training and excellence in fiduciary work. This will require careful study; but as the trust business grows, the people who guide its progress are developing a status which is professional in nature. An American College of Trustmen might be founded on the order of the American College of Life Underwriters. This could dignify the work of trustmen engaged in the professional management of property and help to bring the attention of more people to the value of trusteeship.

The library in Huebner Hall.

The board room in Huebner Hall.

The dedication of Huebner Hall attracted attendance from all over the country. Some eight hundred guests registered for two days of celebration and ceremony.

On the morning of June 1, 1961, the American College Board held a special meeting in the handsome new board room with its view, through floor-to-ceiling windows, of sky and lawns and beautiful trees. The meeting was more a symbol than the occasion for much business. A high light of the session was the presentation to the College of a portrait of Board Chairman Paul F. Clark, a gift from the John Hancock Mutual. The presentation was made by Byron K. Elliott, president of the company. John Hancock Mutual was proud to honor Mr. Clark as the only incorporator of the College still active, and the chairman of his company's Board of Directors. The painting was an admirable likeness done by the famous artist, Alfred Jonniaux. This portrait now hangs in the board room.

Byron K. Elliott unveils the portrait of Paul F. Clark.

Mr. Myrick made a brief talk saluting Mr. Clark and Dr. Huebner as the student and teacher still working "hand in hand" after 50 years. He also reviewed the gratifying progress of the College and complimented the trustees on their faith in the principle of "sound deficit financing" which had worked out so well. Dr. Huebner likewise spoke feelingly on this historic occasion, looking both to the past and to the future. It was Dr. Gregg, however, who turned the trustees' thoughts unitedly toward the future, emphasizing a potential beyond imagination:

> Never in history has the American public needed more the kind of security which can be given through the mechanism of insurance. Never before have those within insurance had a greater potential for service.... [and, quoting David Burnham] Make no little plans; they have no magic to stir men's blood. Make big plans; aim high in hope and work, remembering that a noble, logical diagram once recorded will never die, but long after we are gone, will be a living thing asserting itself with growing intensity.

The official dedication took place that afternoon in a marquee on the campus, following inspection tours of the building. Robert Dechert, counsel of the College and Society and general chairman of the dedication program, presided. The Very Reverend John A. Klekotka, president of Villanova University, gave the invocation. Dr. Katharine E. McBride, president of nearby Bryn Mawr College, graciously welcomed the new neighbors. Dr. Gaylord P. Harnwell, president of the University of Pennsylvania, made a brief dedicatory address. As presiding officer, Mr. Dechert said in part:

> In doing honor today to Dr. Huebner, whose idea was the inspiration for the American College and the American Institute, I feel that we must at the same time do honor to the leaders of the entire insurance industry, who over the years, have had the wisdom and courage through these two institutions to implement Dr. Huebner's inspiration.

> We hear much today of "continuing education" projects for those already active in various phases of professional and business life.

To that end professional associations, educational organizations, and business groups are sponsoring various series of lectures and study courses. This is fine! We give praise to them for thus inspiring continued intellectual growth.

But we must remember that, as an organized matter for an entire industry, *insurance* led the way with a carefully planned and implemented program designed to raise standards of the whole personnel of the industry—or as many of its personnel as could be induced to participate. The program provided incentive through cooperative study and ultimate public recognition, organization of effort, and of printed materials to support such effort, recognition of mental accomplishments, of basic character and of proven achievements in practice as three-fold requirements, and an industry-wide financial support.

First in 1927 came the American College of Life Underwriters, through which the life insurance branch of this industry pooled its resources to increase the stature of its underwriters, and of others who chose to work for C.L.U. recognition. Then in 1941 all the other parts of the insurance business created the American Institute of Property and Liability Underwriters. Together these two have grown, furnishing an example which inspires all other lines of business life to follow.

The process of learning is at its core a lonely one, depending upon the inner fire of inspiration and determination which has been built up in the learner. Here a great industry by its cooperative planning and support, has led the way to encourage and support its own people in carrying the learning process farther forward. Today's events are a memorable landmark in the progress of this combined enterprise.

The most thrilling moment of the occasion came when E. B. Mitchell, of the architectural firm, presented the key of the building to Dr. Huebner. Mrs. Huebner, their children and grandchildren, and the host of friends entertained a flood of memories and crowding hopes as he spoke in response:

I accept this symbolic key officially dedicating this campus and building. It is my hope that this key to Huebner Hall will unlock educational treasures and institutional progress in risk and insurance which is beyond our fondest dreams and imaginations at present. It is my belief that the education and research which will spring from this environment will lead to ever greater security for the people of our nation. And, on behalf of Mrs. Huebner and myself, may I express our deepest appreciation for the honor which has been paid to us by giving our name to this lovely structure.

Writing a few days later about the ceremony at Huebner Hall, one of the trustees reflected the atmosphere of that occasion:

As an interested onlooker, I could feel the electric spark of the significance of those events. The Dedication climaxed another era in the young life of the American College. We have a firm footing for another and longer reach in the years ahead.

Before returning to the city after the dedication, three groups of guests separated for special ceremonies, initiating a new college tradition. In memory of James Elton Bragg, the Class of

John D. Moynahan plants a tree for the Class of 1935, with Mr. Myrick and Dr. Huebner.

1933, Charles W. Campbell officiating, planted a straight, young oak tree. John D. Moynahan and Alice Roché Hare planted an American beech tree for the Class of 1935. Lester A. Rosen, currently chairman of the Million Dollar Round Table as well as the Class of 1936, was assisted by M. Roos Wallis and Benjamin M. Gaston in planting a scarlet oak tree on the south lawn. All these trees have permanent markers, and remind visitors of the hundreds of C.L.U.s whose strength supports as well as beautifies the College.

Devereux C. Josephs was the speaker at the dedication banquet that evening in the grand ballroom of the Sheraton Hotel in Philadelphia. Mr. Josephs is a director and former chairman of the Board of the New York Life. He is widely experienced in the field of education as trustee of the New York Public Library and The Johns Hopkins University, overseer of Harvard University, director and past president of the Carnegie Corporation, and chairman of President Eisenhower's Commission on Education Beyond High School. As he talked about insurance education, he continued the pattern of looking both to the past and to the future:

> It is no longer possible to sell insurance by force or favor. . . . To be sure, the successful underwriters of the long past also continued to learn and grow in wisdom, but there was this very significant difference. They used to learn more and more about how to sell successfully, whereas nowadays the learning process is consciously directed upon the subject matter, the characteristics of the policies, the problems of the insured, his objectives, his family and their problems. Field underwriting has come a long way in the journey to a full profession. Of course, the art of insurance selling is a skill to be developed; however, not as an end in itself, but as the conduit by which knowledge is transmitted and problems solved.

> While the insurance industry has been growing in economic maturity and enlightenment, the policyholder has been doing the same. The public has required more skill and wisdom from the companies, and the companies have more than reacted to the demands put upon them.

Fortunately for the industry, the reaction was broadened, hastened, given direction, and inspired by Dr. Huebner. How fortunate we are to have him with us tonight. Through his personal influence and his teaching and by contagion as well, he has helped transform all types of insurance from a largely commercial operation to one which serves the public better because of his professional standards. In the process he has made Philadelphia and now Bryn Mawr the insurance education center of the country. . . .

Huebner Hall is the symbol of the man who has done most in this century to shape the course of insurance by insistence upon education and research, and it is also the means of carrying out his ideals for the benefit of the industry which he has nurtured and the public that he has sought to benefit.

It is well that through the joining of all sectors of the industry, this building, these schools, and research opportunities have been established. The time, as I have pointed out, has been right. A concatenation of circumstances has made it possible. The leaders pointed the way, the public wanted the advances, the industry needed the development, and education has been the key that fits the lock. Thus a new impetus has been given to the unique institution—INSURANCE.

And so I end by wishing success to all who will use the Hall for training, for further education and research. May they be many—and come often. May Huebner Hall quickly become, and always remain, an integral part of all insurance activities for the better service of the public.

The program for June 2 turned strongly toward the future. The morning double session of the national seminar was a foretaste of the mental stimulus and guidance toward personal development which the College aimed to provide in the years ahead. At noon, the seminar participants were guests of honor at a gala luncheon. The speaker was Erwin D. Canham, well-known editor of the *Christian Science Monitor* and past president of the Chamber of Commerce of the United States. He turned the thoughts of the audience to the nation's basic need for economic growth, and challenged his hearers to recognize that human understanding— man to man and people to people—is fundamental to progress and survival.

Did one ask how far the American College had come since 1927? The Bryn Mawr campus was one answer. The thousands of graduates and the caliber of people such as were brought together on June 2 were another answer. Dr. Huebner well might look at the key to Huebner Hall and express the hope that in the future it would unlock treasures far beyond our present dreams.

Chapter 25

SINCE WORLD WAR II:
AN EPILOGUE

In the years since World War II, what has the American College become? It has demonstrated its vitality in adjustment to dramatic changes in national life and society, and to developments in the insurance industry. With revised and expanded curriculum, with opportunities offered equally to field underwriters and home office personnel, with coverage broadened to serve effectively the needs of health insurance and insurance sales management, with examination techniques modernized, with plans for specialized certificate courses and continuing education for graduates, the C.L.U. program now keys itself to today and tomorrow.

The surge of new candidates and ambitious initiation of service projects immediately after the armistice were all too soon slowed and challenged by disaffection in many places across the country. That the grass roots leadership of the C.L.U. movement as well as the College officials were able to talk those problems out and build a new foundation of devotion to the historic objectives and standards of the College testified to the soundness of the whole concept. The College meets a need. Therefore, it survives and grows. Since 1951, the number of new candidates each year has been increasing steadily. In 1962, 4,063 men and women started work toward the C.L.U. designation, a 14 per cent increase over the previous year.

Most dramatic reaffirmation of faith in the College and its work is seen in the two recent million-dollar drives for capital funds.

The success of these campaigns assures permanent operation of the College, and the money speaks for the donors' belief in what the College is doing. The new Bryn Mawr campus symbolizes the vision of an expanding future.

Since World War II, the American College has continued close and helpful activities with several other educational movements. In the course of the years, the specific associations have waxed and waned, but there remain fundamental ties of related aims, mutual inspiration, and identification of American College personnel with the American Risk and Insurance Association and the S.S. Huebner Foundation for Insurance Education.

The College comes to the end of 1962 with over 10,000 graduates and an accelerating record of growth. A recent survey among 28 companies each having 50 or more C.L.U.s indicated that those graduates had a record of significantly more earnings and production than their contemporary non-C.L.U.s. At latest count, 44 life insurance companies have presidents who are C.L.U.s. More than 750 men and women became C.L.U.s at the 1962 conferment exercises. These people know what the C.L.U. means today, and look to its increasing significance in their tomorrows.

In 1961, Dr. Davis W. Gregg, president of the American College, received the John Newton Russell Award, the highest honor in life insurance. Dr. Huebner had been the first to win such recognition, and other trustees of the College also have been so honored. As Dr. Gregg responded to the presentation, he spoke words that crystallized the accomplishment of the College when he said:

> I am happy to accept this award which I see essentially as a tribute to an idea for which I work. If you could have stood with me on Wednesday night at the national C.L.U. conferment and looked into the faces of the new C.L.U.s grouped before the speakers' table you would have had a new impression of what the C.L.U. means. You would have seen in the faces of these men and women a new commitment to their life work, a new sense of dignity for their vocation, and a new feeling of adequacy for the professional service to which they are dedicated.

Davis W. Gregg. (*Bachrach*)

The American College does not exist merely to award designations. Even its classes and publications are secondary. It has grown through the years because it has given the industry a vision of its own potential. It has become a vital part of life insurance because it has helped men and women to self-fulfilment and the accomplishment of their highest ideals for themselves in their chosen vocation and in service to their fellow men.

In the pre-incorporation years of the College, the leaders of the National Association of Life Underwriters had glimpses of what the business might become. They were searching for ways of implementing their ideas, of presenting a program to their fellow workers that would inspire the participation of great numbers of their associates. The College became that instrument.

As the College was founded to accomplish specific purposes, so through the decades of its existence the trustees and officers have endeavored consciously to work toward established goals. This underlying fact in College history was never more apparent than in the years since World War II. The Stewart Committee and the Zimmerman Committee, at critical stages of College development, analyzed needs, appraised the current services of the College, identified new goals, and pointed out what must be done to assure the accomplishment of new objectives.

Currently, the Beal Commission is working in a similar way. One great strength of the American College lies in its purposeful development. Many institutions grow with little direction, merely carried along by the forces of circumstance. The American College seeks with conscious effort to know the needs of tomorrow and to be ready to serve the public and the industry in meeting new demands and new opportunities.

Let no one think that the American College has been built. To be ever in the way of becoming is the aim of its leaders. This volume is the history of the American College of Life Underwriters—so far—but tomorrow will bring new achievements in service to the American public and to the life and health insurance business.

THE FIRST C.L.U. EXAMINATION

The first series of tests for C.L.U. qualification was scheduled for five successive half-day sessions of three hours each. It was called "the examination," and was held in 14 colleges throughout the United States. The questions in the five parts were as follows:

I. LIFE INSURANCE FUNDAMENTALS

(a) Economics of Life Insurance. (Answer 4 questions.)

1. Give seven (7) specific uses of life insurance for the individual policyholder.

2. What is a trust company? What are the beneficial results of trust company and life insurance company cooperation?

3. Explain the various ways in which life insurance proves helpful in connection with the settlement of estates.

4. State the economic advantages of life annuities.

5. Define so-called "partnership life insurance," and explain briefly the economic advantages derived therefrom.

(b) Principles and Practices. (Answer 4 questions.)

1. a. What objections are customarily raised against term life insurance policies?

b. What is meant by a convertible term policy and explain the reasons for the inclusion of the convertible feature.

2. Contrast ordinary life insurance and endowment insurance, pointing out the differences in purpose and scope of the two types of contracts.

3. From the following data calculate the net annual level premium on a $1,000 five-year term policy, written at age 25:

Age	No. Living at Beginning of Designated Year	No. Dying During Designated Year
25	89,032	718
26	88,314	718
27	87,596	718
28	86,878	718
29	86,160	719

American Experience 3 per cent.

Present values of $1 at 3% due as follows:

1 year	0.970874
2 years	0.942596
3 years	0.915142
4 years	0.888487
5 years	0.862609

(In view of the limited time available, it is not desired that you make your multiplications, additions, and divisions. Merely indicate all answers by letters beginning with "A" and then following continuously with "B," "C," etc. The problem aims to ascertain correctness of procedure and not actual results.)

4. a. What is the meaning of the term "Non-Forfeiture Privileges"? Explain such provisions.

b. What is meant when a company is referred to as a "Legal Reserve Company"?

c. What is the nature of a life insurance dividend and what disposition may the policyholder make of such dividends when payable? Which of these is most expedient to him under ordinary circumstances and why?

II. LIFE INSURANCE SALESMANSHIP

(a) Principles of Salesmanship. (Answer 5 questions.)

1. Discuss the pre-approach.

2. Discuss the approach.

a. Give an example by dialogue of your favorite approach.

3. Discuss the use of "associated interests" in managing the interview.

4. Name six standard objections and your method of meeting those objections.

5. Discuss "testing for the close."

a. Give three examples.

(b) Psychology of Life Insurance Salesmanship. (Answer 5 questions.)

1. In discussing attention, Overstreet refers to a "Putting-It-Up-To-You Technique." What are the advantages of such a method over an expository one?

2. Overstreet says: "No appeal to a reason that is not also an appeal to a want is ever effective." Discuss fully the meaning of this quotation.

3. What are the essential things to remember in trying to give your prospect a vivid imaginative picture?

4. In his chapter on Psychology of Speaking, Overstreet emphasized: voice, mannerisms, and monotony. Discuss these.

5. Overstreet says that to change a person we must change a particular system of habits. Discuss the meaning of this statement.

6. What factors does Overstreet emphasize in his chapter on Diagnosing the Public? How would the intensifying of the following social habits increase interest in life insurance: child welfare, higher education, personal hygiene, thrift?

7. Discuss the technique of humor and the importance of this subject to the salesman.

III. GENERAL EDUCATION

(a) English.

Write an essay of 800 to 1,000 words on any one of the following subjects:

1. Life insurance as an investment.

2. Life insurance as a means of creating and maintaining business credit.

3. Life insurance as a means of creating personal estates through systematic thrift. (The essay will be graded on the basis of all factors essential to the writing of good English.)

(b) Economics. (Answer 4 questions.)

1. Enumerate the factors that tend to fix prices, and explain each briefly with a view to making its significance clear.

2. Define "Production." Outline the several fundamental factors that cooperate in the work of production.

3. a. Define "Monopoly," and state the causes of monopolies.

b. What is meant by "Monopoly Price"? Can the monopolist charge any excessive price he pleases? Explain fully.

4. Define "Interest," and explain how it is possible and why it must be paid.

(c) Sociology. (Answer 5 questions.)

1. a. What interest has the life insurance company in prolonging the lives of its policyholders?

b. What forms of health work have life insurance companies undertaken in this country?

c. How do you account for the greater longevity of annuitants than insured lives?

2. Discuss briefly how life insurance helps women to attain an independent status in present-day society.

3. a. Why should parents guarantee the higher education of their children through the medium of life insurance?

b. Discuss briefly what is meant by "educational insurance."

c. Enumerate the advantages of leaving charitable bequests through life insurance.

4. a. What are the essentials of a successful savings program?

b. How do the assets of life insurance companies compare with those of building and loan associations, savings banks and new security issues?

c. Why is thrift necessary in a country as wealthy as the United States?

5. a. What is meant by the social significance of life insurance company investments?

b. Are life insurance assets growing faster or more slowly than the national wealth?

6. a. Briefly discuss the justice or injustice of life insurance premium taxation.

b. Enumerate the kinds of special insurance taxes and briefly explain each.

IV. COMMERCIAL LAW

(Answer any 10 questions.)

1. Explain briefly each of the elements necessary to a contract.

2. In connection with the discharge of contracts by bankruptcy, explain two of the following:

(a) The method of procedure to be followed by the creditor to obtain a share of his debtor's estate.

(b) The exemptions allowed to bankrupts.

(c) The management of a bankrupt's estate.

3. Explain (a) the agent's obligations to his principal, and (b) the principal's obligations to his agent.

4. Outline the steps necessary for the formation of a business partnership.

5. Outline the rights and obligations of a partner to his fellow partners in the business firm.

6. Outline the steps necessary for the formation of a corporation.

7. Explain briefly the powers of a corporation.

8. Outline the principal rights and liabilities of stockholders in a corporation.

9. As regards a Mortgage of Realty, explain briefly:

(a) The obligations of the mortgagor to the mortgagee.

(b) The obligations of the mortgagee to the mortgagor.

10. Name the parties to a suretyship contract, and as regards each such party outline his essential duties to the other parties.

11. Outline the duties of executors and administrators of decedents' estates.

V. FINANCE

(Answer any 10 questions.)

1. State the following:

(a) Advantages and disadvantages of the business partnership as compared with individual proprietorship.

(b) Advantages and disadvantages of the business corporation as compared with the business partnership.

(c) Advantages and disadvantages of the business trust as compared with the corporation.

2. Classify the essential features differentiating various classes of preferred stock.

3. Explain the different methods of marketing new securities that are employed by corporations to obtain new capital funds.

4. From the standpoint of the merchants' needs, what are the general classes of credit? Define and describe each briefly.

5. What advantages have accrued to business men, from a credit standpoint, by virtue of the Federal Reserve System as contrasted with the old National Banking System?

6. Summarize the advantages of the Federal Bankruptcy Act over State insolvency laws.

7. State and illustrate the basic economic functions of a commercial bank.

8. Outline the principles of procedure followed by commercial banks, when financing business men, in determining the amount of credit that may safely be extended.

9. Explain the fundamental services of an investment bank.

10. As compared with individual trustees, state the advantages of having a trust company administer individual trusts.

11. Classify the major groups of securities (according to the source of issue, such as the United States Government, etc.) that constitute the American field of investment, and with respect to each of the above groups, state any special advantages or disadvantages that may exist.

12. Enumerate the fundamental causes of stock and bond price movements, explaining each sufficiently to make its significance clear.

13. Explain the extent to which stock and bond prices fluctuate during the so-called stock and bond cycle.

THE SECOND SERIES OF
C.L.U. EXAMINATIONS

The C.L.U. tests were given the second time in December, 1928, the only year when two series were offered. The following reproduction of those questions indicates the increasingly high standards for candidates.

I. LIFE INSURANCE FUNDAMENTALS

(*a*) Economics of Life Insurance.

(Answer all questions.)

1. A prospect whom you are soliciting states that he does not regard Life Insurance as a good investment, so has adopted the policy of buying term insurance and investing his other savings in stocks and bonds. What arguments would you advance to demonstrate the fallacy of his attitude towards Life Insurance as an investment?

2. Explain how Life Insurance may be used to influence the credit of a manufacturer—
   (*a*) with producers from whom he buys raw materials.
   (*b*) with investment bankers through whose aid he floats a bond issue.
   (*c*) with the commercial banker from whom he secures working capital.

3. How would you appraise the value of a man's life to his family?

4. Show how the business principles of depreciation, capitalization, and sinking funds may be adapted to the human life value through the agency of Life Insurance.

5. A Life Insurance policy may be regarded as a will which passes the life value of the insured to his beneficiaries. What advantages does such a will possess over the usual type of property will?

(b) Principles and Practices.
   (*Answer all questions.*)

1. (a) Franklin, a bond salesman, age 35, with an income of approximately $6,000 per year, is married and has two children, ages 2 and 5. He owns a $14,000 home with a $7,000 mortgage on it and has $10,000 worth of stocks and bonds, but no Life Insurance. Assuming you represent a nonparticipating company whose rates at his age per $1,000 are $19.91 for ordinary life, $22.28 for 30-payment life, $27.40 for 20-payment life, $41.38 for 20-year endowment, $26.53 for 30-year endowment, and $9.13 for 5-year convertible term insurance, suggest a program of insurance which you believe would best fit his needs.

   (b) Assuming the contract or contracts purchased by Franklin contain the usual optional settlement provisions, advise him as to what you would regard as the most satisfactory method for having the proceeds paid to his wife and children.

2. (a) Contrast the basic principles underlying the operation of the old assessable fraternals with those of a legal reserve "old line" Life Insurance company. Why have these differences resulted in a rapid growth of "old line" companies and in failures of the fraternal assessment plan?

   (b) Show how the nature of the Life Insurance business affects the principles that govern a company in making its investments.

3. (a) Explain (a) the legal and (b) the economic significance of the incontestable clause as used in Life Insurance policies.

   (b) Andrews took out a $100,000 participating ordinary Life Insurance policy when he was 38 years of age. The gross annual premium on it was $2,895. At the end of 20 years the cash value is $36,072. He has been taking his dividends, which are quite substantial, in cash. The last he received (the twentieth) was $1,255. As his health has failed and the cost of supporting his dependents is high, he wants to curtail expenses, so a friend advises that he surrender the policy for cash. Do you consider this advice good? If not, what would you suggest? State your reasons.

4. (*a*) Outline the principal features you would expect to find in a progressive total and permanent disability clause as used in conjunction with a Life Insurance policy. State the reason for each feature.

    (*b*) What does an insurance company agree to do when it writes

        (1) a deferred annuity, and

        (2) a last survivor annuity?

5. Select from the following data the necessary figures and compute the reserve at the end of 3 years on an ordinary Life Insurance policy issued at age 35, using the American Experience Table of Mortality and 3% interest. (Either one of the two customary methods will be acceptable.)

SECTION OF MORTALITY TABLE

Age	No. Living at Beginning of Designated Year	No. Dying During Designated Year
34	82,551	729
35	81,822	732
36	81,090	737
37	80,353	742
38	79,611	749
39	78,862	756
40	78,106	765

Present Values—Life Annuity Due of $1 per Year for the Whole of Life—American Experience Table, 3%.

Age 34	$20.17
35	19.92
36	19.66
37	19.40
Age 38	$19.13
39	18.85
40	18.56

Net Single Premiums
American Experience, 3%

Age 34	$412.63
35	419.88
36	427.36
37	435.04
Age 38	$442.95
39	451.07
40	459.42

Net Level Premiums—Ord. Life
American Experience, 3%

Age 34	$20.46
35	21.08
36	21.74
37	22.43
Age 38	$23.16
39	23.93
40	24.75

II. LIFE INSURANCE SALESMANSHIP

(*a*) Principles of Salesmanship.

(*Answer all 5 questions.*)

1. Discuss the best methods of meeting the prospect's objections.

2. Give an example by dialogue of one of your favorite sales presentations.

3. Discuss difficulties in obtaining a hearing.

4. Discuss the favorite method of prospecting.

5. Discuss the close.

(*b*) Psychology of Life Insurance Salesmanship.

(*Answer any 5 questions.*)

1. Why is it just as important for the salesman to consider his own behavior as it is for him to study the responses of his prospect? Make a list of all of the personality items that you think you should watch in yourself: mannerisms, speech, voice, etc.

2. Distinguish between personality and character. Why are personality attributes so important to the life underwriter? Why is personality not so important to the bookkeeper, carpenter, or civil engineer?

3. Give a psychological explanation of Jones. He has just bought a car but honestly feels he cannot afford Life Insurance. (The car is not used in a business way.)

4. List the emotions you might hope to arouse in relation to Life Insurance.

5. Make a list of all of the suggestive attributes of personality that you wish to possess as an underwriter.

6. List five habits, possessed by nearly everyone, that you could take advantage of in appealing to a Life Insurance prospect.

7. How could Life Insurance companies create a social desire (a habit) for Life Insurance at all comparable to the social desire for the automobile? What disadvantage by way of sensory appeal does Life Insurance have as a handicap over radios or automobiles?

III. GENERAL EDUCATION

(*a*) English.

Select either of the following cases and write a letter to the inquirer outlining the proposal you would offer to solve his problem, and explaining the advantages to be derived. (The letter should be 400 to 500 words in length. It will be graded on the basis of all factors essential to the writing of good English.)

1. Dr. Matthews is a surgeon with a large and lucrative practice. He is now age 56 and his wife is 54. They have two children, James, age 28, and Mary, age 25. As Mary's husband died a few years after their marriage without providing for her support, she and her children, ages 1 and 3, are living at home. James has his own home and is making a good start in the legal profession. Dr. Matthews owns his home and furniture, valued at about $25,000, and high grade stocks and bonds worth approximately $80,000. He is now uninsurable but has $107,000 of ordinary Life Insurance in force. Upon his death Dr. Matthews wants to leave $75,000 outright to his son, but wishes to protect his wife, daughter and grandchildren by some form of an insurance trust. Submit a practical plan.

2. Brown, Evans and Green each own $100,000 worth of stock in a close corporation. The corporation has prospered materially, due largely to the personal interest each has taken in its affairs. All are beginning to realize that the death of any one might result in a transfer of stock ownership which would be prejudicial to the interests of the others. Since each is still insurable, Brown, the president, writes you for information

as to whether Life Insurance could offer a solution. Present a proposal to Mr. Brown for submission to the stockholders.

(*b*) Economics.

(*Answer any 4 questions.*)

1. The assets of a certain business corporation consist of:
    Cash (in bank and on hand)
    Accounts Receivable
    Notes Receivable
    Inventory of raw materials
    Stock of finished goods
    Land and Buildings
    Fixtures and Equipment
    Stocks and Bonds of other companies
    Good Will

If you were preparing a statement of the *capital of the community* in which this business is located, which of the above would you include or exclude? Give reasons. Upon what definition of capital is this division based?

2. Some economists contend that insistence on the payment of the war debts owed by foreign governments to this country is inconsistent with a policy of high protective tariff. Explain. How is the payment of the war debts further complicated by American purchases of foreign bonds?

3. Assuming there is an increase of demand for a given commodity, what will be the effect upon its price over a long period if it is produced under conditions of (a) increasing costs, (b) decreasing costs, and (c) constant costs? Illustrate.

4. (*a*) Explain the meaning of the terms (a) rent, (b) law of diminishing returns, and (c) Malthusian theory of population, as they are used by economists.

    (*b*) Were there no counteracting influences, what effect would you expect the Malthusian theory to have upon the rent of land? Why?

5. To what extent is the life insurance policyholder and his beneficiaries financially affected by the existing (a) state premium taxes, (b) state inheritance taxes, (c) federal estate tax, and (d) federal income tax?

(*c*) Sociology.

> (*Answer any 4 questions.*)

1. What outstanding contributions has the institution of Life Insurance made to the development and betterment of society? Answer in outline form.

2. The President of the Senior Class in a large university has heard that Life Insurance may be utilized as a means of providing endowments for educational institutions. He asks you to outline its advantages and to submit to him a plan for submission to his class. Advise him.

3. What control is exercised by the state over the investments of Life Insurance companies? List the various types of securities in which Life Insurance funds are invested and indicate the relative importance of each.

4. Explain briefly in what ways (a) industrial insurance, (b) group Life Insurance, (c) business Life Insurance, and (d) salary savings insurance, represent the response of Life Insurance to the needs of society.

5. A friend advises you that he wants to carry a Life Insurance contract for the purpose of providing his daughter with a college education. Outline for him a plan of insurance, including the method of paying the proceeds, which you think would best accomplish his desire.

IV. COMMERCIAL LAW AND INSURANCE LAW

> (*Answer any 10 questions.*)

1. Myers is under contract to work three years for Simpson. Warren, a competitor, realizes Myers would be a valuable man to have in his employ, so offers him $1,500 to break his contract and work for him. Myers does this. Can he recover the money promised him? Give your reasons.

2. Maynard wrote Smith: "I will sell you 200 tables at $5 each. Advise by return mail." Smith immediately wrote Maynard that he accepted his proposition and sent the letter by return mail, but it never reached Maynard. Maynard therefore sold the tables to another party and claimed there was no contract. Decide, with reasons.

3. What acts or misconduct on the part of Life Insurance agents are specifically prohibited by state legislation? Why is there

not similar legislation applying to real estate or automobile salesmen?

4. (*a*) Distinguish between the legal status of an agent and a broker.

   (*b*) What does the Life Insurance contract usually state with respect to the right of an agent to modify its terms? Why is such a provision necessary?

5. (*a*) Explain the conditions which may affect the rights of creditors to attach the cash value of a debtor's Life Insurance contracts.

   (*b*) What would you advise a policyholder to do who wishes to safeguard his family from the possibility of creditors seizing Life Insurance carried for family protection?

6. (*a*) What do you mean by the rules against perpetuities and accumulations?

   (*b*) Of what significance are they in connection with the payment of Life Insurance proceeds under the usual optional settlement plans?

7. Smith designates his wife as beneficiary of his Life Insurance contract, reserving, however, the right to change. Subsequently, he assigns the policy to a banker without changing the beneficiary designation. What effect will this have upon Mrs. Smith's rights? Indicate the different lines of court decisions and state which has the preponderance of legal opinion in its favor.

8. On October 5, 1926, Richards applied for a $10,000 Life Insurance policy. In spite of the fact that he had previously spent a year in Denver to ward off a threatened attack of tuberculosis, he stated in his application that he had never had any lung trouble or been forced to make a change of climate on account of his health. The medical examiner did not discover the deception, and the policy was issued. It contained a one-year incontestable clause. On November 8, 1926, Richards assigned the policy to the First National Bank as security for a loan. Two months later he was killed in an automobile accident and the bank endeavored to collect. Learning of Richards' medical history, the insurance company refused to pay. What are the rights of the bank? State your reasons.

9. (*a*) List the requirements for a promissory note or bill of exchange to be negotiable.

   (*b*) Would you classify a Life Insurance policy as a negotiable instrument? Why or why not?

10. Green was a stockholder in the Balank Dye Corporation. The company was enjoying a splendid business but had declared no dividends in 11 years. Green asked permission to examine the books of the company, and on being refused, applied to the court for an order allowing him that privilege. What are his rights?

11. (*a*) What are the usual formal requisites in the making of a will?

    (*b*) If a trust estate is created under the terms of a will, what are the duties, powers and liabilities of the trustee?

12. (*a*) What formal requisites are essential to the validity of a deed to real estate?

    (*b*) If you receive a deed to land which has been drawn up in compliance with these requisites, are you fully protected against other claimants or should you safeguard yourself in some other way? Explain.

13. Daniels, a salesman, hires an automobile by the day from a "Drive-it-Yourself" concern to use in visiting his customers. While driving through a city, he runs down and seriously injures Martin. The injured party sues the company owning the automobile. Decide, with reasons.

V. FINANCE

(Answer any 10 questions.)

1. Account for the growing popularity of the business corporation over the partnership as a form of business organization during recent years.

2. A railroad company has the following types of securities outstanding: collateral trust mortgage bonds, debenture bonds, first and refunding mortgage bonds, preferred stock, and income bonds. Explain what is meant by each of these types of securities and arrange them according to their respective investment security, giving reasons for your arrangement.

3. It is estimated that upward of twelve billion dollars, net, have been invested by the people of the United States in for-

eign securities during the past decade. Account for this growing popularity of foreign investments with the American investor.

4. Differentiate the economic functions of commercial banks, investment banks, and trust companies.

5. State what is meant by underwriting in the investment market, and describe the methods of operation of an underwriting syndicate.

6. Explain two ways in which future bond issues of a growing business corporation may be included under the provisions of a single first mortgage, without impairing the equity of the present bondholders.

7. In recent years there has been a growing tendency on the part of business corporations to issue no par value stock in place of stock with a stated par value. What are the alleged advantages of no par value stock to the business issuing the same, and to the investor?

8. Name and explain the uses of five different forms of credit instruments commonly employed in commercial banking.

9. Explain clearly how the Federal Reserve banks can regulate and control the supply of commercial bank credit.

10. What factors would you consider in determining the advisability of extending commercial credit to an established business?

11. Business cycles, with their alternating periods of prosperity and depression, usually affect the market prices of industrial securities much more than those of either railroad or public utility securities. Why?

12. Account for the wide fluctuations, from time to time, in the market prices of sound bond investments.

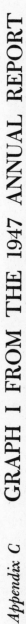
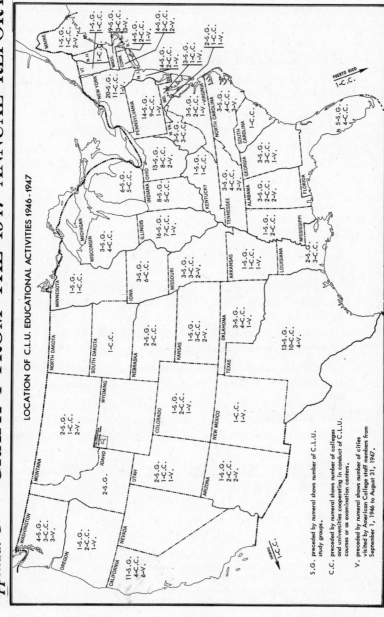

LOCATION OF C.L.U. EDUCATIONAL ACTIVITIES 1946-1947

The notations on this map indicate the extent of the growth of College activity by its twentieth year.

LIFE TRUSTEES, TERM TRUSTEES, AND ELECTED OFFICERS OF THE AMERICAN COLLEGE OF LIFE UNDERWRITERS, 1928-1963

*GEORGE D. ALDER, *General Agent,* National Life Insurance Company, Salt Lake City, Utah—Term Trustee, 1927-29

WILLIAM H. ANDREWS, JR., C.L.U., *Manager,* Jefferson Standard Life Insurance Company, Greensboro, North Carolina—Term Trustee, 1961-

*O. J. ARNOLD, *Chairman of the Board,* Northwestern National Life Insurance Company, Minneapolis, Minnesota—Term Trustee, 1935-50

ORVILLE E. BEAL, C.L.U., *President,* Prudential Insurance Company of America, Newark, New Jersey—Term Trustee, 1957-

HUGH S. BELL, C.L.U., *General Agent (retired),* Equitable Life Insurance Company of Iowa, Seattle, Washington—Term Trustee, 1954-63

*JAMES ELTON BRAGG, C.L.U., *Manager,* Guardian Life Insurance Company of America, New York City—Term Trustee, 1945-58

EDWARD S. BRASHEARS, C.L.U., *Manager,* Union Central Life Insurance Company, Washington, D.C.—Term Trustee, 1927-35

CHARLES W. CAMPBELL, C.L.U., *Senior Vice President,* Prudential Insurance Company of America, Jacksonville, Florida—Term Trustee, 1950-

---

*Deceased

NOTE: Prior to 1938, the governing body of the College was designated the Board of Directors. In 1938 this was changed to Board of Trustees. For the sake of uniformity, all persons in the above listing are designated as "Term Trustees" even though prior to 1938 they were designated "Directors."

First year listed above is the September of year elected; second year listed is September service ended.

GEORGE H. CHACE, *Vice President*, Prudential Insurance Company of America, Newark, New Jersey—Term Trustee, 1938-47

*ERNEST J. CLARK, *General Agent Emeritus*, John Hancock Mutual Life Insurance Company, Baltimore, Maryland—Term Trustee, 1927-38; Life Trustee, 1938-58; Secretary, 1927-28; President, 1928-34; Chairman of the Board, 1934-38

*JEROME CLARK, *Superintendent of Agencies*, Union Central Life Insurance Company, Cincinnati, Ohio—Term Trustee, 1931-36

PAUL F. CLARK, C.L.U., *Chairman of the Board (retired) and Director*, John Hancock Mutual Life Insurance Company, Boston, Massachusetts—Term Trustee, 1927-54; Life Trustee, 1954- ; Vice Chairman of the Board, 1955-60; Chairman of the Board, 1960-

*MICHAEL J. CLEARY, *President*, Northwestern Mutual Life Insurance Company, Milwaukee, Wisconsin—Term Trustee, 1935-44

VINCENT B. COFFIN, C.L.U., *Chancellor*, University of Hartford, West Hartford, Connecticut—Term Trustee, 1949-

PAUL W. COOK, C.L.U., *General Agent (retired)*, Mutual Benefit Life Insurance Company, Chicago, Illinois—Term Trustee, 1944-56

O. SAM CUMMINGS, *General Agent (retired)*, Kansas City Life Insurance Company, Dallas, Texas—Term Trustee, 1931-62

ROBERT DECHERT, ESQ., *Partner*, Dechert, Price & Rhoads, Philadelphia, Pennsylvania—Life Trustee, 1961- ; Counsel, 1936-57, 1959-

DUDLEY DOWELL, *President*, New York Life Insurance Company, New York City—Term Trustee, 1944-53

*WILLIAM M. DUFF, C.L.U., *General Agent*, Equitable Life Assurance Society of the U.S.—Term Trustee, 1928-49

*J. STANLEY EDWARDS, *General Agent*, Aetna Life Insurance Company, Denver, Colorado—Term Trustee, 1927-53; Life Trustee, 1953-55

E. J. FAULKNER, *President*, Woodmen Accident and Life Company, Lincoln, Nebraska—Term Trustee, 1959-

CHESTER O. FISCHER, *Vice President (retired)*, Massachusetts Mutual Life Insurance Company, Springfield, Massachusetts—Term Trustee, 1943-57

*FRANKLIN W. GANSE, C.L.U., Ganse-King Estate Service, Boston, Massachusetts—Term Trustee, 1927-35; Life Trustee, 1938-47; Treasurer, 1927-39

*WILLIAM T. GRANT, *President*, Business Men's Assurance Company of America, Kansas City, Missouri—Term Trustee, 1954-55

---

*Deceased

*DAVID MCCAHAN, C.L.U., *President,* American College of Life Underwriters, Bryn Mawr, Pennsylvania—Term Trustee, 1934-54; Secretary, 1930-34; Dean, 1934-51; Executive Vice President, 1951-52; President, 1952-54

*E. M. MCCONNEY, *President,* Bankers Life Company, Des Moines, Iowa— Term Trustee, 1949-51

BEN S. MCGIVERAN, C.L.U., *President,* The McGiveran Company; Inc., Milwaukee, Wisconsin—Term Trustee, 1961-

*GUY M. MCLAUGHLIN, *General Agent,* Franklin Life Insurance Company, Houston, Texas—Term Trustee, 1927-30; Vice President, 1927-30

CLARENCE B. METZGER, C.L.U., *Vice President,* Equitable Life Assurance Society of the United States, New York City—Term Trustee, 1949-

JULIAN S. MYRICK, *Vice President (retired),* Mutual Life Insurance Company of New York, New York City—Term Trustee, 1929-39; Life Trustee, 1939- ; Chairman of the Board, 1938-60; Chairman Emeritus of the Board, 1960-

CECIL J. NORTH, *President (retired) and Director,* Metropolitan Life Insurance Company, New York City—Term Trustee, 1939-63.

*HENRY E. NORTH, *Vice President,* Metropolitan Life Insurance Company, San Francisco, California—Term Trustee, 1936-58

GERALD W. PAGE, C.L.U., *General Agent,* Provident Mutual Life Insurance Company, Los Angeles, California—Term Trustee, 1955-

*GEORGE A. PATTON, *Vice President,* Mutual Life Insurance Company of New York, New York City—Term Trustee, 1938-44

FREDERIC M. PEIRCE, *President,* General American Life Insurance Company, St. Louis, Missouri—Term Trustee, 1962-

*JULIAN PRICE, *President,* Jefferson Standard Life Insurance Company, Greensboro, North Carolina—Term Trustee, 1930-35

JOSEPH H. REESE, SR., C.L.U., Reese Consulting Services, Rydal, Pennsylvania—Term Trustee, 1943-61; Life Trustee, 1961- ; Secretary 1949-

OWEN B. RHOADS, ESQ., *Partner,* Dechert, Price & Rhoads, Philadelphia, Pennsylvania—Counsel, 1957-59

*THEODORE M. RIEHLE, C.L.U., *General Agent,* Equitable Life Assurance Society of the United States, New York City—Term Trustee, 1935-50

*JOHN NEWTON RUSSELL, *Agency Advisor,* Pacific Mutual Life Insurance Company, Los Angeles, California—Term Trustee, 1927-42

---

*Deceased

MEMBERS OF BOARD OF GRADERS OF THE AMERICAN COLLEGE OF LIFE UNDERWRITERS WITH FIVE OR MORE YEARS OF SERVICE AS OF JUNE, 1962

(The university or business affiliation listed indicates that current during period of grading service)

JOHN R. ABERSOLD, *University of Pennsylvania* (17 years)

LAURENCE J. ACKERMAN, *University of Connecticut* (6 years)

EDWARD M. AIKEN, *Equitable Life Assurance Society*, Pittsburgh (10 years)

GEORGE L. AMRHEIN, *University of Pennsylvania* (10 years)

WILLIAM T. BEADLES, *Illinois Wesleyan University* (20 years) *

IRVIN BENDINER, *New York Life Insurance Company*, Philadelphia (5 years)

KENNETH BLACK, JR., *Georgia State College* (7 years)

EDWARD W. CARTER, *University of Pennsylvania* (12 years)

BERNARD F. CATALDO, *University of Pennsylvania* (9 years)

ROBERT S. CLINE, *S. S. Huebner Foundation; University of Florida* (5 years)

ERNEST W. COLE, *Marshall University* (8 years) *

EUGENE C. DEVOL, *National Life Insurance Company*, Philadelphia (6 years)

---

*Currently serving on Board of Graders in 1963

JAMES J. GALLAGHER, JR., *University of Pennsylvania; American Law Institute* (8 years)*

BENJAMIN M. GASTON, SR., *North American Life Assurance Company,* Philadelphia (9 years)

HERBERT C. GRAEBNER, *Butler University* (5 years)

J. D. HAMMOND, *S. S. Huebner Foundation; Ohio State University* (5 years)

WAYNE E. HOWARD, *University of Pennsylvania* (6 years)

ALAN D. HECHT, *Wolman-Hecht-Schoenfeld, Inc., Baltimore* (5 years)

DAVID A. IVRY, *University of Connecticut* (6 years)

ACIS JENKINSON, 3rd, *University of Pennsylvania* (5 years)

JOHN F. JEREMIAH, *University of Pennsylvania* (33 years)

CLYDE M. KAHLER, *University of Pennsylvania* (20 years)

RICHARD DER. KIP, *University of Pennsylvania; Florida State University* (17 years)

WILLIAM B. KIRK, *Occidental Life Insurance Company of California,* Philadelphia (5 years)

CHESTER A. KLINE, *University of Pennsylvania* (14 years)

HAROLD Q. LANGENDERFER, *University of North Carolina* (5 years)

HARRY J. LOMAN, *University of Pennsylvania* (8 years)

BERNARD J. LYTTLE, *Berkshire Life Insurance Company,* New York City (8 years)*

DAN M. MCGILL, *University of Pennsylvania* (7 years)

EDWARD O. MCHENRY, *Acacia Mutual Life Insurance Company,* Philadelphia and Washington, D.C. (5 years)

WALTER C. MCKAIN, JR., *University of Connecticut* (8 years)

JOSEPH J. MELONE, *S. S. Huebner Foundation; University of Pennsylvania* (5 years)

JONAS B. MITTLEMAN, *S. S. Huebner Foundation; San Francisco State College* (5 years)

ARCHIE J. NICHOLS, *S. S. Huebner Foundation; Butler University* (6 years)

RALPH A. NITTINGER, *University of Pennsylvania* (5 years)

GRANT M. OSBORN, *S. S. Huebner Foundation; Arizona State College* (6 years)

LEROY L. PHAUP, JR., *S. S. Huebner Foundation; University of South Carolina* (6 years)*

---

*Currently serving on Board of Graders in 1963

J. C. PHILLIPS, *University of Pennsylvania* (13 years)

EDWARD L. REILEY, *Mutual Benefit Life Insurance Company*, Philadelphia (5 years)

CHARLES C. ROHLFING, *University of Pennsylvania* (16 years)

DAVID T. ROWLANDS, *University of Pennsylvania* (11 years)

KARL W. H. SCHOLZ, *University of Pennsylvania* (26 years)

DONALD SCOLES, *S. S. Huebner Foundation; University of Southern California; Los Angeles State College* (20 years)*

LEROY B. SCOTT, *University of Pennsylvania* (7 years)*

ELMER E. SELBY, *Berkshire Life Insurance Company*, Pittsburgh (5 years)

HERBERT E. SIM, *University of Notre Dame* (6 years)*

ROBERT H. SKILTON, *University of Pennsylvania* (7 years)

DONALD M. SOLENBERGER, *Connecticut Mutual Life Insurance Company*, Philadelphia (5 years)

CARL STERN, *University of Pennsylvania; Randolph-Macon Woman's College* (10 years)*

ARTHUR I. STERNHELL, *Metropolitan Life Insurance Company*, New York City (6 years)

FREDERICK J. STEVENSON, *Equitable Life Assurance Society*, Pittsburgh (12 years)

THOMAS H. STEWART, *University of Pennsylvania* (5 years)

HOWARD M. TEAF, *Haverford College* (7 years)

W. E. WARRINGTON, *University of Pennsylvania* (15 years)

CHARLES M. WEBER, *University of Pennsylvania* (10 years)

ARTHUR L. WILLIAMS, *S. S. Huebner Foundation; Pennsylvania State University* (7 years)*

LAWRENCE C. WOODS, JR., *Equitable Life Assurance Society*, Pittsburgh (9 years)

AMERICAN COLLEGE STAFF WHO HAVE PARTICIPATED IN THE GRADING

ALBERT H. CLARK, *Director of Examinations* (1959-61)

ROBERT M. CROWE, *Director of Examinations* (1962 to present)

W. W. DOTTERWEICH, JR., *Assistant Dean* (1958 to present)

---

*Currently serving on Board of Graders in 1963

HERBERT C. GRAEBNER, *Dean* (1955 to present)

DAVIS W. GREGG, *Dean* (1950-54)

G. VICTOR HALLMAN, *Director of Educational Publications* (1961 to present)

WILLIAM M. HOWARD, *Director of Educational Publications* (1954-55)

DANIEL P. KEDZIE, *Director of Management Education* (1960-61)

JACK C. KEIR, *Assistant Dean* (1956 to present)

THOMAS J. LUCK, *Director of Management Education* (1956-58)

ARTHUR W. MASON, JR., *Director of College Relations* (1952-56)

DAVID McCAHAN, *Dean* (1929-51)

ROSS M. TRUMP, *Assistant Dean* (1947-49)

Appendix F

MEMBERS OF GOLDEN KEY
SOCIETY AS OF JULY 15, 1963

IRWIN SCOTT ADAMS, JR., C.L.U.
Portland, Oregon

ROBERT S. ALBRITTON, C.L.U.
Los Angeles, California

JONATHAN R. ALDER, C.L.U.
Cleveland, Ohio

ROBERT A. ALFORD, C.L.U.
Des Moines, Iowa

BENJAMIN ALK, C.L.U.
New York City

ARTHUR H. ALLEN, C.L.U.
Murfreesboro, Tennessee

JOHN T. ALLEN, JR., C.L.U.
Denver, Colorado

THOMAS ALLSOPP, C.L.U.
Boston, Massachusetts

HERSCHEL M. ALTON, C.L.U.
Phoenix, Arizona

CARL P. ANDERSON, C.L.U.
Boston, Massachusetts

W. H. ANDREWS, JR., C.L.U.
Greensboro, North Carolina

MILTON E. ASFAHL, C.L.U.
Oklahoma City, Oklahoma

DAVID W. ASHLEY, C.L.U.
Fort Worth, Texas

*BEN P. ATKINSON, C.L.U.
Austin, Texas

MAURICE W. BAEHR, C.L.U.
Philadelphia, Pennsylvania

WILLIAM R. BAGG, C.L.U.
Fort Worth, Texas
In memory of son, Robert Allen

BILL J. BAKER, C.L.U.
Fort Worth, Texas

H. SHERIDAN BAKETEL, JR., C.L.U.
Philadelphia, Pennsylvania

J. HICKS BALDWIN, C.L.U.
Washington, D.C.

JAMES A. BALLEW, C.L.U.
Bryn Mawr, Pennsylvania

BRUCE BARE, C.L.U.
Los Angeles, California

NATHAN BAROCAS, C.L.U.
Portland, Oregon

CHARLES N. BARTON, C.L.U.
New York City

EDWARD B. BATES, C.L.U.
Hartford, Connecticut

W. T. C. BATES, C.L.U.
Orangeburg, South Carolina

ORVILLE E. BEAL, C.L.U.
Newark, New Jersey
In memory of John D. Beal

RICHARD L. T. BEALE, JR., C.L.U.
Sparta, Virginia

RALPH J. BEAVER, C.L.U.
Fort Worth, Texas

ARTHUR L. BECK, C.L.U.
Buffalo, New York

MARTIN J. BECKERS, C.L.U.
Flint, Michigan

HENRY S. BEERS
Glastonbury, Connecticut

*EDWIN J. BEHRENS, C.L.U.
Cleveland, Ohio

*Deceased

HENRY E. BELDEN, C.L.U.
Pasadena, California

MRS. HENRY E. BELDEN
Pasadena, California

HUGH S. BELL, C.L.U.
Seattle, Washington

LLOYD M. BENTSEN, JR.
Houston, Texas

SANFORD M. BERNBAUM, C.L.U.
Seattle, Washington

ROBERT M. BEST, C.L.U.
Binghamton, New York

CHARLES R. BIGBIE, JR., C.L.U.
Tulsa, Oklahoma

WALTER G. BILBREY, JR., C.L.U.
Hartford, Connecticut

KENNETH BLACK, JR., C.L.U.
Atlanta, Georgia

HOWARD E. BLAIR, C.L.U.
Elmira, New York

W. ROBERT BLAKNEY, C.L.U.
Syracuse, New York

BRUCE BLALACK, C.L.U.
Memphis, Tennessee

DAVID M. BLUMBERG, C.L.U.
Knoxville, Tennessee

ARTHUR G. BOARDMAN, C.L.U.
Boston, Massachusetts

JOSEPH E. BOETTNER, C.L.U.
Philadelphia, Pennsylvania

GLENN E. BOGASSE, C.L.U.
Charleston, West Virginia

ROBERT E. BOND, C.L.U.
Cleveland, Ohio

JOHN L. BOONE, C.L.U.
Nashville, Tennessee

ROBERT S. BOWLES, C.L.U.
Chicago, Illinois

ROBERT L. BOYD, C.L.U.
Kokomo, Indiana

CHARLES F. BRADFORD, C.L.U.
Dallas, Texas

THOMAS P. BRADY, C.L.U.
New York City

ELBRIDGE P. BRAGDON, C.L.U.
Harrisburg, Pennsylvania

EARLE W. BRAILEY, C.L.U.
Bethel, Vermont

E. DENBY BRANDON, JR., C.L.U.
Memphis, Tennessee

WILLIAM E. BRANHAM, C.L.U.
Oklahoma City, Okla.

FRANK E. BRENNAN, C.L.U.
Kansas City, Missouri

WILLITS A. BREWSTER, C.L.U.
Cheyenne, Wyoming

DAVID H. BRIDGES, C.L.U.
Oklahoma City, Oklahoma

H. KEITH BRINSON, C.L.U.
Fort Worth, Texas

WALTER F. BRISSENDEN, C.L.U.
Portland, Oregon

JOHN E. BROMLEY, C.L.U.
Battle Creek, Michigan

DONALD BROUN, C.L.U.
Denver, Colorado

GERARD S. BROWN, C.L.U.
Chicago, Illinois

ROYALL R. BROWN, C.L.U.
Winston-Salem, North Carolina

BENJAMIN S. BUCCA, C.L.U.
Highland Park, New Jersey

JOHN D. BUCHANAN, JR., C.L.U.
Newark, New Jersey

CONNER A. BURNETTE, JR., C.L.U.
Knoxville, Tennessee

DICKSON C. BUXTON, C.L.U.
Portland, Oregon

DARRELL L. BYINGTON, C.L.U.
Tacoma, Washington

GEORGE B. BYRNES, C.L.U.
Los Angeles, California

C. B. CAMERON, C.L.U.
Oklahoma City, Oklahoma

CHARLES W. CAMPBELL, C.L.U.
Jacksonville, Florida

CLINTON CAMPBELL, JR., C.L.U.
Knoxville, Tennessee

FRANK J. CAMPBELL, JR., C.L.U.
Philadelphia, Pennsylvania

JOSEPH S. CANNAVA, C.L.U.
Albany, New York

E. VERNON CARBONARA, C.L.U.
New York City

MAURICE I. CARLSON, C.L.U.
Dallas, Texas

ARTHUR B. CARROLL, JR., C.L.U.
Charlotte, North Carolina

EWING CARRUTHERS, JR., C.L.U.
Memphis, Tennessee

AUGUST S. CARSTENS, C.L.U.
Washington, D.C.

W. CLARENCE CARTER, C.L.U.
Richmond, Virginia

ROBERT E. CASTELO, C.L.U.
Champaign, Illinois

WILBERT O. CATTERTON, C.L.U.
Houston, Texas

WALTER R. CAVANAUGH, C.L.U.
Grosse Pointe Woods, Michigan

ROBERT R. CAVE, C.L.U.
Boston, Massachusetts

KENNETH W. CHRISTIANSON, C.L.U.
Los Angeles, California

ROBERT CISAR, C.L.U.
Cleveland, Ohio

PAUL F. CLARK, C.L.U.
Boston, Massachusetts

ROBERT K. CLARK, C.L.U.
Cleveland, Ohio

SCOTT CLAYTON, C.L.U.
Nashville, Tennessee

DAVID B. CLEMANS, C.L.U.
St. Paul, Minnesota

G. FRANCIS CLEMENT, C.L.U.
Roanoke, Virginia

ROBERT R. CLEVENGER, C.L.U.
Houston, Texas

NOBLE E. CLUCHEY, C.L.U.
Tacoma, Washington

JOHN V. COE, C.L.U.
Wichita, Kansas

C. CARLTON COFFIN, JR., C.L.U.
Atlanta, Georgia

S. RUSH COFFIN, C.L.U.
Los Angeles, California

RAYMOND E. COHN, C.L.U.
Fort Worth, Texas

E. PARKER COLBORN, C.L.U.
Syracuse, New York

FRANKLIN C. COMINS, C.L.U.
Flint, Michigan

DOROTHY E. CONNOR, C.L.U.
Tacoma, Washington

PAUL W. COOK, C.L.U.
Chicago, Illinois

SAMUEL W. COOMBS, C.L.U.
Oakland, California

S. BRUCE COPELAND, C.L.U.
Sacramento, California

JOHN P. COSTELLO, C.L.U.
Dallas, Texas

JOHN C. COUGHLIN, JR., C.L.U.
Boston, Massachusetts

MAURICE R. COULSON, C.L.U.
Wichita, Kansas

ROBERT COWAN, C.L.U.
Dallas, Texas

DAVID T. COWLES, C.L.U.
Boston, Massachusetts

RICHARD N. CRAIG, C.L.U.
Joplin, Missouri

ALFRED CRANWILL, C.L.U.
New York City

JOHN W. CRONIN, JR., C.L.U.
Philadelphia, Pennsylvania

CLARE E. CRONKRIGHT, C.L.U.
Detroit, Michigan

ROBERT M. CROWE, C.L.U.
Bryn Mawr, Pennsylvania

MURIEL E. CRUDDEN
Bryn Mawr, Pennsylvania

JOHN F. CURTIS, C.L.U.
Los Angeles, California

CHRISTOPHER F. CUSACK, JR., C.L.U.
Honolulu, Hawaii

EDWARD C. DANFORD, C.L.U.
New York City

JOHN W. DANHOF, C.L.U.
Grand Rapids, Michigan

EDWIN R. DANIELS, C.L.U.
Dallas, Texas

JOHN G. DARLING, C.L.U.
Durham, North Carolina

JOHN M. DARLING, C.L.U.
Kansas City, Missouri

WILLIAM D. DAVIDSON, C.L.U.
Chicago, Illinois

WILLIAM W. DAVIES, C.L.U.
Los Angeles, California

LEIGH H. DAVIS, C.L.U.
Cleveland, Ohio

WALTER W. DAVIS, C.L.U.
Indianapolis, Indiana

ELMER F. DAVY, C.L.U.
Salt Lake City, Utah

DANIEL E. DEAN, C.L.U.
Philadelphia, Pennsylvania

ROBERT DECHERT, ESQ.
Philadelphia, Pennsylvania

ELMER L. DEMAREST, C.L.U.
Newark, New Jersey

F. MASON DeNEFFE, C.L.U.
Portland, Oregon

BEN P. DENMAN, C.L.U.
Richmond, Virginia

NIT DENSKOON, C.L.U.
Bangkok, Thailand

RAYMOND E. DESAUTELS, C.L.U.
Boston, Massachusetts

JOSEPH N. DESMON, C.L.U.
Buffalo, New York

EUGENE C. DeVOL, C.L.U.
Philadelphia, Pennsylvania

ARVID R. DIKE, C.L.U.
Fort Worth, Texas

FREDERICK E. DINEHART, C.L.U.
Meriden, Connecticut

MALCOLM L. DINWIDDIE, C.L.U.
New Orleans, Louisiana

CHARLES L. DOANE, C.L.U.
Omaha, Nebraska

FRANCIS B. DONOVAN, C.L.U.
Peterborough, New Hampshire

FRED J. DOPHEIDE, C.L.U.
Bryn Mawr, Pennsylvania

FINCK DORMAN, C.L.U.
Houston, Texas

WAYNE E. DORMAN, C.L.U.
Washington, D.C.

RALPH S. DORSETT, C.L.U.
Lubbock, Texas

W. W. DOTTERWEICH, JR., C.L.U.
Bryn Mawr, Pennsylvania

ARTHUR E. DOWNER, C.L.U.
Newark, New Jersey

WALTER L. DOWNING, C.L.U.
Boston, Massachusetts

FRANCIS L. DOYLE, JR., C.L.U.
Philadelphia, Pennsylvania

R. WILLIAM DOZIER, JR., C.L.U.
Oklahoma City, Oklahoma

WILLIAM B. DUANE, C.L.U.
Boston, Massachusetts

HENRY W. DuBois, C.L.U.
Dallas, Texas

JACK A. DUCE, C.L.U.
Bryn Mawr, Pennsylvania

RAYMOND A. DuFOUR, C.L.U.
Washington, D.C.

JOSEPH F. DWYER, C.L.U.
Greeley, Colorado

HENRY DYMOND, C.L.U.
Cleveland, Ohio

WILLIAM T. EARLS, C.L.U.
Cincinnati, Ohio

HADSELL STONE EASTON, C.L.U.
Cleveland, Ohio

WILLIAM R. EAVENSON, C.L.U.
Buffalo, New York

RAYMOND A. EBBAGE, C.L.U.
Sacramento, California

RICHARD E. ECKEL, C.L.U.
Harrisburg, Pennsylvania

T. FRED EDMUNDS, C.L.U.
Columbia, South Carolina

CLIFFORD R. EDWARDS, C.L.U.
Tacoma, Washington

HARRY T. EIDSON, C.L.U.
Fort Worth, Texas

ABRAHAM W. EISEN, C.L.U.
New York City

COY G. EKLUND, C.L.U.
New York City

ELIAS B. ELIASON, JR., C.L.U.
San Francisco, California

WILLIAM ELLIOTT
Philadelphia, Pennsylvania

JOE S. ELLIS, C.L.U.
Oklahoma City, Oklahoma

DOUGLAS EMERY, C.L.U.
San Francisco, California

ALBERT R. ENDERLE, C.L.U.
Houston, Texas

IRVING ENNA, C.L.U.
Portland, Oregon

JOHN P. ENRIGHT, C.L.U.
Devon, Pennsylvania

CHARLES H. EVERETT, C.L.U.
Columbia, South Carolina

FREDERICK A. EXLINE, C.L.U.
Columbus, Ohio

ROBERT F. FAHEY, C.L.U.
Buffalo, New York

EDWIN J. FAULKNER
Lincoln, Nebraska

J. CARROLL FEELEY, C.L.U.
Charlottesville, Virginia

BEN FELDMAN, C.L.U.
East Liverpool, Ohio

F. RUSSELL FETTÉ, C.L.U.
St. Louis, Missouri

JACKSON G. FIELDS, C.L.U.
Jacksonville, Florida

A. C. F. FINKBINER, C.L.U.
Philadelphia, Pennsylvania

A. C. F. FINKBINER, JR., C.L.U.
Philadelphia, Pennsylvania

RAYMOND S. FIREBAUGH, C.L.U.
Phoenix, Arizona

C. ROBINSON FISH, III, C.L.U.
Boston, Massachusetts

*H. COCHRAN FISHER, C.L.U.
Washington, D.C.

DAVID C. FLAGG, C.L.U.
East Orange, New Jersey

JOHN T. FLANAGAN, JR., C.L.U.
Philadelphia, Pennsylvania

MEREDITH E. FLAUTT, C.L.U.
Nashville, Tennessee

HERBERT W. FLORER, C.L.U.
Boston, Massachusetts

WILSON L. FORKER, C.L.U.
Des Moines, Iowa

KENNETH C. FOSTER, C.L.U.
Newark, New Jersey

PHILIP J. FOSTER, C.L.U.
Eliot, Maine

THEODORE L. FOWLER, C.L.U.
Boston, Massachusetts

ANTON FOYT, C.L.U.
Wichita Falls, Texas

EDWARD A. FRERICHS, C.L.U.
Lincoln, Nebraska

FRANK FRIEDLER, C.L.U.
New Orleans, Louisiana

ROBERT E. FROOM, C.L.U.
Youngstown, Ohio

ROBERT W. FRYE, C.L.U.
Denver, Colorado

CARL T. FURNISS, C.L.U.
Hartford, Connecticut

LEO R. FUTIA, C.L.U.
Buffalo, New York

LEONARD W. GALLAGHER, C.L.U.
Torrington, Connecticut

HAROLD W. GARDINER, C.L.U.
Milwaukee, Wisconsin

BENJAMIN M. GASTON, SR., C.L.U.
Philadelphia, Pennsylvania

ROBERT P. GATEWOOD, C.L.U.
Washington, D.C.

W. E. GEHMAN, C.L.U.
Bala-Cynwyd, Pennsylvania

GLENN G. GEIGER, C.L.U.
New York City

HERBERT GEIST, C.L.U.
Chicago, Illinois

ELMER V. GETTYS, C.L.U.
Toledo, Ohio

LOUIS E. GIBSON, C.L.U.
Fort Worth, Texas

JACK W. GILLESPIE, C.L.U.
Memphis, Tennessee

BRUCE W. GILMORE, C.L.U.
Grand Rapids, Michigan

STUART A. GOLDFARB, C.L.U.
Jackson, Michigan

HOWARD D. GOLDMAN, C.L.U.
Richmond, Virginia

LEO GOLDSTEIN, C.L.U.
Buffalo, New York

GERALD D. GOOD, C.L.U.
Jamaica, L.I., New York

PAUL GOODMAN, C.L.U.
New York City

SHELLEY S. GOREN, C.L.U.
New York City

RUSSELL F. GORMAN, C.L.U.
Framingham, Massachusetts

*Deceased

WILLIAM H. GOULD, C.L.U.
Los Angeles, California

HERBERT C. GRAEBNER, C.L.U.
Bryn Mawr, Pennsylvania

MILLARD J. GRAUER, C.L.U.
Chicago, Illinois

E. DEE GRAY, C.L.U.
Denver, Colorado

JAMES R. GREANEY, C.L.U.
Boston, Massachusetts

RAY B. GREENE, JR., C.L.U.
Boston, Massachusetts

DAVIS W. GREGG, C.L.U.
Bryn Mawr, Pennsylvania

LEON S. GREGG
Houston, Texas

ARTHUR R. GREMEL, C.L.U.
Philadelphia, Pennsylvania

HARRY K. GUTMANN, C.L.U.
New York City

A. F. HAAS, C.L.U.
Chestertown, Maryland

JOE F. HABEGGER, C.L.U.
Seattle, Washington

ROBERT J. HABEGGER, C.L.U.
Seattle, Washington

RALPH E. HALE, C.L.U.
Framingham, Massachusetts

STANTON G. HALE
Los Angeles, California

ROBERT E. HALL, C.L.U.
New Orleans, Lousiana

G. VICTOR HALLMAN, III, C.L.U.
Bryn Mawr, Pennsylvania

HARRY LEE HAMILTON, C.L.U.
Louisville, Kentucky

WILLIAM J. HAMRICK, C.L.U.
Jacksonville, Florida

DALE W. HARDING, C.L.U.
Santa Ana, California

JOHN R. HARDY, C.L.U.
Jacksonville, Florida

CECIL E. HARRISON, C.L.U.
Frankfort, Indiana

JOHN R. HARTLEY, C.L.U.
Denver, Colorado

PAUL M. HARWICK, C.L.U.
Tacoma, Washington

R. LOUIS HATZES, C.L.U.
Washington, D.C.

JAMES D. HAWKINS, C.L.U.
Richmond, Virginia

ROBERT M. HAWLEY, C.L.U.
Seattle, Washington

ROLLA R. HAYS, JR., C.L.U.
Los Angeles, California

WM. EUGENE HAYS, C.L.U.
Boston, Massachusetts

ALAN D. HECHT, C.L.U.
Baltimore, Maryland

PAUL E. HERBST, C.L.U.
Toledo, Ohio

KENNETH W. HERRICK, C.L.U.
Fort Worth, Texas

RALPH HESTER, C.L.U.
Jackson, Mississippi

HERBERT R. HILL, C.L.U.
Richmond, Virginia

JOHN A. HILL, C.L.U.
Hartford, Connecticut

HENRY F. HINE, C.L.U.
Denver, Colorado

RICHARD A. HITTSON, C.L.U.
Tulsa, Oklahoma

SEWELL W. HODGE
Swarthmore, Pennsylvania

RUSSELL L. HOGHE, C.L.U.
Los Angeles, California

LILLIAN G. HOGUE, C.L.U.
Detroit, Michigan

PHILIP I. HOLWAY, C.L.U.
Hartford, Connecticut

JOHN D. HOPPER, C.L.U.
Harrisburg, Pennsylvania

H. G. HORN
Portland, Oregon

ESTHER M. HORR
Bryn Mawr, Pennsylvania

T. BRAXTON HORSLEY, C.L.U.
Richmond, Virginia

M. JAMES HOULIHAN, C.L.U.
Detroit, Michigan

DOUGLAS B. HOUSER, JR., C.L.U.
Chicago, Illinois

ROBERT C. HOWARD, C.L.U.
Oklahoma City, Oklahoma

JANE A. HOWELL, C.L.U.
San Francisco, California

FRANK W. HOWLAND, C.L.U.
Detroit, Michigan

SOLOMON HUBER, C.L.U.
New York City

JOHN M. HUEBNER
Wynnewood, Pennsylvania

S. S. HUEBNER
Bryn Mawr, Pennsylvania

MRS. S. S. HUEBNER
Merion Station, Pennsylvania

ROGER HULL, C.L.U.
New York City

DAVID G. HUNTING, C.L.U.
Fort Lauderdale, Florida

ALEXANDER HUTCHINSON, C.L.U.
New York City

JAMES B. IRVINE, JR., C.L.U.
Chattanooga, Tenneessee

DAVID A. IVRY, C.L.U.
Storrs, Connecticut

WILLIS JACKSON, SR., C.L.U.
Knoxville, Tennessee

EDWARD C. JAHN, C.L.U.
Newark, New Jersey

STEPHEN M. JAQUITH
New York City

GEORGE J. JOELSON, C.L.U.
New York City

JOHN V. JOHNSON, C.L.U.
Columbus, Ohio

RAYMOND C. JOHNSON, C.L.U.
New York City

THEODORE A. JOHNSTONE, C.L.U.
Kansas City, Missouri

ARTHUR H. JONES, C.L.U.
Syracuse, New York

DEWITT JONES, JR., C.L.U.
Denver, Colorado

H. NEAL JONES, C.L.U.
Sioux Falls, South Dakota

GEORGE G. JOSEPH, C.L.U.
Boston, Massachusetts

ARTHUR F. KEHLE
Seattle, Washington

JACK C. KEIR, C.L.U.
Bryn Mawr, Pennsylvania

JOHN J. KELLAM, C.L.U.
New Canaan, Connecticut

CORNELIUS J. KELLEHER, C.L.U.
San Jose, California

DON C. KENT, C.L.U.
Detroit, Michigan

JOHN G. KHOURI, C.L.U.
Boston, Massachusetts

ISAAC S. KIBRICK
Brockton, Massachusetts
In memory of son,
Herbert V. Kibrick, C.L.U.

JOHN J. KINANE, C.L.U.
Syracuse, New York

CHARLES J. KING, C.L.U.
Kansas City, Missouri

LYMAN E. KING, C.L.U.
Dallas, Texas

GEORGE M. KINGSLEY, JR., C.L.U.
Cleveland, Ohio

WILLIAM B. KIRK, C.L.U.
Philadelphia, Pennsylvania

HENRY A. KIRSCH, C.L.U.
Shreveport, Louisiana

FRED R. KISSLING, JR., C.L.U.
Lexington, Kentucky

JOSEPH J. KLEPPER, C.L.U.
Flushing, New York

CLAYTON T. KNOX, C.L.U.
Buffalo, New York

STUART H. KOCH, C.L.U.
Appleton, Wisconsin

MARTIN E. KOHN, C.L.U.
Philadelphia, Pennsylvania

GERSHEN KONIKOW, C.L.U.
New York City

ARTHUR E. KRAUS, C.L.U.
Los Angeles, California

THEODORE S. KRAUSE, C.L.U.
Bridgeton, New Jersey

KARL H. KREDER, C.L.U.
New York City

THADEUS R. KWARCIAK, C.L.U.
Southbridge, Massachusetts

MERLIN J. LADD, C.L.U.
Boston, Massachusetts

LLOYD LAFOT, C.L.U.
Los Angeles, California

MIRABEAU B. LAMAR, JR., C.L.U.
Philadelphia, Pennsylvania

JOHN B. LAMBERT, C.L.U.
Cleveland, Ohio

ROBERT E. LAMBERT, C.L.U.
Boston, Massachusetts

LONNIE LANGSTON, C.L.U.
Lubbock, Texas

DONALD F. LAU, C.L.U.
Detroit, Michigan

WILLIAM L. LEAVY, C.L.U.
Fort Worth, Texas

AUBREY F. LEE, C.L.U.
Burlingame, California

SIDNEY E. LEIWANT, C.L.U.
Newark, New Jersey

JAMES V. LELAURIN, C.L.U.
Meridian, Mississippi

CHARLES G. LEM, C.L.U.
Madison, Wisconsin
   In memory of Dr. C. H. Webster

LEO H. LESS, C.L.U.
Buffalo, New York

ROBERT L. LEVIN, C.L.U.
San Francisco, California

ALFRED J. LEWALLEN, C.L.U.
Miami, Florida

JACK LIPE, C.L.U.
Wichita, Kansas

JOHN I. LIPPINCOTT, JR., C.L.U.
Houston, Texas

STANLEY LISS, C.L.U.
New York City

D. CONRAD LITTLE, C.L.U.
Norfolk, Virginia

THOMAS E. LIVINGSTON, C.L.U.
Memphis, Tennessee

LOUIS LOFT, C.L.U.
New York City

JAMES B. LONGLEY, C.L.U.
Lewiston, Maine

KENNETH P. LORD, C.L.U.
Binghamton, New York

RALPH H. LOVE, C.L.U.
Hartford, Connecticut

ROBERT H. LOVVORN, C.L.U.
Columbia, South Carolina

FRED A. LUMB, C.L.U.
Boston, Massachusetts

JOHN K. LUTHER, C.L.U.
Hartford, Connecticut

WILLIAM P. LYNCH, C.L.U.
Newark, New Jersey

WILLIAM L. MACARTHUR, C.L.U.
Tacoma, Washington

KENNETH R. MACKENZIE, C.L.U.
Boston, Massachusetts

SAYRE MACLEOD, C.L.U.
Newark, New Jersey

NORRIS MAFFETT, C.L.U.
Hartford, Connecticut

JOHN R. MAGE, C.L.U.
Los Angeles, California

WILLIAM G. MAIBACH, C.L.U.
Peoria, Illinois

HENRY L. MALTENFORT, C.L.U.
Chicago, Illinois

HOLLIS L. MANLY, JR., C.L.U.
Houston, Texas

LAWRENCE MANN, C.L.U.
Los Angeles, California

W. EARL MANNING, JR., C.L.U.
Dallas, Texas

DAVID MARKS, JR., C.L.U.
New York City

SIDNEY L. MARKS, C.L.U.
New Orleans, Louisiana

JUSTIN E. MARSHALL, C.L.U.
Seattle, Washington

LEO C. MASCOTTE, C.L.U.
Fort Wayne, Indiana

A. FREEMAN MASON, C.L.U.
King of Prussia, Pennsylvania

JACK T. MASSEY, C.L.U.
Oklahoma City, Oklahoma

WILLIAM J. MATTINGLY, C.L.U.
Lafayette, Indiana

ROBERT W. MAXWELL, JR., C.L.U.
Hillsborough, California

DAVID MCCAHAN, JR., C.L.U.
Providence, Rhode Island

GRADY S. MCCARTER, JR., C.L.U.
Shreveport, Louisiana

CLARENCE L. MCCOMAS, C.L.U.
Memphis, Tennessee

LAURANCE W. MCDOUGALL, C.L.U.
Cleveland, Ohio

C. WILLARD McDOWELL, C.L.U.
Evansville, Indiana

RICHARD T. McFALLS
Bryn Mawr, Pennsylvania

BEN S. McGIVERAN, C.L.U.
Milwaukee, Wisconsin

THOMAS B. McGLINN, C.L.U.
Miami, Florida

HUBERT M. McLELLAN, C.L.U.
Seattle, Washington
  In memory of Mr. & Mrs. Edward F.
  Henzel and Mr. & Mrs. Hubert B.
  McLellan

MILES W. McNALLY, C.L.U.
Minneapolis, Minnesota

BOB McNEELY, C.L.U.
Fort Worth, Texas

JOHN P. MEEHAN, C.L.U.
Boston, Massachusetts

LESTER J. MEINHARDT, C.L.U.
Madison, Wisconsin

NATHAN METZGER, C.L.U.
Richmond, Virginia

ODD MEYER, JR., C.L.U.
Chicago, Illinois

HORACE H. MICKLEY, C.L.U.
Los Angeles, California

PAUL S. MILLS, C.L.U.
Bryn Mawr, Pennsylvania

EDWARD J. MINTZ, C.L.U.
Salinas, California

DOUGLAS L. MITCHELL, C.L.U.
Seattle, Washington

TOM LYLE MITCHELL, C.L.U.
Birmingham, Alabama

CHARLES M. MOCK, C.L.U.
Jacksonville, Florida

JAMES E. MOGAN, C.L.U.
Denver, Colorado

KENNETH D. MOORE, C.L.U.
Lubbock, Texas

FRANCIS W. MORLEY, JR., C.L.U.
Chicago, Illinois

ROBERT B. MORLEY, C.L.U.
Evanston, Illinois

GUY E. MORRISON, C.L.U.
Indianapolis, Indiana

ROBERT A. MORRISON, C.L.U.
Chattanooga, Tennessee

MARQUARD C. MULLER, C.L.U.
New York City

F. TURNER MUNSELL, C.L.U.
Cocoa, Florida

THOMAS G. MURRELL, C.L.U.
Los Angeles, California

JULIAN S. MYRICK
New York City

EDWIN NADEL, C.L.U.
New York City

EARL P. NEAL, JR.
New York City

HOWARD FREDRICK NEAL, C.L.U.
Los Angeles, California

GEORGE NEITLICH, C.L.U.
Mattapan, Massachusetts

ALBERT L. NEVEUX, JR., C.L.U.
Richmond, Virginia

HOWARD E. NEVONEN, C.L.U.
Los Angeles, California

STANLEY NEWHOUSE, C.L.U.
Scarsdale, New York

CURTIS G. NEWMAN
Oklahoma City, Oklahoma

DONALD C. NEWTON, C.L.U.
Syracuse, New York

FRANKLIN M. NICE, C.L.U.
Reading, Pennsylvania

J. COLGAN NORMAN, C.L.U.
Louisville, Kentucky

RICHARD I. NORTHRUP, C.L.U.
Los Angeles, California

PAUL A. NORTON, C.L.U.
New York City

EDMOND J. NOURI, C.L.U.
New York City

EUGENE C. NOYES, C.L.U.
Akron, Ohio

JIMMIE H. OATMAN, C.L.U.
Wichita Falls, Texas

ROBERT F. OBER, C.L.U.
Chicago, Illinois

JAMES T. O'NEAL, C.L.U.
Indianapolis, Indiana

ROBERT J. O'NEIL, C.L.U.
Peoria, Illinois

D. ROSS OSBORN, C.L.U.
Hartford, Connecticut

PAUL S. OWEN, C.L.U.
High Point, North Carolina

LLEWELLYN G. OWENS, C.L.U.
Chicago, Illinois

JAMES K. PACE, C.L.U.
Memphis, Tennessee

JOHN A. PACKAL, C.L.U.
Cleveland, Ohio

GERALD W. PAGE, C. L.U.
Los Angeles, California

R. MERLE PALMER, C.L.U.
Tacoma, Washington

ALTON C. PARKER, C.L.U.
Fayetteville, North Carolina

JOHN C. PARSONS, C.L.U.
Syracuse, New York

WILLIS M. PARTRIDGE, JR., C.L.U.
Boston, Massachusetts

HENRY J. PEIRCE, C.L.U.
Indianapolis, Indiana

CLARENCE E. PEJEAU, C.L.U.
Cleveland, Ohio

LEONARD A. PENNEY, C.L.U.
Wellesley Hills, Massachusetts

KARL J. PETERSON, C.L.U.
New York City

HOWARD PETITH, C.L.U.
Short Hills, New Jersey

C. R. PETTICREW, C.L.U.
Indianapolis, Indiana

D. MILEY PHIPPS, C.L.U.
Cleveland, Ohio

FRED W. PIERCE, C.L.U.
Los Angeles, California

M. HARRY PIPER
Flint, Michigan

CALVIN L. PONTIUS, C.L.U.
Philadelphia, Pennsylvania

JAMES P. POOLE, C.L.U.
Atlanta, Georgia

WILLIAM F. POOLE, III, C.L.U.
Lakeland, Florida

ROBERT K. POWERS, C.L.U.
Spokane, Washington

WILMER S. POYNER, JR., C.L.U.
Birmingham, Alabama

LAURIE F. PRATT, JR., C.L.U.
Knoxville, Tennessee

ARTHUR F. PRIEBE, C.L.U.
Rockford, Illinois

EDWIN T. PROCTOR, C.L.U.
Nashville, Tennessee

GEORGE N. QUIGLEY, JR., C.L.U.
Los Angeles, California

CHARLES L. QUINN, C.L.U.
Boston, Massachusetts

HAROLD K. QUINN, C.L.U.
Shreveport, Louisiana

FRANCIS J. RADANO, C.L.U.
Philadelphia, Pennsylvania

CALVIN L. RASEY, C.L.U.
Columbus, Ohio

ROBERT J. REA, C.L.U.
Sacramento, California

THOMAS G. READING, C.L.U.
Cleveland, Ohio

HOWARD D. RECTOR, C.L.U.
Fort Worth, Texas

JOHN M. REEDER, C.L.U.
Trenton, New Jersey

JOSEPH H. REESE, SR., C.L.U.
Rydal, Pennsylvania

JOSEPH H. REESE, JR., C.L.U.
Jenkintown, Pennsylvania

CHARLES K. REID, II, C.L.U.
Hartford, Connecticut

ROBERT M. REMICK, JR., C.L.U.
New York City

HERBERT C. REMIEN
Grand Rapids, Michigan

ARTHUR F. RENNING, C.L.U.
Fresno, California

CLARENCE W. REULING, C.L.U.
Peoria, Illinois

JAMES S. RICE, C.L.U.
Cheyenne, Wyoming

HOWARD J. RICHARD, C.L.U.
Boston, Massachusetts

FRANK RIDGE, C.L.U.
Washington, D.C.

BERT G. RIPLEY, JR., C.L.U.
Wichita Falls, Texas

E. PRICE RIPLEY, C.L.U.
Roanoke, Virginia

C. RIGDON ROBB, C.L.U.
Chicago, Illinois

OREM O. ROBBINS, C.L.U.
Minneapolis, Minnesota

ROGER R. ROBERTSON, C.L.U.
Tacoma, Washington

WILLIAM R. ROBERTSON, C.L.U.
Boston, Massachusetts

*CHARLES C. ROBINSON
Hartford, Connecticut

TED L. ROBINSON, C.L.U.
Los Angeles, California

WILLIAM Z. ROBINSON, C.L.U.
Seattle, Washington

SUMNER RODMAN, C.L.U.
Chestnut Hill, Massachusetts

CECIL ROGERS, C.L.U.
Binghamton, New York

HOWARD J. ROSAN, C.L.U.
New York City

BERNARD S. ROSEN, C.L.U.
Denver, Colorado

MARTIN A. ROSOFF, C.L.U.
Merion, Pennsylvania

ARNOLD S. ROSS, C.L.U.
New York City

E. LESLIE ROSS, C.L.U.
Boston, Massachusetts

KENNETH L. ROSS
Nashville, Tennessee

ROWE RUDOLPH, JR., C.L.U.
Denver, Colorado

JOHN M. RUSSON, C.L.U.
Los Angeles, California

HILBERT RUST, C.L.U.
Indianapolis, Indiana

DANIEL C. RYAN, C.L.U.
Boston, Massachusetts

ROBERT J. RYAN, C.L.U.
Detroit, Michigan

FRANK P. SAMFORD, JR., C.L.U.
Birmingham, Alabama

SAMUEL SANDERS, III, C.L.U.
New Orleans, Louisiana

WILLIAM R. SAPERS, C.L.U.
Boston, Massachusetts

T. GALVIN SCANLON, C.L.U.
Kansas City, Missouri

CHARLES H. SCHAAFF, C.L.U.
Springfield, Massachusetts

HERMANN SCHAAR, C.L.U.
Fort Worth, Texas

J. CLAYTON SCHAEFER, C.L.U.
Los Angeles, California

HELEN L. SCHMIDT, C.L.U. Associate
Bryn Mawr, Pennsylvania

KARL H. SCHMIDT, C.L.U.
Akron, Ohio

HARLAND A. SCHULER, C.L.U.
Dayton, Ohio

WILLIAM V. SCHUSTER, C.L.U.
Sacramento, California

VIRGIL A. SCHWARZ, C.L.U.
Tacoma, Washington

C. WILLIAM SCOTT, C.L.U.
Kansas City, Missouri

BERNARD SELDON, C.L.U.
New York City

SAMUEL W. SELDON, C.L.U.
New York City

CROWELL E. SEXTON, C.L.U.
Jacksonville, Florida

REX B. SHANNON, C.L.U.
Los Angeles, California

CHARLES E. SHEARER, JR., C.L.U.
Indianapolis, Indiana

DONALD L. SHEPHERD, C.L.U.
New York City

E. DALE SHEPHERD, JR., C.L.U.
Houston, Texas

MERL E. SHIELDS, C.L.U.
Anaheim, California

DONALD E. SHOPIRO, C.L.U.
Syracuse, New York

CHARLES N. SIEWERS, C.L.U.
Winston-Salem, North Carolina

RALFE O. P. SILVERMAN, JR., C.L.U.
Whitestone, New York

MARGARET T. SIMPSON
Bryn Mawr, Pennsylvania

ROBERT J. SIMS, C.L.U.
Philadelphia, Pennsylvania

NINO SIRACUSA, C.L.U.
Boston, Massachusetts

*Deceased

CLYDE SISSON, C.L.U.
Columbia, South Carolina

LEWIS A. SLEEPER, JR., C.L.U.
New York City

EDGAR R. SMALL, C.L.U.
Peoria, Illinois

ADON N. SMITH, II, C.L.U.
Charlotte, North Carolina

C. CARNEY SMITH, C.L.U.
Washington, D.C.

EVERELL A. SMITH, C.L.U.
Sycamore, Illinois

HORACE R. SMITH, C.L.U.
Hartford, Connecticut

J. CARLTON SMITH, C.L.U.
Dallas, Texas

MYRON E. SMITH, C.L.U.
Boston, Massachusetts

Z. EROL SMITH, JR., C.L.U.
Chicago, Illinois

CHARLES G. SMITHER, C.L.U.
New Orleans, Louisiana

*JAMES W. SMITHER, JR., C.L.U.
New Orleans, Louisiana

LEE T. SNILSBERG, C.L.U.
Mankato, Minnesota

HAROLD C. SONDAY, C.L.U.
Cleveland, Ohio

WILLIAM L. SPENCER, C.L.U.
Youngstown, Ohio

CARL M. SPERO, C.L.U.
New York City

JOSEPH L. SPEYER, C.L.U.
Boston, Massachusetts

WILLIAM A. SPIKER, C.L.U.
Arlington, Virginia

JOHN E. STEGER, C.L.U.
St. Paul, Minnesota

LEROY G. STEINBECK, C.L.U.
Philadelphia, Pennsylvania

B. WILLIAM STEINBERG, C.L.U.
New York City

HILLARD L. STERLING, C.L.U.
Philadelphia, Pennsylvania

MAURICE M. STERN, C.L.U.
New Orleans, Louisiana

RON STEVER, C.L.U.
Los Angeles, California

RICHARD R. STEWART, C.L.U.
Oakland, California

RICHARD T. STITH, JR., C.L.U.
St. Louis, Missouri

JASON C. STONE, C.L.U.
Boston, Massachusetts

JAMES V. STORY, C.L.U.
Wichita Falls, Texas

ALEXIE N. STOUT, C.L.U.
Syracuse, New York

CLARENCE J. STROUSS, JR., C.L.U.
Youngstown, Ohio

*SAMUEL J. SUGAR, C.L.U.
Washington, D.C.

FRANK E. SULLIVAN, C.L.U.
South Bend, Indiana

M. GREELY SUMMERS, JR., C.L.U.
Boston, Massachusetts

WILLIAM I. SUTTON, C.L.U.
Syracuse, New York

ROBERT H. SWANSON, C.L.U.
Chicago, Illinois

CLYDE E. SWIFT, C.L.U.
Atlanta, Georgia

MAURICE S. TABOR, C.L.U.
Buffalo, New York

JOHN R. TELICH, C.L.U.
Cleveland, Ohio

CHARLES IREDELL TENNEY, C.L.U.
Philadelphia, Pennsylvania

LOUIS N. THOMAS, C.L.U.
Plainview, Texas

JAMES R. THOMPSON, C.L.U.
Waco, Texas

MAURICE E. THOMPSON, C.L.U.
Los Angeles, California

P. RUSSELL THOMPSON, C.L.U.
Wakefield, Massachusetts

ANDREW H. THOMPSON, C.L.U.
New York City

CHARLES J. TIENSCH, II, C.L.U.
Newark, New Jersey

ROBERT J. TIFFANY, C.L.U.
Abilene, Texas

*Deceased

JOHN O. TODD, C.L.U.
Evanston, Illinois

BORISLAW J. TODOROVICH, C.L.U.
New York City

LOUIS J. TOIA, C.L.U.
Jersey City, New Jersey

WILLIAM R. TOOKER, C.L.U.
Washington, D.C.

J. RUSSELL TOWNSEND, JR., C.L.U.
Indianapolis, Indiana

GERARD B. TRACY, C.L.U.
New York City

RAYMOND F. TRIPLETT, C.L.U.
San Jose, California

JOHN F. TRUSLER, C.L.U.
Akron, Ohio

KNOX TURNBULL, C.L.U.
Charlottesville, Virginia

FORBES S. TUTTLE, C.L.U.
Syracuse, New York

*JOHN M. UTTER, C.L.U.
Seattle, Washington

ROBERT B. VAN DE MARK, C.L.U.
Tacoma, Washington

S. VAN ELGORT, C.L.U.
Los Angeles, California

FREDERICK T. VAN URK, C.L.U.
Philadelphia, Pennsylvania

LELAND T. WAGGONER, C.L.U.
New York City

CARROLL WALKER, C.L.U.
San Rafael, California

WILLIAM T. WALKER, C.L.U.
Memphis, Tennessee

PAUL A. WALLACE, C.L.U.
Seattle, Washington

M. ROOS WALLIS, C.L.U.
Philadelphia, Pennsylvania

WILLIAM T. WALSH, C.L.U.
Philadelphia, Pennsylvania

CHESTER T. WARDWELL, C.L.U.
Peoria, Illinois

LOUIS D. WASHBURN, C.L.U.
Fort Worth, Texas

HARRY M. WATSON, C.L.U.
Knoxville, Tennessee

STANLEY S. WATTS, C.L.U.
Norfolk, Virginia

GERALD E. WEBB, C.L.U.
Newark, New Jersey

E. CLARE WEBER, C.L.U.
Cleveland, Ohio

MILTON WEINTRAUB, C.L.U.
Pittsburgh, Pennsylvania

CLYDE R. WELMAN, C.L.U.
Montpelier, Vermont

WILLIAM P. WHALEY, C.L.U.
Dallas, Texas

WALTER B. WHEELER, C.L.U.
Bryn Mawr, Pennsylvania

FRED H. WHITE, C.L.U.
Buffalo, New York

GEORGE C. WHITE, C.L.U.
Massapequa Park, L.I., New York

JACK WHITE, C.L.U.
Los Angeles, California

OSCAR WHITEHORN
New York City

TROY N. WHITEHURST, C.L.U.
Houston, Texas

J. HAROLD WHITESIDE, C.L.U.
Tampa, Florida

LAWRENCE A. WHITESIDES, C.L.U.
Long Beach, California

JIMMIE M. WHITMIRE, C.L.U.
Wichita Walls, Texas

FREDERIC F. WIEDEMANN, C.L.U.
Dallas, Texas

FRED B. WILEY, C.L.U.
Seattle, Washington

LAWRENCE WILLET, C.L.U.
Atlanta, Georgia

KENNEY E. WILLIAMSON, C.L.U.
Peoria, Illinois

J. HAWLEY WILSON, JR., C.L.U.
Oklahoma City, Oklahoma

*J. HAWLEY WILSON, SR., C.L.U.
Oklahoma City, Oklahoma

LOYAL I. WILSON, C.L.U.
South Bend, Indiana

JACK C. WINDSOR, C.L.U.
Milwaukee, Wisconsin

*Deceased

ROBERT C. WISMER, C.L.U.
Flint, Michigan

RICHARD C. WOLFF, C.L.U.
Boston, Massachusetts

THOMAS J. WOLFF, C.L.U.
Hartford, Connecticut

SIDNEY L. WOLKENBERG, C.L.U.
New York City

MARSHALL I. WOLPER, C.L.U.
Miami Beach, Florida

E. WAYNE WOOD, C.L.U.
Houston, Texas

R. EDWIN WOOD, C.L.U.
San Francisco, California

ROBERT L. WOODS, C.L.U.
Los Angeles, California

BENJAMIN N. WOODSON, C.L.U.
Houston, Texas

GUS S. WORTHAM
Houston, Texas

THEODORE H. WORTHINGTON, C.L.U.
Wenonah, New Jersey

FORT A. ZACKARY, C.L.U.
Wichita, Kansas

BERNARD H. ZAIS, C.L.U.
Burlington, Vermont

EDMUND L. ZALINSKI, C.L.U.
Philadelphia, Pennsylvania

CHARLES J. ZIMMERMAN, C.L.U.
Hartford, Connecticut

Appendix G

AMERICAN COLLEGE OF LIFE UNDERWRITERS FINANCIAL OPERATIONS 1928-1962

| | INCOME | | DISBURSEMENTS | |
	Budgeted	Actual	Budgeted	Actual
Year				
1928	*	$ 4,835	*	$ 4,500
1929	*	8,842	*	6,812
1930	*	12,215	*	10,696
1931	*	26,073	$ 20,000	19,044
1932	$ 21,825	25,540	21,000	27,521
1933	22,000	26,418	21,410	25,291
1934	*	26,597	29,100	26,900
1935	*	30,967	24,700	29,389
1936	*	31,524	31,653	31,120
1937	*	29,647	34,100	31,559
1938	61,461	91,421	62,262	69,256
1939	64,225	85,414	64,705	76,926
1940	76,832	77,971	81,204	78,785
1941	79,000	86,822	78,740	81,449
1942	74,525	62,642	74,395	63,732
1943	53,250	60,638	57,420	57,962
1944	55,190	65,177	59,557	60,109
1945	63,120	70,422	71,147	66,425
1946	71,650	90,686	83,066	75,907
1947	92,050	131,742	99,485	97,710
1948	115,600	139,186	119,530	134,896
1949	133,900	146,613	140,783	133,384
1950	136,570	149,068	141,433	136,795
1951	143,893	136,095	157,903	142,817
1952	167,970	171,456	173,911	161,356
1953	240,720†	254,149†	268,164†	254,582†
1954	184,160	199,571	222,855	202,445
1955	268,230	310,924	269,369	247,446
1956	322,945	346,006	334,583	314,373
1957	349,650	409,763	344,305	349,612
1958	412,815	442,036	405,994	408,516
1959	444,825	511,366	485,975	471,131
1960	572,396	629,195	558,310	509,327
1961	668,274	681,016	667,128	617,881
1962	729,250	855,684	732,150	781,453
1963	855,550		864,500	

*Figures not available.

† Includes loans for new wing on Walnut Street building and expenditures for same.

C.L.U. CLASS ENROLLMENTS AND COLLEGES AND UNIVERSITIES COOPERATING IN SPONSORING COURSES AND ACTING AS EXAMINATION CENTERS 1928-1962

	C.L.U. Classes		Cooperating Colleges and Universities		
Year	Total Number	Total Enrollment	Number Sponsoring Classes	Enrollment	Serving as Examination Centers
1928	*	*	*	*	14
1929	14	*	*	*	25
1930	29	*	*	*	36
1931	48	*	*	*	49
1932	42	*	*	*	50
1933	49	*	*	*	58
1934	50	1,416	*	*	63
1935	79	1,812	*	*	67
1936	93	1,323	*	*	64
1937	97	1,353	*	*	75
1938	124	1,892	*	*	78
1939	188	3,123	*	*	90
1940	160	2,244	*	*	88
1941	157	2,159	*	*	90
1942	148	1,841	*	*	100
1943	111	1,227	28	*	92
1944	96	1,151	27	402	102
1945	115	1,724	40	707	119
1946	124	2,051	52	1,053	115
1947	187	4,517	100	2,947	121
1948	243	5,046	122	3,269	142
1949	251	4,218	131	2,623	148
1950	259	4,039	134	2,552	155
1951	202	3,281	111	2,031	140
1952	240	3,647	109	1,994	141
1953	222	3,638	100	1,934	132
1954	227	4,088	119	2,339	140
1955	259	5,050	112	2,426	158
1956	291	5,670	126	2,946	164
1957	352	7,251	144	3,589	175
1958	339	7,677	146	3,359	169
1959	398	8,438	158	3,716	194
1960	410	8,572	172	3,624	186
1961	444	8,995	181	3,884	214
1962	528	10,332	191	4,306	210

*Statistics not available.

C.L.U. EXAMINATION DATA
1928-1962

Year	Number of New Candidates	Number Taking Exams	Number Exams Taken	Number Completing	Over-all Passing Ratio
1928	83	66	295	22	76.6%
1929	164	114	509	83	77.9%
1930	242	235	1,007	115	75.6%
1931	470	521	1,758	187	74.2%
1932	440	638	1,701	198	73.9%
1933	407	663	1,536	156	72.9%
1934	408	688	1,534	143	65.5%
1935	463	817	1,770	185	67.3%
1936	594	980	1,952	148	63.1%
1937	423	965	1,760	146	59.0%
1938	600	1,150	2,117	151	58.2%
1939	1,130	1,746	3,125	154	59.9%
1940	742	1,735	2,864	157	62.3%
1941	612	1,616	2,524	212	67.9%
1942	376	1,239	1,660	207	70.5%
1943	233	803	1,019	160	65.5%
1944	260	706	889	125	64.1%
1945	475	952	1,262	117	69.1%
1946	748	1,365	1,749	128	65.7%
1947	1,655	2,564	3,239	205	62.8%
1948	1,494	2,885	3,752	250	64.7%
1949	1,264	2,967	3,944	341	58.6%
1950	1,095	2,794	3,839	449	64.8%
1951	927	2,310	3,201	380	67.8%
1952	1,240	2,539	3,388	367	69.2%
1953	1,320	2,775	3,712	391	66.5%
1954	1,517	3,177	4,142	397	69.2%
1955	1,777	3,630	4,521	407	70.8%
1956	1,906	4,176	5,278	435	61.5%
1957	2,286	5,034	6,202	561	65.8%
1958	2,350	5,396	6,661	641	68.8%
1959	2,755	6,006	7,531	682	64.2%
1960	3,427	6,773	8,499	811	69.1%
1961	3,560	7,394	9,406	1,014	74.3%
1962	4,063	8,194	10,247	802	64.2%

COMPLETING C.L.U. CANDIDATES CLASSIFIED AS TO AWARD EARNED (Cumulative totals) 1928-1962

Year	Number with Credit for All Examinations	Number Holding C.L.U. Designation	Number Holding C.L.U. Associate Designation	Number Holding Certificate of Proficiency	Number Lacking Experience Requirement
1928	22	21			1
1929	105	98			7
1930	220	208			12
1931	407	381		3*	23
1932	605	563		7	35
1933	761	703		11	47
1934	904	830		18	56
1935	1,089	994		20	75
1936	1,237	1,127		23	87
1937	1,383	1,258		29	96
1938	1,534	1,402		33	99
1939	1,688	1,530		38	120
1940	1,845	1,669		43	133
1941	2,057	1,856		64	137
1942	2,264	2,043		77	144
1943	2,424	2,209		77	138
1944	2,549	2,341		73	135
1945	2,666	2,472		67	127
1946	2,794	2,599		71	124
1947	2,999	2,799		78	122
1948	3,249	3,028		81	140
1949	3,590	3,337		88	165
1950	4,039	3,763		92	184
1951	4,419	4,127		106	186
1952	4,786	4,475	103*	29	179
1953	5,177	4,837	121	28	191
1954	5,574	5,215	134	27	198
1955	5,981	5,596	155	27	203
1956	6,416	6,007	175	26	208
1957	6,977	6,526	193	26	232
1958	7,618	7,092	212	26	288
1959	8,300	7,753	236	26	285
1960	9,111	8,521	278	26	286
1961	10,125	9,600	197	26	302
1962	10,927	10,381	201	26	319

*First year awarded.

BIBLIOGRAPHY OF PUBLICATIONS CONCERNING THE COLLEGE OR PUBLISHED BY THE COLLEGE

PERIODICALS

ALDER, GEORGE D. "The American College of Life Underwriters," *Life Association News*, Vol. 21:738 (May, 1927).

"American College Acquires New Home," *Life Association News*, Vol. 42:890–92 (July, 1948).

"American College Alumni Form Permanent Body," *Life Association News*, Vol. 24:849 (June, 1930).

"American College of Life Underwriters Comes Into Being at Mid-Year Meeting of Executive Committee of NALU at Chicago," *Life Association News*, Vol. 21:652–57, 681–87 (April, 1927).

"American College of Life Underwriters Has New President," *Life Association News*, Vol. 22:737, 760 (May, 1928).

"American College of Life Underwriters Proceeding Cautiously," *Spectator*, Vol. 119:8 (July 21, 1927).

AMERICAN SOCIETY OF CHARTERED LIFE UNDERWRITERS. *Official News Bulletin*. Began publication with No. 1, November 15, 1944.

———. *Query*. Began publication January, 1952 to date.

———. *The Society Page*. Published bi-monthly since July, 1962.

BRAGG, JAMES ELTON. "Historical Highlights of the American College," *Life Association News*, Vol. 47:28–30, 82–83 (September, 1952).

CLARK, ERNEST J., SR. "The Founding of the American College of Life Underwriters," *The Journal of the American Society of Chartered Life Underwriters*, Vol. 1:191–200 (March, 1947).

CLARK, ERNEST J. "Professional Education in Life Underwriting," *American Academy of Political and Social Science Annals*, Vol. 161:178–83 (May, 1932).

CLARK, PAUL F. "Dr. S. S. Huebner; An Impression," *The Journal of the American Society of Chartered Life Underwriters*, Vol. 5:64 (December, 1950).

———. "How the C.L.U. Movement Helps Solve Managerial Problems," *Life Insurance Selling*, Vol. 11:18–20, 22, 45 (March, 1936).

———. "Postwar Challenges to the Chartered Life Underwriter," *Insurance Advocate*, Vol. 56:19, 22–23, 26 (September 22, 1945) and *Life Association News*, Vol. 40:149–50, 180–83 (October, 1945). Also issued as a reprint by *Insurance Advocate*.

"C.L.U. Starts Million Dollar Fund Drive," *Life Association News*, Vol. 56:77–78 (January, 1961).

COOPER, F. "Is It Profitable to Promote C.L.U. Studies?" *Spectator*, Vol. 162:49–55 (October, 1954).

CRAIG, WALTER A. "The American College" (editorial), *The Journal of the American Society of Chartered Life Underwriters*, Vol. 1:189–90 (March, 1947).

CUMMINGS, O. SAM. "The C.L.U. Study Program As An Aid to Managers," *Manager's Magazine*, Vol. 8:10–11 (July/August, 1938). Also issued as two-page reprint.

"David McCahan Foundation Announced," *Life Association News*, Vol. 50:34–35 (May, 1955).

DECHERT, ROBERT. "C.L.U. Recognition—Challenge and Responsibility," *Life Insurance Courant*, Vol. 53:8–9 (December, 1948).

"Edward A. Woods Foundation Endowment Plans Announced," *Life Association News*, Vol. 23:229, 264 (November, 1928).

"Eligibility Requirements for Chartered Life Underwriter Revised; Plan for Home Study Courses to Prepare Candidates Lacking High School Prerequisite Arranged by Columbia University," *Life Association News*, Vol. 24:285–86 (November, 1929).

"First Examinations of the American College of Life Underwriters," *Life Association News*, Vol. 22:1034, 1036, 1038 (August, 1928).

FLOYD, FREDERICK W. "For Tomorrow . . . A Look at Yesterday: The Story of the American Society of Chartered Life Underwriters," *Life Association News*, Vol. 47:42–44, 80–81 (September, 1952).

GANSE, FRANKLIN W. "Early Days of the American College," *John Hancock Signature*, Vol. 14:6–7 (September, 1941).

GASTON, BENJAMIN M. "A Quarter Century of Growth and Change," *American Society of Chartered Life Underwriters Journal*, Vol. 15:304–18 (Fall, 1961).

GRAEBNER, HERBERT C. "The C.L.U. Examinations—1959 Model," *The Journal of the American Society of Chartered Life Underwriters*, Vol. 12:375–82 (Fall, 1958).

———. "Objective Testing in C.L.U. Professional Examinations," *The Journal of the American Society of Chartered Life Underwriters*, Vol. 14:277–85 (Summer, 1960).

———. "What Does C.L.U. Do to a Man?" *Insurance Salesman*, Vol. 98:31–32, 47–50 (August, 1955).

GREGG, DAVIS W. "The American College of Life Underwriters," *Life Association News*, Vol. 51, No. 10:45–47 (1956).

———. "The American College of Life Underwriters; What It Is and What It Does," *Life Association News*, Vol. 44:1149–50, 1177–79 (August, 1950).

———. "Changing Subjects With the Changing Times," *The Journal of the American Society of Chartered Life Underwriters*, Vol. 10:258–64 (Summer, 1956).

———. "The Family Life Cycle: A Conceptual Legacy," an introduction to: James H. S. Bossard, "The Concept of the Family Cycle," *The Journal of the American Society of Chartered Life Underwriters*, Vol. 14:308–22 (Fall, 1960).

———. "Keep Your Education Going," *Manager's Magazine*, Vol. 22:9–16 (May, 1951).

GREGG, DAVIS W., and GRAEBNER, HERBERT C. "George Brown Takes a C.L.U. Examination; or How C.L.U. Examinations Are Prepared and Graded," *The Journal of the American Society of Chartered Life Underwriters*, Vol. 9:331–41 (Fall, 1955).

"Gregg Receives John Newton Russell Memorial Award," *Life Association News*, Vol. 56:63–64, 150 (November, 1961).

HILL, GRANT L. "C.L.U.—An Opportunity and a Responsibility," *Life Association News*, Vol. 28:233–35 (December, 1933).

HUEBNER, SOLOMON S. "The American College of Life Underwriters—Completion of the Pioneering Decade—Beginning of the Decade of Expansion," *Life Insurance Selling*, Vol. 12:7–8, 19, 36–38 (May, 1937).

———. "The American College of Life Underwriters: Its Place in American Life Insurance," *Life Association News*, Vol. 24:362–64, 366 (December, 1929).

———. "C.L.U. Movement: Its Growth and Place in Underwriting," *Life Insurance Selling*, Vol. 10:6–8, 43–45 (March, 1935).

———. "Education—The Great Ally of the Life Underwriter," *Spectator*, Vol. 164: Supp. 1–8 (January, 1956).

———. "Edward A. Woods and The American College of Life Underwriters," *Life Association News*, Vol. 23:756–57 (May, 1929).

———. "The First Class of C.L.U.'s; A Brief Recollection," *Life Association News*, Vol. 47:47–48 (September, 1952).

———. "Future Patterns in Life Insurance Distribution—An Educator's View," *Journal of Insurance*, Vol. 24:9–20 (December, 1957).

———. "Growth of the C.L.U. Movement and Its Future," *Life Insurance Selling*, Vol. 11:6–8, 41–45 (March, 1936).

———. "Life Insurance Salesmanship as a Profession," *Life Association News*, Vol. 9:1–4 (March, 1915). Speech to Baltimore Life Underwriters.

———. "The Life Underwriter of the Future—He Will Be A Professional Man and Educator, A Community Leader," *United States Review*, Vol. 160:28–41 (May 29, 1948). Abridgement of address before the C.L.U. luncheon of the annual convention of the Pennsylvania Association of Life Underwriters, May 20, 1948.

———. "A Look Ahead," *American Association of University Teachers of Insurance Journal*, Vol. 15:73–83 (March, 1948).

———. "A Modern Look At the Economics of Life Insurance," *The Journal of the American Society of Chartered Life Underwriters*, Vol. 13:301–13 (Fall, 1959).

———. "The Need for Collegiate Instruction in Insurance," *School and College Placement*, Vol. 2:19–21, 63–72 (October, 1941). Reprinted by the American Society of Chartered Life Underwriters, 1943, 27pp.

———. "New Horizons in Life Insurance," *The Journal of the American Society of Chartered Life Underwriters*, Vol. 1:5–14 (September, 1946).

———. "The Power of Insurance Education," *Federation of Insurance Counsel Quarterly*, Vol. 12:35–40 (Fall, 1961).

———. "The Professional Concept in Life Underwriting," *Life Association News*, Vol. 23:729–32, 774–77 (May, 1929).

———. "A Professional Standard Based Upon a Professional Designation," *Insurance Broker-Age*, Vol. 4:8, 9, 20 (June, 1936).

———. "What a C.L.U. Should Know About A & H," *Life Insurance Courant*, Vol. 60:52–54 (September, 1955) ; 55–57 (October, 1955).

———. "What the C.L.U. Program Has Done for Life Underwriters," *Rough Notes*, Vol. 79:11–12 (September, 1936).

———. "Where Are We Going?" *Best's Insurance News, Life Edition*, Vol. 60:18, 42–45 (October, 1959).

HUEBNER, SOLOMON S., and MCCAHAN, DAVID. "Some Aspects of American College Operational History," *The Journal of the American Society of Chartered Life Underwriters*, Vol. 1:201–16 (March, 1947).

"Huebner Hall: American Center for Insurance Education," *Life Association News*, Vol. 56:75–76 (July, 1961).

"Huebner Hall Dedicated," *The Journal of the American Society of Chartered Life Underwriters*, Vol. 15:197–98 (Summer, 1961).

"Huebner Honored At Dedication of Insurance Education Center," *National Underwriter*, Fire and Casualty Edition, Vol. 65:4 (June 9, 1961). *Ibid.*, Life Edition, Vol. 65:2, 12–13 (June 10, 1961).

Insurance Review (Tokyo), Vol. 10 (May, 1958, July, 1958 and September, 1958). Three issues devoted to Dr. Huebner's 1958 visit to Japan.

JOHNSON, RAYMOND C. "Higher Education in Insurance—Our Growing Strength," *The Journal of the American Society of Chartered Life Underwriters*, Vol. 5:114–24 (March, 1951).

JOSEPHS, DEVEREUX C. "Insurance and Education," *The Journal of the American Society of Chartered Life Underwriters*, Vol. 15:297–303 (Fall, 1961).

The Journal of the American Society of Chartered Life Underwriters, began with Vol. 1, No. 1, September, 1946; quarterly, and has continued to present.

"Keynotes" column, began in *Life Association News*, July, 1954 to date.

LACKEY, GEORGE E. "Education of the Life Underwriter," *Insurance Field*, Life Edition, Vol. 73:16–20 (February 18, 1944).

LUCK, T. J. "C.L.U. Program" (an article concerning Management Education), *Best's Insurance News*, Life Edition, Vol. 58:15–17 (April, 1958).

"A Mark of Distinction; Chartered Life Underwriter," *Life Association News*, Vol. 24:831 (June, 1930).

McCAHAN, DAVID (ed.). "C.L.U. Activities," *Life Association News*. Began February, 1935, continued to September, 1952.

———. "C.L.U. Activities in Wartime," *Journal of Commerce*, Annual Insurance Number, December 28, 1942.

———. "The C.L.U. Educational Program," *Life Association News*, Vol. 33:1005–7 (August, 1939).

———. "C.L.U. Movement in Review," *Life Insurance Selling*, Vol. 12:12–19 (May, 1937).

———. "Getting the Benefits of C.L.U. Education," *Life Insurance Selling*, Vol. 11:10–12 (March, 1936).

———. "The Half-Century in Insurance Education," *American Association of University Teachers of Insurance Journal*, Vol. 18:54–72 (March, 1951).

———. "Life Insurance Education in the Years Ahead," *Weekly Underwriter*, Vol. 150; Sect. 2:52–53, 73, 77, 80–81, 84 (May 13, 1944). Reprint issued by the American College without a date.

———. "Professional Training for Agents," *Weekly Underwriter and the Insurance Press*, Vol. 122; pt. 2:64, 65, 72 (May 10, 1930).

———. "Public and Agency Education in Life Insurance," *Life Association News*, Vol. 24:828–30, 877 (June, 1930).

———. "Solomon Stephen Huebner; World's Foremost Insurance Educator," *Life Association News*, Vol. 34:965–68 (July, 1940).

———. "The Value of C.L.U. Education As An Investment," *Life Insurance Selling*, Vol. 10:11–12, 20 (March, 1935).

McCAHAN, DAVID, and GREGG, DAVIS W. (eds.) "A Collection of Huebnerian Philosophy on Life and Life Insurance; Thoughts from the Pen of Solomon Stephen Huebner," *The Journal of the American Society of Chartered Life Underwriters*, Vol. 6:202–13 (June, 1952).

MILLS, PAUL S. "The C.L.U. Journal—Fifteen Years Later," *The Journal of the American Society of Chartered Life Underwriters*, Vol. 15:293–96 (Fall, 1961).

MYRICK, JULIAN S. "Rapid Expansion Noted in Demand for Broad Educational Facilities," *Weekly Underwriter*, Vol. 156:96 (January 4, 1947).

———. "Value of the C.L.U.," *Insurance Advocate*, Vol. 55:30, 32 (April 15, 1944). Also available as a reprint from *Insurance Advocate*.

NEITLICH, GEORGE. "The American Society of Chartered Life Underwriters," *Life Association News*, Vol. 51, No. 10:51–52 (1956).

"New C.L.U. Associate Designation Adopted in 25th Year of American College," *Life Association News*, Vol. 47:30 (September, 1952).

NORTH, H. "Establishment of $30,000 Fund," *Insurance Field*, Denver Convention Daily Edition, Vol. 66:8 (August 26, 1937).

ORR, CLIFFORD. "The *Journal* is Launched," *The Journal of the American Society of Chartered Life Underwriters*, Vol. 1:3–4 (September, 1946).

QUARTO, PASQUALE A. "The Quiet Man," *Life Association News*, Vol. 49:47–48 (August, 1954). Memorial editorial to Dr. McCahan.

REESE, JOSEPH H. "A Word About the Portrait," *The Journal of the American Society of Chartered Life Underwriters*, Vol. 5:65 (December, 1950).

SMITH, J. CARLTON. "The Handwriting on the Wall," *Life Association News*, Vol. 47:50–52, 79–80 (September, 1952).

SPALDING, ARTHUR M. "Progress of the American College of Life Underwriters," *Life Association News*, Vol. 22:925 (July, 1928).

STASSEN, HAROLD E. "Dr. Solomon S. Huebner," *The Journal of the American Society of Chartered Life Underwriters*, Vol. 6:199–201 (June, 1952).

"Student Topics," Bryn Mawr, Pa.: American College of Life Underwriters (Periodically since 1957).

"Success of the American College of Life Underwriters Assured," *Life Association News*, Vol. 21:835 (June, 1927).

"Teacher Topics," Bryn Mawr, Pa.: American College of Life Underwriters (Periodically since 1952).

WIDING, THEODORE. "C.L.U.—An Investment in Futures," *Life Association News*, Vol. 44:1153–54, 1176–77 (August, 1950).

BROCHURES, MONOGRAPHS AND PAMPHLETS

ADVISORY COUNCIL ON LIFE UNDERWRITER EDUCATION AND TRAINING. *Educational and Training Opportunities for the Life Underwriter; The Story of Three Institutional Programs—Campus Training Schools, Chartered Life Underwriter, Life Underwriter Training Council.* Rev. ed. Hartford, Conn., no date. 20pp.

AMERICAN COLLEGE OF LIFE UNDERWRITERS. *Agency Building Through the C.L.U. Program.* 1940. 15pp.

———. *The American College of Life Underwriters and the C.L.U. Degree.* July 28, 1928. Revised March 1, 1929. 6pp.

———. *Announcement.* Issued 1941/42–1958/59.

———. *Announcement and Directory.* Issued 1931/32–1940/41.

———. *Announcing and Recognizing the New C.L.U.* Revised annually (1953). 6pp.

———. *Announcing the Chartered Life Underwriter Associate; a New Designation to be Conferred by the American College of Life Underwriters.* 1952. 4pp.

———. *Annual Report.* Published 1943 to date.

———. *Building Agency Man Power Through the C.L.U. Program.* 1941. 9pp.

———. *Bulletin and Directory.* Issued 1929/30 and 1930/31.

———. *Capital Giving; a Handbook of Philanthropic Contribution . . ."* Rev. ed. Bryn Mawr, Pa. (July, 1961). 24pp.

———. *Catalogue.* 1959/60 to date.

———. *C.L.U. Development Fund: Annual Report.* Published 1961 to date.

———. *C.L.U. Facts.* 1936. 36pp.

———. *The C.L.U. Program in Building An Agency.* 1938. 15 pp.

———. *The C.L.U. Program in Building Personal Production.* 1938. 7pp.

———. *C.L.U. Yesterday—Today—Tomorrow.* 1960. 7-page brochure for the Development Fund.

———. *College and University Courses in Insurance.* Research project subsequently taken over by the S. S. Huebner Foundation. 1936. 24pp.

———. *The Committee of 1000.* 1962. 8pp.

———. *The Cooperative Fund for Underwriter Education.* 1938. 16pp.

———. *A Description of the C.L.U. Examination Program Beginning With the 1959 Examinations.* 1958. 22pp.

———. *Education the Best Investment.* 1941. 7pp.

———. *Examinations in Life Insurance Agency Management; Announcement for 1932–1934.* 1932. 8pp.

———. *An Expanded National College of Life and Health Insurance . . . and Its Need for a Permanent Endowment Fund.* 1960. 4pp.

——— . *Graphic Survey Illustrating Aims, Trends and Progress of American College Services in "Man Building."* August 31, 1942. Also issued August 31, 1939; August 31, 1940. Became Annual Report in 1943.

———. *Key Men in C.L.U. Instruction 1939–1940.* 1939.

———. *A Message—Interesting Facts About C.L.U.* Published annually since 1958. 4pp.

———. *Organized Study for the C.L.U. Examinations.* 1933. 63pp.

———. *Planning and Promoting C.L.U. Study Groups; A Guide for the C.L.U. Educational Chairman and His Committee.* Prepared by Walter B. Wheeler. Date unknown.

———. *Proceedings of the C.L.U. National Seminar, Management Section, based on "Decision at Zenith Life" by Abram T. Collier,* Bryn Mawr, Pa., c1962. 30pp. Report of the Proceedings: "Election at Zenith Life," *Harvard Business Review,* Vol. 40:176–78, 180, 182, 184, 186, 188, 193–94, 196–97 (March/April, 1962).

———. *Questions and Composite Answers C.L.U. Examinations.* Issued 1933 to date.

———. *Questions, Management Examinations.* Issued 1933 to date; title changed in 1960 to *Questions and Composite Answers, Management Examination.*

———. *Recent Significant Developments in Fields of Knowledge Covered by the C.L.U. Program.* 1943. 1 volume, various paging.

———. *A Revised C.L.U. Curriculum to Meet Changing Times.* 1956. 4pp.

———. *The Revised C.L.U. Examination Program; With Particular Reference to the New Part Entitled Life Underwriting (Comprehensive).* 1941. 19pp.

———. *Suggested Books in the Several Fields Covered by the Examinations for the Degree of Chartered Life Underwriter (C.L.U.).* 1928. 2pp.

———. *They Look to You for Guidance.* 1953.

————. *Topical Outlines of Subjects Covered by the C.L.U. Examination.* Published 1930–1938.

————. *Twentieth Anniversary of the American College of Life Underwriters, Incorporated March 22, 1927.* 28pp. Contains reprints of articles from the March 1947 issue of *The Journal of the American Society of Chartered Life Underwriters,* Vol. 1 (1947).

————. *What Companies Are Doing to Stimulate C.L.U.* September, 1953. 12pp., American College Research Report.

————. *The Why of the Cooperative Fund; Prepared by the Committee on Underwriter Training.* 1950, revised 1958.

AMERICAN COLLEGE OF LIFE UNDERWRITERS—AMERICAN SOCIETY OF CHARTERED LIFE UNDERWRITERS. *C.L.U. Review.* Published 1954 to date.

AMERICAN SOCIETY OF CHARTERED LIFE UNDERWRITERS. *A Blueprint for Growth.* 1959.

————. *Chapter Guide on Public Relations.* 1946.

————. *Chartered Life Underwriter Institute,* Program; The American Society of Chartered Life Underwriters and the School of Business Administration, University of Connecticut. 1946. 12pp.

————. *C.L.U. Chapter Guide.* Looseleaf volume, kept up to date by revision sheets. 1960.

————. *C.L.U. On the March; What This Means to the Public—to the Business —to You.* 1945. 44pp.

————. *Guide for Chapter Administration.* 1948.

————. *How To Conduct a Successful C.L.U. Diploma Presentation Ceremony; A Manual for Chapters.* 1956. 24pp.

————. *The Meaning of C.L.U.* 1962. 7pp.

————. (Philadelphia Chapter.) *Record of Dedication Ceremonies, The American College of Life Underwriters Building, December 7, 1948.* A scrapbook containing program, letters, photographs, news clippings. 1948.

————. *What C.L.U. Can Mean to You.* 1950. 12pp.

————. *What Is A C.L.U.?* 1960. 8pp.

————. *Working Together for Professional Growth.* 1956. 24pp. Revised periodically.

BOSSARD, JAMES H. S. *Large and Small Families—A Study in Contrasts.* David McCahan Foundation Lecture, 1959.

CLARK, PAUL F. *The C.L.U. Program From the General Agent's Point of View.* 16 page brochure issued by National Chapter, Chartered Life Underwriters, also issued in *Life Association News,* Vol. 30:602–5 (March, 1936).

C.L.U. Educational Policies, Programs, and Problems, American College of Life Underwriters. 1931.
1. Clark, Ernest J. Untitled Conferment Address.
2. Duff, William M. "What the C.L.U. Means to Underwriters and the Public."
3. Huebner, Solomon S. "The Three-Year Program of Study." Reprinted in *Life Association News,* Vol. 26:251–52, 254 (November, 1931).
4. McCahan, David. "Properly Organized Review Classes." Reprinted in *Life Association News,* Vol. 26:255–56, 285–86 (November, 1931).

COLLIER, ABRAM T. *Decision at Zenith Life.* Bryn Mawr, Pa., American College of Life Underwriters, c1961. 29pp. Reprinted in *Harvard Business Review,* Vol. 40: 139–40, 143–46, 150–52, 155–57 (January/February, 1962).

DICKEY, JOHN SLOAN. *The American Design.* Bound with Solomon S. Huebner, *Discussions of Implications to Life Insurance.* 1957. David McCahan Foundation Lecture.

GRAEBNER, HERBERT C. *A Survey of the Comparative Data of Production, Income and Persistence of Business of C.L.U.s and Non-C.L.U.s in Full Time Production in Selected Companies for 1959.* American College of Life Underwriters. 1960. 12pp.

GREGG, DAVIS W., and LONGO, MECHTHILD K. *Insurance Courses in Colleges and Universities Outside the United States* (With Summary and Questionnaire Translated in French, Spanish, German, Italian and Portuguese). American College of Life Underwriters, 1960. 73pp.

HUEBNER, SOLOMON S. *The American College of Life Underwriters; Its Aims and Standards.* 1928. 12pp.

———. *Educational Progress in Life Underwriting.* American College of Life Underwriters. 19pp. Speech also printed in *Life Association News,* Vol. 35:202–4, 296–99 (November, 1940).

———. *Professional Progress in Insurance Education.* In *Insurance Lecture Series,* Spring 1954, University of Connecticut, pp. 1–23.

———. *Where Are We Going C.L.U.-wise in the Next 25 Years?* In *A World We've Never Seen,* unpaged pamphlet issued jointly by the American College of Life Underwriters and the American Society of Chartered Life Underwriters, 1958.

Important Aspects of C.L.U. Education. American College of Life Underwriters, 1932. 24pp.:
1. Huebner, Solomon S. "Elevation of Life Insurance Educationally With the Public"; McCahan, David. "Organization of C.L.U. Educational Efforts," and Stevenson, John A. "What the C.L.U. Program Means to Life Insurance."
2. Dr. Huebner's paper also appeared in *N.A.L.U. Proceedings,* 43rd, 1932, pp. 136–45 and *Life Association News,* Vol. 27:69–70, 72, 135–36, 138–39 (September, 1932).

THE INSURANCE FIELD. *About Life Insurance As a Profession.* 56pp. From the Foreword: "Series of fourteen articles . . . compiled for the insurance field for the purpose of interesting the progressive underwriters of the country in the American College of Life Underwriters" (1928).

IRWIN, HAMPTON H. *Hints on Passing the C.L.U. Examination.* Philadelphia, A.S.C.L.U. 1946. 10pp.

———. *Hints on Preparing for the C.L.U. Examinations.* Philadelphia, A.S.C.L.U. 1944. 18pp.

———. *You Can Become a C.L.U.* Philadelphia, A.S.C.L.U. 1942. 16pp.

MARSH, DANIEL L. *The Romance Behind the Name of the American College of Life Underwriters.* Published in a 22-page pamphlet jointly issued by the American College of Life Underwriters and the American Society of Chartered Life Underwriters. Abstracted in *Life Association News,* Vol. 42:259–60 (November, 1947), "The Romance Behind the American College."

MASON, ARTHUR W., JR. *C.L.U. Silver Anniversary Survey; Factual Data on the First 25 Years of the Chartered Life Underwriter Program.* Issued jointly by the A.C.L.U.-A.S.C.L.U. 1953. 59pp.

McCAHAN, DAVID. *The Contribution of the Life Underwriter to American Security.* Issued by National Chapter, Chartered Life Underwriters. 1939. 20pp.

———. *Solomon Stephen Huebner . . . Down Through the Years.* In "Testimonial Dinner in Honor of Solomon Stephen Huebner, Philadelphia, September 26, 1940;

a Tribute to Solomon Stephen Huebner by the Institution of American Life Insurance," 16-page program (1940).

MCCAHAN, DAVID, and KELLY, ANNA M. *College and University Courses in Insurance and Related Subjects.* 36pp. A.C.L.U. Educational Research Bulletin #3 (1940).

OGBURN, WILLIAM FIELDING. *The Family in Our Changing Society.* 1958. David McCahan Foundation Lecture for 1958.

SEEFURTH, NATHANIEL H. *Opportunities for the Advanced Underwriter Today.* Issued by National Chapter, Chartered Life Underwriters (September, 1937). 14pp.

SMITH, J. CARLTON. C.L.U. and You. Published as two booklets: *There Is No Royal Road,* 12pp., and *What Is the Right Road?* 12pp. Philadelphia, A.C.L.U. 1950.

STEINBECK, LEROY G. *Profiles of Excellence.* Bryn Mawr, Pa., Joint Committee on Continuing Education of the American College of Life Underwriters and the American Society of Chartered Life Underwriters. 1961. 28pp.

STEVENSON, JOHN A. *Starting the Second Decade.* Issued by the National Chapter, Chartered Life Underwriters. 1938. 15pp.

Testimonial Dinner to Dr. Solomon Stephen Huebner . . . September 26, 1940. Text of speeches by Julian S. Myrick, S. S. Huebner, Charles J. Zimmerman, Paul H. Musser, Thomas I. Parkinson. 1940. 24pp.

WOODS, LAWRENCE C., JR. *The First Decade, 1927–1937; a Brief History of the American College of Life Underwriters.* National Chapter, Chartered Life Underwriters. 1937. 32pp.

PROCEEDINGS AND REPORTS

THE AMERICAN COLLEGE HOUR:

Bendiner, Irvin. "The Life Underwriter and Human Relations," *N.A.L.U. Proceedings,* 51st, 1940, pp. 85–88.

Dechert, Robert. "Life, the Underwriter and the Lawyer," *N.A.L.U. Proceedings,* 51st, 1940, pp. 74–77.

Lincoln, Leroy A. "The Life Underwriter and Fundamentals of Life Insurance Service," *N.A.L.U. Proceedings,* 51st, 1940, pp. 81–84.

Young, James T. "Finding Life Insurance Facts," *N.A.L.U. Proceedings,* 51st, 1940, pp. 77–81.

AMERICAN COLLEGE HOUR SPEAKERS:

Bendiner, Irvin. "You'd Better Think Twice About It," *N.A.L.U. Proceedings,* 54th, 1943, pp. 51–60; also issued as 19-page pamphlet by American Society of Chartered Life Underwriters. "Bendiner emphasizes life insurance can rise no higher than efficiency of its underwriters." *Life Association News,* Vol. 38:124–26, 200–207 (October, 1943).

CLARK, ERNEST J. "The American College of Life Underwriters." *N.A.L.U. Proceedings,* 41st, 1930, pp. 168–75; reprinted, *Life Association News,* Vol. 25:144–45 (October, 1930).

———. "The First Four Years of the American College," *N.A.L.U. Proceedings,* 42d, 1931, pp. 136–40; reprinted, *Life Association News,* Vol. 26:129–30 (October, 1931).

———. Untitled Conferment remarks, *N.A.L.U. Proceedings,* 39th, 1928, pp. 94–95; 98–99; resumé, without title, *Life Association News,* Vol. 23:103 (October, 1928).

———. Untitled Conferment remarks concerning achievements of the College, *N.A.L.U. Proceedings,* 40th, 1929, pp. 178–81; reprinted, *Life Association News,*

"The Chartered Life Underwriter," Vol. 24:145–47 (October, 1929).

—————. Untitled Conferment remarks at the presentation of C.L.U. diplomas, *N.A.L.U. Proceedings*, 44th, 1933, pp. 108–10; resumé of address, "President Clark Confers C.L.U. Diplomas," *Life Association News*, Vol. 28:211–12 (October, 1933).

CLARK, PAUL F. "The Dollars and Cents Value of the American College of Life Underwriters," *Association of Life Agency Officers* and the *Life Insurance Sales Research Bureau. Annual Meeting. Proceedings*, 1936, pp. 184–99. Reprinted with changes in *Life Association News*, Vol. 31:462–64, 467–68 (January, 1937).

CLEARY, MICHAEL J. "The Importance of Education in Life Insurance," *N.A.L.U. Proceedings*, 47th, 1936, pp. 131–34; reprinted, *Life Association News*, Vol. 31:119–20 (October, 1936).

GREGG, DAVIS W. "The C.L.U. Story," *American Life Convention. Proceedings*, 49th, 1954, pp. 233–40.

—————. "For Education Is Making Men," *American Life Convention. Proceedings*, 57th, 1962, pp. 252–60.

HILL, GRANT L. "C.L.U.—A Decade Hence," *N.A.L.U. Proceedings*, 45th, 1934, pp. 115–23; issued as brochure by National Chapter, Chartered Life Underwriters, *Significance of the C.L.U. Movement to the Public, to the Underwriter, to the Life Insurance Company*. 19 pp. Resumé of paper in *Life Association News*, Vol. 29:197–98 (October, 1934).

HOLCOMBE, JOHN MARSHALL, JR. "The New Professional Concept Represented by the C.L.U. Designation—and Its Influence Upon Public Relations." *N.A.L.U. Proceedings*, 50th, 1939, pp. 117–24; reprinted *Life Association News*, Vol. 34:214–16, 310–11 (November, 1939). Printed also by the American College of Life Underwriters, 16-page pamphlet.

HUEBNER, SOLOMON S. "The American College of Life Underwriters," *Association of Life Agency Officers* and *Life Insurance Sales Research Bureau. Proceedings of the Annual Meeting*, 1929, pp. 100–106.

—————. "The American College of Life Underwriters," *N.A.L.U. Proceedings*, 39th, 1928, pp. 95–98; reprinted in *Life Association News* as "The American College of Life Underwriters Considered from the Educational Standpoint," Vol. 23:158–60, 198 (October, 1928).

—————. "The American College of Life Underwriters," *N.A.L.U. Proceedings*, 40th, 1929, pp. 162–72; reprinted in *Life Association News*, Vol. 24:142–44, 227–29, 231–32 (October, 1929).

—————. "The Conserving Influence of the C.L.U. Program Upon Life Underwriting," *N.A.L.U. Proceedings*, 42d, 1931, pp. 130–36; reprinted, *Life Association News*, Vol. 26:127–28, 221–22 (October, 1931).

—————. "The Contribution of the American College of Life Underwriters to the Life Insurance Institution," *Million Dollar Round Table. Proceedings* 1948, pp. 49–52.

—————. "Financial Value of the Chartered Life Underwriter Course of Study," *N.A.L.U. Proceedings*, 41st, 1930, pp. 158–68; reprinted, *Life Association News*, Vol. 25:141–43, 234–37, October, 1930; reprinted by American College of Life Underwriters as 16-page pamphlet.

—————. "The Human Value in Business Compared with the Property Value," *N.A.L.U. Proceedings*, 35th, 1924, pp. 17–20.

—————. "Life Insurance Education," *National Association of Life Underwriters. Proceedings*, 25th, 1914, pp. 68–80; reprinted in *Life Association News*, Vol. 9:22, 24, 26, 28, 30, 32 (September, 1914).

———. "A New Vision in Salesmanship," *Association of Life Insurance Presidents. Proceedings,* 23d, 1929, pp. 190–94.

———. "Significance of the C.L.U. Movement to the Future of Life Underwriting," *Association of Life Agency Officers* and the *Life Insurance Sales Research Bureau. Annual Meeting. Proceedings,* 1943, pp. 191–204.

———. Untitled Conferment remarks, *N.A.L.U. Proceedings,* 39th, 1928, p. 94.

———. "What the C.L.U. Program Means to the Institution of Life Insurance," *N.A.L.U. Proceedings,* 44th, 1933, pp. 97–108; *ibid., Life Association News,* Vol. 28:155–56, 158–59, 239–41 (October, 1933).

HUTCHISON, RALPH COOPER. "The Qualities of a Profession," *N.A.L.U. Proceedings,* 49th, 1938, pp. 59–64; reprinted, *Life Association News,* Vol. 33:91–93, October, 1938; American College of Life Underwriters, 12-page pamphlet, undated.

JONES, FRANK L. "The Availability of the American College of Life Underwriters," *Association of Life Agency Officers* and the *Life Insurance Sales Research Bureau. Annual Meeting. Proceedings.* 1937, pp. 85–91.

MCCAHAN, DAVID. "University Instruction for Insurance Leadership," *American Association of University Teachers of Insurance. Proceedings,* 2nd, 1934, pp. 9–21.

MYRICK, JULIAN S. "Future Influence of the American College and C.L.U.," *N.A.L.U. Proceedings,* 46th, 1935, pp. 100–109; also published in *Life Association News,* Vol. 30:101–3, 198–200 (October, 1935).

NORTH, HENRY J. "The Coming Decade—A Decade of Expansion," *N.A.L.U. Proceedings,* 48th, 1937, pp. 116–25; reprinted in *Life Association News,* Vol. 32:21–23, 112–13 (September, 1937); reprinted by American College of Life Underwriters as 15-page pamphlet.

STEVENSON, JOHN A. "The American College of Life Underwriters," *Association of Life Agency Officers* and the *Life Insurance Sales Research Bureau. Annual Meeting. Proceedings,* pp. 117–21 (1932).

———. "What the C.L.U. Program Means to the Underwriter," *N.A.L.U. Proceedings,* 44th, 1933, pp. 91–96; *ibid., Life Association News,* Vol. 28:151–53 (October, 1933).

WOODS, EDWARD A. Untitled speech about the American College of Life Underwriters, *N.A.L.U. Proceedings,* 38th, 1927, pp. 25–30.

UNPUBLISHED MATERIAL

AMERICAN COLLEGE OF LIFE UNDERWRITERS. "Factors Affecting C.L.U. Grades" (1940).

———. "How to Use the C.L.U. Study Groups for Training Purposes" (1938).

———. "Publicity Releases," bound in two volumes, covering 1929/37 and 1938/43.

Annual Reports of Various Boards and Committees of the American College of Life Underwriters.

HUEBNER, SOLOMON S. "The American College of Life Underwriters," presented at the Fifth Hemispheric Insurance Conference, Rio de Janeiro, August 19–28, 1954; mimeographed.

"Report of the Committee of the Association of Life Agency Officers for the American College of Life Underwriters." Philadelphia: American College of Life Underwriters. 1937. 13 pp.

SOLOMON S. HUEBNER LECTURE FILMS

"The Human Life Value Concept."

"Life Insurance, A Callable Sinking Fund Bond."

"Life Insurance as a Life Will."

"The Creative Functions of Life Insurance to the Premium Payer."

"Life Insurance as An Investment."

Produced for the American College of Life Underwriters by Aetna Life Affiliated Companies (1962).

BOOKS

AMERICAN COLLEGE OF LIFE UNDERWRITERS. *Significant Developments of the War Years.* 4 Vols. Philadelphia: 1945. Contents. Vol. 1, Life Insurance. Vol. 2, Economic, Government and Social Problems. Vol. 3, Law, Trusts and Taxes. Vol. 4, Corporation Finance, Banking and Investments.

GREGG, DAVIS, W., and MCGILL, DAN M. (Eds.) *World Insurance Trends; Proceedings of the First International Insurance Conference, Philadelphia, Pennsylvania, May 1957.* Philadelphia: The University of Pennsylvania Press, 1959.

HUEBNER, SOLOMON S. *The Economics of Life Insurance; Human Life Values: Their Financial Organization, Management, and Liquidation.* New York: 1st ed., D. Appleton and Co., 1927; 2nd ed., D. Appleton-Century Co., 1935; 3rd ed., Appleton-Century-Crofts, Inc., 1959.

————. *Life Insurance.* New York: 1st ed., D. Appleton and Co.; 1915; 2nd ed., D. Appleton and Co., 1923; 3rd ed., D. Appleton-Century Co., 1935; 4th ed., Appleton-Century-Crofts, Inc., 1950; 5th ed., joint authorship with Kenneth Black, Jr., Appleton-Century-Crofts, Inc., 1958.

HUEBNER, SOLOMON S., and MCCAHAN, DAVID. *Life Insurance as Investment.* New York: D. Appleton and Co., 1933.

STONE, MILDRED F. *The Teacher Who Changed an Industry; a Biography of Dr. Solomon S. Huebner of the University of Pennsylvania.* Homewood, Ill.: Richard D. Irwin, Inc., 1960.

AMERICAN COLLEGE EDUCATIONAL PUBLICATIONS

ACKERMAN, LAWRENCE J. "Fundamentals of Federal Old Age and Survivors Insurance" (1948); subsequently revised, with title "Fundamentals of Federal Old Age, Survivors and Disability Insurance," latest revision by L. J. Ackerman and D. A. Ivry (1962).

AMERICAN COLLEGE OF LIFE UNDERWRITERS. "The Arithmetic of Life Insurance; a Manual of Visual Teaching Aids, 1959–1960," Philadelphia, c1959. 127 pp.

————. "Study Guides," issued 1953 to date.

————. "Study Supplements," issued 1939-1952.

BAXTER, B., and KASHNIG, W. "Life Insurance Marketing Research" (1961); rev. ed. (1962).

BLAIR, B. F. "Interpreting Life Insurance Company Annual Reports" (1956); rev. ed. (1960).

BOMAR, F. "Profit-sharing and Other Forms of Deferred Compensation" (1956); rev. ed. by F. Monar, J. E. McAndrews, and Johannes R. Krahmer (1962).

CHAPMAN. "The Standard Nonforfeiture and Valuation Legislation" (1949).

CLAPP, H. B. "Fundamentals of State Death Taxes" (1953); rev. ed. by H. B. Clapp and P. C. Heady (1961).

EKLUND, COY G. "Organizing An Agency: a Case Example" (1960).

GARDINER, HAROLD W. "The Practice of Life Underwriting" (1956).

GORDON, GEORGE B., and WRIGGINS, JAMES C. "Fundamentals of Federal Income Tax" (1951).

HARMELIN, W., and OSLER, R. W. "Business Uses of Health Insurance" (1960).

HEINS, R. M. "Fundamentals of Property and Casualty Insurance" (1956); rev. ed. (1960).

HOFFMAN, G. WRIGHT. "Investments of Life Insurance Companies—Their Changing Frontiers" (1948). Later revised.

HUEBNER, SOLOMON S. "Economics of Health Insurance" (1956); rev. ed. (1958).

————. "Professional Concept in Life Underwriting" (1952); rev. eds. (1956, 1963).

HULL, ROGER. "The Art in Scientific Management" (1958).

MAYNARD, HAROLD H. "The Place of Personal Salesmanship in Our Economic System" (1951). Subsequent revisions had title, "The Place of Personal Salesmanship of Services in Our Economy." Latest revision, 1960.

MCCAHAN, DAVID. "Fundamentals of Life Insurance Settlement Options" (1949).

MCKAIN, WALTER C. "Social Problems" (1951). Revised, 1961.

MILLER, JOHN H. "Employee Welfare Plans" (1951).

REID, CHARLES K., II. "Fundamentals of Government Life Insurance and Related Benefits" (1948). Various revisions.

RUSSELL, HUGH, and BLACK, KENNETH, JR. "Human Behavior" (1962).

SCHOLZ, KARL, W. H. "Changing Patterns in the Distribution of the National Income" (1948). Later revised.

————. "Inflationary and Counter-inflationary Factors in our Present Day Economy" (1948).

SMITH, J. CARLTON. "Key Man Uses of Life Insurance" (1955); rev. ed., 1959.

SPIEGELMAN, MORTIMER. "Mortality and Morbidity Trends in the United States since 1900" (1951). When revised, title changed to "Significant Mortality and Morbidity Trends in the United States Since 1900." Latest revision, 1962.

SULLIVAN, H. L. "Needs and the Life Underwriter" (1947).

TRUMP, ROSS M. "Developments in Governmental Supervision of Insurance" (1948).

VOLK, HARRY J., and ALLSOPP, THOMAS. "Life Insurance Company Organization" (1955).

THE AUTHOR'S BIBLIOGRAPHY

In personal interviews, many people contributed to the author's information and background for this history, as mentioned in the foreword. Printed source materials of special value were the reports of the annual conventions and committees of the National Association of Life Underwriters and the *Life Association News*, and the files of *The Eastern Underwriter*. Of course the *Minutes*, the *Announcement* and *Catalogue*, and the *Annual Report* and *Annual Review* of the American College, as well as other publications of the College and the American Society of Chartered Life Underwriters were basic and fruitful materials of research.

The following list presents the publications used for background, in addition to those in the bibliography specifically relating to the College, and all those from which verbatim quotations were taken. The annotations for quotations are given by chapter and page in the listing which follows this general bibliography. The author's thanks are hereby extended to all those who kindly gave permission for use of the quotations.

"A.C.L.U. Has a Brilliant Future," *Life Association News*, Vol. 23, No. 1 (September, 1928).

AMERICAN COLLEGE OF LIFE UNDERWRITERS. *A Revised C.L.U. Curriculum.* Philadelphia, 1956.

AMERICAN SOCIETY OF CHARTERED LIFE UNDERWRITERS. *C.L.U. on the March.* Philadelphia, 1945.

———. *The Meaning of C.L.U.* Bryn Mawr, 1962.

———. *Your Vote Will Help Decide.* Bryn Mawr, 1961.

ANDERSON, BUIST M. "The Armstrong Investigation in Retrospect," *Proceedings of the Association of Life Insurance Counsel*, 1952–53, Vol. 11.

ASSOCIATION OF LIFE INSURANCE PRESIDENTS. *Fourth Annual Meeting Proceedings*, 1910.

———. *Proceedings of 23rd Annual Convention*, December, 1929.

BALLEW, JAMES A. "The Man Who Invented Programing," *Manager's Magazine*, Vol. 31, No. 4 (July, 1956).

BROWN, GERARD S. "Why the Chartered Life Underwriter?" *Life Values of the Chicago Association of Life Underwriters*, Vol. 3, No. 21 (October, 1930).

CHICAGO ASSOCIATION OF LIFE UNDERWRITERS. *Life Values*, December, 1933.

CLARK, ERNEST J. "Conferment Address—1931," *C.L.U. Educational Policies, Programs and Problems.* Philadelphia: American College of Life Underwriters, 1931.

———. "Founding of the American College of Life Underwriters," *The Journal of the American Society of Chartered Life Underwriters*, Vol. 1, No. 3 (March, 1947).

————. "Looking Ahead with the American College of Life Underwriters," *John Hancock Signature*, Vol. 2, No. 10 (November, 1929).

CLARK, PAUL F. *The C.L.U. Program from the General Agent's Point of View.* Philadelphia: National Chapter—Chartered Life Underwriters, 1935.

COMMITTEE OF THE ASSOCIATION OF LIFE AGENCY OFFICERS FOR THE AMERICAN COLLEGE OF LIFE UNDERWRITERS. *Report* (October, 1937).

CROWELL, FRED C., JR. "A Product Beyond Reproach," *The Insurance Field*, Vol. 89, No. 46 (November 11, 1960).

DAVID MCCAHAN FOUNDATION OF THE AMERICAN COLLEGE OF LIFE UNDERWRITERS. *The 1957 David McCahan Lecture.* Philadelphia, 1958.

DOWLING, ELEANOR B. *Life Underwriting Training Council—A Ten Year History.* Privately printed, 1957.

DUNSTALL, LESLIE W. *The Story of the Life Underwriters Association of Canada.* Toronto: Privately printed by the Association, 1956.

GANSE, FRANKLIN W. "Early Days of the American College," *John Hancock Signature*, Vol. 14, No. 9 (September, 1941).

GRAEBNER, HERBERT C. "Objective Testing in C.L.U. Professional Examinations," *The Journal of the American Society of Chartered Life Underwriters*, Vol. 14, No. 3 (Summer, 1960).

HAZARD, WILLIS HATFIELD. "Professor Huebner's 'Economics of Life Insurance,' Including an Appreciation of the Series of Technical Books of Which It Is the Foundation Member," *The Standard*, Vol. 102, No. 21 (May 26, 1928).

HENDRICK, BURTON J. *The Story of Life Insurance.* New York: McClure, Phillips & Co., 1907.

HILL, GRANT L. *Significance of the C.L.U. Movement.* Philadelphia: National Chapter—Chartered Life Underwriters, 1934.

HUEBNER, S. S. *Life Insurance: A Textbook.* New York: D. Appleton & Co., 1915.

INSTITUTE OF CHARTERED LIFE UNDERWRITERS OF CANADA. *Regulations and Curriculum, 1960–1961.* Toronto, 1960.

JOSEPHS, DEVEREUX C. "Insurance and Education," *The Journal of the American Society of Chartered Life Underwriters*, Vol. 15, No. 4 (Fall, 1961).

The Journal of the American Society of Chartered Life Underwriters, Vol. 6, No. 3 (June, 1952).

"Key Notes," *Life Association News*, Vol. 50, No. 3 (March, 1955).

KRUEGER, HARRY. "In Memoriam," *The Journal of the American Society of Chartered Life Underwriters*, Vol. 5, No. 1 (December, 1950).

Life Association News, American College of Life Underwriters Silver Anniversary Issue, Vol. 47, No. 1 (September, 1952).

LIFE INSURANCE SALES RESEARCH BUREAU. *Proceedings of the 1929 Annual Meeting.*

Life Insurance Selling, Vol. 10, Nos. 3, 4, and 5 (March, April, May, 1935).

MCCAHAN, DAVID. "C.L.U. Movement in Review," *Life Insurance Selling*, Vol. 12, No. 5 (May, 1937).

"The Million-Dollar Oldster," *Time*, Vol. 75, No. 11 (March 14, 1960).

NATIONAL ASSOCIATION OF LIFE UNDERWRITERS. *Proceedings.* New York: 1913–33.

"$125,000 Scholarship Fund Announced at Testimonial Dinner to Dr. Huebner," *Life Association News*, Vol. 35, No. 3 (November, 1940).

OTTO, INGOLF H. E. "Review of 'Insurance Courses in Colleges and Universities

Outside of the United States,'" *Journal of Insurance*, Vol. 27, No. 4 (December, 1960).

The Pelican, Vol. 43, No. 5 (May, 1945).

RICHARDS, R. G. "Richards Talks on His Preparation for Examinations," *Atlantic Currents*, Vol. 25, No. 10 (October, 1929).

SCOTT, LEROY. "Life Insurance as a Profession," *The World's Work*, Vol. 11, No. 6 (April, 1906).

SMITH, J. CARLETON. "The Handwriting on the Wall," *Life Association News*, Vol. 47, No. 1 (September, 1952).

S. S. HUEBNER FOUNDATION FOR INSURANCE EDUCATION. *Announcement*. Philadelphia, 1941.

STALSON, J. OWEN. *Marketing Life Insurance*. Cambridge: Harvard University Press, 1942.

STASSEN, HAROLD E. "Dr. Solomon S. Huebner," *The Journal of the American Society of Chartered Life Underwriters*, Vol. 6, No. 3 (June, 1952).

Statements of Purpose, C.L.U. Annual Meeting Addresses, Washington, D.C., 1960. Philadelphia: American College of Life Underwriters, 1960.

Testimonial Dinner to Dr. Solomon Stephen Huebner at Bellevue-Stratford Hotel, September 26, 1940. Contemporary verbatim report in manuscript.

The National Association of Life Underwriters. New York: Privately printed by the Association, 1939.

WOODS, LAWRENCE C., JR. *The First Decade*. Philadelphia: The National Chapter—Chartered Life Underwriters, 1937.

AUTHOR'S ANNOTATIONS

(Sources as Listed in the Author's Bibliography)

Chapter 3.   P. 10.   Photostatic copy of the President's letter to N.A.L.U. President Hendley, September 14, 1960.

P. 10.   Leroy Scott, "Life Insurance as a Profession," p. 7391.

P. 11.   B. J. Hendrick, *The Story of Life Insurance*, pp. 3, 4.

P. 12.   B. M. Anderson, "The Armstrong Investigation in Retrospect," p. 237.

P. 14.   J. Owen Stalson, *Marketing Life Insurance*, pp. 551, 552.

P. 16.   B. J. Hendrick, *The Story of Life Insurance*, pp. 63, 64.

P. 16.   J. Owen Stalson, *Marketing Life Insurance*, p. 402.

Chapter 4.   P. 20.   *Association of Life Insurance Presidents Proceedings, 1910*, pp. 30, 31.

P. 20.   *Ibid.*, pp. 35, 36.

P. 22.   *Ibid.*, pp. 113-15.

P. 26.   *24th Proceedings—N.A.L.U.*, 1913, p. 76.

P. 27.   *26th Proceedings—N.A.L.U.*, 1915, p. 170.

P. 32.   *25th Proceedings—N.A.L.U.*, 1914, pp. 66-80.

P. 38.   *Life Insurance*, p. 428.

Chapter 5.   P. 40.   *27th Proceedings—N.A.L.U.*, 1916, p. 48.

P. 41.   *Ibid.*, pp. 49, 50.

P. 43.   *The Eastern Underwriter*, February 21, 1919, p. 12.

P. 44.   *The Eastern Underwriter*, April 4, 1919, p. 5.

P. 44.   *Ibid.*

P. 45.   *The Eastern Underwriter*, August 8, 1919, pp. 7, 8.

P. 46.   J. A. Ballew, "The Man Who Invented Programing," p. 9.

P. 48.   *The Eastern Underwriter*, April 11, 1919, p. 2.

P. 49.   *The Eastern Underwriter*, May 9, 1919, p. 5.

P. 51.   S. S. Huebner, *Life Insurance*, p. 13.

P. 52.   *35th Proceedings—N.A.L.U.*, 1924, pp. 17-40.

	P. 57.	W. H. Hazard, "Professor Huebner's Economics of Life Insurance," pp. 987, 988.
Chapter 6.	P. 61.	*38th Proceedings—N.A.L.U.*, 1927, p. 24.
	P. 69.	E. J. Clark, "Founding of the American College of Life Underwriters," p. 195.
	P. 73.	*38th Proceedings—N.A.L.U.*, 1927, pp. 362, 363, 365-67.
	P. 75.	*38th Proceedings—N.A.L.U.*, 1927, p. 104.
	P. 75.	*The Eastern Underwriter*, December 9, 1927, p. 1.
Chapter 7.	P. 82.	E. J. Clark, "Founding of the American College of Life Underwriters," p. 197.
	P. 83.	*Minutes*, July 28, 1928, p. 66.
	P. 83.	*Ibid.*, p. 73.
	P. 85.	*Ibid.*, pp. 63, 64.
	P. 86.	*Ibid.*, p. 67.
	P. 87.	*39th Proceedings—N.A.L.U.*, 1928, p. 98.
	P. 87.	*39th Proceedings—N.A.L.U.*, 1928, pp. 95-97.
	P. 90.	*Minutes*, February 9, 1929, p. 124.
	P. 90.	*Ibid.*, p. 127.
	P. 90.	*Life Association News*, Vol. 23, No. 6 (February, 1929), p. 494.
	P. 90.	*Minutes*, February 9, 1929, pp. 128, 129.
	P. 94.	*Minutes*, September 10, 1928, p. 102.
Chapter 8.	P. 95.	*Minutes*, February 9, 1929, pp. 117, 118.
	P. 98.	*Ibid.*, pp. 130-33.
	P. 102.	*42nd Proceedings—N.A.L.U.*, 1931, p. 137.
	P. 104.	Chicago Association of Life Underwriters, *Life Values*, December, 1933, p. 1.
	P. 105.	*44th Proceedings—N.A.L.U.*, 1933, pp. 102, 103.
	P. 106.	*Announcement, 1932-1933*, pp. 33, 34.
	P. 106.	*Minutes*, September 26, 1933, p. 355.
	P. 107.	R. G. Richards, "Richards Talks," p. 28.
	P. 109.	*41st Proceedings—N.A.L.U.*, 1930, pp. 5, 6.
Chapter 9.	P. 112.	*43rd Proceedings—N.A.L.U.*, 1932, pp. 12-15.
	P. 116.	Life Insurance Sales Research Bureau, *Proceedings of the 1929 Annual Meeting*, pp. 100-102, 106.

P. 116. Association of Life Insurance Presidents, *Proceedings of 23rd Annual Convention*, pp. 190-94.

P. 118. *41st Proceedings—N.A.L.U.*, 1930, pp. 159, 160.

P. 119. G. S. Brown, *Life Values*, p. 1.

P. 123. *Announcement, 1931-32*, p. 12.

P. 123. *41st Proceedings—N.A.L.U.*, 1930, p. 167.

P. 124. David McCahan, "C.L.U. Movement in Review," pp. 12-14.

P. 127. Woods, L. C., *The First Decade*, pp. 14, 15.

Chapter 10. P. 132. "A C.L.U. Has a Brilliant Future," *Life Association News*, pp. 24, 26.

P. 135. E. J. Clark, "Conferment Address, 1931," pp. 4, 5.

P. 136. *Minutes*, July 28, 1928, p. 70.

P. 136. *Minutes*, March 29, 1929, p. 36.

P. 138. *Announcement, 1932-33*, p. 26.

P. 139. *44th Proceedings—N.A.L.U.*, 1933, p. 104.

P. 140. *Minutes*, July 28, 1933, pp. 342 k, l.

P. 141. *Minutes*, September 23, 1929, p. 177.

P. 143. E. J. Clark, "The Founding of the American College of Life Underwriters," pp. 199, 200.

P. 146. *Minutes*, September 25, 1934, p. 403.

P. 147. E. J. Clark, "Looking Ahead with the American College of Life Underwriters," p. 2.

Chapter 12. P. 152. *Announcement, 1936-37*, pp. 30, 31.

P. 154. *Minutes*, September 16, 1935, pp. 29, 30.

P. 155. Committee of Life Agency Officers, *Report*, p. 1.

P. 157. *Ibid.*, pp. 3-8.

P. 160. *Announcement*, 1940-41, p. 32.

P. 161. *Minutes*, September 16, 1935, pp. 8, 9.

Chapter 13. P. 162. G. L. Hill, *Significance of the C.L.U. Movement*, pp. 5-8.

P. 166. *Ibid.*, pp. 12, 13.

P. 167. *Ibid.*, p. 15.

P. 172. *Minutes*, July 22, 1937, p. 486.

P. 173. *Minutes*, July 30, 1936, p. 453.

P. 173. *Minutes*, September 21, 1936, p. 20.

P. 174. *Minutes*, August 24, 1937, p. 498.

P. 174. L. C. Woods, *The First Decade*, pp. 26-30.

P. 180. *Life Insurance Selling*, March, 1935, cover.

P. 180. *Ibid.*, p. 5.

P. 183. "The Million-Dollar Oldster," *Time*, March 14, 1960, p. 96.

Chapter 14. P. 187. *Minutes*, September 16, 1935, p. 39.

P. 189. *Testimonial dinner report*, p. 1.

P. 193. S. S. Huebner Foundation, *Announcement*, pp. 3-6.

Chapter 15. P. 198. *Minutes*, July 25, 1940, p. 606.

P. 201. *Annual Report, 1943*, pp. 1, 2.

P. 202. *Ibid.*

P. 203. *The Pelican*, May, 1945, p. 22.

P. 204. *Annual Report, 1944*, pp. 30, 31.

P. 207. *Annual Report, 1945*, p. 23.

P. 207. *Eastern Underwriter*, November 15, 1946, p. 9.

P. 208. "Key Notes," *Life Association News*, March, 1955, p. 65.

P. 210. Dr. Gregg's letter to the author, March 18, 1963.

Chapter 16. P. 215. American Society, *C.L.U. on the March*, p. 44.

Chapter 17. P. 222. *Annual Report, 1947*, p. 25.

P. 224. Press release in College scrapbook (undated).

P. 230. *Minutes*, September 13, 1949, p. 1033.

Chapter 18. P. 233. *Minutes*, September 26, 1950, p. 1091.

P. 240. Dr. Gregg's manuscript notes of the meeting, November 14, 1951.

Chapter 19. P. 246. H. E. Stassen, "Dr. Solomon S. Huebner," pp. 199-201.

P. 250. Editorial, *The Journal of the American Society*, June, 1952, p. 193.

P. 250. *The Eastern Underwriter*, September 12, 1952, p. 2.

P. 253. J. C. Smith, "The Handwriting," pp. 51, 52.

Chapter 20. P. 257. *Life Association News*, September, 1952, p. 30.

P. 264. *Annual Report, 1954*, pp. iii, iv.

Chapter 21.   P. 269.   *Minutes,* September 21, 1954, p. 1218.

                   P. 274.   "A Revised C.L.U. Curriculum," pp. 1, 2.

                   P. 276.   H. C. Graebner, "Objective Testing," p. 279.

                   P. 287.   *The 1957 David McCahan Lecture,* p. 1.

                   P. 289.   I. H. E. Otto, "Review," pp. 121, 122.

Chapter 22.   P. 293.   *Catalogue 1962-1963,* p. 6.

                   P. 294.   *The Eastern Underwriter,* June 23, 1961, p. 19.

                   P. 295.   *Ibid.*

                   P. 304.   American Society publicity folder, "Your Vote Will Help Decide."

Chapter 23.   P. 314.   F. C. Crowell, Jr., "A Product Beyond Reproach," p. 30.

                   P. 316.   *Statements of Purpose,* p. 11.

                   P. 317.   *Annual Report 1960,* p. 2.

                   P. 322.   American Society, "The Meaning of C.L.U.," pp. 6, 7.

Chapter 24.   P. 326.   Verbatim quotations are from manuscript transcription of the ceremonies in the files of the College.

                   P. 335.   *The Eastern Underwriter,* October 7, 1960, p. 40.

                   P. 338.   Manuscript transcript.

                   P. 338.   Mr. Dechert's manuscript given to the author.

                   P. 339.   Dr. Huebner's manuscript given to the author.

                   P. 340.   W. E. Hays to Dr. Gregg, June 2, 1961.

                   P. 341.   D. C. Josephs, "Insurance and Education," pp. 299-303.

Chapter 25.   P. 345.   Author's note at the event.

INDEX

Generally in the text of this book the C.L.U. has been omitted, but it is shown with names here where appropriate, and also the year of receiving the designation.

*This book has been set on the Linotype in 12
and 10 point Bodoni Book, leaded 2 points.
Chapter numbers are in 14 point Bulmer italics;
chapter titles are in 18 point Bulmer. The page
size is 25 by 43 picas. Paper is 70# Tone-O-
Paque offset.*